J

Disease and Social Behavior

The MIT Press
Cambridge, Massachusetts, and London, England

Disease and Social Behavior:
An Interdisciplinary Perspective

Horacio Fabrega, Jr.

This book was set in Linotype Baskerville
by Arrow Composition, Inc.
printed on Mohawk Neotext Offset
and bound in G. S. B. s/535/48 "Yellow"
by The Colonial Press, Inc.
in the United States of America.

Library of Congress Cataloging in Publication Data

Fabrega, Horacio.
    Disease and social behavior.

    Bibliography: p.
    1. Social medicine. I. Title.
[DNLM: 1. Social medicine. WA30 F123d 1974]
RA418.F3   1974   362.1'04'220973   73–14752
ISBN 0–262–06052–3

En memoria de mi padre, Horacio Fábrega, and
to my mother, Maria Stewart Fábrega

Contents

Preface

The area of overlap or the meeting ground for the disciplines of social science and medicine—an area concerned with the relations between disease and human behavior—is a rich, dynamic, and complex one, in which diverse traditions, disciplines, and conceptual orientations meet. This book constitutes a brief interdisciplinary journey into this region. Because it is frankly interdisciplinary, it does not grapple with traditional problems related to human behavior, disease, and medical care along the lines carved out and bounded by the orthodox disciplines. Instead, issues bearing on many of the concerns of both medicine and social science are dealt with tangentially and also in a largely exploratory way. The fact that this book is both interdisciplinary and exploratory needs to be emphasized.

Although my own formal training has been in medicine, specifically psychiatry, I am personally deeply committed to the exploration of many difficult problems that fall within the fields of both medicine and social science. In this book I concentrate mainly on the subset of these problems that touch on disease and human behavior. To these problems I bring a synthetic approach. An implicit goal or purpose for writing the book has been to enable me to understand better the linkages between disease and behavior so that old problems can be re-examined in a different light and new ones defined and, ideally, explored in a manner that promises significant gains. I can only hope that what has for me proved a stimulating and challenging interdisciplinary journey will also prove to be of interest and satisfaction to the reader.

Part I of the book reviews and criticizes the recent literature in the fields of ethnomedicine, social epidemiology, and medical ecology; it concludes with a frame of reference designed to guide the reader through the material that follows. In Part II, I examine traditional definitions of disease, propose alternative frameworks in which to consider disease, and present an economic and decision theoretic model of illness behavior. Part III considers the relationship between disease concepts and the organization of medical care, reports on a specific case study in psychosomatic medicine, and discusses the potential contribution of cross-cultural sociomedical study to medicine, the social sciences, and operations research.

The book, then, represents an attempt to bridge the gap between medicine and social science and to interrelate traditional medical issues with those of the social and behavioral sciences that are relevant to them. The reader will also discern some preoccupation with matters properly regarded as "philosophical." This focus reflects two related factors that perhaps should be made explicit here. One is simply a temperamental or personal one: I happen to be interested in theoretical aspects of medicine. The other stems from a felt need, which in my opinion exists among medical students and in medical education generally, for a logical and scientifically based framework with which or from which to interpret and place the content of our daily work as physicians and students of disease. The book, in this sense, may aid in "rounding out" the orientation of those persons in the health-related sciences who, like myself, were unable and at times unwilling to devote attention to theoretical issues. As I read the literature, I find two prevailing schools of thought regarding the philosophy of science: the so-called logical reconstructionists or empiricists (who strive to depict the logic of science independent of content issues) and those influenced by and attendant to developments in the history of science. Both positions are in various degrees reflected in this book, and this pluralism reflects my view that we stand to learn different and equally important matters from each of them.

During my formal medical training at Columbia and Yale, I profited greatly from the serious, disciplined, and scholarly commitments that I observed in my teachers regarding their professional work. Among these I would include: Malcolm B. Carpenter, Elvin Kabat, Robert F. Loeb, Rustin McIntosh, Theodore Lidz, Frederick Redlich, Stephen Fleck, and Daniel Freedman. Several individuals at the Walter Reed Institute of Research were also influential in my thinking, and among these, I would like to mention David McRioch, Edwin Weinstein, and David Marlowe. Wayne Holtzman's guidance at the University of Texas was always positive, incisive, and much appreciated. Shervert Frazier provided me with intellectual stimulation and with the time to pursue research interests and, in addition, always encouraged me along these lines. I wish to express my thanks to him. I am personally very thankful to many individuals whom I have had the benefit of learning from following this period. Among these I would include Herb Hendry, Jack E. Hunter, Peter K. Manning, and Duane Metzger. Peter Manning, in particular, has been a friend and colleague in addition to teacher, and a few of the sections in this book are products of our thinking and working together. My association with Art Rubel was also beneficial and helpful. For a large segment of my academic life I had the privilege and good fortune of having Carole Ann Wallace work for me. Her many talents as well as her diligent, conscientious, and unusually intensive dedication enabled me to process and analyze much empirical data, which have been highly instrumental in affecting my thinking. My secretary, Sherrilyn Boatman, has patiently and most efficiently worked with me during my repeated attempts to get the material of the book formulated and articulated in a relatively coherent way. She has kept herself "cool" and motivated in spite of the many revisions I have presented her. I would like to thank Griffith Freed, who extended me friendship and understanding during portions of my stay in a department that made the pursuit of academic and scholarly ventures extraordinarily difficult. I also wish to express my appreciation to Dean Andrew Hunt of the College of Human Medicine and John Howell, Assistant Provost for Health Programs, both of Michigan State University, who extended personal support to me in a number of instances. Last, without the support and understanding of my wife, Joan, and two daughters, Andrea and Michele, I could not have maintained the frame of mind needed to work on this book.

Introduction

As physicians, we are concerned with the medical problems of individual persons. The patient's aches and pains and his physical and physiological constraints become our concern; and our efforts are directed toward helping *him* achieve a better life. The emotional and social consequences of disease to the individual patient and his family invariably enter the picture also, and in varying degrees our efforts in treatment are affected by these factors. As psychiatrists, we are taught that an analogous set of "medical" issues forms the fabric of our commitment and obligation to the individual patient, although our focus is often more centrally placed on psychological and social aspects of the individual's life situation. At the same time, how we go about carrying out our responsibilities as psychiatrists is affected by our beliefs about how far it is possible for people to change socially and psychologically and how we as persons and psychiatrists are viewed and responded to as a consequence of the very special "treatment relationship" that we form with the patient. Nevertheless, psychiatrists, like physicians, share in the ultimate concern of helping other individual persons deal with the burdens associated with disease. The "clinical" picture of disease that is forged in medical practice is consequently heavily permeated with the personal experiences of individuals from different walks of life.

From their pedagogical training experiences and from repeated clinical encounters with patients, physicians and other students of medical problems are able to abstract a corpus of information about the category "disease" viewed as an entity apart from the individual. This, of course, is the fundamental theme of epidemiology, the study of the causes and distribution of disease, just as it is of the medical investigator interested in the purely physiological, chemical, or clinical aspects of disease. In this context, the term *disease,* which in our work with individual persons is associated with pain, discomfort, disability, and disappointment in a specific person, is made to refer to abstract and impersonal issues, such as physiological mechanisms, socially causal factors, or structural components. We note, then, that different personal experiences and different sorts of happenings and processes are interwoven in and with disease. In subsequent chapters I shall have a great deal more to say about the kinds of things that are ordinarily implied when physicians (and others as well) speak about disease but for now merely point to the varied nature of this central medical concept.

Social scientists, who note and describe the regularities in the way people behave and conduct life and who then study factors that may explain these regularities, have increasingly been drawn to problems associated with disease. As we know, the consequences of disease are problematic to persons, and disease is very often associated with changes in the way people think, feel, and behave. To the social scientists, then, diseases produce patterned, almost predictable disruptions in the social behaviors of persons. Some social scientists may go so far as to state that because diseases are influenced causally by social variables and because their manifestations in turn impinge on the social and psychological sphere, one may properly see disease itself as anchored in the social system. Furthermore, the term *disease* and other medical terms are interesting and important symbols in their own right, symbols that can themselves have profound social and psychological consequences. In probing issues and processes tied loosely under the term *disease,* social scientists have also shown that a great deal of what we as physicians think and do with persons who are sick is affected by variables of a social, psychological, cultural, and economic nature. That is to say that many of the actual decisions of physicians that involve diagnosis and treatment can be traced to characteristics of the person that are, as it were, almost independent of the disease process that can be identified. Nonbiological contingencies that have to do with the person's identity and status thus permeate and strongly influence the work of the physician, leading some social scientists to insist that the practice of medicine itself is truly a social affair. In short, *disease* viewed generically, *physician* viewed generically and in a corporate sense (as a professional group), and *medical practice* viewed as an institution and system of society are all profoundly affected by (actually composed of) variables of a social, psychological, cultural, and economic nature. Medical issues generally, and problems involving human disease and its management specifically, are thus areas of inquiry not only of physicians and biologists but also of social and behavioral scientists.

A number of behavioral scientists are being more direct and insistent about these facts. They are emphasizing that the social sciences are as basic or "required" for the education of the physician as are the disciplines of anatomy, biochemistry, physiology, or pharmacology (Simmons and Wolff 1954, Bloom 1965, and Talbot, Kagan, and Eisenberg 1971). Implicit in these emphases is the view that disease must be seen in behavioral terms. The central premise behind the argument that states that the biological sciences are crucial to medical education, of course, stems from the awareness that the empirically derived knowledge of these sciences enables detecting and controlling many of the consequences of disease and thereby specifying with some reliability the underlying processes and mechanisms of the disease. Social scientists are emphasizing that since what patients seek medical advice and care for is expressed behaviorally, then it follows that behavioral science is equally relevant to a rational understanding of medical problems or "disease."

This argument is supported by an appeal to two general sets of issues that involve the traditional concern of the practicing physician with diagnosis and treatment. First, as regards diagnosis, we can say the following: (1) Not all patients present for evaluation and care with complaints referrable to recognized biologically altered processes or states (Anderson 1963, Von Mering and Earley 1966, Fabrega, Moore, and Strawn 1969, Zola 1972). (2) Some present with complaints that appear to be rooted in and defined by social variables (King 1962, Rubel 1960). (3) Many persons with complaints clearly linked to (1) and (2) do not present formally for scientific medical care but may instead seek other types of help or none at all (Fabrega and Roberts 1972, Kutner, Makover, and Oppenheim 1958). Nevertheless, such persons may be equally in need of scientific care. (4) The manner in which persons perceive, organize, and express disability, *regardless of its origin,* is embedded in behavior; and the form of this behavior, which in many ways is the raw data of medical evaluation, is determined by social, psychological, and cultural factors as well as by biologic, ecologic, or genetic factors (Mead 1947). And (5) decisions affecting what persons do vis-à-vis disability are determined by behaviorally relevant priorities that are also diverse as to source (Rosenstock 1966). The preceding issues, together, give substance to the conviction of social scientists that physicians, the practitioners of scientific care, need to be aware of the many competing factors that impinge on the decision to seek care as well as the many factors that determine the expression of disability.

With regard to the other traditional concern of the physician, namely, treatment, social scientists emphasize the fact that the process of *delivering* and *evaluating* medical care involves the problem of specifying unhealthy behaviors and then planning for their modification or elimination (Skinner 1953, Ferster 1963). The behaviors in question, as already stated, are promoted, maintained, and structured by various factors having social, cultural, and psychological significance. According to the social scientists, then, a physician, in order to make rational and effective use of his knowledge about biological processes to treat a patient, must be aware of the behavioral dimensions and implications of his aims and actions. Stated succinctly, he needs to understand and know how to apply the principles of human behavior in order to treat patients effectively.

These considerations are reflected in the fact that in some quarters the social and behavioral sciences are now being judged as required for the training of the physician. One also notes that departments of community medicine and/or social medicine are being incorporated within medical schools, and these developments are undoubtedly related to the growing awareness of the social and behavioral roots of traditional medical forms. Psychiatrists, traditionally involved in behavioral issues, are becoming more and more oriented to social and community problems, as if these were natural extensions of their "medical" mandate. If behavioral and psychological issues are an integral part of medicine, then surely (the argument runs) the community and the society that nurture the individual must also be considered and involved in "treatment." Clearly, these developments are significant and, I submit, far-reaching, although the implications cannot at this time be fully defined.

In evidence here, then, is a medical revolution of sorts. Activities, obligations, and requirements of physicians, as well as the meanings of key medical concepts and premises, are in the process of being modified. A fundamental thesis underlying this book is that this "revolution" has proceeded with insufficient critical examination. More specifically, I see no exposition of the bases, rationale, and long-range consequences of these seemingly new emphases in contemporary medical theory, practice, and education. This book can in fact be seen as an explanation for and analysis of these developments with the aim of clarifying what they portend. This task will require a review and discussion of contemporary approaches to the study of disease in society and culture, as well as a theoretical analysis of medical concepts. The social factors related to disease, and in particular, the behavioral dimensions of disease, are given principal attention. No attempt is made, in other words, to review basic substantive material of any of the established medical disciplines or to elaborate upon specific medical diseases, procedures, or practices. Instead, the logic and theory of disease and medical practices are examined. From another standpoint, this examination can be regarded as a theoretical analysis of the role of social science in medicine.

Part **I** Review and Criticism of
Traditional Approaches in Social Medicine

Chapter **1** Social and Cultural Aspects of Illness

In this chapter we will review medical studies that employ an exclusive social and cultural perspective toward illness (I use *illness*, rather than *disease*, to indicate that the unit of analysis is a sociocultural category). In contrast to studies that will be reviewed in Chapter 2, in this instance the medical problems are handled in terms of social referents. For example, the beliefs about the causes of an illness, the patterned behaviors and attitudes associated with an illness occurrence, or the social processes that culminate in the treatment of an illness are investigated. Several general books dealing substantively with sociological aspects of medicine have recently appeared (Mechanic 1968, Coe 1970, Freidson 1971). Because these books summarize much of the work undertaken by contemporary medical sociologists in Western urban settings, this chapter will be concerned primarily with medical studies conducted by culturally oriented anthropologists who have worked in nonliterate settings. For comparative purposes, however, I will give some attention to classical sociological studies that are similar in orientation, namely, those that employ a cultural orientation to medical problems.

The majority of the studies reviewed in this chapter follow what can be termed an ethnomedical approach, since medical problems are examined with special attention paid to the form and meaning that these types of problems are given by members of the community. The comparative analytic focus of anthropology and its emphasis on holism, process, and change have classically been employed in the examination of "primitive" medical systems. In such ethnomedical studies an attempt is made to analyze problems of illness and medical care in relation to other cultural activities of the group. Illness, for example, offers an additional opportunity to study how behavior is structured and organized by underlying cultural rules. Focusing on medical treatment, on the other hand, may allow access to the beliefs regarding religious and malevolent agencies as well as statements about the ultimate values that members of the culture hold sacred. How members of the cultural group relate to each other and their views of personal relationships are often dramatically portrayed during occurrences of illness and medical care. A long-range goal of ethnomedical studies, and one that is shared by anthropological studies in general, is to analyze how sociocultural units function and change.

We will consider ethnomedical studies in terms of their focus on the following topics: (1) medical beliefs, (2) beliefs about bodily structure and function, (3) folk illness diagnosis, (4) illness descriptions, (5) the social context of medical problems and medical care, (6) medical treatment, and (7) personality characteristics of the medical practitioner. Finally, we will examine the psychiatric bias of ethnomedical studies and the limitations of current methodology.

Medical Beliefs

The conceptual orientations toward illness of nonliterate peoples have long been a central area of interest of physicians and anthropologists (Clements 1932, Sigerist 1951, Ackernecht 1955). Ideas about the causes and mechanisms of illness are described, and an attempt is made to explain the source of these beliefs and the influence that the beliefs have on what is done about the illness. An often explicit aim of the researcher is to show how a group's medical beliefs are related to its ethical and religious imperatives and to its beliefs about social relations. Beliefs about illness are thus examined in terms of the cultural themes and organized behaviors of the group. An underlying assumption, of course, is that the group does not share the prevailing Western biomedical view of disease and medical care (although all groups everywhere show symptoms and signs that a physician might ascribe to disease). In the absence of this more evolved explanatory base and the corresponding resources and facilities that are employed to combat disease in advanced societies, nonliterate peoples have developed their own orientations and practices that enable them to explain and deal with the manifestations of disease. These explanations invoke supernatural, sociointerpersonal, and naturalistic factors.

Laughlin's (1963) study is an excellent example of the ethnomedical approach of social scientists, especially those who give principal attention to medical beliefs. He begins his report by pointing out that a group's medical knowledge, particularly when viewed from the empirical standpoint, has implications for the study of human evolution. Culture by definition represents a "man-made," socially relevant, experientially derived set of rules for living. A group's medical knowledge and beliefs are a part of this culture and constitute its accumulated understanding of disease, an understanding born of trial-and-error efforts to cope with disease. Laughlin, then, anchors his analysis in the light of the widely held conviction of biologists that biological and cultural evolution need to be seen as interrelated processes, each of which influences the other. His discussion focuses on the Aleuts, a northern and maritime people who (when judged biomedically) show a remarkable degree of medical understanding that encompasses surgery, medical treatment, health practices, and human anatomy. Unfortunately, Laughlin does not review in depth the actual substance of these medical beliefs, and we are left to speculate on the kind of organization and meaning that these matters have *intraculturally* (that is, from the standpoint of the actors' *own perspective*). Laughlin is particularly interested in delineating the general bases for the medical beliefs and understandings of the Aleuts, and he emphasizes the link that these beliefs have with experiences facilitated by their particular environment. He is thus concerned with pointing out some of the general factors that appear relevant in the acquisition of medical knowledge.

Schwartz's (1969) study provides an excellent account of the sociocultural implications of competing medical systems, a factor that she analyzes from the standpoint of "hierarchies of resort" (that is, competing approaches to treatment). The discussion traces the sociohistorical roots of treatment approaches in the Admiralty Islands, Melanesia, and involves a critical examination of the influence of native beliefs and values on these approaches. This paper contains a number of very worthwhile suggestions for analyzing illness (its implications and treatment) in terms of social and cultural change. The many interpretations and definitions that can be given to illness in settings where cultures compete are analyzed. The implications of the observation that illness is construed as a moral category are carefully examined.

The paper by Fabrega, Metzger, and Williams (1970), which relates to the Maya Indians of Tenejapa, also concentrates on the moral bases of illness. In this paper there is greater emphasis on the content and organization of beliefs. The authors explicitly point out how beliefs about illness influence, and in turn are influenced by, social considerations and the status of interpersonal relations. They demonstrate that beliefs about the causes of all types of illness, not just illnesses indicated by exclusively social criteria, explicitly refer to notions of friendship, rivalry, envy, moral worth, and malevolence. The applicaton of the beliefs appeared to monitor the important social events and processes of the community. The study by Fabrega and Metzger (1968) focuses on related concerns among Spanish-speaking "ladino" residents of Chiapas. This report contains more data on social factors and processes linked to what can be termed "psychiatric" issues, that is, illness conditions not indicated by bodily symptoms or signs. The authors, in other words, point out the social and symbolic features of illnesses indicated by exclusively interactional and sociopsychological criteria. The functional consequences for the group of the way in which these beliefs influence behavior are also discussed.

The papers by Currier (1966) and Ingham (1970) are general accounts of the significance of the beliefs about the conditions of the blood in illness in Mexico. The two authors see in these beliefs a variety of symbolic trends that play a role in the process of socialization and in the contemporary interpersonal relationships of the residents. An interesting paper by Panoff (1970) focuses more directly on beliefs about the body and the blood and links these beliefs to the use of plants for remedies. A number of authors have given accounts of the use of botanical specimens for medical problems (for example, Stopp 1963, Grover 1965, Jain 1965, Morton 1968a, 1968b) but tend to de-emphasize cultural patterns and values, particularly as these relate to medical beliefs.

Lieban (1966) studied the relationship between fatalistic beliefs in Christian Philippine society and the often positive medical responses of Filipinos in situations where such beliefs are relevant. He found that such beliefs, even though they assign to supernatural agencies the final work in medical happenings, do not stifle efforts to obtain medical care. Edgerton's (1966) account of beliefs about psychosis in Africa is extensive and includes data about notions of etiology, descriptive features of behaviors felt to indicate psychosis, treatment, and prognosis. Of particular value is the variability that he uncovers regarding behaviors felt to signify psychosis. In a carefully reasoned paper Shiloh (1968) discusses the framework of medical beliefs and practices in the Middle East.

A useful feature of this discussion is his analysis of the way in which the concepts and practices of the Middle Eastern system constrast with those of Western medicine.

Two recent papers by Fabrega contain elaborate information on medical beliefs. In these papers, there is an explicit concern with linking native conceptual traditions about illness with Western scientific medical knowledge. One paper attempts to elucidate, using physical and behavioral symptoms, the general model of illness in Zinacantan, Chiapas, Mexico (Fabrega 1970a). Here Fabrega addresses himself to the question of the specificity of a folk (that is, culturally defined) illness and probes this problem by interviewing a relatively large sample of informants about a number of folk illnesses. By definition, of course, in a cultural group all illnesses labeled X are "specific" in one sense—they are all judged as members of a particular class of illnesses (the class labeled X). Anthropologists have tended to assume that class membership of this sort means that the given instances of the illness possess the same cause, receive the same treatment, and assume the same significance in the group. However, are these illnesses seen as having the same components, that is, symptoms and signs? Stated conversely, in a cultural group can one distinguish *between* folk illnesses in terms of component profiles— are they distinguishable vis-à-vis symptoms and signs? Fabrega showed that in Zinacantan most folk illnesses were believed to be composed of general and systemic symptoms (for example, pain, weakness) as well as symptoms of an infectious nature (such as coughing, chills, etc.). Few folk illnesses were judged highly specific in this component frame of reference. This suggests that in given situations illness terms are not applied on the basis of biophysiologic factors. Presumably, sociocultural factors are important. However, since Fabrega did not study the labeling of actual illness occurrences (only the subjects' general knowledge), the question of how biological factors affect the cultural interpretation of illness must remain open.

Fabrega's second study attempts to arrive at an empirical classification of illness in Zinacantan (Fabrega 1791a). Again working with a substantial sample of informants and using a large number of folk illnesses, he concentrates this time on the way illnesses are interpreted and analyzed in Zinacantan. For this purpose he uses native illness dimensions—that is, culturally specific interpretations involving cause, the condition of the blood, treatment regimens, etc. He shows that, even at this level, there is much overlap in the meaning of folk illness terms. There were, however, interesting relationships between these native dimensions, and, furthermore, some limited correspondences or associations were manifest between Zinacantecan and Western medical "dimensions."

The study of Pridan and Navid (1967) deals with the problems of competing medical systems. An attempt is made to compare the medical knowledge of a group of 10th-grade Ethiopian students with that of American Peace Corps volunteers. Respondents were asked to link test diseases with certain dichotomies having relevance in the native interpretations of illness (for example, acute-chronic, external-internal, etc.). The authors imposed a criterion of 100 percent agreement by the group for a meaningful linkage. As can be expected, large differences were encountered, both in the kinds of dichotomies judged to be relevant by the two groups and the nature of the linkages with specific test diseases. The problem of variability of responses was not dealt with. The authors were able to get some agreements even when complex disease types were used as units (for example, chronic gastritis, typhoid, skin fungus). The implications of this consensus are not discussed. A typology of diseases was developed from the various dichotomies, and an attempt was made to relate this typology to notions of etiology and choice of treatment. Interesting associations between these dimensions were observed. The paper, in brief, represents an interesting exploratory attempt to specify the relationship between cultural background and medical knowledge. However, the details of the knowledge base and cultural orientations of the two groups are not presented; the implications of the results are not dealt with in sufficient detail (for example, What is the meaning of the term "skin fungus" as a label for a disease to a 10th-grade Ethiopian school child?), and there are problems in the method of sampling and in the reliability of the findings. The preceding issues are symptomatic of the fact that the focus of the study is not systematically related to any clearly delineated analytic concern. That differences in medical beliefs exist is by now a truism in the field of ethnomedicine, and attempts to study this phenomenon should reflect a theoretical concern or the aim of resolving a practical problem. However, these authors should not be singled out for special criticism, since their analysis is more refined than most studies in this area. Their study, in short, is notable for its attempt to deal incisively with medical knowledge.

Beliefs about Bodily Structure and Function

With some exceptions, notably the work of Laughlin (1963), most studies of medical beliefs rarely probe the underlying orientations of the peoples toward anatomical or physiological concerns. There appear to be two reasons for this: The first is that investigators judge that ideas about body structure and function are not relevant to an understanding of illness. Illness is frequently seen as a sociopsychological entity or category, and it is mainly moral and social issues that are considered relevant to definition and interpretation (see Chapter 5). The second reason for neglect of these matters might be that investigators lack interest in this domain and see it as somehow unrelated to disciplinary issues such as, for example, cultural dynamics. Quite often, of course, ethnoanatomical and ethnophysiological notions are minimally relevant for understanding native illness taxonomies. That is, how the body is believed to function and its presumed structure are often not factors in how subjects define, explain, and classify illness. In this light, we have seen that physiological symptoms do not appear to be a critical ethnomedical consideration in Zinacantan, Chiapas, Mexico. It is precisely this problem of uncovering the native conceptual categories as regards natural domains (domains commonly studied include plants, trees, and the color spectrum) that is receiving a great deal of attention in anthropology. Cognitions associated with and brought to bear on these domains are believed to be critical for the understanding of the related behaviors.

Ethnoscience is the term used to refer to this area of work, which is aimed at precise and rigorous identification of native taxonomies. Two papers relying on ethnoscientific methods have focused directly on anatomical knowledge. These studies, to repeat, do not bear directly on medical problems per se. However, they reflect the potential contribution that rigorous ethnography can make to ethnomedical studies and to medicine proper. A central fact that we must keep in mind is that although we may "see" and judge the body as integrated in a specific way, how other people "see" the body and distinguish among its parts is a reflection of their own cognitive categories, categories which themselves are culturally determined.

Franklin's (1963) paper reviews the Kewa concepts of body parts using an ethnolinguistic mode of analysis. Results are organized in terms of levels of body systems, with level three constituting the main sections of the physical body, and level four, the contrastive members of each of the main sections of the body. For Kewa anatomy ". . . the greatest number of contrasts that are subordinate to one part occur on level four. Especially significant are those members which are subordinate to the stomach area" (p. 57). Franklin includes in his analysis some of the conceptions regarding the function of body parts (for example, the liver is believed to be the seat of the emotions). Stark (1969) reports his analysis of body parts in Quechua. He limits his analysis to external features of the body. He develops alternative linguistic strategies for arriving at the semantic dimensions of various units within the domain of the body.

Linguistically oriented studies of this type provide an excellent background for an analysis of beliefs about illness and indeed about the nature of the manifestations that associate with altered biological processes. The following questions are suggested: In what manner does anatomical knowledge link with notions of cause and treatment of illness? How are the bodily based symptoms that are recognized by a group experienced and verbalized, and how is the anatomical knowledge possessed by the subjects linked to their perceptions and sensations of these bodily changes? Most ethnomedical studies that focus on folk medical issues, and specifically those dealing with notions of illness cause, definition, and symptomatic components, exclude these and other important questions. Studies that explore how notions of body parts and body function (ethnoanatomy and ethnophysiology) affect the expression and definition of illness would be of significance to both anthropology and medicine. Such studies, in essence, would clarify how culture and cognition filter, organize, and affect the interpretations of underlying bodily processes and changes; thus the potentially invariant behavioral properties of specific disease entities would be further clarified. Culture, in other words, in ordering behavior (including diet, energy expenditure, subsistence patterns, marriage rules, child-rearing emphases, exposure to disease agents, etc.) to some extent orders biology. However, it needs to be emphasized that biological processes themselves are interpreted in terms of culturally specific perceptions, and that the form that the altered behaviors take are to this extent culturally influenced. To state the point succinctly, culture also orders the categories through which biological changes become manifest.

Of course, we need to keep uppermost in our minds the fact that beliefs and concepts about bodily structure and function have implications that stretch far beyond strictly medical matters. The critical influence that language has in ordering an individual's orientation to his world and the centrality as well as the extensive interconnections that concepts about the body have in this orientation have not been more incisively probed than in the work of Friedrich (1969). Involving himself with the Tarascan language, Friedrich explored the fundamental meanings of body-part or corporeal suffixes, limiting himself to denotative (as opposed to connotative) aspects. He was particularly interested in uncovering the abstract and spatial nature of the underlying signification of a small set of complex body-part suffixes. Each of these suffixes denotes at least one body part, and some enter also into many of the expressions that are analogous to our adverbs of place, such as *beneath* and *beside*. In general, native Tarascans when confronted with body-part suffixes appear to have no conscious idea of the meanings of them. This is related to the fact that the suffixes are said to be structurally covert— the suffixes cannot be discussed in isolation. Furthermore, the semantic categories signified by the suffixes are obligatory, since the speaker in coding and reporting his experience by means of these categories is guided in a necessary fashion by choices tied to location, dimension, and shape. The body-part suffixes are a subset of what Friedrich terms (p. 7) "a larger set of 32 mutually exclusive morphemes [roughly, words]," which he calls the suffixes of space, because they are complementary to classes of suffixes equally fundamental in orienting the individual (such as suffixes of time, motion, person, etc.). A body-part word or an expression about some aspect of the body actually expresses one realization of a formula that is composed of various classes of grammatically and semantically distinct units (such as nonsuffixal roots, suffixes of voice, and inflectional units of tense, person, etc.), one of which is a suffix of space. So-called simple corporeal suffixes, besides contributing to specific body-part words, can also enter into the formation of expressions signifying function of a body part, gross bodily postures and positions, localized states and aspects of bodily segments, and socially contextualized idioms that metaphorically draw on a bodily part. On the other hand, the semantically more complex body-part suffixes extend broadly into any number of domains and are by nature more abstract. They signify such notions as narrowing, undersides of entities, edges of orifices, surfaces, and portions of enclosed spaces. Last, in everyday use, these abstract and rather complex body-part suffixes lead to the formation of expressions having psychosocial meaning (involving desires, memories, etc.) as well as referents in such "natural" domains as house parts, pottery, and farming. Body-part suffixes, in short, enter into the creation of meaning in a whole range of situations that are of central importance to Tarascans.

We observe in these more complex suffixes, then, the concrete and essentially symbolic *interconnectedness* of the world of the Tarascans and how central meanings tied to the body are to them. When elaborated upon, such meanings allow the individual to forge for himself a cognitive orientation in physical and even psychosocial space. In short, we have in beliefs and concepts associated with the body the units that anchor an individual in his universe. We must assume that the body as a three-dimensional and physiologic entity has a distinctive structure and function, which, however, is coded in a unique and variable way by means of the instrumentality provided the individual by his language. To quote Friedrich: "All languages presumably use what are apparently or primarily corporeal units (body-part words, and so forth) to signal various shape, locative, spatial, and deictic features" (p. 45). The way in which these corporeal units are used—the meanings given to them—differs depending on the language. Nevertheless, such a portion of an individual's language provides for him the basic map or set of metaphors that he symbolically draws on in his attempt to order and explain to himself the world around him.

The body must also be assumed to furnish the individual with a collection of rather elemental sensations that he draws on to give meaning and substance to his psychological and even social life. In this light, we must recall that illness in a fundamental sense reflects an alteration of the body—its shape, function, and feeling—and that for this reason, it also reflects and may trigger an alteration of the fundamental cognitive units that anchor the individual in his world. One is thus allowed to say that in changing the status and integrity of the body, the biological processes we have come to equate with disease are associated with or mediate changes having wide-ranging implications, precisely because the body is composed of those fundamental verities that constitute for the individual the symbolic and/or cognitive units that in a phylogenetic and ontogenetic sense have created structure and order for him. Studies that probe basic meanings about the body thus promise to clarify not only what is universal and what is culturally variable about illness and/or disease but also the central role that these intertwined notions have in man's perceived relationship to his ecosystem.

Folk Illness Diagnosis

A rare and brilliant attempt to understand how native people diagnose and categorize actual illness occurrences was made by Frake (1961), who studied the Subanun in the Philippines. This paper certainly must be placed high on the list of required readings in the rapidly expanding field of social science and medicine. Frake begins by distinguishing between an illness (what in this book I refer to as an illness occurrence) and a disease name or diagnostic category (what I earlier referred to as an illness term). Illnesses in a sense exist through time and at different points have different manifestations, and for this reason the illness can be called by different names (see Chapter 6). Frake shows that these considerations are *formally* a part of the Subanun medical taxonomy. Thus, although every disease term can be made to designate potentially a terminal stage (that is, vis-à-vis death or recovery), some terms are actually prodromal of other terms, which then function as "terminals." In the paper, Frake examines general features of taxonomies, particularly the fact that they are often hierarchic, and gives special attention to the medical one. Taxonomies divide phenomena horizontally (by discrimination) and vertically (by generalization or inclusion). Disease terms in Subanun can function at different levels of contrast. At any one level, of course, one finds what Frake refers to as diagnostive contrastive categories, that is, diagnostic types, each of which is potentially applicable in the labeling of an occurrence and which, for this reason, contrasts meaningfully with the others.

Frake then reviews the task of the ethnographer: given a set of disease names or terms that are contrastive, what rules govern which disease name is actually applied to an illness occurrence (that is, a "diagnostic situation")? To answer this question, Frake states that the investigator can rely on rules that are what he refers to as analytic, perceptual, and explicit in derivation. By a suitable coding device or grid, the investigator can apply to a given occurrence of illness external or independently derived markings that are from his standpoint distinctive. He then sees how this occurrence gets labeled by the people. Any illness occurrence, in other words, can be equated with two dimensions of meaning and labeling: the investigator's own (for example, his distinctive markings may include such things as physiological system involved, degree of behavioral interference, etc.) and the native's (which are unknown and to be discovered). Exhaustive markings of this type allow the investigator to determine analytically what important markers appear to coalesce in or underlie the use of a particular native diagnostic term. By analyzing the native taxonomy using these independent "distinctive" markings, the researcher can make intelligent guesses about the bases for and rationale of the native system of naming and ordering. Perceptual criteria are involved when the investigator tries to determine the actual stimulus discriminations made by the subjects when they categorize illness occurrences. However, since cues can be "internal" (may inhere in altered bodily sensations or in convictions about social occurrences), it is sometimes difficult to follow this route. Among the Subanun, Frake used careful elicitation techniques and asked informants about their "explicit" definitions or criteria of diagnosis. He thus isolated a limited number of diagnostic questions and criterial answers that the Subanun themselves use in classifying illness.

I cannot go into further detail here about Frake's substantive findings, and those interested should read his original document. It is significant that he concludes with the (debatable) point that disease or illness terms are mutually exclusive, and, furthermore, that informants, although they may disagree in *applying* their taxonomy in a given instance, *never* disagree about its inherent structure and meaning. He feels, in other words, that medical diagnostic types and taxonomies could be equivalently shared by members of the culture. Fabrega's studies in Zinacantan, reviewed earlier, cast doubt on the generality of this proposition. At least he found substantial variability in the way subjects used disease names or terms in Zinacantan. Frake's more general point is well taken: he proposes that to native subjects, ideally every illness occurrence can be placed into one or into a conjunction of two or more diagnostic categories. Furthermore, although disagreement may be encountered about which category a given occurrence falls into, the fact that the occurrence belongs in some category of the taxonomy is axiomatic. Failures at "proper" placement are seen as a consequence of deficiencies in the subjects' knowledge, and *not* as deficiencies in the taxonomy. Every illness occurrence, in other words, has a name; the problem is to find the correct name, since this usually dictates the responses to the occurrence (for example, treatment). Although other investigators have examined the problem of diagnosis among nonliterate peoples—see, for example, Schwartz (1969), Press (1969), and Fabrega (1970*b*)—none has made it the central focus of his efforts. Frake's emphasis, when combined with his careful and incisive methods of procedure, contributes to what must be regarded as a model study.

Illness Descriptions

From the standpoint of the field of medicine and human biology, a payoff of studies dealing with the medical problems of nonliterate peoples is that such studies might give clues that will clarify the various behaviors that are universally associated with illness. In subsequent chapters I will deal explicitly with the underlying question of what constitutes a disease—for example, what sort of ontological "entity" it is. Here, the problem of disease and behavior can be phrased as follows: Are bodily changes, such as gastric ulceration, universally perceived by all subjects? If so, which of these changes are viewed as illness? When is a chronic suppurative cough associated with weight loss invariably seen as an abnormality that is deemed to require care and treatment? Is there such a "thing" as schizophrenia in all cultures, and, if so, what are its universal indicators? Do the indicators of "mental illness" necessarily refer to social adjustment, or are reports of special perceptual experiences or evidence of cognitive dysfunctioning, which are not accompanied by poor social adjustment, sufficient for labeling someone as ill? Questions of this type may be answered if we conduct meaningful cross-cultural studies of illness.

Perhaps because *social* behaviors are easily observed and interpreted, whereas *physiological* ones seem to require additional specialized knowledge for their understanding, field studies of illness among nonliterate groups seem consistently to touch on the question of mental illness. As we shall see, most such studies operate on what we could term a psychiatric bias—illness states are presumed to have no bodily correlates (or at least these seem to be disregarded by the investigator). To be sure, there have been some outstanding reports of how specific illnesses are actually expressed and interpreted by nonliterate peoples, and these need to be discussed.

Notable among these descriptions and analyses of what are currently termed *culture-specific syndromes,* or "folk" illnesses, are the ones by Newman, Langness, and Rubel. Newman's (1964) report of "wild man" behavior in New Guinea contains a wealth of detail dealing with the behavior of one individual who demonstrates features of a culture-specific syndrome. The fact that this behavior is described situationally, with attention given to the chronology of events antedating the "disturbed" behavior and with a minimal number of psychological inferences, enhances the value of the report; how the behavior is organized and linked to social circumstances is described intricately, and this objective reporting allows the reader to supply his own theoretical interpretation. Following this lengthy description, Newman presents a balanced evaluation of factors bearing on the etiology of this "wild man" behavior. This evaluation provides a succinct and scholarly review of the various factors that are believed to be important in the organization of psychopathological behavior. In contrast to earlier scholarly accounts of similar issues (see Parker 1962), then, Newman's report includes firsthand observations and ranges across distinct but complementary explanatory paradigms.

Langness's accounts (1965, 1967*b*) also include rich detail about socially relevant situations. His study elaborates on the type of behavior described by Newman and provides an evaluation of its dynamics that includes reference to Western psychiatric principles. His report also includes a review of similar syndromes that appear to bear a structural relationship (that is, hysteria) to the case he discusses. The implications of the relationship among these various syndromes are discussed. Both of these investigators adhere rather closely to a sociopsychological mode of explanation.

Rubel's (1964) account, on the other hand, although lacking a detailed description of the content of the behavior labeled as *susto*, includes an analysis of the history and distribution of this illness or syndrome. *Susto* (in some places termed *espanto*) is an illness that is found throughout Central America and parts of South America as well. The word signifies "fright" and is a clue to the cause of the illness. An unsettling experience, such as a fall, bad dream, or encounter with an animal in a secluded location, is believed to dislodge the individual's soul, which in turn causes and is reflected by certain physiologic, psychologic, and sociointerpersonal changes. Thus, the individual suffering from *susto* is characteristically said to be restless, weak, to sleep poorly, to withdraw socially, and to not feel well. (The reader is referred to the excellent paper by G. M. Foster [1953] for an analysis of the sources of the beliefs about this illness, which stems from Spanish folk medicine.)

To Rubel, a folk illness embodies a changed sociopsychological state and at the same time symbolizes a culturally significant pattern or trait. He sees the *susto* complex as referring to an illness per se (that is, a set of symptoms that locate in an individual and exist through time) and to a mode of explaining an illness. In a broader vein, the illness *susto* draws attention to a set of ideas and beliefs about man's relatedness to supernatural agencies, which contribute to his vulnerability. Rubel does give explicit attention to the several different types of social factors that might bear on the genesis of the *susto* complex, discusses these by means of illustration from field notes, and concentrates somewhat (though superficially) on illness components.

We should emphasize the irony and integrity implicit in Rubel's work on *susto*. He takes a folk illness (that is, a non-Western illness having its own culturally specific etiology, treatment, meaning, etc.) and handles it in the same way as would an epidemiologist. He assumes, in other words, that the "illness," in addition to functioning as a culture pattern, also represents an entity of sorts that exists in time and place and *across* culture groups. *Susto,* in short, is handled as though it were malaria or onchocerciasis—as a specific disease entity having its own discrete distribution, which bears (in the broadest sense) on environmental contingencies. Diagnostic criteria, of course, rest on cultural factors as opposed to microbiological ones. In the paper, Rubel suggests that *susto* also has a purely sociocultural etiology—personal stress engendered by the perception of failure in carrying out the behaviors and responsibilities of a particular intracultural role. To Rubel's way of thinking then, the illness *susto* has a functional importance in the sociocultural system—it represents a cultural pattern as well as an illness, which furnishes individuals who are experiencing "role-stress" social and psychological protection: by becoming ill and entering this sick role, as it were, the individual is released from the demands of his normal, "well" role. This is not the place to criticize this particular position. In later chapters I will examine more carefully the implications of adopting such an exclusive sociocultural frame of reference in matters having to do with health and illness. Rubel's study, though, does illustrate nicely the classic ethnographic approach to medical studies, and his observations and thinking are in this sense exemplary.

O'Nell and Selby (1968), following ideas set forth by Rubel, conducted a controlled study in two Zapotec villages, which involved relating the prevalence of *susto* to the amount of stress associated with the performance of sex-role duties. Here, in other words, the epidemiological method is employed to gain empirical support for the hypothesis regarding the etiology and functional significance of the ethnomedical entity *susto*. Women, who are believed to experience considerably more stress than men and who, in addition, are provided fewer sanctioned outlets for the expression of stress, more frequently tended to report having suffered from *susto*. O'Nell and Selby did not attempt to relate folk illness prevalence either to disease problems defined in terms of alternative frameworks or to disturbances in biological systems. Neither did they take into consideration the frequently reported finding that in epidemiological survey studies in general women tend to report more illness (see Fabrega et al. 1967, Fabrega and Wallace 1967). This general finding, of course, weakens the thrust of this particular study on *susto*. Nevertheless, this study moves beyond ordinary descriptive accounts of folk illnesses and makes a more incisive attempt to relate illness to cultural patterns.

Several additional studies of culture-specific illnesses have emphasized different facets of the behaviors that signal illness diagnosis. Rodrique (1963), for example, reports on the psychological disorder called *lulu*, which is found in Papua. The manifestations of this disorder are very similar to those of "wild man" behavior described by Newman and Langness. Rodrique's account contains a rich array of clinical findings that he obtained by examination and historical research. These data draw attention to motor disturbances during the illness phase and also suggest that changes in level of awareness (for example, confusion, disorientation) are part of this disorder. Koch (1968), also working in New Guinea, describes the condition termed *nenek*. He notes similar types of motor and psychological abnormalities and includes considerable detail on the behavior of individuals showing the condition. His report is notable for its inclusion of material dealing with folk etiology and treatment. Cawte (1964) has contributed a balanced report of the ethnopsychiatric concerns he observed among the Kalumburu people in Australia and has compared Western and aboriginal perspectives toward psychopathology, classification of psychiatrically relevant behaviors, and medical management. His classification on the basis of predominant symptom pattern contains some insightful observations but is only schematically developed; he does not present actual clinical material or descriptions of behaviors that serve to indicate illness and that underlie the process of diagnosis. Hoskin, Kiloh, and Cawte (1969) reported on their observations of *guria,* a term used to designate various "shaking syndromes" found in New Guinea. They include in their discussion clinical features as well as native beliefs regarding the source and mechanism of these syndromes. In their discussion, the relationship of these syndromes to possession behavior and to disorders having a documented central nervous system malfunction (such as epilepsy or seizure disorders) is also probed.

Many investigators have focused on the phenomenon of spirit possession. The report of Freed and Freed (1964), as an example, contains an
excellent description of the situational reactions to an illness episode.
Their analysis is in terms of the traditional concepts of hysteria. Hamer
and Hamer (1966), focusing on spirit possession in Ethiopia, drew attention to the many physical complaints that are subsumed under this
label. Their report also includes excellent data dealing with the family's
reaction to the individual showing possession behavior. Their interpretation, however, again follows a rather traditional sociopsychological
paradigm: ". . . it is apparent that personality dissociation still remains
a satisfactory technique for many individuals in adapting to frustrations
and failures of their everyday existence" (p. 407). Lewis (1966) and Wilson (1967), on the other hand, tend to emphasize purely social and structural factors as causative forces of possession behavior.

The reader wishing to obtain further material on possession states
is urged to consult the collection of papers edited by Prince (1968),
especially the chapters by Bourguignon, Ludwig, and Van Der Walde.
The first of these presents a comprehensive framework that allows organizing the large amount of data that has accumulated about trance
and possession behavior. The application of this framework, however,
might prove to be problematic in individual instances, since there are
no clear indicators or guidelines that allow one to differentiate reliably
between trance and possession behavior. Ludwig's chapter contains an
excellent review of the components, native explanations, and probable
etiologic factors that are regularly found to be associated with altered
states of consciousness. Van Der Walde's account reviews etiologic
notions about trance using data about hypnosis as background. The
theoretical paradigm of ego psychology forms the foundation of his
analysis.

The recent reviews by Kiev (1969), Kennedy (in press), and Yap (1967,
1969) make unnecessary further review of substantive work relating to
the culture-specific syndromes as judged from the psychiatric standpoint. All of these reviews are extensive and of very high quality. The
reviewers approach the examination of these syndromes from a traditional Western medical perspective. The prevailing Western biomedical mode of differentiating among types of illnesses and medical prob-

lems is salient in their approach: they demonstrate a persistent concern with typing disorders or illness (that is, organic versus psychiatric, schizophrenia versus depression versus hysteria, etc.). For certain types of questions this approach is, of course, necessary. However, many disagreements among workers in this field seem to overemphasize Western typological concerns and have the effect of clouding what can be a potentially important area of study for both social science and medicine (Salisbury 1966a, 1966b, 1967, Langness 1967a). Any illness episode makes possible a careful description of the factors leading to the recognition of an altered behavioral or biological state, to the illness behavior itself, the manner of onset, progression, and resolution of the illness episode, to an assessment of the contribution of different apparent etiological factors, and to a careful analysis of the meaning given the behavior by members of the group. A careful inspection of the rather extensive reports of illness problems in various cultures will disclose that these rather basic ethnographic elements of illness episodes are usually overlooked. The greater the number of case analyses that include material on the situations evoking illness as well as on descriptions of the illness per se, the more we will be able to learn about factors influencing behavioral reactions. A follow-up of individuals who have had these reactions, a survey of the frequency and distribution of occurrences, and a specification of the social context and of how the behavior differs from other behavioral reactions that may or may not be viewed similarly by members of the group would allow a better understanding of the meaning of these reactions.

The Social Context of Medical Problems and Medical Care

Studies that describe the social context of medical problems and care, either in nonliterate settings, preindustrial cities, or in situations of contact between competing cultures, are numerous. Wolff (1965), in addition to describing the beliefs that organize medically relevant behaviors, illustrates nicely the manner in which contrasting medical care systems are relied upon conjointly. Solien De Gonzalez, although her focus extends beyond strictly medical concerns, provides an interesting description of the family's manner of coping with the health problems of infants and children in Guatemala. The kinds of health problems recognized by the mothers, their explanations of these problems, and their manner of reaching decisions about the health of children are discussed. In another paper, De Gonzalez (1966) touches on the theme of competition between medical systems and includes an analysis of the type of medical behaviors (deemed advantageous or adaptive from a Western medical standpoint) that appear to be thwarted or not rationalized by folk traditions of care. Shiloh (1965) presented a case study involving leprosy and its management among the Hausa of northern Nigeria. The native beliefs and orientations toward leprosy are first contrasted with those of Christian missionaries who attempted to treat leprosy. Then, the reasons for the success of the government's treatment program, which involved Western scientific methods, are reviewed. The study represents a clear illustration of how competing medical traditions can interact in a positive way and lead to the control of a serious health problem.

Maclean's paper (1966) focuses more intensively on the phenomenon of competing medical systems. She illustrates how residents use, in a complementary fashion, medical facilities and personnel attached to care systems that are conceptually opposed. She includes a description of the existing Western scientific medical care system that presents an alternative to the use of traditional healers in Ibadan. Her data were obtained as part of a survey funded by the British Empire Cancer Campaign, and the study provides an example of the increasing reliance on social scientists for analyses of medical care practices. Use of facilities and remedies prescribed by both medical traditions is compared by sex and social grouping. Results indicate that the "emerging middle class" does not respond to treatment of illness differently from the group living in the traditional Yoruba pattern. In these studies (see also Maclean 1965a) she gives attention to the local population's acceptance of hospitals and the extent of their continued dependence upon traditional forms of treatment. An interesting finding was that close to 50 percent of the households in the traditional area relied on native medicines as a prophylactic and treatment for fits or convulsions in children. In a separate paper Maclean (1969) focused more directly on the use of traditional healers by female clients, and her analysis of illness behaviors is linked with conceptions of pregnancy. This paper discusses in a very detailed way the native system of curing. Press's (1969) study in Bogota, Colombia, is similar in focus and contains a very useful analysis of the patterns and implications of the use of dual medical systems. It includes an awareness of the expressive factors that play a role in the use of lay medical care facilities and personnel.

As I shall indicate in later chapters, one reason for studying medical problems cross-culturally and with an ethnographic focus is to arrive at a more insightful and well-rounded picture of disease. This potential of ethnomedical studies has been implicit in many of the discussions of the current chapter. V. Turner has illustrated in rich detail one particular form that these insights can take in his publication on Lunda medicine (1963). The Ndembu, he informs us, conceive of disease as a type of misfortune, on a par with such issues as bad luck at hunting, loss of property, etc. (see Fabrega, Metzger, and Williams 1970 for an elaboration of related matters among the Maya of Tenejapa). Some illnesses are believed to result from the breach of a ritual prohibition, which is actually disclosed by the nature of the symptoms of the illness. Turner shows how various features of physiological symptoms (for example, level and type of pain, appearance of a lesion, nature of physiological dysfunction) are symbolically elaborated upon by the people in their responses to it. In a sense, bodily abnormality, ritual practice, and cognitive interpretation are fused, and the totality of these considerations constitute what the disease "is" for the Ndembu. Color symbolism is prominent in this elaboration. In a given instance the associative links between medicines and the feature of the illness that is the object of symbolic elaboration are "sympathic" (the symbol shares an aspect of the object's existence or state) or "contagious" (the symbol is or has been an actual part of the object it signifies or in physical contact with it). The former is illustrated by the use of the white gum that is secreted by the root of a plant to treat gonorrheal infection (symbolic link with pus), the latter, by the use of portions of the ant bear's diaphragm to cure tuberculosis (the animal's strong chest, it is believed, will strengthen the chest of the patient). Turner's report is a virtual collection of such instances of physiologic-socio-cognitive elaborations and provides the reader with a refined picture of how disease is woven into the fabric of social life among the Ndembu.

Medical Treatment

The classic studies of Ackerknecht (1942*a*, 1942*b*, 1943, 1945*a*, 1945*b*, 1946*a*, 1946*b*, 1947) led to important insights in the study of primitive medicine and represent a convenient point of reference for the discussion of lay medical treatment. These early contributions of Ackerknecht in many ways must be regarded as transitional ones; they were the first attempts to review critically and analyze a large body of information (much of it anecdotal, impressionistic, and highly biased) that had been accumulating about the medical practices of nonliterate people. Individuals like Clements (1932), Evans-Pritchard (1937), and Rivers (1924) had dealt with conceptual styles of "primitives" in a variety of contexts though with considerable focus on medical concerns. Ackerknecht reviewed their assumptions, clarified their logic, and developed a perspective that, despite its occasional ambiguities and inconsistencies, is still valuable today. (For subsequent developments of this theme, see Erasmus 1952, Simmons 1955, Frake 1961, Fabrega and Metzger 1968.)

What Ackerknecht first pointed to was the need to attend to the premises and the assumptions that underlay much of primitive medical beliefs and practices. He first emphasized the imprecision and ambiguity associated with the attempt to distinguish the concept of supernatural causes from that of natural causes, indicating that elaborations of the "natural" usually contained supernatural premises, and, conversely, probing for explanations of the "supernatural" often involved an appeal to events or interpretations that could be labeled naturalistic. In an attempt to resolve this intellectual dilemma, he suggested that what often appeared to be "natural" in an explanation or conceptual style and belief was merely habitual, meaning that there appeared to exist an absence of urgency and, at the same time, an "automatic" character to the way in which the medical explanations were offered. Ackerknecht appeared to arrive at this position as a result of his conclusion that natives used "natural" explanations to explain illnesses that were nonproblematic, highly visible, and very common.

The critical limitation in Ackerknecht's early work was his confusion (a legacy from the earlier, biased impressions of others) about what constituted rationality in medical explanations. At times he equated rationality with the Western or the valid, at other times with the "natural," at other times with the desirable or modern in the native's mode of thinking. Quite obviously, an explanation that a subject offers may be considered "rational" if it follows the rules of logic regardless of the epistemological status of its premises. The confusion evident in Ackerknecht's early work stems in part from confounding the structure or logic of explanations with the status of the premises.

I will not treat here in more detail the relevance of Ackerknecht's early contributions, but I wish to make several points regarding his intentions. The utility or purpose of classifying and differentiating medical explanations is clear when the goal is to assess the medical "value" or "correctness" of native medical practices and beliefs, that is, when the investigator, assuming Western medical principles to be valid, tries to determine the degree to which native beliefs and practices approximate Western ones. In other words, when evolutionary issues or questions of ecologic persistence are at stake, this paradigm is critical. However, such an evaluation can be accomplished only when the knowledge and methods of the biological sciences can be used to analyze and interpret what takes place in settings where primitive medicine is practiced. Ackerknecht's goal and accomplishment was to sensitize the observer to the necessity of distinguishing between, on one hand, what is believed to actually transpire in primitive medical transactions when one interprets phenomena using a biomedical framework and, on the other, what the natives believe or surmise has taken place. In other words, he drew a distinction between the instrumental value of a belief or action in a particular setting and the interpretation placed on it by the subjects themselves. When the investigator focuses on the subject's point of view and classifies his beliefs, one purpose for differentiating between the natural as opposed to the supernatural, assuming this distinction can be agreed upon, may be its usefulness in the explication of behavior and conduct that accompany the differing interpretations. There are, of course, any number of reasons or purposes for differentiating or typing the nature of the premises that are being used in medical explanation; these will depend on the analytic intentions of the investigator.

The ideas of Frank (1961; see also Kiev 1964) must also be considered in any evaluation of the medical value or therapeutic efficacy of curing ceremonies in preliterate settings. What Frank lucidly illustrated is that there are a variety of emotional states that accompany the condition of disability that is brought about by underlying disease processes of a bio-medical nature. These emotions are analogous to those we label as hope-lessness, despair, and anxiety. The consequences of these emotions for the sick person are negative; probably through the hormonal imbalances with which they are associated they contribute to a deterioration of phys-ical status; at the same time, the behavioral correlates of these emotions can interfere with proper rest, hydration, and nutrition, which serve to aid the body in its attempts to ward off some of the effects of the disease process. (The reader is urged to consult Schmale 1972 for a succinct summary of these issues from the standpoint of contemporary psycho-somatic medicine.)

Frank emphasized the strong social and psychological effects that ceremonies can have: the ceremony draws key personal objects of the patient together and enhances his self-esteem by promoting the sym-pathy and good intentions of his group's comembers at the same time that he expiates and atones for past sins. In addition, he pointed out that these sociopsychological effects occur in a culturally meaningful context that generates hope and anticipation of help and improved well-being. The result is that the negative emotional correlates of dis-ease, emotions that can retard improvement and also promote deterio-ration, are counteracted and replaced by those that have a beneficial ef-fect. The patient gains confidence and hope that others, including the important spiritual agents, are working and demonstrating in his behalf through the mediation of the curer. These factors, Frank implies, proba-bly affect the disease process itself by altering hormonal balances and thus promoting the body's natural recuperative powers. Some improve-ment in nutrition and hydration follow when previously withdrawn and isolated individuals begin to show an interest in food, activity, and their social environment generally, as a result of the enhanced self-image that is promoted by the ceremony.

Frank's rationale, then, is aimed at explaining the beneficial effects that curing ceremonies have on individuals who are suffering from mor-bid pathophysiological processes. If to this list of potentially beneficial factors we add the possibility that an undefined subset of individuals improve simply because the purely social basis and *definition* of their illness is eliminated as a result of the curing ceremony, we complete the picture of how curing ceremonies can promote healing in nonliterate settings. Many persons, no doubt, experience distress and are labeled as ill by themselves and by group members without having underlying structural or serious disease processes. Several reports have drawn attention to the role that purely social factors can play in generating illness conditions. Whether these persons adopt the "sick role" (Parsons 1951a) or the symbolic categories of illness merely for socially expedient reasons, to what extent this adoption is rationally or *consciously* determined, and what the concomitant bodily sensations and *biological processes* are that lead persons to choose this role are questions that are difficult to answer.

The analytic framework of Frank underlies many recent studies. The chapter by Kiev in the book that he edited (1964) contains a useful summary of the many issues that influence the success of medical treatment practices and focuses more centrally on specific problems bearing on folk "psychiatric" treatment. The Kiev collection contains several illustrations of how psychological features of treatment ceremonies promote healing (for example, the work of Murphy, Fuchs, and Madsen). The studies by Holland and Tharp (1964), Balikci (1963), and Kiev (1966) are in the same tradition. The paper by Kennedy (1967) deals more directly with psychological illnesses, and his recent general discussion of "primitive" psychotherapies (in press) is very complete and should be consulted for details of this paradigm for explaining treatment.

A number of studies have followed a different approach to explaining folk curing. Metzger and Williams (1963) in a concise report ". . . examine the role of the curer, placing particular emphasis on the characteristics and performances which not only define the role but which also, in their internal variation, are the basis for evaluation of curers and selection of one curer rather than another" (p. 216). Using rigorous methods of elicitation, they report on the method of diagnosis, the sequence of performances in curing, the social evaluation of curers, and the conditions and procedure for seeking a curer. Romano's (1965) description of curers and healing in southern Texas also shows a sensitivity to social factors: he anchors his analysis in what he terms a "healing hierarchy," which includes family and friends of the person needing help. He then proceeds to elucidate higher levels of this hierarchy and includes features of healers having great renown. Maclean's (1965b) report describes in some detail the curing personnel in Ibadan together with their methods of approach and is notable for its comprehensiveness. Nash (1967a) provides a careful description of curing, beginning with diagnosis and continuing through the rituals and practices that are believed to constitute the treatment. The description is accompanied by a presentation of the "logic" or theory of illness, which rationalizes the procedures that take place in the cure. Buchler (1964) in examining medical care practices presents data in support of the symbolic importance of the physical form of the medicine used in treatment.

Fabrega (1970b) examined the process of folk treatment in Zinacantan and gave particular attention to the implications of the interaction between healer and client for the treatment process. These interactions were viewed as involving the gathering and exchange of information between healer and patient, and in the analysis of this communication system the author drew attention to the competing medical resources that are available to Zinacantecans. He describes a system of medical care that is "open" in that there are many equally legitimate options, each of which may be used by the patient and his family. The obligations of both healer and patient are quite flexible and fluid, and either can and frequently does interrupt the process of diagnosis and medical care. In contrast to our own culture, where explicit rules and an institutionalized code of ethics seem to in principle bind the physician to his patient and his problem, in Zinacantan the shaman is allowed priorities (such as farming duties, family obligations) that can override the requests for his services no matter how pressing these may be. From a sociopsychological standpoint, the existence of such formal and explicit options appears to be functional, for these alternatives allow the shaman to withdraw from those encounters that bode ill for him and/or the patient. We must recall that such "folk" systems of medical care are anchored directly in everyday social relations and are permeated by notions of morality, malevolence, and personal involvement and liabilities. Shamans treating a "witchcraft" case are seen as exposing their very person to the evil that is symbolized by the illness. Should outside individuals in fact wish harm to the patient or his family, then the shaman becomes vulnerable himself should it appear that the illness (that is, the evil) will be undone. Illness, in short, is not simply a physical or physiologic state; it is symbolic of moral issues that implicate the patient and others in a web of social rivalries and jealousies. Similarly, should a patient die (even one not initially suspected of being bewitched), then the shaman involved in his "case" can be held responsible and may in fact be accused himself of being a witch and have his life threatened and in some instances taken. One observes, then, the highly personalized, inciting, and socially encompassing character of folk systems of medical care. These systems contrast starkly with our own, which are impersonal and almost "technological." Related issues touching on the social implications of illness and medical care will be discussed in more detail in later chapters.

The book by Lieban, *Cebuano Sorcery* (1967), illustrates in a very clear manner the framework that is often used by culturally oriented anthropologists when they examine medical treatment. A number of dimensions of a lay medical system are presented in this book. Of special note is Lieban's presentation of how illness and human experiences tied to disease articulate with and form a part of social activities and processes in the setting. Beliefs about the causes of illness are developed, and the ways in which these beliefs motivate the use of sorcerers and other medical practitioners in urban segments of the Philippines are presented. Illness constructs and related behaviors, as well as practices mediating medical care, are depicted as socially relevant phenomena that are culturally structured. Consequently, considerable attention is also given to different types of problematic social behaviors that are independent of (although often coexistent with) illness and disease and that also occasion the use of sorcery. The way in which concerns about disease (biologically defined) provide a matrix for the controlling functions of sorcery and the activities of practitioners is described, thus paving the way for an analysis of the presumed function of this system of medical care. Throughout the book the reader is kept informed of the way in which individuals oscillate between and relate to the two prevailing and quite different medical traditions, namely, the ethnomedical and the Western biomedical. Lieban, in other words, keeps in focus throughout his account the various components or aspects of disease, illness, and medical care. By means of illustrative field notes (abbreviated case analyses, if you will), he describes in rich detail actions having both an expressive (that is, actions that are their own justifications and that tend to carry heavy symbolic meanings) and instrumental (actions designed to achieve specific medical purposes) import on illness and medical treatment. In a separate report, Lieban (1965) studied the activities of practitioners from the standpoint of social control. The maintenance of shamanism was explained by Lieban as related to weaknesses and limitations in the formal system of social control, particularly in the area of maintenance of property rights and marital obligations.

An unfortunate deficiency of most studies of folk treatment is the regular absence of data regarding the behavior and symptoms of the person who is sick. Although quite often, of course, the concern of the researcher is not on specifics of the sick person but on general facets of curing practices, detailed descriptions of persons who are sick—beginning with the initial recognition of illness and ending with the outcome of culturally prescribed curing practices—would be useful in rounding out the treatment analysis. Also, the linkages between competing systems of care already well described by Maclean (1965a, 1965b, 1966, 1969), Fabrega (1970b), Press (1969), and Schwartz (1969) need to be broadened to include individual instances of illness viewed along a more extended time framework—illness "careers," so to speak. In-depth, qualitative studies of how folk modes of treatment link with Western medical modes are also needed. For example, what are the available folk remedy options, which ones are chosen (and in what order) for specific illness manifestations, and, similarly, at what point and in what manner do other types of treatment modalities enter? Data along these vectors, if extensive and suitably analyzed mathematically, will enable building a rigorous model of medical treatment, which will be valuable to both anthropology and medicine (see subsequent chapters for an elaboration of these issues).

The question of the efficacy of folk medical treatment is frequently raised. The impression one gains from reading the literature in ethnomedicine is that investigators do not deal with illness occurrences longitudinally and in depth. In other words, attention is not given to the long-term consequences of ceremonies as viewed from multiple frameworks (that is, biological, behavioral, emotional, etc.). It should be stated that such analyses are, in a practical sense, very difficult to undertake. First of all, obtaining permission merely to observe a ceremony is quite problematic since these are, above all, private affairs touching on highly intimate and personal life concerns that are usually seen as fraught with potential danger to the patient, family, and the healer. Similarly, the general tenuousness of the moral and physiological health status of the patient following a ceremony renders a visit and interview with even the family of the patient equally problematic. Third, it frequently is difficult to obtain information regarding who is developing illness in a hamlet so that one often cannot determine early in the "career" of sick persons the nature of the symptoms and signs present. This difficulty stems in part from the general exclusiveness with which subjects often guard private and moral concerns as well as from the fact that quite often the label of illness (together with the decision to seek treatment) is applied rather abruptly, being determined by social and private contingencies as well as by the magnitude of the experienced discomfort. The literature suggests that occasionally judgments about illness are made when minimal objective evidence is present, but more often the judgment is reached at a later stage in the "natural history" of the disease. A final impediment to obtaining a critical medical evaluation (from the Western biomedical standpoint) of a person receiving treatment within the native system of care is the difficulty of obtaining consent for examination. Such consent, if granted, comes later or at critical stages in the career of the patient when the family may decide that Western forms of treatment are appropriate. Such a group of patients, quite understandably, is biased in the direction of serious illness and usually includes those who have experienced no benefit from traditional treatment practices.

One final comment needs to be made in order to round out this discussion of the issues and problems associated with the evaluation of folk medical treatment practices. Frequently, the groups studied have ready access to the many and varied pharmaceutical products that are sold commercially in nearby towns and cities. These products extend along a continuum from the pharmacologically active (for example, antibiotics and steroid preparations) to the (apparently) physiologically innocuous (such as salves, powders, or home remedies). Friends and relatives of a sick individual receiving folk treatment frequently obtain these commercial products as well as the more "traditional" remedies prescribed by the healer. This exposure to multiple types of medicinal preparations, some of which might be pharmacologically efficacious, others directly harmful, and still others likely to mask or confuse the clinical status of the patient, create an additional and somewhat formidable impediment to any attempt to evaluate systematically and empirically the healer's activities. In summary, the attempt to examine critically the medical value of folk medical practices is a most difficult undertaking since it requires accurately and repeatedly evaluating the physiological status of the patient, the pharmacologic value of the remedies that he uses, the unique sociopsychological consequences of the ceremony, and the therapeutic contribution that is being offered by contacts with and the use of products of the Western medical care system.

The reader should be aware that the attempt to evaluate the quality or effectiveness of medical care even in Western settings is quite problematic (Kerr and Trantow 1968, Last 1965, Weinerman 1966). The developing literature in this field of medicine has pointed to the many unresolved conceptual issues that exist, the central ones being the definition of concepts such as *health* and *illness,* as well as the definition and selection of an operational measure of *quality* (for example, should it be improved well-being, exposure to competently trained physicians, or the administration of medical procedures judged to be optimal or acceptable?). The methodological difficulties that attend the attempt to evaluate the quality of medical care are equally impressive and have been recently reviewed (Donabedian 1966).

Personality Characteristics of the Medical Practitioner
The behavior of "native healers," "medicine men," and shamans has long intrigued travelers and missionaries and has received considerable attention from behavioral scientists. Central issues in the field of psychiatric anthropology dealing with the relationship between culture and mental illness have been approached through the paradigm of the adaptation of the shaman. A persistent question has been whether sha-

mans are socially deviant persons with an underlying psychotic personality whose pathology is somehow protected and concealed by the behavioral requirements of their role. Silverman (1967) has recently reviewed the literature pertaining to this general topic. He elaborated on the ideas of Devereaux (1956) and Wallace (1961b) and, using psychiatric knowledge about the syndrome of schizophrenia, developed a five-stage cognitive model to explain and compare shamanism with the schizophrenic process. An explicit assumption of this model is that a potential shaman undergoes a significant and quasi-pathological change in personality adjustment during the process of consolidating his identity as a shaman. The current psychological health status of practicing shamans was not an explicit concern of the model. Handelman (1968) has stressed the need that exists in this general area for psychological data. He emphasized the importance of distinguishing between the role behavior of the shaman and behavior directly traceable to personality dynamics. Handelman suggests that many of the impressions and inferences about shamans stem from the analysis of behavior that has been consciously produced in compliance with socially shared definitions about the shamanistic role, rather than from psychopathology per se. These two frames are not mutually exclusive and thereby cause analytic and methodological problems for the researcher interested in evaluating behavior. How an individual "uses" a role, in other words, can also reflect psychopathology.

Initially, impressionistic and scattered observations served to link shamans with psychopathology. Single case studies or life histories of shamans, although often used for structural-functional analyses of sociocultural units, provide a profile of personality dynamics and functioning. The picture that emerges from some of these studies is hardly one of pathology. Case studies, unfortunately, cannot answer the question of whether shamans as a group tend to demonstrate psychopathology. In order to establish this in any one culture group as a whole, more extensive and controlled psychological studies are needed. There are actually few reports of investigations that have dealt with a group of shamans by use of systematic interview and testing methods, however.

A notable exception is the work of Boyer (1962, 1964; Boyer et al. 1964; Boyer et al. 1967), who studied the personality configuration of

Mescalero Apache Indians using a sample that included shamans, pseudoshamans, and "normals." Boyer relied on anthropological methods and techniques and psychoanalytically oriented interviews and, in addition, administered Rorschach tests, which were scored using the Klopfer method. His initial impressions, which were felt to be validated by the Rorschach analyses, were that "the typical Apache of the Mescalero reservation suffers from a hysterical personality disorder with attributes of the impulse neurosis" (Boyer 1962, p. 248). In addition to personality configurations of this type, the shamans in general were felt to have strong oral and phallic fixations and to possess traits of the impostor. The general conclusion, however, was that Apache shamans are not individuals who have disguised serious psychological illness, but on the contrary, that "based upon their greater capacity to test reality and their ability to use regression in the service of the ego, they are healthier than their societal co-member" (Boyer et al. 1964, p. 179). By employing a large group of Apaches as a control group, Boyer and his colleagues have presumably anchored their analyses of shamans on culturally relevant psychological baselines. The use of a group of cultural comembers in this fashion overcomes many of the problems associated with evaluating psychological material cross-culturally, since the characteristics of a group of persons gain saliency from the perspective of the particular culture and not from that of a totally different one.

However, several methodological and conceptual issues need to be taken into account in evaluating these results. The first involves the choice of a projective technique. The Rorschach is a valuable test for clinically assessing the dynamics of personality. The low reliability of its measures, however, limits the utility of the test when it is used for research purposes. Second, Boyer and his colleagues have not reported ample data on the social characteristics and experiences of their subjects so that the comparability of the groups cannot be established on this dimension. Consequently, one cannot determine in what fashion or to what extent the reported "personality" differences are due to differences in the social backgrounds (for example, acculturative exposures) of their study groups. Related to this is the fact that Boyer et al. have not sufficiently linked their analysis of the projective material with knowledge of the role behavior of their subjects. It is possible that psychological data they evaluated purely from the standpoint of the health-pathology continuum could be better interpreted from a perspective that accounts for the unique learning experiences of the groups. Thus, group differences on particular Rorschach measures, rather than exclusively reflecting greater "health" in the psychodynamic sense, may in part be a result of unique learning experiences that have accrued from the performance of the shamanistic role. Last, the conclusions of Boyer et al. regarding the greater adjustment or health of Apache shamans appear to rest entirely on psychological grounds. Information derived from analyzing the projective material has not been explicitly linked with information bearing on social adjustment. Because of this, problems that may result from the cross-cultural invalidity of the test cannot be excluded.

The recent empirical paper by Fabrega and Silver (1970) manifests a related clinical concern. They compared Zinacantecan shamans with nonshamans on a variety of social background and psychological characteristics. A projective test, the Holtzman Inkblot Technique (HIT) was used to evaluate clinically the personality of shamans. Shamans tended to score lower on acculturation indices. They also scored higher on a number of measures, including anxiety, hostility, and pathognomic verbalization. The exigencies of medical care and practice that bear on the role duties of the shaman were taken into account in the analyses of responses to the projective test. This point requires elaboration. As I have indicated, in nonliterate settings illness is a sociopsychologically inciting event or episode in the life of the patient and his family, involving issues of morality, sin, and personal responsibility. In Zinacantan, shamans are the culturally designated individuals who are empowered to deal with illness, and they consequently intrude into this emotionally charged "space." Furthermore, as spiritual as well as bodily healers, they become involved directly with supernatural agents of diverse types. Long-term involvements of this nature, or more precisely, experience in diagnosing and treating illness in a setting governed by these particular premises, was felt to predispose shamans to see in the undifferentiated ink blots various entities, such as gods, witches, and people, and to elaborate upon these in a socially and psychologically consequential manner. Fabrega and Silver argued that perceptual tendencies of this type that are picked up and measured by the HIT as anxiety or hostility cannot be viewed as personality traits in the classic sense. Instead, the personal experiences of the shaman in the process and dynamics of medical care (that is, his performance of a distinctive social role) must be seen as contributing to the responses that he volunteers in the testing situation. These kinds of experiences, in other words, are important factors in what shamans see in the essentially formless ink blots. The authors concluded that little evidence of psychopathology was present among Zinacantecan shamans.

In general, most studies of lay or shamanistic medical practitioners tend to focus on personality attributes and on the health status of the shaman viewed from a psychological standpoint. Few researchers have dealt with the shaman as a provider of medical care and focused on his activities from the standpoint of his duties as a medical practitioner, that is, as a player differentiated on the basis of his knowledge of illness and remedies, the task of diagnosis, his manner of evaluating clients, etc. The following are examples of studies that do focus somewhat on this medical care dimension.

Margetts (1965) extensively reviewed the practices of the traditional Yoruba healers. He does not give attention to the underlying beliefs that organize and structure medical care but stresses the personalistic motivations and intentions of the healers. Fabrega (1970a), in contrast, compared the medical knowledge base of a group of shamans and nonshamans in Zinacantan and found no differences when symptomatic components of various illnesses were used as referents. However, when dimensions of illness (that is, notions involving cause, severity, mode of treatment) were focused upon (Fabrega 1971a), he observed group differences involving both content and response tendencies. Shamans tended to state more frequently that deities were the cause of illness and also that illnesses were treatable and, specifically, treatable by native practitioners. In addition, there was evidence that as individuals shamans tended to demonstrate greater consistency with themselves across the series of questions that were asked. As a group, then shamans were in many ways like their comembers as regards knowledge, although they *used* this knowledge differently. This is an important finding and bears on the general problem that was attacked by Frake (1961), as we have already seen.

The medical knowledge of lay subjects in certain folk or nonliterate settings, thus, may not differ on a group basis from that of healers and medical practitioners. Beliefs about the cause and treatment of illness are simply shared among the members of the culture. This system contrasts sharply with our own culture, where the difference in knowledge between laymen and physicians is very large. In folk settings, it appears that the role of the healer (his social and spiritual validation, as it were) and his charisma are what give him and his actions credibility and stamp him as unique in the culture. Furthermore, as we have just reviewed, shamans may have evolved distinctive styles in the way they use their cultural knowledge, and this is reflected in the relatively consistent pattern of responses they volunteer when questioned about their knowledge of illness.

The paper by Handelman (1967) presents a life history study of a Washo shaman. An emphasis in this account is on the ways Henry Rupert (the shaman) reconceptualizes Washo cosmology in his own terms, introducing innovations in curing procedures. Within the stress of an acculturative situation, Rupert was able to provide synthesis and bring a creative touch to an established role. This study by Handelman makes a significant contribution to culture and personality studies. It is included here because it illustrates lucidly the many psychocultural factors that surround the curing activities of folk practitioners.

Employing a unique research plan, Carlos Castaneda (1968) studied a Yaqui shaman, or man of knowledge, in an attempt to understand the implicit rules that govern the actions of the curer in that culture. The book is presented as an essay in which the author, largely unknowing, is guided through a series of learning experiences under the tutelage of the shaman. Castaneda, however, fails to achieve confirmation in an important test of his commitment to the role. Perhaps the central contributions of the work are its close reporting of the shaman's actions and their culturally embedded explanations and the author's attempt to develop the implicit or structural rules that govern his actions and beliefs. The essay, or "data," is reported as it is given; thus it is presented from a culturally specific perspective. The rules that are extracted, however, are presented from the perspective of the outside observer. This combination of perspectives makes for an interesting kind of anthropological research.

Osgood, Hochstrasser, and Deuschle (1966) presented extensive information on the characteristics of lay midwives in eastern Kentucky. Personal and social features of nine female and one male practitioners were described, including the background, experience, form of training, and characteristics of their current practice. This article also contains a useful analysis of social and structural aspects of the system of medical care of the region that maintains the activity of midwives. Tenzel (1970) studied the context of illness (beliefs, practices, and treatment regimens) in a Mayan Indian village in the highlands of Guatemala. Brief descriptive data on the characteristics of shamans are presented, including the basis of their curing powers and their assumptions about health and illness. Tenzel examined several patients who were suffering from *susto,* all of whom apparently demonstrated evidence of physical disease. He emphasizes the need for caution when generalizing about the nature and processes underlying common folk illnesses. Turner's accounts of practitioners in Africa (see, for example, his articles of 1967 and 1968) should be carefully consulted in any attempt to understand the activities of the practitioner as these relate to treatment situations. In contrast to the typical psychodynamic emphases that are common in most accounts of shamanistic behavior, Turner emphasizes how the shaman creatively links social processes and situations with the mutilvalent meanings of culturally relevant symbols during his attempt to meet his obligations and responsibilities.

Emphasis has been given in this brief discussion of folk practitioners to personality dynamics and to aspects of medical care and practice. Clarification of the former issue relates centrally to current concerns in the fields of transcultural psychiatry and psychological anthropology. An additional purpose for studying the practitioner, however, is to allow for a more rational understanding of the role of his behavior in medical care. To recapitulate, delineating the nature of the medical knowledge and judgments of the practitioner should make explicit the relevance of different types of symbolic categories in medical transactions, and clarifying the influence of personality factors and social patterns of functioning should lead to a better understanding of why and how he applies these categories. This information, of course, needs to be supplemented by analyses of the actual process of medical care. Despite an extensive literature on various facets of medicine in preliterate settings, there is surprisingly little information dealing with the processes and the dynamics of medical practice in these settings. An example of this bias is the lack of attention that is given to the various stages of the practitioner-patient relationship, which mediates the delivery of medical care. As I have suggested earlier, the implicit model that most investigators rely on could be termed time limited and sociopsychological. That is, the modification of social and psychological factors that are assumed to relate to health status is regarded as central to the eventual healing that takes place. Factors promoting this healing or treatment, however, are believed to be set in motion during a sharply demarcated time interval. Such a model does not include discussion of the many considerations and events that antedate a curing ceremony and that also follow it. These events involve the particular healer and patient as well as other key persons and health-focused relationships, relate to the unique sociocultural patterns that structure medical practice in the setting, and importantly affect the nature of any healing or treatment that may take place. Issues of this type have been examined in our society, but a comprehensive understanding of medical practice requires that such phenomena be studied in other settings as well.

The Psychiatric Bias of Ethnomedical Studies and Limitations of Methodology

Issues discussed earlier no doubt make clear the affinity that culturally oriented studies of illness (that is, ethnomedicine) have always had with psychiatry. For when instances of illness are examined, principal attention is given to changes in behaviors, general bodily complaints, and verbalizations regarding the perceived change in identity, which, it is frequently said, signals and represents the illness. Given this model or definition of "illness," the concern of the social scientist seems to be to explain the illness—its genesis, mechanism, descriptive features, treatment, and resolution—as an event having cultural significance. Similarly, most indicators of psychiatric diseases involve behaviors, feelings, beliefs, modes of thinking, etc. Most psychiatrists will acknowledge that social and psychological factors are important in the etiology of psychiatric diseases, and features of the disease are examined by them and given meaning and significance in psychological and sociobehavioral terms. Last, an important modality of treatment of psychiatric disease is psychotherapeutic and/or sociointerpersonal. Thus, the significant clinical features and dimensions of psychiatric diseases (for example, cause, form, treatment) involve data and happenings that cultural anthropologists have always dealt with comfortably. To be sure, this interest on the part of anthropologists in clinical psychiatric concerns has been very fruitful. Prominent characteristics of American psychiatry today must in fact be seen as a consequence of the incisive contributions of American anthropologists (Weakland 1968). However, the long-standing close association between these two disciplines has had the effect of imparting a distinct orientation to ethnographic studies of medical problems, and that is that instances of illness (that is, "folk illnesses") have been regarded as culturally patterned sociopsychological happenings. Stated differently, instances of illness have been described and analyzed in large part as if they were "psychiatric."

Peculiar aspects of Western medical science (rooted in its historical development) allow for the existence of the category "psychiatric disease." The application of this paradigm to nonliterate settings is problematic, since the limited biomedical facilities and resources of these settings as well as the imperfect understanding of the sociocultural system simply do not allow the investigator to evaluate health status clearly and hence to apply unambiguously a diagnosis of psychiatric disease type. Nevertheless, the implicit assumption adopted by the researcher is that he is dealing with a disorder that is either typically psychiatric or at least psychiatric-like. Excessive preoccupation with this dimension on the part of culturally oriented anthropologists has tended to obscure the influences that biological components have on (culturally defined) illnesses. Consequently, the potential of examining the reciprocal influences that psychocultural and biological factors have on instances of illness occurrences (as defined and categorized by subjects) has been missed.

Thus, we are not in the position to say for certain which symptoms and signs of disease are universal, that is, which ones are invariably defined by the actor as problematic and systematically incorporated into a socially meaningful episode that represents the culturally defined illness. Perhaps certain bodily changes are consistently judged not only as indications of illness but as an indication of an illness of a certain type, which means that the actor and his group give an instantiation of these bodily changes distinctive symbolic markings. More importantly, we have no way of assessing which symptoms and signs of disease escape notice and are simply viewed as trivial or "natural" accompaniments to living in the distinctive ecological setting of the actor. The fields of ethnomedicine and social medicine in general are in need of formulations that are anchored in both social and biological categories so that theories of illness and disease can be developed.

Unfortunately, social scientists and even psychiatrists (who should know better) when they study problems of illness cross-culturally seem fixed on the view that only psychological and perhaps sociointerpersonal factors are sufficient to explain medical phenomena. This one-sided view of illness seriously constrains the framework needed to analyze medical happenings in the field and has thereby limited the contribution that social scientists and psychiatrists as well have thus far made in this area of study.

It is regrettable that many cultural anthropologists interested in ethnomedicine have not heeded the advice of Mead (1947) and the example of Wallace (1961a) in approaching the study of illness with a framework that includes both bodily happenings and behavioral changes. This perspective is also illustrated in papers by Rohrl (1970), Mazzur (1970), and Katz and Foulks (1970). Given a concern with behavior and its organization and a desire to probe medical issues in an incisive manner, an awareness of the biological components of disease would appear mandatory. It is in this particular area that anthropology has barely begun to tap its potential to contribute not only to the field of medicine but also to a science of man. The vocabulary of Western scientific medicine is replete with linguistic forms (for example, pain, nausea, onset, natural history, weakness, etc.) that require examination and interpretation by means of a comparative orientation toward medical happenings. Ethnomedical inquiries using structural linguistic methods, an ecological approach, or a processual paradigm (to name a few techniques) would serve to enhance greatly our understanding about human behavior, about medical problems, and about their interrelation. If medically relevant behaviors are linked in a systematic fashion with even rather general biological parameters of illness, it should be possible to construct a typology of illness that bridges the sociocultural and biomedical frames of reference, and which in time might allow anthropologists to develop models of medical care.

The psychiatric bias of ethnomedical studies may result largely from a limitation of methodology. By and large, mainly social anthropologists or those associated with the field of culture and personality have worked on medical issues. The problems of methodology in these subfields of anthropology and cross-cultural psychology are legion and have recently been reviewed and criticized rather pointedly (LeVine 1973). Anthropologists who do employ refined and culturally more appropriate methods of procedure are the ethnoscientists. However, with the exception of the study by Frake reviewed earlier (which actually is limited principally to some rather general characteristics of how the Subanun organize a subset of dermatological conditions), the most incisive contributions that ethnoscientists have thus far made involve the analysis of native schemes for classifying areas such as firewood, plants, animals, kinship relations, and the color spectrum (Berlin, Breedlove, and Raven 1968, Conklin 1955, Metzger and Williams 1966).

The task of the ethnoscientist is to describe and render intelligible the way in which natives classify a domain. Native taxonomies of various domains have in fact been worked out elaborately, and even some general propositions about the structure as well as growth and differentiation of the taxonomic schemes have been developed (Berlin and Kay 1969, Berlin, Breedlove, and Raven 1973). The search in this field of ethnosystematics is for laws that will eventually explain in a rigorous fashion how and why man conceptualizes his natural and social environments the way he does. One hopes that the skills and insights of individuals with this training will be brought to bear on the domain of illness and disease; and for reasons to be developed presently, I suspect that a set of biobehavioral units or segments will have to be worked out in order for them to articulate such laws of illness. For one observes that these domains that have been mapped with fidelity consist of elements that have either physical extension or can be tied to stimuli or anchor points in the "external" and public world. Plant specimens, for example, can be presented to the native subject for him to name and classify as can color chips of various sorts. The subject and investigator are witnesses to the same item and process of classification. Similarly, most persons in an actor's relational field can be marked by the external grid of gender, age, generation, biological parentage, etc., thereby allowing the investigator to code independently and precisely the actual persons that in the culture are viewed as kinsmen. When devices of this sort exist or, stated differently, when the investigator works in the "right" domain, he is allowed to assign his own independent meanings to the native categories, thereby providing for himself anchoring points that will eventually allow him to reconstruct the actor's classification system. But thus far, no such analogous markers or anchoring points exist or have been developed for the study of illness and disease (see Fabrega and Silver 1973, Chapter 8, for recent methodological approaches to this problem). Since a great deal of what signals, determines, and semantically distinguishes an occurrence of illness occurs internally, that is *within* the actor, the investigator is a priori deprived of the relevant observational material. As mentioned earlier, I believe that a suitable vocabulary of illness-relevant components (that is, biobehavioral segments) will need to be constructed inductively for just this purpose (see Chapter 6).

In general, then, the investigator wishing to study how illness is defined and classified is forced to adopt one of two strategies. He may either analyze subjects' responses to a natural occurrence of a disease (which is problematic given that illness attacks are infrequent, judged to represent crises, and regarded as private) or rely on data derived from interviews conducted after the fact. The consequence of these factors is that it is difficult to obtain precise and reliable data about the actual indicators that underlie illness definition and classification. Stated differently, the investigator wishing to study how native subjects classify medical phenomena is usually constrained by his general inability to have access to specific and concrete instances of this domain.

An equally serious limitation of ethnomedical studies that deal with illness conditions, and one not unrelated to the preceding consideration, is that medical data elicited and organized as part of an ethnographic inquiry are rarely analyzed in terms of or with reference to external systems of meaning that bear directly on the domain under investigation (Goodenough 1957, Pike 1954, Wallace 1962). This is to say that native medical categories and classification schemes are not ordinarily compared in a systematic fashion to similar phenomena that are classified by alternative frameworks. Attempts to achieve this type of comparative focus have provided answers to some of the theoretical questions that are of concern to social scientists, although in each instance the alternative classificatory framework (in this case, Western medical knowledge) has been applied to information generated from interview data. The items classified, in other words, have been reports of illness dimensions and not observable manifestations of disease (see, for example, Fabrega 1971a). One consequence of analyzing folk medical beliefs or perceptions without the precise and rigorous use of reference points that are external to the native system and grounded in theoretical frameworks dealing with the biological correlates of disease is that some critical questions that are of concern to medical ecologists and population biologists cannot be meaningfully answered (see Chapter 2, especially the review of Alland's work).

Chapter 2 Social Biology of Disease

In this chapter we will review some of the approaches and findings of investigators who examine the relationship between disease (considered now as a biomedical condition or entity) and social and cultural factors. Disease, in other words, in contrast to the way it is usually handled in ethnomedical studies (see Chapter 1), is defined in terms of traditional Western biological science. However, the simultaneous use of a sociocultural level of analysis means that emphasis is also given to the dynamics and organization of human behavior. The studies we will be concerned with, thus, examine the mutual influences that exist between diseases and the behaviors of persons and groups, the latter organized in terms of social science concepts and variables. The information to be described falls within the subdisciplines of medical epidemiology and medical ecology.

Medical epidemiology is the study of the distribution of disease in relation to physical, biological, or sociocultural features of the environment. In this chapter we will focus specifically on social epidemiology, which concentrates on the sociocultural aspects of the environment. Most studies in this field are conducted in industrialized settings, tend to employ linear-deductive and quasi-experimental designs, make use of survey methods and data from agency or hospital records, and aim to develop and refine hypotheses about the causes of disease. The reader who desires a lucid and at the same time highly sophisticated review of the logic of epidemiology, that is, how epidemiologists go about designing studies and analyzing findings in order to draw reasoned judgments about the causes of disease, is urged to read the book by Susser (1973). The literature on epidemiology, even the portion of epidemiology emphasizing sociocultural factors or the medical problems of non-Western groups, is very extensive. This literature will not be reviewed here in its entirety since this is not necessary for our purposes. The reader desiring a lucid introduction to the descriptive and analytical facets of traditional epidemiology is directed to the book by MacMahon and Pugh (1970). Feinstein (1968a, 1968b) has recently emphasized the close linkages that exist between traditional epidemiology and clinical medicine and has argued for a clinical epidemiological orientation to the problems of disease and medical care. Such an orientation would be addressed to the diverse biophysical and social patterns that antedate the onset of disease and which assume relevance during the conduct of treatment. Feinstein urges that disease be handled as a clinical and statistical entity and that its implications be linked to the person as well as the population.

Medical ecology will be viewed here as a somewhat narrower and more specialized segment of the field of medical epidemiology. In addition to concerning themselves in a general way with the distributions of disease and its relations to various environmental factors, medical ecologists are principally concerned with the more specific issues of environmental biology, population genetics, and human evolution. Medical studies that can be termed ecological in this sense are usually conducted in preliterate settings where non-Western groups are found and particularly among small, highly isolated groups, which ordinarily demonstrate quite elementary or what can be termed primitive forms of social organization. The nature of the physical and geographic setting, the habits of the residents of these settings, as well as the problem being studied, often require that a more holistic, multilevel, and exploratory orientation be adopted in these studies. See, for example, Tromp (1963), Sargent (1966), Dubos (1968), May (1960), and Shimkin (1970). Thus, in what I shall refer to as medical ecological studies, such issues as the diet of the subjects, their energy expenditure, their blood types, antibody levels, etc., as well as apparent and manifest health status, are given attention; similarly, demographic characteristics (manner of forming sexual unions, group composition, pattern of group dissolution, etc.) and features of the environment (for example, climate, animal life, composition of flora, etc.) that affect adaptation levels, health status, and social organization may be emphasized. As can be seen, then, a broad framework is used to evaluate medical problems. It should be emphasized, however, that the ecological framework or approach has always been an inherent feature of medical epidemiology (see Gordon and Ingalls 1958, Rogers 1962, and Kartman 1967), and that distinguishing between these two approaches is somewhat arbitrary. Particularly important is the fact that medical studies of this genre (that is, what I have termed epidemiological and ecological) tend to disregard the perspective of the actor, the rules and values of the people, the meanings that illness has, and the way subjects orient and respond to illness or disease occurrences. The principal questions tend to be causal, and consequently the disease itself (that is, its occurrence, prevalence, and incidence) is seen as the endpoint. Causal studies of this type must be seen in the context of the (correctionistic) goals of Western medical science, which are to control disease.

Social Epidemiology

The systematic search for factors bearing on disease has classically involved analyzing a variety of features of the physical environment of man. The term "social epidemiology" may be used to define studies that attempt to relate social and cultural factors to specific diseases found in a population or social group. An immediate aim of these studies is to demonstrate that the prevalence and/or incidence of disease and its distribution in space or in a social system bear a relationship to such factors as cultural exclusivity, ethnic identity, social class, or any other variable that may be linked to social processes. An ultimate aim of such studies is to uncover leads that will help clarify how these types of factors may contribute to the causes of disease. A critical requirement of a social epidemiological study is that the social and/or cultural variables that are examined (variables that in the logic of the study's design are termed "independent") be precisely identified and measured and that the influence of these variables in the web of causation of disease be analytically specified (see Scotch 1963a).

The rationale of social epidemiology was clearly explicated by Cassel, Patrick, and Jenkins (1960) and Cassel (1964). The investigators point out that current preconceptions and investigative strategies regarding the "causes of disease" are products of historically successful identifications of infectious diseases, diseases that are amenable to a closed-system mechanistic and single-cause model. They suggest that such a model, in addition to its limitation to certain types of diseases and its dependence on historically bound analytic strategies, is clearly inappropriate for the bulk of diseases that are prominent today (the so-called chronic or degenerative diseases). Given our ignorance about the nature of these diseases, they insist, we should adopt an open, multilevel and multicausal model that admits of social, psychological, and cultural factors. They point out that the association of a particular disease (D_i), for example, tuberculosis, indicated by specific signs and symptoms (S_i), in this case, of a respiratory nature, with a unique cause (C_i), the tubercle bacillus, is partly a tautology or an analytic determination, rather than an accurate reflection of human biological functioning. The linkage between S_i, C_i, and D_i, in other words, is an analytic and somewhat arbitrary consequence of our having successfully identified one specific etiological agent of what then comes to be viewed as a particular type of disease. Biological changes in no way unique to that disease actually need to be identified, but the application of the causally relevant "disease" label to those changes seems to create a myth that something unique and specific has been uncovered. Rather than portraying the correct or "true" relationship that exists between a "disease" picture and its many etiologically relevant factors, then, the association simply reflects the very process of definition. This particular analytic paradigm (C_i causes D_i, which is indicated by S_i) creates the illusion that an empirical fact of nature has been uncovered, a "fact" from which we tend uncautiously to generalize. This means, in particular, that the notion that each disease has a precise biophysiologic identity that needs to be discovered in order to be able to specify its equally precise cause is fallacious. Our search for the etiological factors or processes that contribute to impaired health and our attempts to understand them in a refined way are consequently hampered by the inappropriate use of a closed model and a descriptive nosological system that ties us to "disease entities" that may in fact not exist as independent and biophysiologically self-contained units having a single cause. What is needed then, are new, flexible models of or approaches to health, approaches that allow us to examine the consequences of potentially noxious stressful conditions, which we have reason to believe antedate impaired health. Rather than working back from a presumed disease entity D_i, we should work forward from identified (or potentially) stressful circumstances (C_i) and expect various pathological consequences (S_i). In short, a given disease should not be defined simply as though it represented a conjunction of a C_i and a set of S_i, with no further investigation; we should, instead, explore relations between a range of C_i (for example, crowding, malnutrition, the tubercle bacillus) and alternative sets of S_i (for example, social isolation, poor school performance, and respiratory problems) and then term the whole network D_i.

Tyroler and Cassel (1964) have used an open-system multicausal model to examine the effect of urbanization on coronary heart disease mortality in North Carolina. The size of the population of the largest city in a county was used as an index of the extent of urbanization of that county. An ordinal four-point scale was devised using various population ranges as values. Mortality rates were compared among rural and urban residents of the counties across a four-point urbanization gradient. The prediction that rural white males would exhibit an increase in mortality from coronary heart disease as the index of urbanization of the county increased was empirically supported by the data of this study. This finding is explained in terms of the incongruity that rural residents experience in their culture and social situation as urbanization increases. In this study, then, cultural change resulting presumably from urbanization is believed to affect the quality of life of rural residents and to contribute to coronary heart disease mortality.

For other examples of epidemiologically oriented studies that focus on the influence of cultural factors on diseases of the circulatory system, the reader can consult Cruz-Coke, Etcheverry, and Nagel (1964), Fulmer and Roberts (1963), Mann et al. (1964), Syme, Hyman, and Enterline (1964, 1965), Bruhn et al. (1966), and Sievers (1967). These authors all rely on indicators of cultural factors—for example, urbanization, migration, other types of sociocultural change, cultural exclusivity—and examine how these factors affect rates and the distribution of arteriosclerotic and hypertensive heart disease. Recent social epidemiological studies focusing on these diseases have tended to rely on more refined independent variables—for example, incongruity in social status and degree of manifest hostility (Shekelle, Ostfeld, and Paul 1969, Ibrahim et al. 1966). For reviews of studies of this type the reader should see Sprague (1966), Antonovsky (1968), Lehman (1967), and the Milbank issue edited by Syme and Reeder (1967). An excellent review of the literature dealing with hypertensive diseases is the one by Henry and Cassel (1969). They surveyed the recent epidemiologic literature and literature relating to animal experiments that bear on hypertensive disease. A large number of studies dealing with hypertension that examine the influence of cultural variables are also reviewed. Henry and Cassel find evidence to support the view that psychological factors are involved in the cause of hypertension. In their words, ". . . a dissonance between the social milieu in later life and expectations based on early experiences during the organism's developmental stages may be one of the critical factors" in the cause of hypertension (p. 196).

Relying on an open-system type of approach, Scotch and Geiger (1963) evaluated the usefulness of the Cornell Medical Index (CMI), a symptom questionnaire that contains items that may reflect various types of system disorders, as a general measure of the health of a social group among a Zulu population (and subgroups therein). Again, these investigators were interested in probing relations between health status and sociopsychological variables. They relied on mortality rates and elevated diastolic blood pressure levels as independent indicators of health status (see also Scotch 1963b). CMI scores bore an appreciable degree of correspondence to mortality rates and morbidity indices. The CMI scores of various subgroups differentiated on the basis of social criteria (age, sex, place of residence, belief in witchcraft, etc.) revealed significant contrasts. Urban residents demonstrated higher scores, as did male respondents in general. These findings were explained as correlates (or perhaps outcomes) of the greater stresses that individuals in the various categories experience. An impressive degree of interaction was noted between age and belief in witchcraft, with younger believers demonstrating higher CMI scores. The design employed did not allow determining if illness led to espousal of witchcraft beliefs, if believers are especially prone to medical problems, or whether both of these issues were "caused" by another factor or factors. The logic of this study and the discussion provided by Scotch and Geiger illustrate the traditional social epidemiological concern of establishing relationships between social factors and health indicators in groups presumably exposed to potentially stressful circumstances. The actual findings contribute significantly to an understanding of hypertensive disease and must be seen as enhancing the validity of the CMI. The authors also suggest that the index may be used to develop hypotheses concerning sociocultural processes: ". . . in the hand of the anthropologist-physician team, the CMI may serve not only to give a crude health profile of a population but also to point to puzzles, points of stress, or areas of apparently high risk that deserve further exploration both medically and by the methods of social science" (p. 311). Their suggestion, then, is that the CMI (or indices of a similar nature) might be used by social scientists as "diagnostic" instruments of social phenomena that may be stressful to individuals.

The rationale followed by Scotch and Geiger, of course, is similar to that used in field studies of untreated mental disorder. In these studies, symptom questionnaires (and other questionnaires focusing on social and demographic variables) are administered to a probability sample of a population. Later, the symptom scores are clinically rated or judged by a panel of psychiatrists. The estimates of illness or disability that are obtained are then related to social and cultural factors (presumably measured independently) that are hypothesized to have a potential causal influence on psychiatric health status. The studies of A. H. Leighton et al. (1963) and D. Leighton et al. (1963) are typical psychiatric epidemiologic studies that follow this rationale. In these studies particular attention is given to the effects of social disorganization. Empirical findings support the belief that communities that can be described as culturally stable and socially organized or integrated are associated with lower measures of psychiatric ill health. For a discussion of the assumptions as well as the framework of social epidemiologic studies of psychiatric disorder the reader should consult Leighton (1955, 1959a, 1959b, 1969), Leighton and Hughes (1961), Leighton and Murphy (1965), Savage, Leighton, and Leighton (1965), and Dohrenwend (1966). (For a general picture of the issues involved, the reader should also consult the highly critical review by Mishler and Scotch [1965] on epidemiological studies of schizophrenia.)

Psychiatric epidemiologists, as a reading of the preceding empirical and analytic studies will disclose, have resolved the central problems of clearly identifying a case or instance of disease in a manner that is most problematic (see Dohrenwend and Dohrenwend 1969). In the first place, the preoccupation of these epidemiologists with "cutoff points" (that is, the line in symptom profiles that distinguishes between health and disease) underlines the somewhat arbitrary and ultimately social basis of disease definitions. (Most biological traits, of course, also require such arbitration.) As we shall see in later chapters, there are additional, what we could term ontological, problems associated with the entity "psychiatric disease," and furthermore there are special methodological problems that plague attempts at precisely identifying occurrences of these types of "disease" (see Chapter 3). Consequently, the attempt to quantify amount of disease in a bounded social group and then to relate this amount to ("independent") sociocultural events or categories (which themselves are difficult to measure precisely) must be evaluated rather cautiously. These studies, in addition, are constrained by their partial reliance on the previously discussed closed-systems mechanistic model. Ironically, although the studies admit of only one ontological type of disease, the operational indicators of disease span across behavioral, psychological, and physiological systems. It needs to be emphasized, however, that field studies that attempt to link social or cultural factors with "disease entities" of any sort encounter related problems of inappropriate exclusivity—that is, problems of disease definition and disease measurement (this point will be elaborated upon subsequently) —and that for this reason psychiatric epidemiology is in no way unique.

Recent studies in psychiatric epidemiology not only have demonstrated an awareness of the pernicious influences that observer biases have on the attempt to uncover or diagnose psychiatric diseases but have creatively exploited this awareness in order to arrive at an understanding of far more fundamental issues. Thus Katz, Gudeman, and Sanborn (1969) working in Hawaii have been concerned not only with the different ways in which ethnic groups show or manifest schizophrenia when Western biomedical standards are applied by trained raters in the hospital but also with how these same patients were judged by their relatives in the community *prior to* hospitalization. In addition to offering insights about the processes that lead to hospitalization, studies of this type also offer the potential of clarifying how cultural patterns affect behavioral organization, maintenance, change, and deviation. They are consequently addressed to rather basic sociobehavioral issues. Why are certain forms of behavior judged as abnormal or aberrant by members of an ethnic group, whereas others (perhaps equally pathological from the observer's standpoint) are viewed as appropriate? Similarly, why do ethnic or cultural groups differ radically on these parameters, and what can we learn about behavioral dynamics from these issues? These questions highlight the fact that the behavioral expressions of psychiatric disease (assuming for the moment that such diseases are what biological psychiatrists claim they are, namely, truly psychobiologic entities) must be evaluated in the light of the cultural rules that organize and pattern what passes as "normal" behavior among members of the ethnic group. Such questions, often bypassed, are going to have to be answered before we can answer others, such as what and how social variables cause psychiatric disease. Studies in this vein, although ostensibly social epidemiological and psychiatric, must be seen as contributing to our understanding of more fundamental questions that are of concern to the fields of medicine and social science (see also Katz, Cole, and Lowery 1969, Katz and Lyerly 1963, Draguns and Phillips 1971).

An associated limitation of most social epidemiological studies is that sociocultural variables are handled in a rather abstract and static manner. Stated more specifically, in these studies the processes and dynamics of social events tend to be imprecisely captured, as do the behaviors of the person bound in these processes. The papers by Graves (1966, 1967, 1970) are substantively related and employ a framework similar to those just described in that what could be termed "maladaptive" behaviors (for example, excessive drinking, police arrests) presumed to follow or express psychological stress are studied in a rigorous manner. However, these papers by Graves are notable for their emphasis on process and for the sensitivity with which they capture the social circumstances in which the actors find themselves. Although the content of these papers cannot be viewed as typically "medical," they are mentioned here because they do represent attempts at analyzing how social and cultural factors affect adjustment, and they focus on behavioral processes that are the outcome or expression of stress.

The medical consequences of certain unusual cultural practices have received explicit attention. For example, Ahluwalia and Ponnampalam (1968) addressed themselves to the potential effects of betel-nut chewing among plantation workers of South Indian origin. They obtained relevant medical histories and personally conducted examinations of the oral cavities of 168 workers. No evidence to support the hypothesis that betel chewing causes oral cancer was obtained, but a definite association between chewing and various lesions of the mouth was noted. In their report, no clear picture of the sampling frame is presented, and thus the generalizability of their findings must be regarded as tentative.

The paper by Buck et al. (1968)—also included as a chapter in their book—reports on some of the physical health correlates of coca chewing, a widespread practice in parts of South America, particularly the Peruvian Andes. In this study coca chewers were matched with non-chewers on the variables of age, ethnic affiliation, and sex. Coca chewers showed a poorer nutritional status, more evidence of hookworm anemia, and poorer personal hygiene and rated higher on indices suggesting serious illness. Buck et al. attributed these findings to the influence that cocaine has in maintaining a state of malnutrition. The assumption here is that cocaine reduces the sensation of hunger, thereby eliminating or reducing appetite and ultimately food intake. A long-range consequence of this is malnutrition, which reduces "natural" defenses against infection. However, a variety of other factors distinguished their control and experimental groups, and since some of the factors (for example, alcohol consumption) have clear health implications, the exact influence of coca chewing must remain open. Related to this interesting cultural practice is the work of Negrete and Murphy (1967) in Bolivia, who found indications that coca chewers, compared to non-chewers, demonstrate evidence of psychological deficit, although the nature of the deficit and the exact role of coca in the clinical picture could not be determined. Sampling problems encountered during the conduct of this particular study also limit the extent to which results can be generalized. (For a discussion of social factors associated with coca chewing, see Goddard, DeGoddard, and Whitehead 1969). These studies, then, address themselves to a culturally significant practice and examine the adverse consequences in terms of narrowly defined physical and psychological indices.

A number of investigators have attended more generally to the medical problems that are found in specific cultural and socially differentiated groups. Chowdhury and Schiller (1968) and Chowdhury, Schad, and

Schiller (1968), for example, studied the prevalence of intestinal helminth in religious groups in a rural community near Calcutta. The prevalence of ascariasis was significantly greater in Muslims, whereas hookworm infections were more prevalent among Hindus. The authors were not able to offer a satisfactory explanation for these differences. Using mainly secondary literature sources Worth (1963a, 1963b) reviewed the health problems of contemporary rural China and indicated some of the government's efforts to combat these problems. Walker (1969) reviewed the general literature bearing on the amount of coronary heart disease among the Bantu of South Africa and Indians living in India as well as other countries. He concluded that the differences observed probably stem from "racial" factors. Graham et al. (1970), working in the United States, reported on the results of the tristate leukemia project, which examined the association between religion and ethnicity and leukemia. Jews (especially Russian Jews), Russians, and Poles all demonstrated significantly elevated risks. Horowitz and Enterline (1970) studied patterns of mortality from lung cancer among ethnic groups in Montreal and related these to knowledge about the smoking histories of the groups. In a carefully performed investigation, Reed, Labarthe, and Stallones (1970) studied Chamorro natives of the Mariana Islands who had migrated to a different cultural milieu and found no evidence to support the hypothesis that migration and Westernization are associated with an increased prevalence of a variety of diseases. Jelliffe and Jelliffe (1963) and Price and Lewthwaite (1963) studied the prevalence of malaria in various parts of Uganda and reported high figures of plasmodium in children. Terespolsky and Yofe (1965) described the pattern of hospital admissions in a geographically bounded community of immigrants in Jerusalem, giving attention to the country of origin of the residents. Feldman et al. (1969) and Kamath et al. (1969) reported the results of following through time the health status of families in semiurban areas of Vellore, South India. They worked with public health nurses and had physicians available to perform medical evaluation. They noted that the amount of illness in the families varied a great deal and did not relate clearly to family income, family size, or geographical section. A seasonal pattern could be discerned in the incidence of skin infection and respiratory and diarrheal illness. The study by Ashley (1968) represents an interesting attempt to equate genetic exclusivity ("Welshness") with amount of specific diseases. Welshness was indicated by language and surname, and these indicators were associated with particular medical problems. The authors are of the opinion that insofar as environment and occupation are similar in the two groups studied (Welsh and non-Welsh), their results touching on differences in disease incidence can be ascribed to genetic differences. For other epidemiologically oriented studies the reader may wish to consult Florey and Cuadrado (1968), Adelstein (1963), Norman-Taylor and Rees (1963), Miall et al. (1967), Robson (1964), Rabin et al. (1965), and S. B. Levine et al. (1970).

It should be mentioned that by employing a framework that includes general social and cultural variables, studies described here implicitly admit that these variables may be related to etiology. A long-range goal is the accumulation of diverse evidence regarding associations between disease and social categories, which when suitably organized and analyzed will point out distributions of disease, which in turn will suggest hypotheses for more focused studies. However, although this goal underlies the work, it is notable that units that might make a sociocultural category relevant are left out of analysis. In other words, from the standpoint of medicine and especially for a refined understanding of disease, we should adopt a critical posture toward categories such as ethnic group or social class, high-level categories that leave unspecified social processes and behavioral practices that are likely to have a more direct influence on biological functioning. For this reason epidemiologists who include social categories in their designs would do well to enumerate more precisely unitary behaviors and practices that are glossed over by higher-level abstractions.

A converse problem is revealed in certain epidemiological studies that examine the prevalence and distribution of various infectious and parasitic diseases in preliterate groups. These studies, although potentially capable of contributing to a broad understanding of how diseases and environmental factors are interrelated, do not employ at all what could be termed a social and cultural perspective, nor do they focus on behavioral concomitants of the diseases. The aim of the investigator appears to be to specify strictly clinical and descriptive aspects of diseases as well as the amount of disease present in the group; how the various diseases are related to discrete behavioral practices, or how cultural patterns affect the expression, definition, or management of the disease in the group is not a salient concern (see Price et al. 1963, Scrimshaw et al. 1966, Bergner 1964, Reed, Struve, and Maynard 1967, Haddad 1965, Mata et al. 1965, Salomon, Gordon, and Scrimshaw 1966, and Mackenzie 1965). A number of investigators who do focus on behavioral aspects do so strictly from the standpoint of how existing behaviors may "mechanically" affect the distribution and spread of disease. In other words, the influence of cultural orientations, which presumably organize and give meaning to the behaviors, is given little attention. The lack is felt by social scientists who are thereby limited in their efforts to develop theories of how sociocultural factors influence disease and medical care.

The paper by Bruch et al. (1963), for example, specifies in some detail the various sources of infection and the behavioral practices that affect the prevalence and distribution of diarrheal diseases in Guatemalan highland villages. The perspective of the actor or group member vis-à-vis these diseases is not delineated. Indeed, the whole dimension of the consequences of disease, which includes the native perceptions and coping responses of villagers, is not considered. (The paper by Scrimshaw et al. [1969] contains a bibliography of the many articles produced by this study program.) Kourany and Vasques (1969) conducted a similar study in Panama but dealt exclusively with the influence of type of dwelling on prevalence of enteropathogenic bacteria. Ch'i and Blackwell (1968) have traced the cause of an endemic peripheral gangrene disease in Taiwan (termed blackfoot disease) to the consumption of deep well water that contains appreciable amounts of arsenic. Generally speaking, then, in these studies various social and behavioral practices of the group have the effect of bringing persons into association with unique features of the setting, and the results are certain disease pictures. However, the influence of such issues as values, beliefs, or general orientation to life on the outcomes or consequences of the disease are not described.

Studies that focus on the factors promoting or hindering the utilization of medical facilities in Western settings bring to light a related limitation of a strict epidemiological approach. In addition to features of disease (duration, level of severity, etc.), four types of factors seem to be consistently invoked in attempts to explain the processes underlying the use (or lack of use, or delay in use) of medical care resources and facilities: (1) economic (for example, the "demand" for care, the capacity of the consumer to pay for services, the coverage offered by different types of medical insurance), (2) sociostructural (for example, distance constraints, transportation impediments, inefficient organization of care institutions, type of professional practice arrangements), (3) sociodemographic (for example, age, sex, social class, ethnic identification, etc., of consumers), and (4) psychosocial (for example, perceived health status, perceived need for care, attitudes toward physicians, salience and definition of illness). Quite obviously, factors (3) and (4) bear rather directly on cultural considerations and for this reason are frequently examined by social scientists interested in medical phenomena. The literature dealing with this general problem area is rather voluminous, and no attempt will be made to review it here. It should be clear, however, that since behaviors related to use of medical facilities are generated and organized by orientations dealing with health, illness, and medical care, a number of issues ordinarily confined to ethnomedical studies bear on this question of utilization. For an excellent (though now somewhat dated) review of the literature the reader is referred to the paper by Rosenstock (1966). The monograph by Andersen (1968) and papers by Kasl and Cobb (1964, 1966a, 1966b) also deal with this general problem.

An examination of the many interrelated factors that affect use of medical facilities provides, in a sense, a meeting ground or boundary setting for studies that incorporate epidemiological and ethnomedical frameworks. This is the case because the specific biomedically defined problems or processes that lead to the decision to seek care (that is, the potential analytic units of an epidemiologic study conducted in a hospital or clinic) are given meanings and interpretations along the lines delineated by cultural categories (that is, by "ethnomedical" concepts and practices). More specifically, among the factors leading diseased persons to avoid using medical facilities (thereby affecting a disease rate) are the contrasting meanings and action implications that are given to manifestations of the disease. Epidemiological findings, in a sense, are embedded in the perceptions and behaviors of people. For this reason a complete depiction of a community's level and distribution of disease requires delineating the influences of these "ethnomedical" dimensions of disease.

Medical Ecology

In this section I review disease studies that are anchored in a broad ecologic approach. The interactions between human groups and their environment are handled holistically, for attention is given not only to disease pictures but also to the myriad of additional sociobiologic factors that influence human adaptation and persistence. In a sense, such studies are addressed to central concerns of the field of population biology and have an added feature, that of exploring the role of Western biomedically defined diseases. Studies of the type under discussion are wide-ranging, have diverse emphases, are conducted in non-Western and pre-literate settings, and are all ultimately related to basic questions that center on man's evolution. There are, however, differences in the principal issues with which the various studies are concerned, and for this reason I have divided this section into three parts: the first deals with general and theoretical issues in population biology; the second brings together studies that focus principally on historical and evolutionary implications associated with human disease; and the last contains a discussion and review of more elaborate and fine-grained empirical studies conducted in isolated human groups. It should be understood, however, that the material in each of the various sections is related to that of the others. Given the interconnectedness of the ecologic approach, this overlap in content is to be expected.

THEORETICAL STUDIES INVOLVING DISEASE-SOCIAL SYSTEM INTERRELATIONS

Hughes (1963) reviewed in considerable detail the kinds of behavior and life situations in preliterate groups that are relevant to health status. The paper did not address itself to particular historical periods but merely discussed general issues. The effects of magico-religious devices, empirical preventives, personal hygiene habits, cosmetic and mutilation practices, housing and settlement patterns, manner of waste disposal, and food habits on the prevalence and persistence of disease in human groups were discussed. An attempt was made to describe the mechanisms whereby these factors affect health status. Hughes's study is a masterful summary of the then current literature dealing with those features of a group's environment (including cultural) that influence level of health and is framed very aesthetically and eloquently within the ecological mold. His chapter is very insightful and is particularly recommended to those who desire a broad public health approach to medical problems with emphasis on this ecologic perspective.

Perhaps the best example of how sociocultural systems affect and in turn are affected by biological systems is the case involving the relations among the disease malaria, the sickle-cell trait, and the agricultural practices of groups in Africa. In careful work involving abnormal hemoglobins, Livingstone (1958, 1967) has demonstrated how specific cultural practices have changed and are still changing the genes affecting hemoglobin types among African populations. His most striking findings involve the sickling trait. The basic problem was: If individuals homozygous as SS gene carriers (hemoglobin S, which accounts for the abnormal sickling) die early, thereby decreasing the frequency of the S gene, then why does one observe such a high frequency in the general population of Africa of the S gene? The disease malaria has proven to be responsible—the S trait (heterozygosity) confers a form of "genetic" immunity on the individual and population. Falciparum malaria is less lethal in individuals showing the trait, and such individuals show higher fertility indices. In other words, the disease, which is endemic among groups with distinctive agricultural practices (the slash and burn agriculture facilitates the breeding of the malaria parasite), has a lowered morbidity among persons carrying the S trait. (The reader is urged to consult the chapter by Allison [1968] for an excellent summary of the background leading to the discovery of the malaria-sickle cell disease linkage.)

In an excellent study Wiesenfeld (1967) addressed himself to this general problem involving malaria, sickling, and sociocultural functioning. He raised the question of whether different agricultural systems might have different effects on the development of malaria and the sickle-cell trait. By drawing on data from the *World Ethnographic Survey* Weisenfeld supported his claim that the development of a particular agricultural system (termed Malaysian) was in fact bound to rather specific changes in the gene pools of populations using this system. These issues he discussed in the distinctly cultural-ecological manner alluded to earlier: the feedback between sociocultural happenings and biological changes was seen as allowing population groups to more efficiently apply and extract energy from a particular ecosystem. The sequence, in other words, seems to be cultural (for example, agricultural) development, endemicity of malaria, "abnormal" hemoglobin development tied to genetic changes, gene-pool changes, lowered morbidity of malaria, sociocultural and biologic persistence.

Hudson's (1965) account of how treponematosis has accommodated to man throughout his social history has a narrower scope but employs a related socioecologic perspective. Evolutionary concerns are not directly in salience in this analysis. Nevertheless, this is a model study that affords an illustration of how disease, culture, and environment are believed to interact. Treponemal infections, which many view as producing separate and distinct disease "types" each caused by a "different" type of treponemal microorganism, are described by Hudson as specific outcomes of the interplay between social practices, climatic conditions, degrees of endemicity, and essentially only one type of pathogenic microorganism. In developing this analytic position Hudson reviews the literature and discusses results of his earlier work.

Three recent books by Buck, Sasaki, and Anderson (1968) and Buck et al. (1970a, 1970b) having a predominantly epidemiological focus are notable for their comprehensiveness and careful presentation of findings. These books are excellent examples of what current medical technology allows in the field of international health. In addition to presenting data dealing with amounts of various systemic and localized parasitic and infectious diseases, the authors report on such issues as community organization, demographic patterns, environmental health parameters, hygiene practices, nutritional habits, and other social activities that have potential medical import. The many types of information collected are related mainly to rather traditional concerns of public health and epidemiology. In other words, the amounts and distributions of disease, the characteristics of the setting, and the living habits and behaviors that are of relevance to morbidity are given principal attention. Little attempt is made by these authors to analytically link culturally organized beliefs and life patterns to the causes of the diseases that are found, to disease manifestations and interpretations, and to medical care.

The books, in short, are outstanding contributions to the fields of international and community health as well as medical ecology and epidemiology. Seldom has such detail and care been employed in delineating the medical problems and health-related parameters of bounded social groups. What is more, a great deal of attention is paid to social and demographic concerns as these bear on health.

However, what is lacking in these studies is a delineation and exposition of the preceding in a manner that reflects the human and culturally organized concerns and behaviors of people. For example, on page 216 in their volume on Chad (Buck et al. 1970*b*) the authors point out the discrepancy that exists between the high *level of disease* that they have uncovered and the quite low *level of perceived illness* as judged by respondents. Insights of this type, which are of great interest to the social scientist and physician interested in examining behavioral correlates of disease states, are not systematically analyzed, let alone elaborated upon in the book. For example, what are the activity levels of persons who can be diagnosed as having a particular disease but who themselves do not claim or acknowledge illness? Similarly, if disease states that are not formally recognized by residents are nevertheless associated with different modes or levels of social and economic adaptation on the part of particular persons in the community, how are these differences in attainment rationalized? Questions of this type, unfortunately, simply are not entertained by Buck et al. Consequently, from a behavioral standpoint these books are somewhat unsatisfactory. In all fairness to the authors, it needs to be said that their intention was to focus primarily on public health issues of a biomedical sort and not on sociocultural ones.

Few books can begin to approach the range and depth that Dubos' *Man Adapting* (1965) manages to convey about the many interrelated factors that affect man's biological adaptation and that underlie and coexist with recognized health problems. Dubos summarizes and critically examines biomedical information from many diverse fields, such as microbiology, human development, genetics, nutrition, clinical medicine, and bioclimatology. It is important to emphasize that this book is not just "another" general and discursive review of "basic" ecologic issues that are relevant to health. Rather, it provides a refined analysis of the many complex factors involving man's biological nature and the physical aspects of his environment that have a bearing on his health and adjustment. Disease to Dubos is not a discontinuous qualitative state that man simply enters into or passes through. Instead, disease is viewed as a term that we arbitrarily use to label what in actuality constitute temporary setbacks in the perpetual struggle between man and the forces of nature. Man and the human group are viewed as standing in an "open" relationship with nature, each an interdependent part of the other. This means that the biological and social levels of human activity are, in a literal sense, structurally and functionally interwoven with nature (that is, with viruses, bacteria, waste products, climatological features, periodicities, etc.). Man is thus viewed as always "diseased"; the relevant question becomes in what particular way and to what extent at this moment in time. Dubos' book, in summary, reviews recent findings of a substantive nature dealing with the many issues that affect health and adaptation; at the same time, the book articulates a truly holistic framework, which is required in order to analyze and interpret fully these issues. This book is certainly required reading for all those interested in a systems approach to the problems of human disease and adaptation.

In a series of publications Alland has discussed in further detail the potential influence that ecologically oriented medical studies can have in the study of human adaptation. In an article published in the *American Anthropologist* (1966) he reviews in a very general way how ". . . medical anthropology may serve as a major link between physical and cultural anthropology, particularly in the areas of biological and cultural evolution" (p. 40). An outline is presented for viewing the reciprocal influences among biological parameters (for example, disease rates), cultural practices that have medical implications, and the adaptation of populations. In this paper he mentions that ethnomedical studies can contribute knowledge about the natural history and spread of various diseases in specific groups. In a subsequent book Alland (1967) discusses basic principles of genetics and biological evolution, notes the general relevance of studies in population genetics and evolution for cultural anthropology, and touches tangentially on the implications of medical studies.

In a more recent book Alland (1970) is directly concerned with the relevance of medical studies in anthropology. Here Alland develops in some detail the view that culture is an adaptive response to environmental pressures, and he emphasizes that as man changes his environment through the adaptive mechanism of culture, this changed environment then acts as a selective agent on man's physical structure as well as on his behavior. The effectiveness of adaptive traits must be measured in relation to increases in carrying capacity and concomitant increases in population. Within this framework, the epidemiological patterns that vary among populations provide interesting material for the analysis of the adaptive process. Any change in the "behavioral system" (Alland's term, which is roughly equivalent in meaning to "culture") is likely to have medical consequences, and in addition, induced or natural alterations in the environmental field provide new selective pressures relating to health and disease, which must be met through a combination of somatic and nonsomatic adaptations. Alland discusses in some detail the relationships among a range of biological and cultural phenomena that affect health and disease, focusing on infectious and parasitic diseases, nutritional disorders, and stress. This book is notable for its provocativeness; it contains a number of ideas about the influence of disease in the adaptation of human groups and, as already mentioned, the relevance of medical studies for the study of biological and cultural evolution. Alland suggests that a game theoretic framework can be used in these studies, a game in which the participants include a population and an environment, the latter composed of specific flora, fauna, and also the set of "diseases" that are endemic in the area. From the standpoint of the population, economic exploitation, efficiency, and population growth serve as indicators of gain. The fact that various diseases are endemic in an area means that population groups must overcome health hazards (the potential losses of the "game") in order to persist and grow. Alland proposes that *ethnomedical practices* and other *cultural practices* and values that affect morbidity and mortality be examined from this population standpoint—specifically, which "practices" promote adaptation and which ones hinder it. Alland emphasizes that the functional (and expressive) values that appear to inhere in various ethnomedical or other cultural practices must be analytically distinguished from the potential biological consequences (vis-à-vis disease distribution) that the practices can have on the group. His field experience in Africa suggests that seemingly unimportant cultural practices (some of which may have nothing to do with medical issues as defined in the group) may nevertheless have major influences on the spread of disease within the group and ultimately can be expected to affect the population structure. This book must be seen in the context of the ferment in the field of human ecology generally and more specifically under the rubric of "cultural ecology." Its contribution is that it reviews a number of ideas and studies from diverse fields that bear on the phenomenon of disease and relates them analytically to problems of human and cultural evolution.

It should be mentioned that Alland does not address himself to the analytic and methodological problems that are logically entailed by a multilevel framework such as the one that he draws on in his writings. Problems implicit in analytic schemes of this nature will be reviewed in subsequent chapters. There I shall show in more detail that for the construction of sociomedical theories (for example, a series of related propositions that explain relations between sociocultural matters and medical ones) it is necessary to study the *reciprocal* relations that obtain between disease and society. Some way must be found, in other words, that allows one to move analytically, in a logically consistent fashion, and with theoretical precision in and out of the category disease (however we choose to define it) into the categories of the social system.

At this stage of theory building, ecological medical studies and writings offer insights in this regard. (The reader may wish to read the review by Cornell [1971] of Alland's book for some of the problems of contemporary interdisciplinary efforts.) Boyden (1970a, 1970b, 1972) has recently written a series of very provocative articles, which suggest the directions that such socioecologic and sociomedical theories may take. Boyden discusses how societies have coped with disease and the hazards of the environment across time. Though he focuses mainly on recent trends, he does employ a broad historic and sociologic approach. He draws attention to the different levels of "adaptation" (each with its own implications for health, disease, and social system functioning) that social systems can reach when viewed against their ecosystem and suggests that health-related behaviors of all sorts need to be considered when social systems are examined from the adaptational point of view.

Now is perhaps a convenient time to emphasize a point only briefly mentioned in the previous chapter about the need that exists in ethno-medicine for descriptions of illness that would allow investigators to draw inferences that have biological as well as social implications. We saw there that as a result of the psychiatric bias, mainly psychological factors are singled out for attention in description of illness. Investigators have simply not been concerned with probing into bodily components of illness, and we have ascribed this to problems in methodology, in particular, the lack of a suitable vocabulary or framework for the description and retrieval of significant biobehavioral correlates and consequences of disease. Rigorous ethnography, we saw, seems to require "hard" and public anchoring points. The work of medical ecologists just reviewed here has in general demonstrated an awareness of the need for linking culturally specific practices involving orientations to illness and disease with analytic requirements of population biology in order to develop incisive formulations of how cultures persist and change. Thus, a question that has been repeatedly raised is how diseases operate or may have operated as selective agents in the course of evolutionary human history, and more importantly, how cultural factors have influenced this population-environment exchange.

There are at least two general strategies or analytic procedures that may be used to arrive at answers to questions such as these. In the first one, general cultural practices or institutions that may significantly bear on the development, propagation, or treatment of specific endemic diseases are analyzed in relation to population trends and distributions in particular geographic settings. In analyses of this type, the interaction between cultural groups and a particular disease or group of diseases is generally approached at a rather high level of abstraction, and, consequently, the issue of whether members of the culture recognize either the value of a particular medical practice or specific features of the disease that they may be controlling is left out of focus. On the other hand, with the view of generalizing to earlier historical periods, one can analyze how representatives of particular "preliterate" cultures actually respond to medical phenomena, that is to say, how they define illness, how they treat it, and how they organize their social lives when they judge it to be in their midst; especially important in this approach is a consideration of potential biological consequences for the group of the various actions that are taken in response to native categories of meaning (Vayda and Rappaport 1968). The requirements of this latter analytic strategy are quite different from those of the former one, since the emphasis is on specific groups in space and time, and the task ordinarily necessitates that the investigator be present in order to make direct observations. Since the investigator hopes to demonstrate that cultural responses to disease have significant consequence to the group's survival, it is naturally imperative that he be able to systematically compare his observations regarding native classification with knowledge of the actual biology of disease. Stated more succinctly, studying the influences of cultural practices of a population group on the effects of disease requires a careful delimitation of native categories of meaning in the domain of illness using biologically significant components of disease as referents. This, then, underlies the close link that exists between medicine and population biology on the one hand and the rather traditional concerns of a field such as anthropology for rigorous ethnography on the other. In subsequent chapters I will deal more directly with the problems of studying the feedbacks between sociocultural and disease-related changes.

STUDIES HAVING A HISTORICAL AND EVOLUTIONARY FOCUS
Another segment of medical ecological studies focuses directly on questions involving man's evolution. The assumption is that the habits and adaptational styles of current nonliterate groups approximate those of early man; thus insights gained from contemporary studies can be used to make inferences about early man and his forms of adjustment.

Two papers by Polgar (1963, 1964) focus in a very general way on the probable medical problems that characterized human groups during the various stages of biological and cultural evolution. In these papers the influence of living conditions generally and of specific issues such as physical and faunal characteristics of the environmental setting, size and density of human groups, permanence of habitation sites, behavioral practices, etc., on types and patterning of diseases is discussed.

In an elegant and concise manner Dunn (1968) has focused more directly on the medical problems of an important type of human grouping, the hunter-gatherers. The term *hunter-gatherers* has imprecise meanings but can be used roughly to refer to nonliterate persons who are nomadic as opposed to settled, who subsist directly off the land (that is, do not farm), and who are organized socially in small groups or bands. It is generally conceded that man's earlier history was characterized by this mode of social organization, and that, consequently, important biological characteristics of man (including disease resistance and vulnerabilities) have to be interpreted in the light of the demands presented by this mode. In his review of the medical problems of these people, Dunn first presents the sources of data that human biologists can use to evaluate the health status of prehistoric hunter-gatherers. The influence of disease and other environmental factors on the structure of the population is considered. Then, current literature dealing with the health problems of contemporary hunter-gatherers is used to evaluate the kinds of diseases that are common among them. Infectious diseases are most important. Attention is given to factors that affect the mortality of hunter-gatherers. The influence of ecological diversity and complexity is given specific attention in the attempt to explain rates of parasitic and infectious diseases. Dunn's chapter in this excellent book is very useful since it addresses itself systematically to a variety of summary propositions about medical features of hunter-gatherers (such as frequency of starvation, traumatic death rates, and the question of mental illness). The reader who wishes to go further into this general problem of the relations among ecological factors, social organization, and health status is urged to read Dunn's empirical paper on the Malayan Aborigines (1972). A segment of the succinctly written paper by Goldstein (1969) reviews the recent literature focusing on those diseases that are encountered in present "primitive societies," particularly, the hunter-gatherers.

The publications of Cockburn (1963, 1967, 1971) are related to those discussed here and deal additionally with a more specialized aspect of the problem, namely, the potential of this field to contribute knowledge about human evolution. Cockburn is interested in the distribution of particular parasites and microorganisms in primates and man and uses knowledge about this distribution to clarify issues of man's phylogenetic relationship to other primates. The history and evolution of infectious diseases, particularly those that have affected man, receive emphasis. Cockburn is interested in clarifying the influence that infectious disease has had on man during different evolutionary periods and how both man and parasites have been affected biologically by living together.

Here, the contrast between the approach of the ecologist and that of the social scientist interested in cultural matters is graphically illustrated. The relevant features of a group, for example, are its population size and density, particularly as these relate to the persistence of a pool of microorganisms that allow for continued epidemics. Estimates of this size are offered, and the influence of mode of life on disease propagation is examined. Yet the way disease may affect the quality of social life is not explored, nor are the people's ways of responding socially to the disease considered relevant. Cockburn's first book (1963) reviews in considerable detail related but purely ecologic issues and also contains excellent chapters dealing with the problem of eradication of infectious diseases. The contents of this book spans the fields of paleopathology, paleoepidemiology, virology, parasitology, and evolution. A later, edited book (Cockburn 1967) elaborates upon the preceding issues. It contains numerous chapters dealing with the various specific types of diseases that have affected man through his history. In addition, the book contains chapters on related biological issues that bear on evolution and the influence of disease. Thus, two chapters review thinking on the origins and early manifestations of life, another deals analytically with the theory of a natural focus of disease (depicting disease agents as natural features of an ecological unit), and one chapter discusses the development of insecticides. The chapters in this book, which tend to be discursive and general, also attempt to review the literature.

A common subject of writings on the health problems of contemporary preliterate and prehistoric human groups is the diseases found in and carried by other forms of life in intimate contact with man. Quite frequently, the medical diseases found in nonhuman primates receive particular attention, since the resulting picture bears on questions of evolution as well as on the potential of transmission to humans. However, the problems involved in interpreting findings dealing with infections in nonhuman primates are numerous and infrequently discussed. The work of Dunn (1965, 1966, 1970), who was already cited with regard to health problems of hunter-gatherers, and that of Dunn, Lim, and Yap (1968) also deals with the general question of the distribution of disease and parasites in subhuman primates and their implications for issues of human biology. In his papers he discusses critically the problems of interpreting data reported by others. In addition, his papers should be consulted for an appreciation of the logic and strategy of analyses in this field as well as for their substantive information. In his essay dealing with the antiquity of malaria, for example, he summarizes the literature dealing with the distribution of this disease and then critically examines hypotheses purporting to explain this distribution. Such an analysis requires him to examine the distribution of the malaria parasite in subhuman primates and to explain this prevalence with respect to the prevalence of malaria in man. (The papers by Pimentel [1961, 1968] deal generally with the reciprocal relations between host and parasite and the genetic feedback between the two; although analyses are set in a broad evolutionary framework and do not deal directly with problems of human diseases, they are relevant to the general problem of evolution that is in focus in most medical ecological studies.) The reader who wishes a general exposition of the logic and rationale of comparative medicine should consult the monograph by Beveridge (1972). His is a lucid account of how the study of diseases in animals has benefited man in the past and can be expected to continue to do so in the future.

The paper by Otten (1967) reviews in a quite thorough and very critical manner a portion of the literature dealing with the relations between man (viewed in terms of the immunological properties of his blood group antigens and sera) and microbial agents capable of causing clinical infections. The problems discussed in this paper are central to such issues as human evolution, population stability, the influence of disease in recorded human history, and so on. This is the case because the paper focuses on rather basic biological characteristics that influence the relative vulnerability of man to infectious disease agents. Otten feels that the literature does not support the claim that the distribution of ABO blood group frequencies is related to the possible selective actions of specific infectious disease agents. She discusses the influence that antibody formation in various parts of the body can have on the development of infectious diseases and raises the possibility that ABO blood types may create different susceptibilities to intestinal microbiota.

More general analyses and reviews of the literature dealing with the disease problems of earlier human groups and civilizations are plentiful. The Brothwell book (1963) is an introduction to the field of paleopathology. In a succinct and lucid manner, he describes the types of skeletal specimens that can be encountered, the procedure for uncovering remains, and characteristics of specimens that enable drawing inferences about disease. The book by Wells (1964) is similar in scope, although it includes more detail on pathological characteristics of bones and also reviews historical issues. The book edited by Jarcho (1966) is a collection of essays on selected problems in the field of paleopathology; it also contains chapters dealing with data from recent excavations and others that review the recent physiologic and allied research findings in osteology, which may have potential value in further analyses of skeletal remains. The article by Kerley and Bass (1967) is a lucid, rounded, and succinct statement about the field of paleopathology; its scope, methods, and concerns are discussed. The Brothwell and Sandison volume (1967) contains general summaries of the literature dealing with the medical problems of ancient populations and with those of preliterate groups (both contemporary and ancient). This book represents a summary and assessment of the field of paleopathology. The chapters cover a number of issues—general systemic medical diseases, diseases caused by specific microorganisms, congenital anomalies, arthritic problems, the practice of trephanation, and others. The book should be consulted by anyone interested in capturing the scope and complexity of this field of activity.

EMPIRICAL STUDIES OF ISOLATED GROUPS

Small groups living in relative isolation offer a particularly good opportunity to examine the interplay among environment, culture, population changes, and disease. As we have already emphasized, such groups are believed to represent the best existing approximation of the types of conditions that presumably gave rise to human variability and thus allow focusing on theoretical questions that may yield insights into human evolution. Multidisciplinary, systems-oriented studies dealing with isolated groups have been numerous in the recent past. The concerns of the International Biological Program include an examination of the influence of disease in the adaptation of isolated groups (see Baker and Weiner 1966). The general comments offered by Gajdusek (1964, 1970a), Neel and Salzano (1964), and Neel (1970) dealing with the potential of these studies from the standpoint of medicine and population biology should be consulted. Medically oriented studies of small, isolated groups having "primitive" forms of social organization are often conducted within a framework similar to that used to examine the adaptations of various peoples to different types of harsh environment (Baker 1966). This framework has been termed by Lasker (1969) the "ecological approach" in physical anthropology.

The series of papers on the Xavante, Makiritare, and Yanomama Indians, three South American hunting and gathering groups (Neel and Salzano 1967, Neel et al., 1968a, 1968b, Niswander 1967, and Weinstein et al. 1967), contains a great deal of information on factors related to disease. Information derived from physical examinations, analysis of peripheral blood specimens, dental examinations, and examination of sera, urine, and stool specimens has been reported in various publications. The Xavante are, in general, in an excellent state of physical health, and observations indicate the same picture with regard to the Makiritare and Yanomama. For reasons that are not entirely clear, Xavante women appear less healthy than men. There is an unresolved paradox brought about by the apparent excellent health of the young and the absence of elderly individuals in the group. Infant and childhood mortality rates are high when compared to highly civilized countries but low when compared to underdeveloped nations such as India at the turn of the century. Stool examination and serologic evidence suggest that these groups have experienced extensive contacts with certain potentially disease-producing, infectious agents. The ecological setting, and, in this particular case, the microorganisms and foreign proteins in it, uniquely determine what characterizes the individual's blood proteins and, by implication, health status. The many biological attributes of these subjects in a sense mirror the physical environment. Newborn infants, who appear to possess rather high measures of maternal antibody acquired transplacentally, are from very early in life exposed to a variety of pathogens. The rather long period of lactation and the excellent nutritional status of the child allow for a relatively smooth transition from passive to active immunity. A number of additional observations on the health status of these subjects have been included in several of the papers. The studies conducted by Neel and his group, of course, have a broad and diversified focus and in addition to dealing with disease agents per se include such issues as cytogenetic changes, the distribution of genetic markers, and considerations of the movements and changes in population groups. A rather high degree of intratribal genetic differentiation across Indian villages has been documented (Ward and Neel 1970). This finding is believed to reflect stochastic events as well as more socially structured factors, such as the fission-fusion pattern of village propagation, the nonrandom pattern of intervillage migration, and the genetic consequences of the differential fertility that is maintained by polygamy. Among the Yanomama, intercourse taboos, prolonged lactation, abortion, and infanticide have the effect of reducing the effective live-birth rate to about one child every four to five years during the child-bearing years. This has led Neel to propose that a form of prudent control of the population base characterizes these Indian groups.

These studies, then, represent excellent examples of how interdisciplinary research efforts, which involve anthropologists, biologists, and physicians, can be developed and coordinated in the attempt to examine problems of disease and population genetics. Clarification of these problems may answer questions dealing with man's early history. In related studies conducted by the same group, the response of the Yanomama Indians to a measles epidemic is lucidly described (Neel et al. 1970). Viral agents such as measles have shown an unusual pathogenicity in American indigenous groups. Although a genetic susceptibility has been presumed, some observations have challenged this presumption and raised the possibility that other factors are involved. An implication of Neel's recent observations is that secondary factors (such as the behavior of the subject during the infection—in particular, his apathy—the absence of fluid replacement, and the general consequences of an essential collapse of village life during the epidemic) probably account for much of the morbidity and mortality associated with this disease. A serologic follow-up on a small scale revealed that ". . . the ability of the Indian to form antibodies to an antigen to which he may not previously have been exposed appears no different from that of the much exposed Caucasian" (p. 427). Thus, the long-held view regarding an innate "susceptibility" to measles in the American Indian is seriously challenged by this data. (Additional data on the health status of the American Indian can be found in the chapters by Nutels, Burch et al., Miller, Galanter, and Pribram, Giglioli, Riviere et al., and Barzelatto and Covarrubias in the publication of the Pan American Health Organization [1968], *Biomedical Challenges Presented by the American Indian*.)

The studies of Gajdusek and his group on *kuru*, the fatal progressive degenerative disease of the central nervous system, are also illustrative of the direction these studies can take (see Alpers and Gajdusek 1965, Zigas 1970, Alpers 1970, and Gibbs and Gajdusek 1970). In this instance, the study of an unusual syndrome in an isolated group (New Guinea Highlanders) has led to brilliant explorations of the relationships between culture, environment, and a specific disease. What is more, biomedical knowledge generated by the study of *kuru* has had an important influence in stimulating work that has led to the development of refined hypotheses about the cause of a variety of human diseases. The disease *kuru* is confined to members of the Fore linguistic group of New Guinea and those with whom they intermarry. The disease, which accounted for the mortality of over 2 percent of the population each year, affected mostly women and children, often producing a male to female ratio of 3:1. Salient features of the distribution of this disease have been explained by means of hypotheses that invoke genetic and environmental factors. The disease is caused by a slow "latent" virus for which there is a genetic susceptibility. The third factor in the expression of the disease appears to be the practice of cannibalism, which is believed to expose susceptible individuals to contaminated human segments. Striking changes in the sex and age incidence of the disease have occurred, and these are believed to be due to socioenvironmental changes in the region, in particular the curtailment of the practice of cannibalism among the Fore. Some of the social consequences of this disease are described by Gajdusek (1963). The mode of search for the etiology of *kuru* reflects clearly the multilevel and holistic approach of human ecology. The study of *kuru* has stimulated the search for similar types of viruses in other degenerative diseases of the central nervous system (see Petrov 1970, Mathai 1970, and Yase 1970).

Some of the striking biomedical characteristics of people living in societies of New Guinea have also been provocatively discussed by Gajdusek (1970*b*). These include extremely slow growth patterns and delayed puberty, which together with a short life expectancy mean that many New Guineans have spent over two-thirds of their life attaining full sexual maturity. The characteristic early aging of many New Guineans is not accompanied by the vascular changes and high blood pressures of aging civilized societies. Those who exhibit extreme growth retardation are regularly found to be suffering from malnutrition with low total protein and caloric intake, although they frequently do not show clinical manifestations of malnutrition. It is unclear to what extent the pigmoid build of some New Guineans is determined by genetic factors as opposed to environmental ones. The land-locked New Guineans in the interior valleys live in a sodium-scarce environment. Compared to "civilized" peoples, these New Guineans demonstrate a reversal of the expected values of urinary sodium and potassium excretion. Excessively low salt and protein intake lead to low urinary amino acid and sodium excretion and to daily urinary output values that are extraordinarily reduced. The wiry build of these people with little subcutaneous tissue suggests a high degree of adaptation to heavy work requirements, with low-weight body frames that are believed to be ideal for the rather high load-to-body-weight ratios. An unusual insensitivity to pain has also been observed. Instances of relatively unusual behavioral practices (for example, headhunting, cannibalism, scarification, and mutilation) have been described, though the full psychological or behavioral implications of these practices remain to be explored. The implications of some of these observations cannot be overemphasized, since they dramatically illustrate the *biological plasticity of man*—the extent to which his anatomy, physiology, and biochemistry are products of his physical and social environment.

A series of studies conducted in the village of Keneba in West Africa illustrates further the potential contribution that culturally and ecologically oriented studies of medical issues can make (A. M. Thomson et al. 1966*a*, 1966*b*, 1968, B. Thompson 1966, 1967*a*, 1967*b*, B. Thompson and Rahman 1967, B. Thompson and Baird 1967*a*, 1967*b*, 1967*c*, and McGregor et al. 1968, 1970). One study examined activities and events surrounding the first two weeks of life. The activities of pregnant women, cultural attitudes toward pregnancy, the process of childbirth, and the care and feeding of the newborn were presented in rich detail. It was shown that immediate wet nursing and demand feeding from birth had no obvious ill effects on the neonates, a finding that tends to weaken a prevailing view that newborns should be deprived of milk during their first days of life because of potential ill effects. The time of the year when birth occurred was shown to have significant consequences for such issues as child care, feeding, and even survival. In another study, the weight changes in pregnant and lactating women were evaluated as a function of time and season of the year. Changes noted were related to work and leisure characteristics, which reflected behavioral patterns imposed by the culture as well as availability of food, which is tied to features of the ecosystem. The paper by Brazelton et al. (1969) is another illustration of how biologically relevant data about human development can be enriched by being related analytically to the cultural framework. These investigators report their results of observing childbirth routines and early developmental phases of children in Zinacantan. Characteristics of adult Zinacantecan behavior were felt to be mirrored in these early developmental sequences.

Studies of this type, which involve "filling in" the details of how biologically significant events are structured by culture and environment, can offer a contribution to social science in a purely descriptive sense and also to the extent that the events and processes examined (which represent universal points of emphasis or crises in human groups) are analyzed with reference to the functioning of the sociocultural system. In addition, however, studies documenting the basic physiological changes involved in these processes make an obvious contribution to human biology. Data of the type produced in these studies have heretofore been lacking; medical knowledge has simply lacked details of how sociocultural factors interrelate with biomedical events and processes. Studies of a similar nature have been reported by Marsden (1964), Potter et al. (1965), Simpkiss (1968), and Cravioto (1968).

Historical Studies of Disease
Another way in which theoreticians have discussed the influence of various diseases in earlier periods is by availing themselves of historical ac-

counts and records, describing morbidity pictures in various population groups at distinct points in time, and then making inferences about the sources and types of disease involved. Indeed, this highly descriptive and anecdotal approach is the hallmark of attempts to evaluate the impact of disease in population groups. The works of Sigerist (1951, 1961), old classics in the field, hardly need mentioning. The more recent book by Ackerknecht (1965) also provides disease histories. He reviews in varying degrees of detail clinical features and background knowledge pertaining to a number of diseases that have played important roles in recorded history. The natural history, manner of spread, consequences, and eventual control of such diseases as plague, typhus, and yellow fever are described. Historical aspects and the geographic distribution of the diseases are particularly stressed. The recent book by Cartwright and Biddiss (1972) has a similar focus but gives greater emphasis to historical and especially social details accompanying disease. The new edition of Burnet and White's (1972) classic book should be consulted for related analyses of important infectious diseases. Here, the disease itself viewed across time is examined. This book focuses incisively on immunological aspects of these diseases, and the author employs a distinctly ecological framework.

An interesting use of the historical approach to the study of disease in society is to focus on one disease and trace how concepts and interpretations about that disease have changed over time. The book by Veith (1965) is an excellent example of this type of study. She concentrates on the "disease" hysteria and reviews historical writings beginning with ancient Egyptian sources and carrying her analysis through medieval and early modern Western European history up to the preliminary stages of the psychoanalytic movement in the late 19th century. Hysteria, as is well known, was of central importance in the evolution of Sigmund Freud's thinking about intrapsychic processes. Less well known, perhaps, and insightfully analyzed by Veith, is the long-standing association that this "disease" has had with ideas focusing on female sexuality. In a sense, Freud's formulations about hysteria are but analytic extensions (with theoretical implications of a profound sort, to be sure) of a theme that runs through Western European medical thinking to the effect that sexual problems cause or bring about the complex psychosocial and psychosomatic changes that consistently have been given the label hysteria. Veith's analysis sensitizes the reader to the intellectual sources of contemporary medical thinking about what has come to be seen as a neuropsychiatric entity. Her book, in short, must be seen as making an important contribution not only to medical history per se but also to our understanding of the background of an important intellectual theme of contemporary society, namely, psychoanalysis.

The book has additional merits. Because it is detailed and richly interspersed with sections taken directly from significant writings, the reader gains firsthand knowledge of how Western-trained physicians at different points in time have viewed interactions between what have come to be seen as the mental and the somatic domains. Waxing and waning throughout the pages of this book is the dualistic approach to disease, an approach that has come more and more to divide the disturbances of man into the physical and mental sides. Assuming for the moment that hysteria is a disease that persons in earlier periods suffered from just as they do today, then we are forced to claim that it is a psychosomatic or psychobiologic entity. Thinking about hysteria, then, becomes illustrative of Western man's thinking about how his body and his mind are related and interact. The reader wishing to delve into this facet of man's attempt to explain to himself how his emotional and thinking side relate to his corporeal one is urged to read this book. To be sure, Veith does not view the problem this way but is more centrally concerned with tracing and reviewing formulations about this disease itself. Consequently, it becomes quite difficult for one to draw firm conclusions on just when and how Western medical thinking shifted toward a reductionistic and dualistic mold. Nevertheless, the richness of her material does allow the interested reader at least to pose and entertain questions of this sort. Those who wish to pursue in greater depth related matters are urged to read the books by Riese (1959) and Temkin (1971).

The book by Klibansky, Panofsky, and Saxl (1964) is a scholarly account of the thinking that has surrounded the entity "melancholia," which must be seen as a forerunner of our "depression." The authors trace the unfolding of humoral theory through the medium of the writings of the classicists. Here one sees in rich detail the original Greek unified conception of or approach to disease, which involved bodily matters (that is, the various humors), psychological matters (that is, personality types and mood states, which were said to depend on the humors), and behavioral dispositions of various sorts. Even in Western culture, then, the entity "disease" initially possessed these integrated aspects. Indeed, the idea that mind and body are different and each potentially capable of influencing the other is a *late* Greek idea, as Snell (1960) has lucidly documented. Subsequent developments in intellectual European history had the effect of dichotomizing these domains into separate, almost mutually exclusive divisions of the person. Sarbin (1968), although ignoring Greek sources of a dualistic orientation, has offered a speculative analysis of how the notion of anxiety as a mental state grew in Western psychology. He has suggested that the idea of an eschatological soul was influential in orienting psychologists (and, by extension, physicians) to the realm of the mind as an explanation for behavior. His analysis of scientific change can be termed sociolinguistic insofar as he emphasizes that important social processes surrounding the use of various linguistic forms serve to create new domains of intellectual focus. These studies all point to the historical bases of our conceptions about how man functions and becomes diseased, underscore the extent to which we ourselves may be intellectually trapped by prevailing paradigms, and alert us to the possibility that contemporary approaches to man and disease may have outlived their usefulness. At the same time, we need to understand that to a considerable extent the behavior of persons showing changes one may term disease is affected by the paradigms and explanations that society (that is, the scientific community) provides them. I shall return to related issues in later chapters.

We should note in passing that theoreticians who inform us about disease in past historical epochs very often assume implicitly that the disease under examination had an "existence" then just as it does now. In other words, the prevailing view is that disease X (cancer, hysteria, typhus, tuberculosis, etc.) is a universal "thing" that has existed in time with a precise and unvarying identity that "we" now know or have access to. In most instances, such an *ethnocentric* assumption is harmless and, given the immediate aims of the analyst, perfectly justified. However, this assumptive view overlooks or at least minimizes two related issues that are worth making explicit at this juncture, since they (when properly examined) will be seen to contain biases that militate against effective theorizing in the field of social medicine.

The first issue is that, in a nontrivial sense, at any point in time diseases are what persons suffering from and treating them say they are. Perhaps nowhere is this better demonstrated than in the very scholarly writings of the noted American historian of medicine, Lester S. King (1963, 1971), who has concerned himself with tracing the evolution of Western man's thinking about disease. The fact that King is a trained pathologist eminently qualifies him for this task, since a sound contemporary medical training is used as a basis for examining earlier ones. King is thus able to depict how changing intellectual traditions contribute to the formulation of what passes as a medical fact. Tuberculosis, for example, didn't "exist" as such prior to certain needed refinements in biological science. Neither did the nephrotic syndrome, congestive heart failure, nor ascites due to postnecrotic cirrhosis. What did exist, instead, were such things as dropsy, cachexiae, tartaric diseases, and the like. Reality, in the viewpoint we are adopting here for heuristic purposes, is made up of the symbols, paradigms, and concepts available to people in time and space that enable them to perceive, organize, and make sense of the world around them. We see, make contact with, and treat as real those things that our social system defines for us. This particular position, of course, is the cornerstone of a prominent and increasingly important tradition in the history and philosophy of science (Kuhn 1970, Schappere 1966) and is and always has been a fundamental tenet of culturally oriented anthropologists.

If we assume this position, and from a certain theoretical standpoint we are indeed compelled to, then it follows (and this is the second and related issue mentioned previously) that the diseases we are now seeing and treating (and ethnocentrically projecting backward and generalizing about) are in an equivalent sense socially constructed and/or arbitrary "things." In a specific sense, this fact is in evidence when biologists fret about the proper indicators of disease. Feinstein (1967) has demonstrated in a most compelling way how Western man's taxonomies change, their whimsical, often inconsistent bases, and the problems that they create for epidemiologists wishing to establish "true" prevalence or incidence figures. More generally, the symbols and conventions of a society or social system are to some extent what determines ontologies. Ours tell us that we have to believe in the scientific method and accept the findings and propositions generated by it. This rule applies to our conceptions of what disease is, which ones are real, and how we should treat them. Scientists and theoreticians of the future may condemn us for the naïvete that we unknowingly show when categorizing disease much the same way that many of us condemn those (*equally knowledgeable*) before us.

When we come to view disease in this fashion—as an entity we have defined for ourselves—then it follows that we should examine critically the processes that underlie these definitional efforts as well as the implications that devolve from them. At the very least we should come to appreciate that because disease definitions are socially sanctioned enterprises they entail commitments about how to go about dealing with them. We should also become alerted to the utility of seeing in disease definitions devices and programs for the accomplishment of variable ends. In subsequent chapters, these and related issues will be examined in greater depth.

Disease as an Independent Variable

This section reviews medical studies that in general examine the influence of sociocultural factors from the additional standpoints of what is done about disease, what the manifestations of disease are, and the social consequences of discrete disease types in specific groups. Thus, in contrast to those epidemiologic and ecologic studies that treat specific diseases largely as dependent variables, in the studies to be reviewed diseases (or biomedical problems in general) tend to be handled mainly as independent variables. This then leads to the examination of sociocultural issues as they affect outcome or effects (that is, as dependent variables).

An excellent example of the contribution of this framework for viewing medical problems is illustrated in a series of papers by Schofield. Two initial papers coauthored with Parkinson (Schofield and Parkinson, 1963a, 1963b) describe beliefs and practices that have a bearing on health status among peoples of the Sepik district of New Guinea. In many ways, the focus of these studies is similar to those that were reviewed in the preceding chapter. The principal difference, however, is the attention paid to native orientations and practices that have an important influence on specific types of biomedical and public health problems. The aim of these studies, in fact, can be described as an attempt to arrive at a comprehensive view of medically relevant dispositions and behaviors, since biomedical categories are articulated with reference to the sociocultural perspective. Thus, Schofield reviews beliefs about the cause of illness and important physiological events (such as pregnancy) and also attitudes toward hospitalization and other Western forms of medical treatment. His intent is to show how these influence the behaviors of the people and constrain any attempt to introduce public health measures. In another paper Schofield et al. (1963) report on their studies of *tinea imbricata,* a skin disease that is common in the lowland section of New Guinea. Several factors that bear on the potential etiology, onset, and distribution of the disease are discussed. Personal habits (particularly, degree of cleanliness, diet, and closeness to infected persons) and living conditions are reported to be factors affecting the risk of primary infection. Although the disease appears to have no biological effect on the fertility of married women, the social effects of *tinea imbricata* do reduce the crude fertility rate of infected women since they are judged to be less desirable wives and tend to marry later. The disease also contributes to bachelorhood in males and appears to cause economic and educational handicaps as well. In a later paper, Schofield (1970) reports on his observations in the Ethiopian highlands and discusses some of the distinctive social and psychological reactions to the presence of leprosy. Schofield et al., in summary, starting with either specific Western disease types or generic medical and public health issues, examine social and cultural factors not only etiologically but also as they bear on the course and effects of the disease. To some extent, these studies represent a fusion of the perspectives of medicine, ecology, and cultural anthropology.

An interesting use of the social science perspective in medicine involves examining the influence that social and cultural factors have on the orientations and behaviors of persons vis-à-vis a particular disease that is categorized in terms of Western biomedical science. In other words, a Western biomedical entity (disease X) is examined in terms of how members of a cultural group apprehend, define, and explain this "entity" (now termed illness Y by members of the culture). Thus, Imperato (1969) studied orientations toward measles in the Republic of Mali. His material came from specific case investigations as well as questionnaire responses of medical officers who had been instructed to interview villagers. The various tribal names for measles, the presumed cause, and the attitudes of families toward active cases were obtained. He shows that a number of clinical features of measles are recognized by the group as being criterial in this disease, and that various folk practices are used with reference to these features. The deleterious consequences of the practice of withholding food during the active phase of the disease (rooted in culturally specific conceptions about illness) are reviewed. Topley (1970), who worked in Hong Kong, analyzed in detail traditional ideas about and treatment of measles. Her information derives from direct interviews with informants, and she includes in her account a more detailed presentation of the historical background and the current cultural orientations of the peoples in the area of medicine. The analysis of measles is undertaken in terms of traditional beliefs and patterns of the group; the category measles is treated, not so much as a Western disease type having specific morbidity features and treatment regimes, but as a normalized cultural category that is integrated with other behavioral prescriptions and orientations of the group. The latter part of Topley's paper focuses on another specific folk illness that also affects children and includes a personalized analysis of the mechanism for folk illness labeling.

Imperato and Traore (1968), who worked in the Republic of Mali, discuss the content of beliefs held about smallpox. Beliefs regarding the cause and mode of treatment of smallpox were examined. The authors point out that although ideas regarding "why" a disease occurs may be grounded in traditional supernatural notions, these ideas may coexist with Western scientific views of "how" the disease developed. Hoeppli and Lucasse (1964) traced the history and distribution of native beliefs about the cause, symptoms, and treatment of sleeping sickness, a usually fatal trypanosomal disease, in West Africa. They showed that a number of features about this disease that are regarded as criterial in Western scientific medical knowledge had been recognized and acted upon by residents of the area.

The papers by Gussow (1964) and Gussow and Tracy (1968) also focus on a Western-defined disease type—namely, leprosy—but involve an analysis within the framework of processual and interactionist sociology of how persons adjust to this disease. The sociological constructs of medical "career" and social stigma prove central in this analysis, though the authors also give attention to physical and physiologic issues as well. This type of study of disease is a spin-off from the work of social scientists interested in the general problem of social deviance, marginality, influence of social symbols on interpersonal relations, etc. In other words, these researchers start with a given diagnostic name or label, which is applied to an individual, and examine the *consequences* that accrue to him by virtue of his acquiring this label. This form of social analysis—actually called labeling theory as well as phenomenologic sociology—is quite prominent in contemporary sociology. It has most classically been used in the study of "mental illness" but applies as well to all diseases that have important stigmatizing effects. Sociologists have been able to explain much of the behavior of patients in terms of this labeling paradigm—that is, how "having" a disease places individuals in distinct social categories and situations that create special problems for them above and beyond those attributed to the purely physiological ones. Some of these researchers' analyses tend to suggest that little of "disease" remains when we "peel off" these social factors (see Scheff 1966), a suggestion that, although interesting, is highly questionable.

Another and rather fundamental way in which social science has contributed to our understanding about disease has been by facilitating analyses that show that different diseases are responded to differently and in fact *mean different things* to people in different walks of life. These studies, which to some extent share a cultural framework, are actually quite numerous and are reviewed in the books by Coe, Friedson, and Mechanic referred to earlier. Thus, Bronks and Blackburn (1968) reported on the social and psychological problems experienced by persons with hemophilia. Elder and Acheson (1970) reported on a study dealing with the influence of social class on the responses and behavioral patterns of persons suffering from osteoarthrosis. Studies of this type—namely, those that show that to understand the psychological and behavioral consequences of disease one must take into account the social and cultural identity of the person—are seen as providing the most compelling reason for including social science in the training of health service professionals. A person, in other words, embodies among other things a collection of *social identities*—social class, ethnicity, roles, obligations, styles of living, etc.—each and all of which need to be taken into account in appraising why he has a disease, how he thinks and feels about it, and what he does about it. This theory, particularly when enunciated in this simplistic manner, is slowly becoming a truism.

Continuing with the review of studies that begin with the category disease and then examine its social effects, we come to a study such as the one by Gelfand (1966), who is intent on showing how a biologically construed disease entity (schistosomiasis) can be expressed or manifested differently in individuals having different cultural and physical characteristics (in this case, Europeans versus Africans). This particular study has shortcomings. Sampling problems, for example, limit the generalizability of the findings, and some of the categories used as indicators of the disease are rather general and hence problematic. However, the logic and intent of this study is interesting and deserves discussion. Gelfand showed that Europeans, who tended to demonstrate fewer excreted eggs, also tended to show greater physical effects of the parasitic infestations —in particular, more frequent reports of fatigue. Africans tended more frequently to report abdominal complaints. The study concurs with Honey and Gelfand's previous (1962) experience indicating that a number of urological findings associated with this disease differ in cultural groups. (Traditional epidemiologic investigations demonstrating that a particular disease type manifests different pathophysiologic profiles in different social or cultural groups bear on this same issue of disease comparability—see, for example, Blackard, Omori, and Freedman 1965— though these particular investigations never appear to question the integrity and specificity of the particular disease category under examination.) Studies of this type, in short, bring into sharp focus the question of *what constitutes a disease* or, more specifically, what framework should be used to define a disease. Gelfand uses a strictly biologistic framework (that is, his indicators of disease are egg counts of particular parasites); yet a behavioral or manifestational framework (that is, one that relies on symptoms and expressed disabilities as indicators) might have led him to conclude that different diseases were actually being compared.

The imperfect correlation between diseases and disease outcomes (that is, the fact that similar biologically defined "disease processes" may have different expressions and individualistic consequences) should alert us to the arbitrariness and, hence, limitation of any one disease definition and suggest not only that many interrelated factors must be taken into account in the study of disease but also that biology and psychosocial matters heavily influence each other. To be sure, the problems posed by the existing nosology of disease are currently receiving a great deal of attention. There is no reason to expect current disease "types" to have a precise identity in nature. As was mentioned earlier, Feinstein has discussed at length the pernicious consequences for clinical epidemiology of changing disease classification schemes and has presented cogent arguments in favor of the view that "diseases" need to be seen as sets of clustered biological facts, rather than as unitary phenomena (see Feinstein 1967, Chapters 1–7; 1968a, 1968b). Furthermore, we have now seen how models of disease causation that rest on inappropriate nosologies might constrain research strategies. It needs hardly be emphasized that cultural factors (as expressed either at the level of behavior per se or at the level of perceptual and cognitive processes) must also be seen as contributing to the variability and imprecision with which disease "types" occur in nature. Stated differently, at any one point in time a Western disease type is likely to be expressed in ways that are affected by culture just as its course and development will be culturally patterned. In subsequent chapters we shall examine more closely this question of disease ontology and the problems stemming from levels at which a disease is to be articulated. The problem of pain, of course, poses similar conceptual and methodological issues (see Zborowski 1958, 1969, and Wolff and Langley 1968), as does any biologically specified process that has social and behavioral accompaniments and consequences. Thus, Solien De Gonzalez (1964) has reported persuasive observations leading her to question traditional assumptions about lactation. Similarly, Obeyesekere (1963) analyzes the relevance of sociocultural factors for the expression of pregnancy "symptoms" in a Sinhalese village. What is more, an attempt is made to analyze the functional consequences and implications for the group of what must be seen as a biocultural complex. (See also the papers by Hanson [1970], Kupferer [1965], and Newman [1966].)

By way of summary it can be said that these studies illustrate nicely the way in which biological processes (for example, the disease schistosomiasis, "pain" stimuli, lactation, pregnancy) can serve as a matrix or foundation for the elaboration of what can be viewed as biocultural categories, and they offer compelling evidence for the need to employ alternative frameworks in order to understand fully the phenomena of disease and human adaptation. Socioculturally oriented studies of health and disease thus not only have a bearing on traditional epidemiological concerns but must also be seen as clarifying the many consequences of disease and indeed as clarifying the central set of premises that serve as the basis of our definitions of disease. An examination and analysis of those issues that bear on this point will be undertaken in the coming chapters.

Chapter 3   Critique of Traditional Approaches in Social Medicine

As the previous two chapters have shown, a basic distinction in socio-medical studies is whether disease and illness are analyzed using conceptual categories that draw on contemporary Western *scientific medical knowledge* or, instead, whether the *native (cultural) framework* is followed. The kinds of orientations followed can be seen as involving alternative disease frameworks. Studies employing the Western perspective can be further distinguished by the way in which they type or classify the particular health impairment that is in salience. In other words, in defining or specifying the basis of an impairment, investigators often attempt to draw a distinction between physical disorders and psychiatric disorders. We will examine this question of disease definitions in a more formal manner in subsequent chapters. For now, I wish to emphasize that for the investigator seeking to comprehend in a refined way problems involving health and illness, particularly as these involve social factors, there are definite limitations in focusing on only one type of medical orientation and in strictly maintaining a logical distinction regarding type of illness. Stated differently, continuing to study medical problems in relation to social systems by means of the existing traditional approaches creates analytic problems that limit clarification of the mutual influences that culture, the environment, and illness have on each other. What is more, relying on these approaches has practical disadvantages.

Limitations and Deficiencies of Ethnomedical Studies

An examination of the literature in cultural anthropology dealing with medical problems reveals that instances of illness or disease are usually handled analytically in one of three ways: (1) An episode of illness indicates a point or area of stress and dysfunction in the sociocultural system. This dysfunction (that is, illness) is itself viewed as determined either by sociocultural factors or stochastic ones in the sense that random and poorly understood "natural or physical forces" are involved. This dysfunction in the sociocultural system then provides an opportunity for specific institutions and/or other culturally patterned processes to bring about a reparation or control of the illness. (2) An illness episode involves persons who are suffused with emotion and concern and consequently provides an opportunity to demonstrate how religious and other "supernatural" ideas get expressed in symbolic actions, rituals, practices, etc., that exercise powerful influences on the behaviors of the sick one and his family. Although this frame of reference is not exclusive of the "functional" one illustrated in (1) previously, it is analytically distinguished, since the main effort of the ethnographer appears to be devoted to processual and symbolic issues. (3) An instance of illness shows how sociocultural patterns "shape" the expression of disability itself as well as general aspects of illness and medical care contingencies (regardless of whether the medical occurrence is determined or stochastic as in (1) above).

Thus, a largely descriptive interest often seems to motivate the anthropologists. Regardless of which of these analytic approaches is used by the cultural anthropologist, it is usually the case that the components of illness (that is, the varied behaviors and symptoms of the illness and their meanings) are not differentiated in any refined way such that the account allows others to build on the impressions of the ethnographer. The fact that the illness is often viewed as "psychiatric" also presents serious obstacles to cross-cultural comparisons (see Chapter 1 and also the next section). Even if this is not the case, the illness is usually described as an exotic, generic, and culturally specific occurrence that is patterned across time. This rather common way of handling illness has two related disadvantages. First, descriptions of illness in ethnomedical studies characteristically reflect cultural relativism: because the illness is culturally marked, it is different from illnesses found in other cultures. Such a position simply does not allow for comparisons of medical matters across cultural groups. Second, descriptions of illness in ethnomedical studies give the impression that all illnesses that are similarly labeled by the group are equivalent and have the significance that the ethnographer attributes to the particular one he examined. In a sociocultural unit, a particular illness type obviously varies as to manifestations, modes of onset, and type of treatment. An occurrence of the illness is related to social and other medical contingencies. A realistic appreciation of the reciprocal influences that cultural factors can have on illness and disease requires a more fine-grained depiction of medical happenings.

What is not altogether clear is what transpires situationally prior and subsequent to a clearly defined illness-treatment episode: the sequence of events (or processes) that precede the "social" definition of illness; the early behavioral manifestations of illness and the actions taken to curtail them; and the duration and progression of physiologic symptoms. The past social and medical history of the person experiencing the early manifestations of illness must also be specified. Analyses of these various issues would clarify what factors precipitate illness occurrences and answer questions centering on the kinds of social and bodily manifestations that persons tolerate or do not act upon.

Similarly, it is important to clarify what transpires after a curing or treatment procedure. Some reports suggest that as a person's illness abates, previously ruptured (or problematic) social relationships are reestablished, leading to a diminution in tensions. Much more likely, of course, is that some ill persons continue to deteriorate medically, others remain unchanged, and still others begin slowly to improve. In this context, the linkage between sociocultural and biologic factors needs to be specified. Similarly, regardless of what does follow a treatment procedure, including death, it is clear that a social process is involved. It is notable that the recent anthropological literature contains few descriptive or theoretical statements regarding the processes that lead up to and follow a "natural" death in a particular sociocultural unit (Nash 1967b).

If the preceding type of information is generated, together with an accurate portrayal of the meanings and interpretations given to these happenings, then it should be possible to begin to construct a broader picture of the way in which sociocultural processes affect and are affected by medical processes. Much of the literature suggests that most illness episodes are simply another type of critical incident in the life of a family, the explanation of which follows from the current status and degree of social integration of the family or sick person. The data necessary to determine clearly if this is the case are sadly lacking. These issues, of course, take on a more diversified significance when a situation involving the contact between cultures (and contrasting traditions) is made the setting for a study.

To a very large extent, then, investigators in ethnomedicine have relied on rather general and discipline-centered approaches to illness and disease and have undervalued and/or neglected the need for the development of a new language or set of concepts that can be used to describe and compare medical matters cross-culturally. The application of such a set of concepts would lead to the accumulation of knowledge valuable to anthropology and to medicine. A place to begin might be in the construction of a typology of illness stressing its social features and/or the development of a model of the decisions and behaviors associated with an occurrence of illness. I will have more to say about these issues in later chapters. Suffice it to say here that the implementation of these *analytic procedures* could accomplish two things: First, it would allow investigators to formally describe and empirically retrieve an occurrence of illness in a social system in terms of the associated behaviors or social responses of the sick person. Second, if the behaviors and their bases are represented in a sufficiently abstract way, the procedures would allow anthropologists and public health physicians the opportunity to study in a systematic and theoretically productive manner how in various settings cultural happenings are related to illness occurrences. The disciplines of anthropology and medicine stand to gain by developing such frameworks for examining illness. By formulating illness and disease-related behavioral responses in new ways, it may be possible to preserve a measure of cultural specificity and at the same time allow for comparative analyses. An opportunity may thus be provided for constructing a broad, cross-culturally relevant picture of medical care. Other parameters of interest to anthropologists and physicians might thus be linked analytically with the medical system, the latter immersed securely in culture and behavior.

Glick has already made an excellent beginning in this direction in his portrayal and analysis of medicine in the New Guinea Highlands (Glick 1967). He suggests that power be the central concept around which one organizes ethnomedical studies. Illnesses are in many instances seen as caused by entities with power, and treatment involves overcoming this power or strengthening the sick person, who is believed to be in a weakened state. The papers by Press (1969), Schwartz (1969), Fabrega (1970b), and Colson (1971) contain observations and formulations that bear on this matter of how illness and social processes could be related. The papers by Devereux (1963) and Hallowell (1963) contain useful observations and inferences regarding illness definition and behavior, although they employ a largely psychiatric framework. Weaver's interesting study (1970), which traces the unfolding of illness behaviors in the family, seems to be motivated by the desire to root illness in social situations and illustrates some of the practical implications of analyses evaluating disease using alternative formulations. The classic studies by American sociologists such as Freidson (1960), Mechanic (1962), Suchman (1965a, 1965b, 1965c, 1967), and Zola (1966) contain excellent analyses of illness behavior in Western industrialized settings that would allow sensitizing any new formulation of illness and medical treatment with elements that are likely to contrast in different sociocultural units. The papers by Kasl and Cobb (1964, 1966a, 1966b) and Chapter 4 in Coe's (1970) book contain analytic schemes that rely on the preceding body of sociological work and should be consulted for details.

Empirical Problems of Field Studies in Epidemiology

An epidemiologist who intends to study medical problems in relation to social or environmental variables is required to have at his disposal some procedure for measuring his dependent variable, namely, a medical "fact" of some sort. He needs to know, in other words, how many diseases (or disease-related "effects") exist and where these are located in the social unit he is studying. It is only against a reliable picture of an identifiable and measurable "medical" problem that he can bring his analytic skills to bear in his search for the *causes* of these problems (see Lilienfeld, Pedersen, and Dowd 1967, Hobson 1969, MacMahon and Pugh 1970, Holland 1970, Kessler and Levin 1970, Fox, Hall, and Elveback 1970, and Susser 1973). I must emphasize here that this problem does not necessarily require knowledge of a disease in the contemporary sense of medical diagnosis, for as a matter of fact any number of extraordinarily important health-promoting social changes have been instituted following findings by epidemiologists who lacked a knowledge of what we may now view in a biased way as the "disease entity" being investigated (see Susser 1973 for examples). Of course, as biomedical knowledge has progressed, more and more epidemiologists have come to focus on discrete diseases in these studies.

It is because of this basic requirement that epidemiological studies are ordinarily easier to perform in industrialized settings, for these have the facilities necessary for such precise identification. In these settings one finds agencies that keep records of vital health-related events (such as births and deaths) as well as the type of medical resources (such as hospitals and privately licensed physicians) needed to mark unambiguously the instanciations of the medical problem or disease. It is thus not surprising that a great number of epidemiological findings center around the records of hospitals, physicians in private practice, and mortality records. These records, in fact, are the researcher's *anchoring points*, markings that we must be quick to emphasize have significance within the framework of Western biomedicine.

Field studies in epidemiology move out and away from the hospital or physician's office and into the community itself. The task that confronts the field epidemiologist is how to find instances of his medical problem or disease in a setting where the individuals concerned either may not be aware of having any problem or, if they are, choose to minimize it and "keep it to themselves." It is in the light of just this empirical problem confronting the field epidemiologist that one must appreciate his reliance on survey analysis, probability sampling, and precise case definition methods. Household surveys can be designed that might allow the researcher to infer distributions in the group at large, but how will the survey "pick out" all and only those who have the problem in the subgroup sampled? It is usually not feasible and becomes very costly to examine the individual sampled (and, of course, he may not wish such an examination even if it were made available).

The traditional procedure that has been followed by the epidemiologist is to have or construct a test that reliably identifies for him his cases. This test can be a simple physiologic one (for example, a blood pressure reading) or, more commonly, a set of questions, the answers to which allow the researcher to identify reliably "caseness" (Feldman 1960). Unfortunately, few simple and reliable physiologic tests exist that allow the field epidemiologist to draw compelling inferences about disease pictures or important medical problems. The empirical issue thus becomes which questions reliably tap experiences associated with the specific disease or problem that is of interest to the field epidemiologist, and

furthermore, how such questions should be phrased so as to relate meaningfully to the assumptive world of the subject. The problem is perhaps
a trivial one when a cooperative, intelligent, and personally self-con-
scious person is being interviewed—what physicians and medical students term a "good informant." It is far from trivial, however, when the
person being interviewed is simply not oriented to the assumptive world
of the epidemiologist, and it becomes particularly problematic if the
subject is a member of an altogether different culture.

Epidemiologically oriented investigators who wish to measure disease
in a particular society or group and who use interviews typically employ
a set of questions that inquire about the subject's perceptions about his
bodily state. The investigator assumes that certain biological changes
that are characteristic of the disease in question give rise to specific
bodily sensations and perceptions, and it is these that he inquires about.
In the ideal instance, a subject who reports that he has perceived such
bodily changes in himself may then be regarded as a case. Implicit in
this rationale is the belief that persons who may actually have had such
bodily changes not only noticed them but also paid attention to them
such that they can recollect the perceptions when subsequently probed.
The investigator, in short, assumes that perceived bodily sensations are
stored in the individual's memory in "raw form" and can be readily recalled. Anthropological data and recent research findings involving emotional states to some extent challenge this formulation (Schacter 1971).
Such information suggests that the cognitive structures of the actor,
themselves a product of socialization, are critical factors that affect how
bodily changes and sensations are labeled and interpreted. Presumably,
it is this elaborated and complex experience that is remembered, and
not the highly discrete raw sensations themselves. Similarly, empirical
data indicate that persons (even within our own culture) differ in terms
of how responsive they are to bodily changes (Valins 1970). By way of
summary, then, we can say that field epidemiologists who use answers
to questions about bodily symptoms as indicators of disease must take
into account the following: First, they must consider the general problem of equating the perception of raw bodily sensations with what passes
as a biomedical disease, something that touches on the definition of disease, which we shall go into in greater detail in subsequent chapters.

Second, they must not assume that bodily sensations are necessarily stored in raw form and are easily recalled by the person. They must, in other words, take into account the role of individual differences in bodily responsivity and the role played by the individual's cognitive structures in elaborating upon and to some extent modifying raw sensations.

Interestingly, field epidemiologists heavily influenced by Western biomedical notions whose well-intentioned motive is to clarify how social and cultural factors influence the expression and genesis of disease are trapped in a quagmire of problems that devolve from the reductionistic and dualistic system of thought that permeates Western medicine. Rigorous adherence to this mode of thought constitutes a bias and is particularly evident among those who study the cross-cultural distributions of psychiatric disease.

A particular psychiatric syndrome that is being explored cross-culturally, for example, is often assumed to be "functional" (which means "not organic") and socially determined, and there is usually a strict reliance on a psychocultural framework of analysis. Sometimes this bias will be revealed by the fact that certain illnesses are disqualified from consideration because they are said to have an "organic" basis or because they may include symptoms indicating specific physiological disturbances. Factors bearing on the etiology or expression of the illness may consequently be disregarded. At other times, a converse tendency is in evidence: Any syndrome or symptom cluster that appears to be psychological is assumed to have no "organic" basis. The analysis of the syndrome is then pursued entirely at the psychocultural level, although it may well represent an expression of or a way of coping with structural bodily changes.

No segment of behavior, of course, regardless of whether it is judged to be "normal" by members of a culture or claimed to be "abnormal" in a "psychological" sense by a panel of physicians, is devoid of a biological or physical basis (Durrel 1973). In just the same way that the limitations inherent in rigidly maintaining the distinction between genetically determined versus environmentally learned capacities or traits led modern biologists to formulate an interdependent basis for understanding or conceptualizing the nature and behavior of man (Dobzhansky 1962), persons studying medicine cross-culturally may be led to see the utility of dealing with the phenomena of health and disease in a comprehensive and unified way. Thus, regardless of whether there can be theoretical advantages to distinguishing between types of analytic frameworks, I will argue subsequently that sociocultural studies of medical issues require multiple levels of analysis. I believe that preliterate peoples, because they rely on alternative patterns and categories of experience, offer an opportunity to examine how sociocultural processes and ecologic givens uniquely structure or shape human adaptation and its failures in the form of illness. Employing a medical orientation in this regard involves applying, in a rational and theoretically productive manner, the concepts of health, illness, and medical care to the life circumstances of these groups. One way to accomplish this meaningfully is to employ a frame of reference that does not require a dualistic typology vis-à-vis disease. Such a frame of reference should allow equating contrasting definitions of health and illness and, in addition, should avoid prejudging phenomena and forcing medically relevant observations and data into the dualistic mold.

I should make explicit here a related set of problems that surround the work of those field epidemiologists who study disease in relation to social systems. These are largely outgrowths of the dominating influences that the Western disease model itself has on the effort to draw social meaning from disease occurrences or pictures, and the problems are manifest in studies of both psychiatric and nonpsychiatric diseases. First, we shall concentrate on the psychiatric case.

We saw in Chapter 1 that a variety of unusual or atypical syndromes occurring in various non-Western settings has been described. The exact status or "nature" of these disorders is typically said to be "unclear." A particular syndrome, for example, may be said to be either a unique clinical entity or a different type of neurosis (Parker 1962). Preoccupations of this type, it will be argued, constrain investigation and limit the potential value of studying illness and disease in relation to social systems. More specifically, it would appear that the logical problems involved in mixing medical orientations (that is, in not keeping the scientific and the native conceptual perspectives separate) have not been fully considered.

Very often, investigators studying the so-called culture-bound syndromes implicitly or unknowingly assume the concepts and, in some instances, the universality of the *premises* of scientific medicine. They begin, in other words, with a preconceived picture of the nature of illness and disease. Then, having defined categories of disease according to Western scientific principles, they attempt to unmask or unravel the cultural *factors* or *contributions* from the "true" or "essential" disease process that is felt to underlie the particular native syndrome under investigation. Implicit, then, is the view that disease types (biomedically categorized) are universal or transcultural entities, which are somehow being obscured by culturally specific categories, symbols, and behavioral prescriptions. Stated more succinctly, the orientation of these studies appears to inadvertently confound the Western biomedical and native perspectives. The search is for a biomedically defined *disease type;* what is found and analyzed is a culturally defined *folk illness.* The attempt is then made to determine whether the two are actually equivalent.

This attempt to equate a biomedically specified disease with a folk illness involves a misuse and misinterpretation of both the relevance and significance of the cultural perspective. Although there are exceptions (see Marsh and Laughlin 1956), in general we have seen that native explanations of illness do not, to any significant extent, involve notions of how the body functions or whether the mind as opposed to an organ is affected. Thus, while adopting the cultural framework regarding the unit of analysis (that is, the folk illness), the investigator overlooks the native rationale for explaining the illness and substitutes his own, which involves different categories and premises. The result is a mixing of logical types. More importantly, the unique effects that the cultural patterns and definitions can have in affecting the way persons respond to stress or to changes in bodily processes (in the form of symptoms or clusters of symptoms) are disregarded. Symptomatic responses are instead coded using the referents of scientific medicine. In other words, the linkage between cultural patterns and expressions of problematic human adjustment (that is, illness) should be made the focus of analysis and not eliminated from consideration by exclusively applying the traditional Western model of disease. The application of this model of disease means that "atypical" or unusual features of the folk illness under investigation are likely to be overlooked, attributed to nonrelevant factors, or, at the very least, considered conceptually ambiguous by the investigator, who is intent on rigidly typing the "true" basis or nature of the syndrome in terms of his a priori (and perhaps inapplicable) model of disease. (The reader is referred to the next section for a further analysis of problems in cross-cultural psychiatric studies.)

I wish to emphasize that biases created by strictly adhering to the Western disease model are not unique to field studies of psychiatric disease. We have seen that even when medical "diseases" with clearly specifiable structural bodily changes are studied in Western settings, conceptual and definitional problems are present (see Geiger and Scotch 1963, Scotch and Geiger 1962, 1963). A comprehensive inquiry into the "cause" of the disease is likely to uncover psychological factors. Furthermore, a realistic evaluation of the impact of the disease is likely to show that behavioral symptoms play an important role. (See Fabrega, Moore, and Strawn 1969 for an example of how these symptoms can influence treatment.) Moreover, both causal factors and manifestations are likely to vary depending on social class and ethnicity (Scotch and Geiger 1962, 1963, Zborowski 1958, and Zola 1966). In earlier chapters, the problems and biases created by existing nosologies were reviewed, and indeed Feinstein (1968a, 1968b) has addressed himself formally and in depth to these matters. All of these considerations emphasize the limitations of assuming that so-called organic diseases haxe a fixed nature or that they can be unambiguously marked. If the field epidemiological study is conducted in nonliterate settings, an additional factor that makes it difficult to understand in a socially refined way a particular disease is that the accompanying biological changes will be interpreted and expressed differently, depending on native patterns of perception and behavioral organization. The behavioral effects or consequences of the disease, as it were, will vary in relation to physical and cultural aspects of the environment. It would appear useful, then, to approach the study of "nonpsychiatric" medical problems also with other than a fixed orientation toward the nature of disease. If the application of exclusive or arbitrary criteria allows making reliable diagnoses, the observer is left with the critical problem of explaining how the disease and the manner in which it is dealt with express the group's attempt to cope with its environment. The latter requires specifying the way manifestations of the disease are defined and treated, the social criteria used to evaluate its impact on the group, and the possible role that these issues have on the functioning of the sociocultural system. To accomplish this analysis, a broader description of medical phenomena than that afforded by results of specific laboratory tests is needed.

Problems Involved in Handling Psychological Data

Even when confined exclusively to "diseases" that involve purely psychological matters, the study of medicine in relation to social systems presents distinctive conceptual and methodological problems that require closer examination. Let us assume that in a particular native setting, the group designates certain segments of behavior that are rather atypical (x_1, x_2, x_3) as indicative of an illness and gives this illness a specific label X. Let us avoid the problem discussed in the earlier section by assuming that X seems to consist entirely of elements that refer to disturbances in psychosocial adaptation (that is, the criterial features of X do not include "physical" symptoms such as nausea, vomiting, or blood in urine). Moreover, let us also assume that some of the segments of behavior or symptoms that make up X (x_1–x_j) appear analogous to symptoms we recognize as typical or "diagnostic" of a "disease" that we wish to investigate, such as schizophrenia. For purposes of discussion, then, we will assume that schizophrenic-appearing behavior seems to be included among the behaviors that are symptomatic of a particular folk "psychiatric" illness. The task now becomes one involving methodology, namely, how to find or pick out "schizophrenic" subjects from among the group of subjects with the folk illness labeled X. Several problems become immediately apparent. Do the investigators have knowledge of and training in psychiatry? Do they fluently speak the language or dialect that is spoken in the native culture? What is more, do they understand the culture? Are they able, in other words, to communicate with representatives of the culture and meaningfully inquire about aspects of behavior, experience, and social situations using categories and symbols that translate between the scientific and native cultural systems? If schizophrenia is made the focus of the inquiry, additional requirements become the ability to explain and interpret the perceptions and beliefs of the subjects, since much of what is currently felt to be salient about schizophrenia is in this realm (McGhie and Chapman 1961). Do the investigators know the culture well enough to be able to recognize when an individual's verbalized belief is actually a "delusion," or when a report of a certain perception or experience is "atypical" in terms of what others characteristically report or act upon?

It is evident that to carry out this type of analysis a great many labels or terms of the language system should be known, and by this I mean that the conceptual boundaries should be carefully delineated. What is atypical or abnormal about an individual's statements or understanding of "reality" can only be known if one also knows what the typical or normal happens to be, assuming for the moment that there is a core of experience that members of a culture share and which is capable of being learned by individuals not of that culture. The task of learning a native culture in a rigorous manner such as is required to meaningfully study "mental illness" in that culture is a current concern in the field of anthropology (Frake 1962, Goodenough 1957, Wallace 1962).

To study psychiatric "disease" in a native culture, a procedure or approach like the one referred to earlier may perhaps suffice. If the goal of the investigation is to inquire more carefully into the relationship between psychiatric disease and the sociocultural environment, however, several additional conceptual problems become apparent. Not all individuals manifesting behavior that happens to be symptomatic of a psychiatric disease such as schizophrenia (even behavior that is atypical or unusual within the culture) will necessarily be said to be "sick" with a particular folk illness. A controversial issue in psychiatric anthropology, for example, is that which deals with the psychological status of the shaman or healer. The literature on this particular issue was already reviewed (see also Fabrega and Silver 1970). Briefly stated, much of the behavior of shamans has been felt by some to indicate the presence of a schizophrenic disease. If this is the case, then why are not these individuals viewed as having a folk "psychiatric" illness? The topic touched by this question is, of course, a very complex one. I wish to point out simply that to study in a comprehensive manner a psychiatric disease such as schizophrenia in a native culture, this topic needs to be probed or dealt with.

What about other individuals of the native culture who are generally regarded as atypical not only because of their marginal social adaptation but also because of their peculiar beliefs and rather strange or humorous convictions? On close evaluation, these persons may likely be found to qualify as "schizophrenic." What exactly is it about their "schizophrenic symptoms" that escapes the label pathological in the folk medical system? Finally, a portion of the set of behaviors and actions that fall within the sphere of sorcery and witchcraft is relevant to one's goal of inquiring into the relationship between culture and schizophrenia. Personal misfortunes, doubts, suspicions, and rivalries at times often come together and produce behavior that may have "clinical" import. Homicides or suicides that later are interpretable as socially expedient may be promoted by underlying morbid psychological processes on the part of the victim or assailant. These psychological processes on close inspection may prove to be manifestations of a schizophrenic disease. Persons who behave in this manner should logically be examined in any investigation that involves schizophrenia. In summary, many additional problems become apparent when the distribution of psychiatric disease is evaluated in a native culture, and any inquiry into the relationship between psychiatric disease and a native culture is incomplete without an appreciation of these problems.

Social Limitations of the Biomedical Framework

In this section I will try to indicate more directly why I think the biomedical framework of disease has limitations for what will be termed refined *social analyses* of medical issues. The limitations of this framework will be illustrated by concentrating on two of the principal ways in which it is used by social scientists, namely, in the fields of epidemiology and symbolic interactionism.[1] Some general comments about the

[1] The two emphases singled out here for special attention by no means encompass all of the contributions that sociologists have made to our understanding of disease in society, nor do I mean to imply that a rigid conceptualization of disease has always been salient. I shall have occasion, in Chapter 6, for example, to review briefly several studies addressed to the processes surrounding the use of medical facilities, that is, the factors implicated in what has come to be called illness behavior. In this instance, the influence of social factors on disease manifestations and desire for treatment is directly considered. Similarly, Freidson in his insightful book (1971) makes pre-

juxtaposition of biomedical forms with those of role theory in sociology will also be offered. A premise that is implicit in the argument to follow should be clearly understood. The contemporary biomedical definition of disease has allowed man unprecedented control over nature: it represents the fundamental reason why he can prevent and cure much of disease. For answering questions of disease causation and control, thus, such a "language" of disease is indispensable. In the efforts to control disease by the use and elaboration of this language, analytic epidemiology has been a useful and valuable tool of science, and studies of this sort have contributed extraordinarily valuable knowledge to medicine and society. Social epidemiology, furthermore, constitutes an area of work that has relied heavily on the cogent and constructive efforts of social scientists. The value of this work, then, is unquestioned and cannot be faulted. Similarly, I do not wish to imply that the body of work in sociology dealing with the social aspects of disease, such as symbolic interactionism, role theory, and deviance, is lacking in theoretical usefulness. For as a matter of fact, some of the most incisive theoretical contributions in sociology have devolved from analyses of disease and medical care (see Freidson 1971, Lemert 1951, 1967, Mechanic 1968, Parsons 1951a, Goffman 1963.) These social scientists have availed themselves of the existing paradigm for framing disease and proceeded to analyze insightfully how this paradigm is used and functions in society.

I do believe, nevertheless, that social epidemiologists and social theorists have stopped short of directly probing the entity "disease" in a way that would allow posing and perhaps answering more generic questions about relations between disease and social systems. More specifically, I would claim that the existing sociomedical explorations do not approach problems of disease, medicine, and human behavior in a manner that allows clarifying fundamental questions about man as a

---

liminary efforts to challenge biomedical definitions and to construct socially consequential ones by elaborating on Parsons' (1951b) notion of conditional legitimacy and responsibility. There are, in fact, empirical studies that have tested out these various notions (see, for example, Petroni 1969). Despite these efforts, which reflect an appreciation of the variegated social meanings of disease, I still maintain that sociologists by and large tend to rely quite heavily on traditional nosological thinking when studying disease, and that they do not view their efforts as requiring alternative conceptualizations.

biocultural animal and about his unique status in sociocultural systems. Furthermore, I believe that this limitation stems from an overly strict reliance on the biomedical framework of disease and a failure to explore new definitions of disease. I will elaborate upon these assertions presently. Additional considerations bearing on these and related points will occupy us in subsequent chapters.

Sociologists have a long history of productive involvement with problems of health and illness. In important contributions, they have explicated many sociostructural aspects of the medical profession as well as peculiarities of its economic functioning. With regard to problems of disease and medical care, it can be said that the major proportion of work in epidemiology is either directly conducted by sociologists or strongly under the influence of their formulations and earlier empirical findings. The realization that rather complex social processes intervene in and in fact account for the differential use of medical facilities is largely a product of the efforts of social scientists working in urban settings who have documented with fidelity the contrasting meanings, interpretations, and action consequences that medical problems can have. It can be argued, however, that as regards the study of disease and medical care, the work of sociologists (and similarly oriented urban anthropologists) has thus far merely contributed to the clarification and refinement of what are essentially biomedical disease concepts. In other words, these social scientists have largely accepted categories of disease that are formulated on the basis of a biological framework, and they seem to view their efforts as directed toward elaborating upon this framework. However, if the immediate aim of an inquiry into problems of health and disease is to explicate social influences and eventually to develop a comprehensive picture of a social frame of reference about medical issues, or what one might wish to term a sociomedical theory, there are reasons for not adopting such a biological framework of disease and for employing instead formulations that allow more direct linkage with human behavior.

A rate produced by a social epidemiologic study represents primarily a biomedical fact: it informs us that certain social and cultural factors ("independent variables") have an influence on the distribution and/or frequency of a biomedically specified disease entity (the "dependent variable"). To the extent that the rate is construed as an attribute of a sociocultural unit, it quite obviously enhances our understanding of that unit. Similarly, since disease implies the existence of human disability and discomfort, both of which have psychological and social dimensions, quite obviously knowledge about a disease rate in a sociocultural unit conveys information about characteristics of the members of that unit. In this sense, then, disease rates can be seen as a form of social facts, although facts made meaningful because of their linkage with biomedical categories and frameworks. This same reliance on a biomedical framework is demonstrated by sociologists making use of labeling theory and by role theorists (Goffman 1959, Gordon 1966). They have cogently pointed out various sociopsychological consequences that accrue to persons by virtue of the acquisition of disease labels as well as the varied implications that devolve from transactions with the medical care system. Figure 3.1 illustrates how disease is related

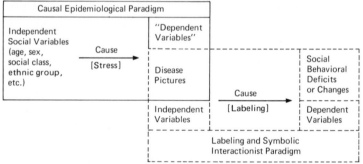

Figure 3.1 Current conceptualizations regarding disease-society relations

to social variables in traditional sociomedical studies. Overlapping boxes and differential markings symbolize the alternative influences ascribed to disease pictures and to social variables in each analytic paradigm. I will argue that, at this juncture in the development of sociomedical inquiries, studies that indicate that working classes have a higher rate of disease X, or that diabetics and tubercular patients are likely to be discredited by virtue of carrying these nominative forms (or to show changes classifiable as "sick role"), do not yield information that is sufficiently precise to be used to develop formulations about how social systems affect and, importantly, are affected by medical happenings. Let me elaborate on this assertion.

In specifying the distribution and incidence of disease in a society, epidemiological studies do inform us about how social systems influence medical problems. Explanations about distribution and incidence patterns of disease can reveal that characteristics of the way social systems function or change can *cause* certain medical problems. Thus, by *implication*, epidemiologic studies suggest how social systems and medical problems affect the lives of persons. However, strictly speaking, epidemiologic information does not inform us about the social consequences of disease, about how illness and disease are resolved at the social level, or about how medical problems influence social system functioning. For this type of analysis, one needs to know *who* is diseased, also *how* he is diseased—that is, the behavioral consequences of disease—and, last, how social responses link with and feed back on the "disease." Interactionistic medical studies, on the other hand, reveal potential social consequences of disease (for example, stigmatization) but do not show how societies influence disease pictures (for example, in terms of causation, intensity, distribution, incidence, resolution, etc.). Disease pictures point to biomedical changes in persons, and interactionist studies begin with these changes (or at least the labeling of these changes) as givens. Social scientists making use of role theory also use the category disease as an independent variable and then extrapolate about social behavior. Concepts such as *sick role* and *patient role* have been used, for example, as a way of describing and explaining the behaviors of persons who are marked as diseased in our society. Here again, I would claim that much of the social data of "disease" is lost by using such concepts. For one thing, the actual interferences and changes occasioned by the disease, which may in fact bring on the patterned behaviors signified by concepts such as *sick* or *patient role,* are simply left out of analysis. Furthermore, the use of such concepts reflects a reification of "disease," since the term is used as though it referred to a single category or thing, when in fact only certain diseases can be assumed to occasion patterned behaviors; and the empirical task, in my estimation, should be finding out which ones, under what circumstances, how, and why.

Briefly, then, I claim that a refined and *direct examination* of medicine-society (that is, disease-social system functioning) interrelations at
the level of social relations cannot be usefully carried out by means of
the existing analytic paradigms and approaches of sociomedical studies,
and this is the case because in large part a biologic and nonsocial way of
defining and measuring disease is manifest. As we shall have occasion to
see in subsequent chapters, the category marked by the biomedical language, namely, *disease,* simply has an ontological identity different from
that of those categories ordinarily used in social studies. From the standpoint of social science and medicine this ontological (and epistemological) problem involving the definition of disease has important empirical consequences.

Sociological medical studies as they are currently undertaken do not
allow describing or predicting in a refined way how groups or persons
showing disease profiles behave or, stated differently, the ways in which
their lives will be affected and changed. Clearly, disease states such as
diabetes and tuberculosis are not unitary "things"; each disease (that is,
biomedical category or form) varies as to components, intensity, and
spread, which is another way of saying that the symptoms and physiologic effects will be highly variable. It is these latter issues that may
allow inferring about behavior. Thus, traditional epidemiological facts
when extrapolated probabilistically to individuals stand in some uncertain relation to the actual burdens and/or social consequences created by disease (that is, social behaviors) and thus will constrain sociomedical inquiries of the type herein under discussion—those involving
reciprocal relations between disease and social systems at the level of
social relations.[2] At the same time, interactionistic and role theoretic
studies will be limited in what they can reveal about how disease affects
persons; factors such as the visibility or potential for concealment of
symptoms as well as complex behavioral changes in many spheres quite
obviously will affect the extent to which the person who is diseased ac-

---

[2] Epidemiological inquiries deal with group phenomena; the distribution, or rate,
of disease in a population or subgroup is described. However, incidence rates can
be used to make estimates about individuals. For example, if the incidence rate of
acute leukemia in a group is three per thousand per year, then we may judge that
the rough likelihood of any one person's developing the disease is 0.003.

quires the associations and symbols suggested by labeling and role theories. Moreover, since the social and psychological attributes of the persons who are medically diagnosed are likely to vary, the symbolic consequences of social labeling are likely to be affected in a significant manner (augmented, neutralized, etc.). Finally, interactionist studies simply do not address questions involving how social processes bring about disease. To repeat, these types of studies are simply not concerned with disease causation, and the investigation of *reciprocal* relations between disease and social systems requires that attention be given to causal factors.

The preceding issues, then, suggest that the writings of sociologists who focus on epidemiologic concerns and on social correlates of disease specify causally relevant social and cultural aspects of disease viewed biologically, and/or that a functional relation exists between disease labels, terms, and medical care contingencies on the one hand and socially significant processes and consequences on the other. However, the outcome of this function in specific instances is problematic and remains to be empirically determined. To put the matter succinctly, the pictures presented by medical sociological studies that stem from the biomedical tradition are often rather general and abstract because (1) their analytic unit, disease, bears a loose and ambiguous relation to social categories and/or (2) in pointing to potentially significant social processes they suggest that certain behavioral issues are inevitable or constant, when in fact they are merely possible outcomes of problematic situational contingencies. Furthermore, since any one person can be included in several classificational categories of disease, association between disease type and human behavior is made even less predictable. In other words, for the purposes of linking disease with the behaviors of persons, the language of biomedicine lacks precision, since its categories or forms (that is, specific disease entities) are *not* mutually exclusive and in fact are often related logically and empirically. Those interested in studying in a refined manner human behavior under conditions of illness and disease are thus in certain ways constrained by having to rely on the traditional biomedical framework as a way of marking disease.

These matters involving disease and behavior will not be pursued further here, since their full exploration requires an examination of fundamental properties and assumptions involving disease and disease frameworks. Such formal analyses will be conducted in subsequent chapters. There we shall see that by exploring different ways of defining disease we clarify meaningful issues involving relations between medicine and society.

I wish to emphasize again that the criticisms I offer here must be seen in the context of the need that I feel exists for different and somewhat specialized lines of inquiry in social medicine, issues that will occupy us later. I maintain that traditional sociological studies contribute fundamental information about disease and are much needed. With regard to the discipline of psychiatry, the labeling perspective toward mental illness, in particular, presented very incisive criticisms. These criticisms, in fact, focus on such elemental matters that they need to be discussed separately. In this regard, we may ask the following questions: How is one to respond to the challenges posed by this perspective toward "psychiatric disease"? What are the implications that can be drawn from this labeling and essentially behavioristic view of the psychiatric domain, a domain powerfully influenced by the notion of disease and of the differences between mind and body? First, it needs to be emphasized that psychiatrists, like other physicians, unquestionably aim to precisely identify "diseases," because it is assumed that only in the light of such a refined understanding can disease be effectively controlled. Robins and Guze (1972) and Winokur (1973) have briefly but cogently summarized the rationale and value of pursuing a rigorous "nosological" approach vis-à-vis the disease depression (see also Katz, Cole, and Barton 1968). Similarly, working within a dualistic framework that acknowledges the unity and interconnection between the domains "mind" and "body," psychiatrists espousing a psychophysiologic position have succeeded in bringing about a better understanding of human disease generally, not just the so-called psychiatric ones. An approach, and let us term it the *medical approach,* that has been successful in general medicine and which stems from sound biological principles should not be discredited a priori on epistemological grounds without a careful evaluation of its accomplishments. Thus, to the extent that one acknowledges some success in the effort to control and treat various psychiatric diseases—and modest success has unquestionably been achieved (see, for example, the collection edited by Mendels 1973)—to that extent one must grant a measure of validity to the approach in question. The strong claim of the labeling theorists that psychiatric diseases are myths, falsely created entities, and *nothing but* changed social relations powerfully embedded in and responsive to the social system has to be dismissed in the light of the successes so far achieved. The reader wishing a critique of the labeling perspective that focuses primarily on theoretical matters is urged to read LeVine's analysis (1973). The weaker claim of labeling theorists remains, and it is a cogent one. There is unquestionably some misguided and careless use made of psychiatric terms and paradigms. Such misuse raises perplexing social and political questions. At the same time, it must be granted that symbols and labels generally, and especially those that fall into the classes termed medical and psychiatric, powerfully shape behavior and can mark in important ways persons associated with them. In this light, persons espousing a labeling perspective have performed a service to the profession by underscoring the social rootedness of behavior generally, and psychiatric practice specifically, and by sensitizing practitioners to the fact that their terms and paradigms also function as social symbols. As a result, such critics have probably succeeded in bringing about a more rational *medical* application of behavioral science principles and knowledge. The related matter of the conflicting frames of reference that have been used to study disease will be covered in later chapters.

A Guiding Frame of Reference for the Study of Illness and Medical Care

In the following chapters, contemporary approaches to the study of disease in relation to society, culture, and social behavior will be analyzed, and specific attention will be given to the logic underlying these approaches. Prior to entering into this analysis, it seems useful to present a general and orienting perspective toward disease that may help to organize and place the material to come.

The following set of propositions, which are offered in the form of an outline, explains a frame of reference that is designed to minimize problems that are often generated as a result of studying medical problems using strict disciplinary emphases. The frame of reference is introduced here as a pedagogical device and should be seen as prescriptive *only* in the limited context of the reviews and analyses to be undertaken in this book. The implications of assumptions behind this perspective will receive more central examination later. A tenet of this frame of reference is that individuals often respond to disease in a unified way and do not necessarily distinguish between mental or physical problems, nor do they fully understand issues formulated in terms of contemporary biological science. In Western nations, for example, although persons may readily use biomedical terms, the language of disease and medical care used to rationalize illness is often social and emotional. Among peoples of non-Western nations (and the frame of reference is general in the sense of encompassing medical developments there as well), the social and interpersonal aspects of communications about illness are more evident, since persons ordinarily do not employ biomedical terms. A fundamental assumption of the frame of reference is that bodily changes and physiologically based symptoms of some sort are in most instances central ingredients of the medical problems that persons experience, and for this reason biological concerns need to be linked to lay medical categories and to the sociocultural level of analysis. The latter is facilitated if general views regarding health and illness are followed.

1 The Labels *Sick* and *Normal*

1.1 The labels *sick (S)* and *not sick* or *normal (N)* will be construed as social labels or categories that individuals use to refer to segments of behavior. In the broadest sense, they label the level of a subject's adaptation to his environment. Although these categories are frequently acted upon implicitly as if they were continuous and overlapping (that is, as if one can "be" both, as is the case with someone who has diabetes or gout but is described as normal), explicitly and in a formal sense they tend to be viewed as mutually exclusive.

1.2 *Normal* and *sick* can be seen as designations of a person's behavior by himself (a self-concept) or as designations by others, that is, as an imputed *identity*. These two, self-designation and other-designation, may vary independently in given instances. These designations of identity may be viewed as the bases for a *role*—a set of expectations mobilized by an identity in a situation.

1.3 Given these designations (or their equivalents in different sociocultural systems), the investigator must set for himself the task of learning how they tend to be applied. In other words, how do people become differentiated and individuated over time by means of the categoric designations *well* or *sick*? How do people come to act in accord with the sick role, or how do they cease to act in accord with this role and come once again to be viewed as normal?

1.4 The designations or labels listed here are assumed to be applied as part of an interactional process that is culturally structured. Culture in this context refers in part to such inferences from behavior as values, norms, attitudes, and "rules of thumb" or uncontested assumptions.

2 Relevant Behaviors

2.1 *Normal* and *sick* are both highly abstract terms, each of which refers to and is thus indicated by clusters or sets of behaviors (B_i) which in a given situation have relevance and validity in terms of the underlying assumptions listed in (1.4). Thus, the category termed *sick (S)* is assumed to be indicated by a subset of relevant behaviors which in combination are taken to indicate that a state of illness prevails. (Thus in the set consisting of B_1, B_2, B_3, . . . , B_n, $S = \sum_{i=1}^{k} B_i$, where k designates any proper subset of n.) It is assumed that the label *normal* (that is, not sick) is applied when these behaviors are no longer evident.

2.2 Clusters of behavior labeled either *normal* or *sick* are located in time, in geographical space, and in discernible segments, sections, or processes of the sociocultural system delimited by these coordinates. To further simplify my meanings, I claim that the labels are applied in social situations. What is described as sick in one time and place and with a given audience may not receive the same evaluation in a different configuration of time, place, and audience.

2.3 A working assumption is that there is a functional relationship between units of the sociocultural systems (2.2) on the one hand and the behaviors of the category S on the other. For example, certain behaviors that indicate a state of illness may be linked to work situations, others to intimate, private, or family situations, still others to situations we might term religious. These behaviors, of course, are actualized in processes alluded to in assumptions (1.2), (1.3), and (1.4).

3 The Bases for Relevant Behaviors

3.1 The behaviors categorized as normal or sick may be traced to *individual actions* or *utterances,* to externally (socioculturally) *patterned circumstances,* or to *situational contingencies* (1.4, 2.2).

3.2 In a great many instances, sickness-related individual actions and utterances may be a result of or be accompanied by the perception (by the self or by others) of altered bodily functioning that can be verified by biologically based analyses. It is to be emphasized, however, that sickness need not be associated with altered states as these are defined currently by Western biomedical science.

3.3 The behaviors subsumed under the designations *normal* and *sick* bear an important relationship to the manner in which the members of a sociocultural unit construe the functioning of their bodies. By this it is meant that the form and content of the behaviors labeled by these terms are determined by the manner in which persons evaluate, perceive, and respond to various levels of bodily function.

3.4 The form and content of these behaviors are linked to the normative range of function (and deviations therefrom) that characterizes the various physiological systems of the body. This normative range of function is itself a function of the group's sociocultural patterns, gene-pool and breeding history, and the ecological characteristics of the setting. Physiologic normative ranges of function are not equally delimited cross-culturally. At the very least, to obtain a multilevel appreciation of the meaning and function of health-relevant transactions, the functional status of the systems of the body needs to be specified, on an individualistic and group basis.

3.5 Behaviors judged to reflect sickness may also be a consequence of an individual's perception that he is in a state of relational disequilibrium with himself, his family, other primary groups in which he participates, and/or the sacred elements (individuals, religious personages, etc.) of his society.

3.6 The relationships, implicit or explicit, among (1.1), (1.2), (2.2), (3.2), and (3.5) are *problematic* and therefore require investigation to discover what criteria or rules are used by people in the culture or situation to judge the health status of other members.

3.7 The health-relevant conditions delineated by (2.2), (3.3), and (3.5) may exist independently or may coexist.

3.8 Only by repeated observations and recording of behavioral events will the investigator be in a position to uncover the nature of the relationship that exists among sociocultural, psychologic, and physiologic levels of function as these relate to the category *sick*.

4 Judgments of Behavior Segments

4.1 Individual behaviors judged to constitute illness, thus, probably contain references to disturbed feelings, bodily sensations, or culturally patterned beliefs or convictions. At the same time these behaviors may symbolically communicate the individual's inability to function productively and in conformance with the implicit rules, attitudes, and goals of his group. The judgments and interpretations made about the behaviors provide the basis for decisions concerning the different action alternatives or imperatives possible.

4.2 The behaviors of S may be reacted to with varying degrees of disapproval and, in some instances, approval. They are judged and interpreted in terms of native medically relevant dimensions, for example, cause, severity, consequences, implications, etc., and they associate with differing action imperatives aimed either at eliminating the perceived sources of the underlying illness or, in rare instances, at perpetuating the illness source for purposes of expiation, punishment, or shamanistic recruitment and verification.

4.3 The various dimensions and action imperatives that members of a sociocultural system associate with the behaviors that indicate sickness are the bases for their differentiating among types of sicknesses. If careful ethnographic work has yielded the set of relevant sickness behaviors and the dimensions or characters that are used to interpret and classify these behaviors, then it should be possible to develop the native *taxonomy of illness* (that is, the folk or primitive medical system of the group).

4.4 The goal the investigator should set for himself is to make explicit the content, form, and duration of those behavioral segments that comprise S, the relevant dimensions on the basis of which these behaviors are interpreted, and last, the action imperatives that they elicit in the immediate family and elsewhere in the group. As already stated, this is equivalent to the delineation of the folk taxonomy of illness (4.3).

5 The Consequences of Judgments of Behavior as Sick

5.1 In an urban society, a rational, scientific medical system provides one set of *alternatives* that compete with inactivity, peer advice, family definitions and responses, neighborhood experts and quasi-medical personnel (pharmacists), and other lay advisors and religious figures.

5.2 In preliterate groups, a native medical care system can be delineated. Such a system consists of personnel, resources, facilities, practices, and a body of knowledge that enables persons to obtain treatment.

5.3 The action choices available in the various curing or medical systems may involve attempts at (1) eliminating the symptoms, (2) eliminating the perceived causes of the illness, or (3) perpetuating the illness for purposes of expiation or punishment.

5.4 The consequences of particular responses (4.2) that are made to behavior judged to constitute illness vary. The sick person, generally speaking, is *affected* by both the *nature* of the responses and the conditions (2.2) under which they are generated.

5.5 The sick person, as a result of this response and in conformance with implicit rules and values of the culture, will consciously modify, shape, or structure his subsequent behavior in ways that the investigator needs to make explicit.

5.6 Because the behavioral effects of this modification and shaping have synchronic or cross-sectional properties, they can be grouped and said to constitute a *role* (that is, a set of behavioral expectations or prescriptions) for the sick person.

5.7 Because the behavioral effects of this modification and shaping have diachronic, developmental, or time-bound properties, they can be seen as a *career* for the sick person.

6 The Career of the Sick Person

6.1 The concept of a career highlights the truism that the sick person is continually involved in interactional sequences (that is, between self and others). A career implies a potential beginning, intervening stages with distinctive properties, and, equally important, an end.

6.2 The investigator should set for himself the task of delineating in depth characteristics of the sick person's career. The task involves data bearing on (1–5) as listed previously. In a concise fashion, this entails making explicit the interrelationships between features of *disease* (altered functioning of the body as determined by direct evaluation of biological status) and *illness,* the socially structured results of the alternatives chosen in the light of factors (1–4) and consequences as seen in (5).

6.3 The sick person's behavioral participation in or execution of the action imperatives of (4.3) constitute what one could term the *explicit* features of his career.

6.4 The investigator must also attempt to delineate *implicit* features of the sick person's career. These may not necessarily be tied to the goals of eliminating or perpetuating the illness but involve issues such as morality, perceived self-worth, and other symbolically altered interactional sequences that indicate that the sick person's identity has been individuated and differentiated in the social setting.

6.5 The content, form, and duration of these career features must be delineated as well as their effect on the original illness behaviors of (4.1).

7 The Return to Normality

7.1 The termination of the sick person's career and his return to a non-sick status involve, to some extent, reversal of the previously listed experiential and physiological modes. The exact relationship among these modes, the interactions involved, and the shared meanings that mediate them must be delineated.

7.2 The investigator should assume that there are definite *behavioral consequences* to having been sick, that is, to having experienced and completed one of the possible symbolic types of illness careers suggested in this scheme.

7.3 These consequences (7.2) might involve putative residues of the cultural stereotyping that associates with having been at one time sick or deviant.

7.4 These consequences (7.2) may lead the person to re-enter the illness cycle beginning again with (1.1), while carrying the symbolic burden of the initial cycle. The investigator must study the extent of overlap and recycling of illness careers as well as the internal variations in their interactional content.

7.5 Participation in illness chains, or cycles of health and illness, is un-ending for the individual and in a given group or culture. It is useful, however, to assume that groups do distinguish endpoints, and the nature of these culturally defined endpoints should be explicated by the investigator.

Part **II** Analytical Foundations of Sociomedical Studies

Chapter 4 Disease Definitions: Traditional Perspectives

When we as physicians evaluate bodily systems using established biomedical procedures, we rely on information (for example, X rays, blood chemistries, auscultatory findings) that, from a semantic and logical standpoint, is sharply different from that contained in the everyday language of social relations. Much of this biological data, furthermore, lends itself to classification usually by nominal category schemes if not by means of interval measurement scales. This type of data, namely, numerically expressible descriptions and estimations of neutral (biological) domains or systems, has of course been made possible by "scientific" developments, which are themselves a consequence of social sanctions. The collection of this data in various contexts and settings, always under the prevailing guidelines of biological theory and science, has allowed describing, in the form of frequency distributions, the biological parameters of groups and populations. Analyses of these distributions using related information obtained on diseased persons have produced the "norms" and "cutoff points" that articulate what are now seen as harmful deviations in these parameters. We will see that these deviations constitute the essence of what can be described as disease indicators and (by extension) disease states. The straightforward if not simplistic manner in which cutoff points and deviations are sometimes formulated contributes to the impersonality and austerity of medical inquiries. The end result of these kinds of biological developments, in short, is a neutral and value-free "language" of disease.[1]

1 The word *language* is used here in a multivalent way, and the various meanings that this word can have and often will be given in the book need to be pointed out. In one sense, we will use *language* to signify the terms and rules by means of which communication is possible. Although the lexical units of language will be given some attention, we will not examine the actual rules that are embodied in a language, neither those that are of a syntactic or semantic nature (Chomsky 1965, Katz and Postal 1964), nor those that can be developed and inferred from what are termed illocutionary acts (Searle 1970). Often, however, the word *language* will also be used to refer to logical calculi or frameworks by means of which it is possible to partition and organize phenomena. In this latter, more specific sense, we allow expressions such as "language of physics" or "language of biology" to signify the concepts, premises, and rules of inference by means of which physicists and biologists describe and explain phenomena falling within their respective domains. The word *language* in this latter sense is close in meaning to that associated with the word when it is used by logicians. Logical or empirical positivists, for example, repeatedly attempt

We note, however, that this neutral and "scientific" language of bio-medicine is employed, interpreted, and acted upon in a highly social and personalized context, namely, a doctor-patient relationship. It is most difficult (some would say *impossible*) to exercise objective and value-free judgments in such a context. Thus, although the biomedical language *qua* language (that is, the lexical forms used, the concepts and categories implicated, the scales and rules of inference that are presupposed) is impersonal and materialistic, its use involves the mediation of highly personal, subjective, and, for this reason, moral considerations. A further factor that tarnishes our efforts to be "objective" by capitalizing on the neutral and value-free biomedical language stems from a central philosophic and phenomenologic fact: People don't feel X-ray shadows, blood chemistries, or auscultatory findings. Rather, people feel or report weakness, coughing, and excessive urination. In this domain —the domain of experience and personal awareness—biological categories and forms can be applied only with great difficulty. This state of affairs obtains not only because of this very real logical "barrier" but also because every indication suggests that the domain of experience and personal awareness is highly determined by social and culturally programmed experiences.

The working physician thus occupies a unique position in the stream of daily life. As an expert on the biological concerns of the very private and "mysterious" domain of the body, he is capable of ascertaining highly personal, significant, and fundamental aspects of human functioning. However, although his focus of inquiry and the ultimate source of his authority are principally the body viewed as a biophysical system, he carries out his work by assuming a dominant role in social transactions that are heightened by emotional poignancy and concern. Given the nature of his work, then, his judgments and decisions frequently have profound social and psychological impact on the lives of his clients.

---

to formally develop languages by means of which they may describe succinctly and unambiguously the operations of reasoning and thought that underlie all of the sciences. For a discussion of these issues, the reader is urged to consult Scheffler (1963), Mates (1965), Lounsbury (1969), Quine (1965), Graham (1967), Fishman (1960), and also the chapters by Lyons (1972), MacKay (1972), and Leach (1972) in the recent book edited by Hinde (1972).

This impact, because it can modify and redirect human orientations, usually exercises a controlling influence on behavior. The physician, in brief, mediates between and has important influences on two logically separate domains of human activity: the bodily-organic and the sociobehavioral (Henderson 1935).

A growing awareness of this unique and pivotal position of the physician, and more directly an appreciation of the fact that he exercises a compelling *behavioral* influence on the lives of patients, has promoted the channeling of behavioral science knowledge into medicine. The growth of the medical specialty of psychiatry since World War II is a development that must be seen as both a cause and a consequence of the growing relevance that has been attributed to the behavioral sciences and to the physician's sociopsychological impact (Morgan and Engel 1969). An additional important factor indicating this fertilization of medicine with behavioral science data is the developing body of work in social epidemiology and health services research (MacMahon and Pugh 1970, White 1968, Rutstein 1967), which was reviewed earlier. However, despite developments that seem to have crystallized in the view that behavioral science furnishes an important and relevant body of work that medicine and medical educators must take into consideration, the knowledge that is being channeled into medical curricula and practice often seems to lack clear points of correspondence with the conventional medical tasks of diagnosis and treatment, which are central to the role of the physician. Furthermore, the way in which this knowledge is introduced to and assimilated within medicine creates problems, since it often challenges traditional assumptions about the nature of medical data. This is here seen in large part as a consequence of the contrasting and often conflicting meanings that are given to the term *disease* by physicians and behavioral scientists.

A common viewpoint, and, as we have seen, one that behavioral scientists and physicians frequently share, is that disease is a fixed and enduring biological category that can be applied across individuals ("many persons can develop disease X"). The patient in "coping with" or "adjusting to" disease is seen to have his behavior modified in more or less predictable ways (for example, terms such as *sick role, patient role,* etc., are used to describe behavioral responses to disease). The prevailing view, then, is that disease and behavior constitute logically distinct or independent domains that are capable of influencing each other. The principal task of the medical educator is thus to inform the student physician about the science of human behavior as it applies to aspects of disease so that he may optimally undertake his medical duties and responsibilities. Problems are generated when the fundamental nature of disease is probed and, in relation to this, when the principal aims of the physician are brought into focus. (For example, must a disease be located exclusively in tissues or must it be recognized and felt by the person first? How must a person who claims to be diseased but who demonstrates no "organic pathology" be viewed?) Furthermore, since psychiatrists and/or behavioral scientists working in psychiatric departments are usually the persons who instruct the student in the behavioral sciences, the many logical problems surrounding the nature of psychiatric disease can further confuse the student and the practitioner alike about the value and relevance of behavioral science for medicine (see Szasz 1964).

The aim of this and the subsequent chapter is to formally bring into focus fundamental aspects of the Western biomedical and behavioral science perspectives as these relate to the idea of disease. I hope to clarify, compare, and perhaps systematize relations between these two medical perspectives. This will be attempted by analyzing from a logical standpoint semantic and syntactic features of the term *disease*. In this chapter fundamental and generic features tied to the term are first discussed. Then, the definitions of disease that are prominent in contemporary medical theory are reviewed. In the next chapter alternative conceptualizations about disease and human behavior are probed. There it is argued that one way of gaining a greater appreciation of the relevance of behavioral science for medicine is to attempt to conceptualize disease as a behavioral category. We shall see in later chapters that such alternative definitions of disease have implications for medical care and practice and also for the development of sociomedical theory. The problems implicit in this type of logical analysis, however, are many, and these will be reviewed. One immediate consequence of the analysis undertaken in these two chapters will be to make clearer how behavioral science concepts and orientations can sensitize the physician to the social nature of his work, and this should serve to deepen his appreciation of the many behavioral influences that he may have on patients. This will also lay the groundwork for more theoretical discussions to be pursued later.

Logical Implications of the Term *Disease*

Part of the difficulty of discussing the meanings of disease stems from the fact that the term itself can function semantically and syntactically in a number of different ways. The term *disease* can be used as follows:

1. As an abstract general term, purporting to refer to each or any number of the members of the class of "diseases" that includes hypertension, diabetes, etc. For example: (a) "Diseases found in this community tend to be more serious." (b) "Diseases due to bacteria have always plagued mankind." In each instance the term *diseases* functions as a general abstract term. However, the meaning provided by the context of each sentence differs, serving to narrow the focus of the term: (a) a subgroup of diseases that are serious and (b) any and all diseases caused by bacteria.

2. With a singularizing modifier, purporting to refer to exactly one thing. For example: "That disease has an abrupt onset" or "the disease that he has." In these instances, the term with the singularizing modifier together function as an abstract singular term.

Two different and independent manners of classifying the term follow:

3. As a denotative term, purporting to *refer* to things. For example: "The disease had an abrupt onset." Here the abstract general term *disease* is conjoined with a singularizing modifier *the* and forms a denotative term that refers to a specific disease.

4. As an attributive term, purporting to *apply* to things. For example: "You could see that he was diseased." In this instance, the term is used to qualify things.

Two particular features seem to contribute to ambiguity in attempts at specifying the meaning and logical features of the term *disease*. The first is ambiguity as to whether it is being used as a general or singular term. Thus, in the statement "Man must constantly guard against disease," the term appears to function singularly and refer to one specific thing or to an actual quality, namely, "diseasehood." Here, then, the idea of an abstract *singular* entity or property that people take on or acquire is suggested. Yet, as used in the statement the term may very well purport to refer to any of several diseases, and in this latter usage the term would be used as an abstract *general* term. Changing the term *disease* to *diseases* in the statement makes this latter usage clear. The second feature contributing to ambiguity stems from the experience of studying the manifestations and properties of various diseases. This leads to the tendency to use the term as if it referred to concrete objects, having spatial and temporal extensions. Strictly speaking, there is no object or concrete thing that is a disease, although there are tissues, hearts, livers, and respiratory passages that many demonstrate or reflect the manifestations and characteristics that we would attribute to disease. In summary, it would appear that in everyday discourse the term *disease* can contribute to ambiguity because it raises questions touching on the philosophical problems of universals, an aspect of what Quine (1969) refers to as the "ontological problem." On the one hand, the term suggests the existence of an abstract entity that has an existence separate from that of the concrete world as well as an abstract quality or property that people take on or acquire. Conversely, the term can sometimes suggest the existence of concrete entities, or subjects located in space and time.

It is important to emphasize that a principal characterization of medical activity is that it is on the one hand evaluative and on the other correctional. Thus, a normative orientation guides the practitioner: he seeks to uncover, define, and rectify that which *deviates* from norms or levels that are held to be optimal or "healthy." With this in mind we may view the term *disease* as a theoretical term that is used to designate or label harmful deviations (or "disturbances") from optimal human functioning and adaptation.[2] Disease in this view, then, represents an incontrovertibly *valued term* regarding human functioning. The term also must be seen as the focus of medical activity, the core

[2] I am here equating disease with some "thing" (condition, state, etc.) that has "negative" consequences for a person. I believe most people intuitively would agree with this. It is of course often difficult to specify in the short run (and even in the long run) what is "negative" for the individual, and an elaboration of this facet of the problem takes one to the heart of considerations involving the philosophy of science and the sociology of knowledge. An evaluation of a set of changes yielding the designation "negative" (in this case, disease) is made by the individual himself or by others (friends, relatives, practitioners, etc.) and is invariably grounded on the past and anticipated experiences and values of those doing the evaluating. Further theoretical aspects of disease definitions will be explored later.

concept around which the practitioner organizes and continually monitors his inquiry and evaluation.

At this juncture I would like to make explicit a so-called "real" (as opposed to stipulative) definition of disease. I submit that as generally used by social scientists, physicians, and lay persons as well, the term *disease* appears to signify a person-centered undesirable deviation or discontinuity in the value of one or more of any number of different measures that can characterize an individual through time. A state of "disease" is usually said to exist during the time that this deviation exists, and for this reason, it appears that disease is a temporally extended undesirable deviation of a human characteristic or set of characteristics. The fact that the deviation is undesirable usually means that it gives rise to a need for corrective action. Diseases are also unplanned, unwanted, and usually dysfunctional occurrences in human groups. All activities or considerations that bear on this temporally extended undesirable deviation in the characterization of the person can be termed *medical*.

Using this definition of disease, we will now consider the logical grammar of the term. Here, two ways of viewing how language terms are used and interpreted might prove useful. We must distinguish between the sense (intension) and denotation (extension) of a term (Mates 1965). The sense of a term is what must be grasped in order to understand the term when it is used; it tells us what criteria or essences phenomena must have in order to be properly labeled by the term in question. The defining characteristics of a term thus summarize and inform us about the sense of a term. On the other hand, by the denotation of a term we shall mean the group or class of all those entities to each of which the term properly refers or can be said to apply. By relying on agreed upon indicators, we are able to correctly apply a given term in a particular situation or context. In light of these considerations, then, the sense or meaning of *disease* is represented by a set of *defining characteristics* that inform us about the inherent nature of things to which we apply this term. In particular situations, the use of *indicators* of disease allows us to correctly identify phenomena that potentially warrant the term, and the members of the class of such phenomena constitute the denotation or extension of the term.

With each disease D, regardless of its defining characteristics, we can associate a set of indicators $(I_1, I_2, \ldots, I_n)$. In order to correctly label ("diagnose") phenomena as "disease," we must determine if the indicators in question are present in or characterize the phenomena. What types of logical relationships exist between disease and disease indicators? Two considerations will prove helpful here. The first involves the appropriateness of indicators. In the simplest case, a finite set of indicators may be associated with a disease, and all indicators may be needed in order to make judgments about disease:

Disease: D_1
Relevant indicators of D_1: I_1, I_2, I_3, and I_4.
Requirements for ascertainment: the presence of $I_1 + I_2 + I_3 + I_4$.

Alternatively, we may envision a more complex situation wherein various possibilities of association between disease and disease indicators exist:

Disease: D_2
Relevant indicators of D_2: I_1, I_2, I_3, $\ldots$, I_{10}.
Requirements for ascertainment: the presence of either $I_1 + I_2 + I_3 + I_7$ or $I_1 + I_2 + I_6 + I_{10}$ or $I_2 + I_4 + I_5 + I_9$, etc.

A second consideration bearing on the relationship between disease and disease indicators can be illustrated by examining the logical structure of the following statements (Quine 1960):

"If a person demonstrates indicators I_1–I_k, then he has disease D_3." This conditional statement enunciates that the presence of I_1–I_k together constitute *sufficient* conditions for someone to be said to show (or "have") disease D_3.

"If a person has disease D_4, then he demonstrates indicators I_1–I_j." This conditional statement asserts that the presence of I_1–I_j constitute *necessary* conditions for someone to be said to show D_4.

"A person has disease D_5 if and only if he shows indicators I_1–I_m." (This is logically equivalent to the conjunction of "if a person demonstrates indicators I_1–I_m, then he has disease D_5" and "if a person has disease D_5, then he demonstrates indicators I_1–I_m".) This biconditional statement asserts that indicators I_1–I_m constitute *necessary* and *sufficient* conditions for someone to be characterized as having or showing D_5.

From a logical standpoint, we may view the process of diagnosis of disease as involving the making of a classification. Diagnosing phenomena means properly classifying such phenomena. Alternatively, we may say that a diagnosis involves making a claim as to which classificatory class (that is, diagnostic class or category) the phenomena properly belong. In either case, the conceptual operation or process can be represented formally as conforming to a valid deductive or inductive argument (see Skyrms 1966 for a lucid introduction). This means that a set of premises, when incorporated in an argument we describe as valid, leads to the assertion that someone has a particular disease. In these particular arguments a set of true statements informs us about particulars: for example, at t_i, person X, who is such and such type of person (that is, relevant demographic characteristics), demonstrates indicators $I_1, I_2, \ldots$, etc. A statement of the type listed earlier, which we could describe as a law-like generalization, or a related statement that includes probability estimates occupies a critical position in the argument. The statements asserting true particulars together with the generalization can be described as constituting the premise-set of the argument. In the case of deduction, the conclusion of the argument is a statement asserting that person X has (or does not have) disease D_i. However, if statistical generalizations are used in the argument, that is, if the argument is an inductive one, then the result is a probabilistic statement describing the likelihood that person X has disease D_i. We may illustrate this as follows (only the deductive pattern will be illustrated):

At t_i, John Smith, who is a male aged 47, was examined medically and showed $I_1, I_2, \ldots, I_j$.

If a 47-year-old man demonstrates indicators $I_1, I_2, \ldots, I_j$, then he has D_j.

At t_i, John Smith has D_j.

This pattern is obviously idealized and simplified for purposes of this exposition. Critical issues confronting philosophers of science regarding the formal structure of explanation and prediction are germane to a discussion of diagnosis. Readers interested in these logical issues are urged to consult Hempel (1965, 1966), Graham (1967), Scheffler (1963), Scriven (1959), Salmon (1970), Engle and Davis (1963), and Engle (1963a, 1963b).

Clarifying what is meant by "indicator of disease" involves probing issues that are largely implicit in much of medical practice, just as it touches on the very essence of what we mean by "disease." In a preliminary fashion a "disease indicator" may be defined as a measure, level, or state of a particular human trait or characteristic that experience has demonstrated bears an *empirical relation or association* with impaired social productivity, in some instances being detrimental to life itself.[3] In most cases, disease indicators are viewed as analytically linked to or expressive of the underlying processes that represent the defining characteristics of the disease in question. In our discussion we will exclude abnormal traits or indicators present since birth and assume an antecedent or baseline state of nondisease. With this in mind, it would appear that in order to be judged as an indicator of disease, the trait or characteristic in question usually meets three basic requirements: Its value or measure deviates from *group norms,* it also deviates from *personal norms,* and the deviations are seen as *undesirable* by the person or by significant others. By *group norms* I mean the norms or statistically observed values for the trait in question that characterize the group formed by persons sharing the relevant social background features of the index person. By *personal norms* I mean the norms (or values) of the trait that have characterized the index person through time. This definition is, of course, quite broad and not ideally as precise as it could be. However, this imprecision is

---

3 Several features of this definition that admit of the changing nature of disease need to be made explicit. The expression "level or state of a particular human trait," for example, clearly suggests a historical dimension, since what passes for a significant trait and measure at a given point in time or in a given culture is quite obviously dependent on the prevailing standards and viewpoints of the (medical and scientific) community. The expression "experience has demonstrated" reinforces this historical and cultural dependence. The expression "bears an empirical relation to or association with" also emphasizes the theory-dependent (and thus also sociohistorical) nature of the definition: what is judged as related to or associated with something quite obviously depends on the frame of reference, paradigms, presuppositions, or background theory of the persons making the judgment. Finally, the expression "impaired social productivity ... [or] detrimental to life itself," in addition to its dependence on or embeddedness in a theoretical frame of reference, also indicates that what are more traditionally referred to as the *values* of the community are implicated in the definition. In other words, at what point one judges life and/or productivity to be impaired obviously depends on how highly we value or disvalue pain, weakness, felt incapacity, interruptions in social functioning, etc.

necessary at this juncture since we are attempting to isolate logical and formal properties of "disease." [4]

It is very important to emphasize that these formal or generic issues implicated by the term *disease* need to be seen merely as necessary conditions for the appropriate use of the term. In other words, if person X can be (or has been) properly said to be diseased, then it follows that the aforementioned issues (deviation, undesirability, etc.) obtain. However, not all instances of person-centered undesirable deviations constitute disease, and thus these issues do not constitute a sufficient condition for the proper use of the term. Why these conditions are not sufficient in a given instance for labeling someone as diseased requires examination. The fact that these conditions function in this manner is not only interesting but highly important for a critical understanding of sociomedical affairs. A specific example will illustrate this point. In India (Stevenson 1954, Harper 1964) if a person violates certain ritual taboo practices he is said to enter a state of ritual pollution. (Incidentally, whether he violates these by choice or not appears to be irrelevant, so that the issue of personal responsibility does not appear critical.) Not only is he so characterized, he must "cleanse" (or cure?) himself in order to be free (and well enough?) to conduct the social business of life. During the time that he is said to be ritually polluted (a person-centered undesirable deviation in his sociomoral status) he is apparently not considered to be sick or ill—although illness itself can be a form of ritual pollution, and "contamination" with someone who is sick (or his emanations) can be polluting to the actor. In short, in India the condition

---

[4] A person-centered human characteristic that deviates from *individual and group norms* in the manner outlined allows fixing disease to time and place and also helps exclude much of what is ordinarily termed "social deviance" by sociologists. As regards *biological matters*, we have seen that biological processes are highly responsive to features of the environment, and that what appear to be bizarre or deviant characterizations viewed against Western standards are actually statistically normal in the group (see, for example, Gajdusek 1970*b*). Similarly, as regards *social psychological matters*, many forms of behavior when viewed against the prevailing standards of the society are deviant but when judged against the background of the individual's socioethnic group are normative. It makes little sense to label these behaviors "disease." It is the existence of problematic situations such as these that seem to point us in the direction of associating "disease" with deviations from both personal and group norms.

termed by social scientists "ritual pollution" represents an undesirable person-centered deviation in a person's sense of self (and we can assume that if the condition is "serious" enough, one could identify altered biological parameters) which, however, is not regarded by the people themselves as illness.

A sociomedical analysis should strive to clarify why this is the case. In other words, what are the native distinctions between illness and disease on the one hand and "ritual pollution" on the other? How do these two conditions compare and interact in given instances and what are the reasons for this? Similarly, in our own culture, an individual who commits a crime or engages in a dishonorable action, though we could say his behavior constitutes an undesirable deviation in group norms or that he himself is in such an undesirable state, is not invariably said to be "diseased" or "have a disease." We should, however, note that if such actions, although socially deviant and egregious, represent a new commission or omission by the actor (that is, also represent a deviation in personal norms), then the matter of its representing an indication or manifestation of disease becomes relevant. Such a state of affairs prevails today, when psychiatrists are called in to render "expert" opinion regarding unusual behavioral actions. We have in these types of psychosocial matters (what sociologists term *deviance*), then, the cutting edge or boundary between the moral and the medical—a boundary that fluctuates and is subject to arbitration. We note, by way of summary, that the previously mentioned formal or generic issues can be said to constitute necessary but *not* sufficient conditions for correctly applying the term *disease*. Furthermore, explaining why some conditions are properly viewed as disease and others, which from a formal standpoint appear related, are not involves fundamental aspects of the relations between social system functioning and medical matters.

Evidence indicates that until recently, in preliterate societies to some extent and especially in literate Western ones, sensations, characteristics, and/or traits having to do with the body's condition have invariably been associated with matters termed "medical" or involving "disease." Thus, until the growth of biological science, bodily experiences and ideas about the structure and functioning of the human body have been a principal *source* for the language and metaphors that have been used to describe, evaluate, and explain "disease." Disease may have been viewed in purely social and/or moral terms, but it was usually experiences tied to the body that prompted inquiry into or evaluation of these matters.

At this juncture, in pursuing our inquiry into the logic of disease indicators, we will continue to rely on this tradition. As an example, we may take an individual who shows an "elevated blood sugar." A certain point on the continuum of concentrations of blood sugars is judged as critical, and levels beyond this are viewed as "elevations." The term *elevations* points to the essentially normative and rather arbitrary nature of a disease indicator at the same time that it reveals an essential circularity. An elevation is a level beyond one that is arbitrarily "normal" or "healthy." It is viewed as relevant or significant precisely because experience has shown that there is an association between "elevated" blood sugar levels and a set of bodily processes and changes that account for or coexist with impaired productivity and shortened life span. The latter set of changes is termed *diabetes*. However, as has been pointed out by others (Israel and Teeling-Smith 1967), there is no reason to expect human traits such as these to conform to discrete categories (high versus low, normal versus abnormal, or healthy versus nonhealthy). Rather, our expectation is that blood sugars form a continuous distribution in nature. Some individuals typically demonstrate low levels, others high levels. A person who has *always* shown a slightly elevated sugar level (or, alternatively, an elevated temperature) is viewed somewhat problematically. Such an individual deviates from group norms but not from personal norms. He may be suspected of showing a disease indicator, or he may be viewed as merely on the "high side" of normal with regard to the process in question (that is, carbohydrate metabolism). Equally problematic is the person whose sugar level has risen substantially from earlier levels but who remains "within the normal range." Thus, traits showing deviations from *either* personal *or* group norms stand in some uncertain relation to our concept of disease. Clearly, a person whose blood sugar level rises beyond what it was at an earlier point in time and furthermore now exceeds the arbitrarily defined normal level (deviates from *both* group *and* personal norms) is judged as showing the indicator in question. It would appear, thus, that a key characteristic of a disease indicator is that the value of the trait in question is found to deviate from both group and personal norms. In subsequent discussions, when the phrase "indicator of disease" is used, such characteristics are assumed.

The preceding logical considerations, then, illustrate the relationship that obtains between disease conditions and disease indicators. To recapitulate: With each disease term there is associated a set of statements that together enunciate the defining characteristics of the disease in question, that is, what the disease term means and what processes, conditions, or changes must be present in order to correctly use the term. However, it is by demonstrating the presence of a set of disease indicators that particular diseases are recognized or diagnosed. Each disease indicator may be viewed as a sign that points to the disease in question. With each disease condition there is associated a set of disease indicators, these indicators in turn constituting either necessary, sufficient, or necessary and sufficient conditions for establishing the presence of the disease. Clearly, then, the defining characteristics and the disease indicators together describe and point to the nature or essence of a particular disease. It should be emphasized that although thus far the biomedical language has been used to examine aspects of disease, we are principally concerned here with logical and generic issues, and that from this latter standpoint the term *disease,* while conforming to previously discussed *formal requirements,* can have varying ontological identities. Subsequently and in the next chapter, different frameworks or languages that can be used for the definition of the term *disease* will be suggested. Here, it is important to emphasize merely that the logical entity denoted by the term *disease* can be made to refer to different matters. We turn now to the traditional biomedical framework or "language" of disease.

Disease Viewed as a Biologistic Category
In what will be called here a *biologistic* perspective, the term *disease* signifies a medical concept whose meaning or intension involves an abnormality in function and/or structure of any part, process, or system of the organism. The framing of the organism's "normal" functioning or structure is accomplished by means of the concepts, findings, and premises of Western biological science. The range of application of the term or the class of things to which it applies—its extension—would include such things as appendicitis, schizophrenia, hypertension, depres-

sion, or diabetes. In any particular instance of its use, the term might refer to one of these items.

The logical grammar and meaning of *disease* viewed within this framework may be illustrated by focusing on diabetes. The following conventions and rules will prove useful:

1. D = the disease diabetes.

2. P_i = defining characteristics of D (for example, P_1 = disorder of carbohydrate metabolism, P_2 = disturbance in normal insulin mechanism, P_3 = abnormality of the pancreas, etc.).

3. Q_i and R_i = indicators of D (for example, elevated blood sugar, glycosuria, polyuria, ketonuria, retinitis, etc.). $\{Q_i\}$ is used to represent the subset of sufficient indicators, and $\{R_i\}$, the subset of necessary indicators.[5]

4. X has D if and only if $\{P_i\}$ is true of X.
This is a biconditional statement that specifies the analytic definition of D. Observe that the statement is true (by definition) in the two component forms of the biconditional:
If X has D, then he has $\{P_i\}$.
If X has $\{P_i\}$, then he has D.

5. If X has $\{Q_i\}$, then X has D.
This is a conditional statement that, if true, specifies that the presence of $\{Q_i\}$ constitutes a *sufficient condition* for X to have D. Note that asserting a true conditional statement of this form does not allow assigning a truth value to its converse; that is, if X has D, it does not follow that he must show $\{Q_i\}$.

6. If X has D, then X has $\{R_i\}$.
This is a conditional statement, that, if true, specifies that the presence of $\{R_i\}$ constitutes a *necessary condition* for X to have D. Note again that the truth value of the converse of this conditional statement cannot be assigned; that is, $\{R_i\}$ need not constitute a sufficient condition for D.

It is to be emphasized that the indicators used in the logical forms of sections (5) and (6) are drawn from the same set but in general are not the same; that is, specific indicators $\{Q_i\}$ are not usually identical to specific indicators $\{R_i\}$. Thus, if X has symptoms highly suggestive of diabetes together with an elevated fasting blood sugar and glycosuria,

[5] Q_i and R_i are the individual indicators; $\{Q_i\}$ and $\{R_i\}$ are subsets of indicators. For example, for i = 1, 2, 3, 4, $\{Q_i\} = \{Q_1, Q_2, Q_3, Q_4\}$ and $\{R_i\} = \{R_1, R_2, R_3, R_4\}$. However, Q_1 and R_1 need not be identical. $\{Q_i\}$ and $\{R_i\}$ are used here to signify differing subsets of the set of relevant biologistic indicators of disease.

then we might be reasonably sure that he has diabetes. However, if X has diabetes he may or may not demonstrate all of these features. The aim of scientific medicine is to reach a state of affairs where these two sets of indicators are in fact identical: a state of affairs where the biconditional form could be applied, but expressed in terms of indicators instead of defining characteristics. If this were the case one could then speak of diseases as having indexical definitions (Leonard 1967). In contrast to the analytic definition provided in (4), this can be viewed as an empirical definition. There is reason to believe that indicators such as those obtained from a glucose tolerance test will come to serve this function in the case of diabetes.

In a *biologistic* framework, then, the defining characteristics of specific diseases refer to biological processes. The necessary and/or sufficient conditions that allow inferring the presence of diseases are expressed in information pertaining to such things as blood sugar levels, electrographic patterns, chest X rays, or microscopic specimens of tissues. This information is interpreted by means of the empirically derived knowledge about human biological functioning. Indeed, the operations used to generate such information have meaning in terms of such knowledge. This particular framework for defining disease, then, quite obviously grows out of and is tied to historical developments associated with the Western scientific tradition. It should be noted that on occasion, particular verbal reports or behaviors may serve as ("pathognomonic") indicators of a disease, as, for example, the report of types of pain such as of myocardial infarction or dissecting aneurism, the reports of a migraine syndrome, or the history of sudden lapses into unconsciousness. In some instances these types of indicators are necessary, and in rare instances, sufficient. As a rule, however, verbal reports are neither necessary nor sufficient for establishing the presence of disease. The application of sophisticated technology to human biological functioning has had the effect of enabling physicians to slowly replace these reports by indicators that more directly and reliably reflect biological processes and changes.

Psychiatric "diseases" occupy an ambiguous position when considered against a strictly biologistic framework. Their defining characteristics involve mentalistic concepts or entities, such as feelings, impulses, drives, ego strength, psychological defenses, etc. Their indicators consist of inferences about these matters, which are reached following standardized interviews or tests. In most instances, no direct information about the body's structure or function is used. If these latter considerations are viewed as criterial of a biologistic framework, then they would suggest that psychiatric diseases have little to do with biological happenings. However, since judgments about psychiatric diseases are reached in terms of representative psychological formulations about human behavior and experience (according to many, in terms of formulations about the way the mind functions), they can be and are viewed by many as dealing with biological happenings but at different levels or in terms of different organizing principles. One defense of this position would state that, in a procedural sense, reliance on verbal reports (referring to key "symptoms") as indicators of *any* disease represents activity that is equivalent to psychiatric diagnosing. In other words, physicians regularly interpret and reach decisions on the basis of verbal reports of their patients, and regardless of the type of report, the physician is concerned with marking deviations. Moreover, physicians must also interpret and make decisions based on given reports of laboratory results. In each of these instances, the argument would run, physicians are using their knowledge of human biology (viewed broadly) to make judgments about function and dysfunction. The way medical information (such as laboratory reports, physical exam or interview data, psychological test data) is used by physicians thus can be described as being similar from an instrumental standpoint, regardless of the type of disease. This argument has as its conclusion a proposition to the effect that any examination and systematization of life can be said to be biologistic especially if it is conducted by a certified physician. Ultimately, clarification of this issue leads to central problems in the philosophy of science as well as the sociology of knowledge, which will not be pursued here. Suffice it to say that psychiatric diseases are somewhat problematic when considered against a strictly biologistic framework as it is defined here.[6]

---

[6] Despite the fact that psychiatric and nonpsychiatric diseases are viewed by many as similar in their ontologies (that is, as equally "biologic"), it cannot be disputed that their social and psychologic implications generally, and for the person in particular, are vastly different. In our culture, indicators of nonpsychiatric disease by and large refer to an impersonal body (perhaps weakened and disabled) but are not taken to

Assuming that these issues are clarified satisfactorily, a consequence of applying or using such a biologistic framework regarding disease is that specific diseases can be said to be *universal* or transcultural occurrences.[7] We have seen that this is clearly the way in which biologists and epidemiologists view disease, and from a certain standpoint they are correct. In other words, if the current norms physicians use in determining whether disease is present represent a reliable and valid framework from which to generalize, then indicators of biological function reflecting a deviation therefrom constitute *prima facie* evidence of disease.

It is necessary to emphasize that recent analytic developments and empirical investigations in fields such as population genetics, physical anthropology, and human biology in general (material reviewed in Chapter 2) weaken this claim somewhat and force one to reinterpret the biomedical framework or language of disease. Stated more directly, theoretical developments in genetic theory and comparative research findings in medical ecology throw into sharp relief what can be described as the subjective, biased, and ethnocentric assumptions and procedures of Western human biomedicine. A simple statement of the issue here under

---

reflect a failure of the person's self. The matter is of course radically different in the case of "psychiatric disease," as a number of investigators have pointed out (Goffman 1969, Szasz 1961, Fabrega and Manning 1972a). One observes that the indicators of psychiatric disease, although framed in the language of biology, in a very obvious sense refer to the very essence of a person's self—his motivations, feelings, beliefs, actions, and dispositions. Furthermore, in the present context, these matters are often interpreted socially and psychologically as signifying a failure and discreditation of the person himself. The reader is urged to read the accounts of Foucault (1965) and Rosen (1968) in order to appreciate the historical bases of these matters (see also Chapter 8 in this book).

[7] Here I use the term *universal* with some reservations that need to be made explicit. Quite obviously, to the extent that scientific knowledge and theories change across time, the key terms and concepts of the theory also change. In this sense, then, biologistic diseases as currently articulated are not so much universal as they are changing and being constantly refined. Furthermore, as we shall see subsequently, even if knowledge were fixed, disease definitions are outgrowths of prevailing norms of biological competence, and which reference group is to be judged as the "normal or "healthy" one is highly problematic, especially when we evaluate man's adaptation phylogenetically and in relation to a prevailing ecosystem. These two considerations, then, limit the claim of universality. However, to the extent that a scientific and medical community reflects the best or "truest" understanding of a domain and furthermore is socially legitimated in some unproblematic sense, it is permissible to judge their claims as (temporarily and geographically, at least) universal.

discussion would go as follows: Refined judgments about biological parameters and disease states are first of all reached in the context and against the background of our most unnatural ecological setting. We were not made biologically to live in cities, in polluted environments, and removed from other species of the living world. Our life patterns and biological parameters are from this standpoint uncharacteristic if not highly deviant. The way in which our biologic systems are structured and how they function must for this reason be interpreted cautiously. The distinctness of our own biological systems should prompt care and restraint in our often uncritical tendencies to view them as "normal" or "correct" and, by comparison, those of other societies as abnormal or diseased or less well developed. Although we live longer, our biological systems are simply subject to different challenges and for this reason break down differently. At the very least, comparative research findings in human biology and medicine should lead us to appreciate the valuational, arbitrary, and culture-bound bases of what we view as "normal" (or diseased) biological systems. Our norms, cutoff points, and deviations, in short, are interwoven with (or expressions of) our specialized, if not *deviant*, biological modes of adaptation. Exporting these to other peoples and applying them in other cultures entail logically the false assumption that similar modes of adaptation obtain there. Clearly, assessment of other peoples' biological systems requires the collection of suitable data and the creation of appropriate norms from which to generalize. Deviations or indicators of disease, in brief, need to be articulated against the background of what are the empirically encountered distributions of traits which themselves are expressions of distinctive adjustments to highly specific ecologic constraints (see Gajdusek 1970b and Neel et al. 1968b).

To recapitulate this point, then, one can say that we have available a relatively refined, value-free, precise, and "scientific" language or framework for describing what biological systems are: their structures, how they function and how they break down. Even here, however, we find that we lack a value-free or "scientific" context from which we can judge impartially and unproblematically what biomedical diseases "are" and "where" they can be said to exist. Our cherished norms and cutoff points (the foundations of disease definitions) are simply some of many found in nature even today and furthermore presuppose our own deviant and perhaps "unbiologic" adaptations. Any efforts to apply these norms presupposes that our form of life constitutes the legitimate one from which to generalize and arbitrate, whereas any rational assessment requires standardization of biological parameters under differing ecological conditions. In a sense, then, disease formulations are by definition enterprises that from a logical standpoint are tied to time, place, and culture. Consequently, when discussing the advantages of an "objective" framework or language of biomedicine one should not lose sight of the fact that its use or application can involve ethnocentric assumptions.

The Unified or Systems View of Disease

The biologistic definition of disease reviewed earlier has been substantially modified as a result of contemporary developments in the field of psychosomatic medicine (see Lipowski 1967b, 1968, 1969). Originally, the term *psychosomatic* was used to characterize certain specific diseases whose etiology, it was believed, was importantly influenced by psychological factors. Psychiatrists and internists shared concern with the treatment of such diseases as peptic ulcer, bronchial asthma, and ulcerative colitis. Within the speciality of psychiatry, interest in these "psychosomatic diseases" led to formulations about how various intrapsychic and personality factors contributed to identifiable bodily changes. Various theories about how and why these interactions between body and mind occur have in fact been propounded. We are not interested here in these particular matters but rather in some of their general consequences. The psychosomatic approach to disease has evolved and led to a general concern on the part of physicians with the multifaceted aspects of an individual's functioning and life situation. The *unified view* of disease, which is an outgrowth of the psychosomatic position, is perhaps the most widely held view of disease among contemporary medical educators and theoreticians.

The writings of Engel (1960, 1970b), Hinkle (1961), and Wolff (1962) are examples of the psychosomatic perspective. Engel's key articles to a large extent emphasize the unique psychosocial and experiential components of all conditions labeled as disease. The patient's earlier experiences with disease fuse with those now at hand and thereby significantly color the meaning of symptoms and disabilities. Emotional and other psychological factors, thus, not only bear on how and when disease occurs but also on the very essence of what the person experiences when diseased. Engel stresses the need for a broad view of disease, termed by him *unified,* and has lucidly described the arbitrariness and pernicious consequences of other, more truncated and narrow definitions. In a fashion reminiscent of human ecologists, Engel argues that health and disease, rather than representing discrete "states" or conditions, need to be seen as phases of the continuously changing multilevel set of processes (cellular, chemical, physiological, behavioral) that at any one moment constitute human striving. Hinkle and Wolff, on the basis of their now classic longitudinal studies of individuals of varied ages and backgrounds, have described the manner in which illnesses cluster in individuals and in time. The ecologic perspective is clearly in evidence when they probe in depth a person's adjustment to his social environment, his work habits, his emotional responsiveness, as well as his physical status through time with the goal of arriving at a broadly grounded meaning of health and illness. The framework proposed by Howard and Scott (1965) for the analysis of stress, insofar as it is multileveled, holistic, and concerned with both the internal and external environments of man, can be seen as congruent with the ecological approach to disease. Significantly, Hinkle, Wolff, Engel, and Howard and Scott, although they concern themselves with phenomena that are obviously "medical," carefully avoid the concept of disease as traditionally employed. Instead, the organism's attempts at mastery, that is, its attempts to successfully solve problems that are posed to it by its environments, receive analytic emphasis. Failure in mastery leads to excessive energy expenditure, and this in turn leads to a state of tension or stress, which in the long run is deleterious to the organism.

The view of health and illness developed in these writings bears an obvious relationship to recent theoretical developments in the social and biological sciences. General systems theory, a corpus of organized concepts and approaches to the evaluation of regularities in the empirical world, has recently been applied more directly to the study of medicine in society (von Bertalanffy 1968, Rutstein and Eden 1970, Sheldon, Baker, and McLaughlin 1970, Buckley 1968, and Miller 1965, 1971). An attempt has been made to depict the health care delivery network as an abstracted system. When applied to the disease concept, this systems view of disease appears to correspond to and strengthen the unified view described earlier. In this perspective, disease is not viewed as a discrete and discontinuous state that attaches to an organism in space and time. What obtain, instead, are systems in articulation—molecular systems within cells, biochemical energy-processing systems at the tissue level, homeostatically geared systems at the organ-physiologic level, biopsychologic and sociopsychologic systems at the level of the self, sociointerpersonal systems at the family and institutional level, etc. All levels of this complex, hierarchically organized system are described as being implicated in the processual stream of life.

It is important to emphasize that in a unified or systems view of disease, not only are the *manifestations* or expressions of what we term disease seen as interconnected and hierarchically organized (that is, as segments of a whole), but in addition, the *determinants* of disease are also conceptualized holistically. Disease is seen as a natural consequence of man's open relationship with his physical and social environment. Styles of coping are seen as rooted in patterns of neuromuscular and humoral integration, and difficulties in coping are expressed in altered biological processes that give rise to symptoms or signs of disordered function, that is, "disease." Thus, cause is multifactorial, processes are interconnected, and manifestations are multifaceted. What we can observe are systems showing different degrees of adaptation and equilibrium. A "symptom" or a "sign" of dysfunction, then, appears to be equally medical whether it occurs at the biochemical level, the psychological level, or the social level. Similarly, emphasis on processes that are interconnected means that temporal and spatial boundaries become less clear and less relevant when applied to disease. For example, "locating" a disease in tissues or body fluids is no more correct than locating it in, say, the relationships and motivations that contribute to the bodily alterations. General systems theorists emphasize the linkages that exist among subsystems implicated in any disease process; the unit of organization to which attention and effort are to be directed is determined by the particular aims and goals of the practitioner or planner.

The systems or unified view of disease, then, because of its emphasis on processes, interconnectedness, holism, and hierarchy tends to blur the boundaries between the various factors or components of disease. To put the matter succinctly, the ontology, location, and/or boundedness of disease, in both a spatial and a temporal sense, become ill defined and problematic; and, as we shall see later, these particular considerations have important implications for how medical care is practiced and organized. However, for now I merely wish to point out that the unified view of disease is associated with important medical research that has led to enhanced understanding and knowledge of man's attempts at adaptation. The utility of this framework for conceptualizing health and disease is, thus, unquestioned. What does appear to require more immediate consideration are the problem of linkages among the various systems and, especially important from our standpoint, the problem of clarifying how behavioral factors relate to disease. Although the unified or systems view clearly includes behavioral dimensions, it leaves unspecified how these aspects are to be conceptualized and organized. In the next chapter an attempt will be made to analyze further and systematize how behavioral factors can be linked with disease. We shall see that this effort can lead to what in essence are alternative definitions of disease.

Chapter 5 Disease Definitions: Toward Alternative Formulations

The purpose of this chapter is to explore and analyze different ways of conceptualizing the relations between disease and behavior. We have observed that in traditional approaches to disease and human behavior, the primary referents of disease are usually biological happenings; behavioral factors are examined insofar as they elaborate on and clarify the causes and consequences of these happenings. Assumptions about how mind and body can interact culminate in a systems view of disease, which, although quite broad, leaves unspecified and unclear how behavioral dimensions are to be formulated. In this chapter considerations bearing on the formulation of disease as a *behavioral category* are discussed. I use the term *behavioral* broadly to signify physicalistic actions, symbolic and socially rooted conduct, verbal reports of internal states or bodily centered concerns, and/or rationalized explanations of perceived changes in the individual's orientation in his relevant world. Three different behavioral frameworks for conceptualizing disease are presented and analyzed. Some of the implications for medicine and social science of viewing disease in this fashion are also probed.

Disease Viewed as a Phenomenologic Category

We have seen that in a broad intellectual context, the idea of disease or illness does not logically entail any particular type of *understanding* of bodily function, nor does it require that the users of the concept regard the body's mode of functioning as a salient consideration. In earlier chapters we considered the problematic issue of psychiatric diseases, whose defining characteristics refer to psychological processes involving social relationships and mental functioning. These latter features are frequently only loosely tied to or even viewed as independent of particular understandings of bodily function. Ethnomedical studies afford still further insights into alternative meanings given to "disease." Earlier studies have made clear that what illness or disease means in non-Western groups must be examined from the perspective of the general cultural beliefs and explanations that prevail, particularly as these relate to the domain of the body, the self, and the various supernatural agencies that are viewed as causing and determining events in nature.

Although an individual's ideas about the body have been studied in relation to the phenomenon of pain and as part of general psychological studies (Szasz 1957, Schilder 1950, Wapner and Werner 1965), the relationship that exists between the experience or sensation of the body and the understanding that subjects or groups have of bodily processes and functioning remains relatively unexplored. The work of cognitive anthropologists (see Chapter 1) who rely on the methods of structural linguistics has documented with fidelity the contrasting meanings associated with domains having concrete and publicly shared referents. Richness of language terms brought to bear on a particular phenomenal domain generally tends to reflect the salience or relevance of that domain to members of the group. The body as an anatomical entity quite obviously "exposes" only a portion of its features to the inspection and hence recognition of the self and others. Much remains hidden "beneath the surface," so to speak. Nevertheless, the number of anatomical terms in use, their organization, and the importance that is attached to them differ across cultural groups and tend to reflect the nature of the subsistence patterns and occupational roles that characterize the culture (Franklin 1963). Similarly, the degree of access that subjects have to the interior of the human body is a cultural trait that differs substantially across cultures (Laughlin 1963).

The language or knowledge of the body's functioning together with the experience of significant past events involving the body will no doubt influence the role and importance that the body is given in general discourse and, more importantly, the nature of the "reality" that subjects will attribute to the body. Sensations and feelings that are linked to biologically altered states must be viewed as a function of these symbols and meanings that involve the body, so that a consideration of how the body is *experienced* will not necessarily provide a framework or common denominator that might serve to unify our thinking about illness and disease. It *is* likely, however, that such bodily states as fractures, lacerations, and contusions, which stem from observable and externally induced events, will to a large extent be experienced similarly across individuals and groups. This is the case because, in addition to the stimulation of particular types of pain fibers, touch receptors will be stimulated, thus aiding in fixing the locality and the "sociality" of the sensation (Engel 1970a). Clearly, the pattern and type of nerve stimulation is similar in these instances, and, more importantly, the stimulation is linked to phenomenological "events" that share formal characteristics, for example, discrete onset, traumatic cause, heightened anxiety, visible abnormality, etc. It should be emphasized, however, that pain, involving such issues as its quality, its localization, its spread and reference, and its relationship to bodily events is far from being rigorously understood (see Merskey and Spear 1967, Wolff and Langley 1968). Individuals who study the neurophysiology of emotion are frequently forced to rely on tautologies, in part because the mind-body dichotomy and our language demand it, in part because the bulk of the experimental subjects who furnish reports of pain are all members of related cultural and language communities, and, last, because of the obvious inability to capture precisely the essence of the sensation. The result is that there is no unambiguous manner of depicting pain, and thus one can expect to find much variability even in descriptions of bodily changes originating in the surfaces of the body and in areas richly innervated.

If one excludes these particular bodily events (generally speaking, traumatic bodily changes), one is left with a multitude of biologically altered states that will be *experienced* in a variegated (ultimately idiosyncratic) manner. Obviously, diverse interpretations can be attached to these experiences. Only a subset of these is likely to be viewed universally as evidence of illness or disease. Table 5.1 illustrates two sets of

Table 5.1 Clinical Happenings Having Diverse Responses Cross-Culturally

Cultural Masking	Cultural Invariance
Particular avitaminoses	Acute asthmatic attack
Sensory paraesthesias	Cerebrovascular accident
Chronic bronchitis	Grand mal seizure
Early stages of malignancy	Acute glaucoma
Moderate to mild anemia	Renal colic
Mild diabetes	Acute pancreatitis
Trichuriasis	Fracture of femur
Pulmonary tuberculosis (early)	Acute pulmonary edema
Chronic brain syndrome	Hemoptysis

clinically relevant happenings that are likely to be judged as illness by different individuals or groups with varying degrees of uniformity. Items on the right of the table, which, in general, constitute typical medical and surgical emergencies, are likely to be regarded as evidence of abnormality or illness in a large proportion of instances. Clearly, the prior experiences of the subject or actor are likely to be minimal in affecting the judgment that an abnormality is present, although, of course, the general significance that the group will assign to that disturbance would depend on the repertoire of explanations available for dealing with personal crises. On the other hand, those abnormalities listed on the left of the table will likely be subject to considerable cultural masking or "distortion," with the designation of illness or abnormality applied more variably. Items on the left (and the list could obviously be expanded) are likely to underlie the bulk of medical complaints that physicians practicing in industrialized nations are called upon to treat. It is these clinical manifestations that are the substance of medical practice, the manifestations that physicians would like patients to notice and seek prompt relief for. Since these manifestations will be judged by the actor (and, by extension, his significant others) in terms of available existential symbols that link with the body, psychological factors will prove important in their interpretation and action consequences. Whether these manifestations are noticed or ignored, the manner in which they are defined (for example, as illness, fatigue, or part of the aging process), and, last, the actual form that they will take are likely to be influenced by psychological factors. This is to say that, although terms such as weakness or nausea may have straightforward clinical implications, it must be emphasized that they are rooted in differing phenomenologic complexes. For example, what causes nausea and how it is conceptualized, experienced, and reported will differ according to meanings people attribute to their body, to their food, and to vomiting and also according to whether they believe it is due to a poisoning or a punishment.

The influence that social and cultural patterns have in shaping the way in which subjects experience and define medical issues suggests an alternative framework for the understanding of "disease," one we could term *phenomenological*. The defining characteristics of "disease" formulated within this framework would include changes in the *states of being* (for example, feeling, thought, self-definition, impulses, etc.), which are (1) seen as discontinuous with everyday affairs and (2) believed to be caused by socioculturally defined agents or circumstances. Indicators would represent statements of modified phenomenologic states (or culturally specific behaviors symbolizing such states) cast in symbolic categories having multivalent meanings. These individualistic statements judged to constitute or reflect "disease" might contain reference to disturbed feelings, bodily sensations, beliefs about how the body functions, self-derogatory convictions, imputations of moral guilt, etc., which together would designate an altered conception of self-identity. Thus, altered bodily sensations fuse with their sociomoral implications and interpretations to form a culturally relevant picture that symbolizes a disarticulation of the self. Biological indicators and behavioral parameters, although theoretically related and, perhaps, empirically embodied in this changed identity, should be regarded as independent of the categorization process, because the units rationalizing an inability to function productively and in conformance with the implicit and explicit rules of the group usually refer to features of the person's self-identity.

Concentrating on these experiential dimensions associated with states or conditions variously labeled as illness or disease, we can suggest the outlines that such a "phenomenologic framework" of disease might take in Western settings. Four dimensions relevant to an individual's altered self might be selected: discomfort, disability, discreditation, and danger. Each of these can be thought of as contributing to the formation of a continuum of human experience associated with states of illness. For purposes of analytic exposition, the dimensions will be treated as signed and dichotomous. Each state of illness, in other words, can be seen as associated with either a positive or negative value, that is, with discomfort (+) or with no discomfort (−). In the same vein, an illness may be associated with social and moral discreditation, danger with regard to outcome or resolution, and with disability or impairment of life duties and functions. Categorizing each of these four dimensions into one of two values yields 16 logical types. However, only 15 illness types result, since the type consisting of four negative values is the individual's normal state. An illustration of such a framework of disease follows:

1. D_i = a disease construed in phenomenologic terms.

2. P_i = defining characteristics. Two diseases will be illustrated:
P_1 = much discomfort and disability but very little sense of discreditation or danger. (This disease type can be seen as glossing behaviors and
experiential states variously labeled as "indigestion," colds, sprained
backs, grief states, etc. In other words, persons afflicted with D_1 experience pain, malaise, weakness, disconnectedness, and isolation from on-
going affairs; however, there are no associated feelings of threat, no
doubts regarding survival, no sense of worthlessness, etc., nor feelings
of shame and embarrassment.)

P_2 = little discomfort or disability but considerable discreditation and
danger. (The person afflicted with D_2, in other words, experiences a personal threat to his being and additionally considerable shame and moral
opprobrium. However, there is little pain, discomfort, or impaired activity levels. Participation in life events and demands is possible but
takes place under altered premises and orientations. An example of
this type of disease is early tuberculosis or cancer.)

3. X has D_i if and only if he shows $\{P_i\}$. (This statement constitutes the
analytic definition of D_i.)

4. Q_{ij} = disease indicators. Again, two diseases will be illustrated:
Q_{11} =Person complains of much malaise, pain, and weakness; Q_{12} =
experiences an unwillingness or inability to carry out tasks or undertake "usual" responsibilities; Q_{13} = shows preoccupation with his body's
state, integrity, and functioning; Q_{14} = evinces loss of interest in leisure
activities; Q_{15} = physical activity level is diminished; Q_{16} = complains
of various unwanted somatic sensations; Q_{17} = feels disconnected and
isolated; Q_{18} = suffers from nausea and vomiting, etc.

Q_{21} = Person experiences embarrassment in settings where others
"know" of disease; Q_{22} = avoids revealing or exposing his "disease";
Q_{23} = develops resentment and humiliation at being socially excluded
from work or valued leisure activities; Q_{24} = shows preoccupation and
concern with his continued physical existence; Q_{25} = alters his will and
plans to visit friends and relatives so as to re-establish old ties; Q_{26} =
verbalizes statements about the meaning and purpose of life; Q_{27} =
shows increased interest in formal religion; Q_{28} = verbalizes a sense of
worthlessness and guilt.

5. X has D_i if and only if he shows $\{Q_{ij}\}$. (This statement constitutes the
empirical definition of D_i.)

In this framework, it is likely that no conjunction of *types* of bodily
sensations and malfunctions would constitute a sufficient condition for
a person to have a particular disease, although some of these types of indicators might be necessary. Important factors in determining disease

would be the manner in which the person perceives or judges himself vis-à-vis others and various institutions. By focusing on four sociopsychological dimensions underlying the phenomenologic experiences of persons who are ill, we have thus been able to develop a typology of disease. Clearly, other "dimensions" of experience might have been selected, just as a more refined procedure for partitioning each dimension could have been developed. The important point I wish to emphasize, however, is that a phenomenologic framework such as the one illustrated articulates types of altered *experiential states* that indicate disease. A variety of biological changes and associated social processes may underlie and/or form a part of any one experiential state that represents disease in this framework. They are joined and handled together precisely because they share a common socioemotional theme.

A Task-Action Framework of Disease

If it were possible to list in a relatively exhaustive manner the activities and tasks that persons engage in regularly and that occupy them during the daily conduct of their lives, this listing would provide a basis for the construction of a grid that could be used to map their degree of behavioral participation in life affairs. The various tasks and actions, in other words, would serve as coordinates or "units" of this grid. These units, in turn, could be organized in some systematic fashion so as to form a framework that would define types of behavioral actions. The units could also be employed to evaluate how the behavior of individuals varies and changes in response to or in association with various processes that are external or internal to the organism. In other words, the various actions and tasks that made up our grid could serve to identify types of behavioral deviations. If we chose to conceptualize these behavioral deviations as "medical" happenings (perhaps because the deviations were so often correlated with discomfort and evidence of bodily malfunctions), then our grid would in effect serve as a framework of disease.

A requirement for this framework of disease, in other words, is a set of disease indicators that refer to discrete actions and tasks, these construed in behavioral terms. The following are illustrations of actions and tasks that could be used: sleeping, eating, walking, talking, moviegoing, lifting and carrying, performing household tasks, etc. A broad and representative set of actions and tasks such as these could be used for the purpose of developing indicators in this particular behavioristic framework of disease. By then applying such a framework (that is, coding or measuring a person's degree of participation in the various work units of this grid through time), a *level* and pattern of participation could be obtained. This, in turn, would provide a basis for classifying and quantifying behavioral *changes* or *deviations,* which could be studied both internally and with respect to external events or processes.

The defining characteristics of a disease formulated in terms of such a task-action behavioral framework would then include changes in physicalistic behaviors, and the indicators would refer to specific behavioral segments. Diseases defined on this basis might take the following form:

1. D_i = a disease construed in task-action terms.

2. P_i = defining characteristics. Three types of diseases might be described:

P_1 = the regular features of the way X behaves in response to social demands are curtailed.

P_2 = the regular features of the way X behaves in response to social demands are quantitatively affected (that is, the intensity and activity are either increased or diminished).

P_3 = the regular features of the way X behaves in response to social demands are qualitatively affected.

3. X has D_i if and only if he shows $\{P_i\}$. (This statement constitutes the analytic definition of D_i.)

4. Q_{ij} = disease indicators.
Indicators of D_1 might include: Q_{11} = refuses to participate in social and leisure activities; Q_{12} = stays in bed a large proportion of time; Q_{13} = does not go to work; Q_{14} = food intake is significantly diminished; ... Q_{1n}.

Indicators of D_2 might include either: (a) Q_{21} = spends much time sitting; Q_{22} = walks more slowly, appears less active; Q_{23} = speaks less frequently and more slowly; Q_{24} = eats less frequently and smaller amounts; Q_{25} = work output diminished; ... Q_{2n}; or (b) Q_{21} = prefers to stand and walk; Q_{22} = walks faster, appears more active; Q_{23} = speaks more frequently and rapidly; Q_{24} = eats more frequently and in larger amounts; Q_{25} = work output increases; ... Q_{2n}.

Indicators of D_3 might include: Q_{31} = talks about irrelevancies; Q_{32} = now violates social conventions; Q_{33} = utters statements that disregard logical and/or empirical principles; Q_{34} = cries frequently and appears sad; Q_{35} = is argumentative; ... Q_{3n}.

5. X has D_i if and only if he shows $\{Q_{ij}\}$. (This statement constitutes the empirical definition of D_i.)

It should be evident that this definitional framework could be substantially refined so that each unit or category is made to refer to more specific behavioral sets. Thus, D_1 could be further subdivided as follows:

1. Defining characteristics:

P_{11} = the regular features of the way X behaves are curtailed as a result of visible structural faults.

P_{12} = the regular features of the way X behaves are curtailed, but there are no visible structural faults.

2. Disease indicators:

of D_{11} = same Q_{11}–Q_{1n} as for D_1 plus Q_{1n+1} (in this case, denoting faulty or unmovable extremities); Q_{1n+2} (here, faulty extremities that can be moved only with much labor and verbalization about pain).

of D_{12} = same Q_{11}–Q_{1n} as for D_1 plus Q_{1n+1} (in this variation on D_1, reporting pain); Q_{1n+2} (here, reports feeling weak and having no energy), etc.

Further differentiation might yield for D_{11}, P_{111}, faulty lower extremities, and P_{112}, faulty upper extremities; and for D_{12}, P_{121}, associated problems in bowel function, and P_{122}, associated problems with breathing, etc. By a procedure analogous to this one it should be possible to develop a branching classification scheme of task-action behavioral diseases, such that a "species" of disease located at the terminal locus of a branch is indicated by discrete and specific sets of behavioral elements. Careful analytic work might yield a refined scheme that would be exclusive, and whose categories could approximate segments of the biologistic and/or the phenomenologic framework. However, despite the possibility that the frameworks might bear a systematic relationship to each other, they would refer to different sorts of phenomena. That is, disease in one framework would refer to biological or phenomenologic processes; in the other it would refer to behavioral manifestations construed in terms of tasks and actions.

The preceding point implies that what we have thus far termed loosely a "behavioral disease" would, from the standpoint of alternative explanatory schemes, represent a heterogeneous category. To illustrate this point, let us assume that the application of a task-action disease framework reveals that certain individuals are prone to develop relatively abrupt, short-lasting episodes during which they fail to carry out particular tasks and actions in their usual behavioral way. For example, during such episodes individuals might be noted to (1) stay in bed longer, (2) engage in routine tasks around the house sporadically and with diminished intensity, (3) avoid engaging in strenuous physical activity, (4) report feeling tired and not interested in current goings-on, and (5) be prone to behave abruptly when they are engaged in conversation. We might term such a "disease" D_7. It should be clear that a subset of individuals labeled as "having" D_7 might be viewed, were a biologistic framework applied, as suffering from an acute upper respiratory infection. Others might show a viral gastroenteritis. Still others, and this is the important point, might be viewed as emotionally upset and depressed or simply as wanting to avoid facing certain problems in their lives. Regardless of the factors that contribute to the development of D_7 or the processes that mediate it, the employment of a task-action framework would force us to view episodes of the type described as equivalent. Thus, a behavioral framework must be seen simply as a device for specifying ways of classifying deviations in behavior that persons are observed to develop through time. The *type* of behavioral change and the *duration* are key dimensions of such episodes, not the causes or "reasons" for them. The implications of labeling behavioral deviations "disease" and of handling deviation types equivalently, regardless of etiology or cause, are obviously quite profound and cannot be pursued in depth here. Clearly, to avoid the sort of social dilemmas posed by "problem" or "functional" patients—patients who claim illness and behave as if ill but who do not demonstrate "organic" pathology (Von Mering and Earley 1966, Fabrega, Moore, and Strawn 1969) —and the dilemmas created by psychiatric diagnosing—where persons often are diagnosed as ill strictly on the basis of specific behavioral decrements (Szasz 1961)—we would need to modify the system of beliefs and values that link strictly medical issues with societal traditions, conventions, and norms.

A Role Enactment Framework of Disease

Instead of partitioning behavior using specific tasks and actions, we might attempt to use the concept of *social role* as the theme around which to develop a behavioral framework of disease. Several social dimensions or coordinates may be used to depict the totality of a person's behavior using such a paradigm. In this regard the following concepts may prove useful: social position, social role, role set, role relationship, and institution. As participants of any social system, individual persons may be said to repeatedly enter in and out of *social positions,* such as that of drugstore client, clerical employee, patient, father, husband, and novelist. To each position are attached specific duties and obligations that are expected and demanded by others who occupy counter positions in the social system, as well as prerogatives or entitlements that may be expected of others. The behaviors through which the duties, obligations, and prerogatives of a social position get enacted may be termed a *social role,* although the term *role set* might be more accurate insofar as it emphasizes that a group of behaviors (each of which may be thought of as directed to a counter position) is attached to a particular social position. Any behavior transpiring between the occupants of two social positions may be termed a *role relationship,* it consequently being clear that many such role relationships are attached to social positions. It is, in fact, possible to evaluate each social position or role relationship in terms of general factors such as intensity of involvement, frequency of interactions, number of duties expected, etc., but an elaboration of this type is not necessary for our immediate purposes (Marwell and Hage 1970).

The social "space" wherein behavior gets enacted has thus far been assigned such nodal points as social position, social role, and role relationship. It remains to be emphasized that sectors of the space (alternatively, subsets of the behaviors enacted therein) may be delimited on the basis of the types of institutional concerns that characterize them. Thus, a subset of shared concerns can be grouped under the rubric "economic" or "occupational" and delimit specific types of behavioral activities and responsibilities. Four types of roles can be enunciated: occupational, familial or kinship, recreational, and religious. These types of roles are relatively straightforward and conform to the usual content-based classifications of role behaviors employed by behavioral scientists (Sarbin and Allen 1969).

It should be very clear that when we use role performances as the basis for evaluating changes in behavior, we are forced to analyze more carefully the symbolic and social rootedness of behavior. To elaborate on this point, let us recall that a task-action framework is concerned in large part with the physical performance of specific acts. The fact that these acts may occur in social situations and consequently differ as to meaning is not important. What is important is merely whether a person evidences changes in these activities. When emphasis is given to the performance of roles, on the other hand, the meanings and symbols that actors use and act upon in different social contexts become important in the evaluation of behavior. For example, the *meanings, "reasons for,"* and *implications* of performing or not performing certain acts are what is critical for the overall evaluation of a person's occupational or family role behavior. In this evaluation, as in the evaluation of disease indicators in other frameworks, the concept of deviation assumes central importance in two respects. The first is deviation construed diachronically and on a personalistic basis; the second, deviation viewed synchronically and with reference to group norms. Individualistic behaviors that form a part of the performance of a role are enacted in particular social situations. In these situations, an individual's behavior that we may regard as deviating from personal norms may not necessarily be viewed by others as a deviation. Only if the behavior in question also violates norms involving a specific social position or role is it judged to represent a group deviation. I will posit that a role behavioral indicator of disease consists of a behavior segment that deviates from both personal and group norms. (The reader wishing to gain an appreciation of how information related to role behaviors can be used in social psychiatric studies is referred to Katz and Lyerly 1963, Ruesch and Brodsky 1968, Ruesch 1969, Paykel et al. 1971, Hogarty and Katz, 1971, Weissman et al. 1971, and Paykel and Weissman 1973, as well as the writings of Leslie Phillips 1968).

Let us consider a behavioral framework of disease using instances of role enactment as the analytical units. Figure 5.1 illustrates both the traditional and role enactment paradigms. In the traditional paradigm, disease state is separated from but assumed to be the basis for "new" role behaviors. In the role enactment paradigm, ordinary role behaviors are believed to be interfered with or altered, and the whole complex of role changes constitutes the illness. An R with a subscript signifies traditional role behaviors (economic, familial, etc.). An R with a superscript signifies a sociological framework (for example R^1 = sick role,

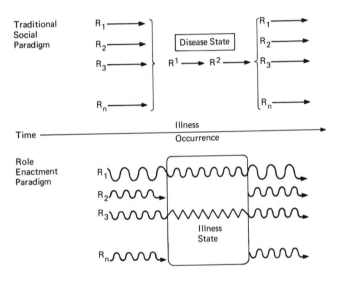

Figure 5.1 Disease and social roles

R^2 = patient role, etc.). As already stated, in this paradigm role behaviors will be classified into four types: occupational, familial, recreational, and religious. Deviations in role enactment in each of these four spheres will be evaluated by analyzing the symbolic content of the behavior. By *symbolic content* I mean whether behaviors are (a) appropriate to the social position, (b) socially proper and correct, and (c) convincing. For purposes of exposition, deviations in enactment of each of the four role types will be evaluated by means of a dichotomous scale (deviation versus no deviation), and the presence of deviation will constitute a disease indicator. (Evaluating role enactment in each role sphere along the three symbolic coordinates separately could be proposed, but the effort is too cumbersome for our immediate purposes.) Since an actor may demonstrate changes in none, some, or all role behaviors, we again are provided with 15 logical possibilities (there are actually 2^4 or 16 logical types, but the type showing no change in any of the four role spheres obviously does not represent a deviation).

1. D_i = a particular disease construed in role enactment terms.

2. P_i = defining characteristics.

P_1 = changes in the symbolic content of family and kinship role behaviors.

P_2 = changes in the symbolic content of occupational role behaviors.

P_3 = changes in the content of role behaviors in all four spheres (familial, occupational, recreational, and religious).

3. X has D_i if and only if he shows $\{P_i\}$. (This statement constitutes the analytic definition of D_i.)

4. Q_{ij} = disease indicators.

Q_{11} = A father preoccupied with an unspecified problem behaves inappropriately with his children, treating them alternately as strangers and as antagonists; Q_{12} = complains of various somatic ailments, demonstrates alienation, antagonism, and lack of interest in activities of wife; Q_{13} = ceases to be respectful of his parents, stating that his physical needs are unmet; Q_{14} = spends little time in the home, preferring to stay at work or engage in leisure activities; Q_{15} = while home, avoids conversing with wife or attending to needs of his children; Q_{16} = "forgets" important family events, refuses to attend family gatherings.

Q_{21} = A salesgirl becomes distant, aloof, and disinterested in relating to fellow employees, stating that she is feeling ill and wishes not to be disturbed; Q_{22} = becomes forgetful of duties; Q_{23} = avoids counting total sales at end of working day; Q_{24} = takes longer breaks during the day; Q_{25} = is impatient, disrespectful, and highly impersonal toward customers; Q_{26} = chooses not to answer questions asked about products she is selling; Q_{27} = appears distracted and uninvolved during duty hours.

Q_{31} = A car mechanic who complains of his "liver condition" behaves inappropriately toward customers; Q_{32} = forgets to carry out functions; Q_{33} = spends increasing amounts of time on breaks; Q_{34} = appears uninterested in work and distracted, claiming his health is failing; Q_{35} = is distant, aloof, preoccupied, and resentful in home; Q_{36} = fails to show interest in and respond to needs of family; Q_{37} = claims his poor health does not allow him to enjoy television, movies, and parties; Q_{38} = shows no anticipation toward weekend leisure activities; Q_{39} = becomes intensely preoccupied with religion; Q_{310} = constantly attends church, verbalizes need for involvement in church activities.

5. X has D_i if and only if he shows $\{Q_{ij}\}$. (This statement constitutes the empirical definition of D_i.)

The preceding disease types are offered as illustrations of a role enactment framework of disease. Three things should be noted. First, it is quite likely that the three symbolic dimensions that were mentioned earlier and then collapsed for the sake of brevity (that is, whether the behaviors were appropriate, proper, and convincing) may in different circumstances show different degrees of independence from each other. In other words, alterations in one dimension may at times be associated with patterned changes in another dimension, while at other times, such a correlation may not be observed. In a more refined role enactment framework, important symbolic axes of the type mentioned (and any others deemed equally or more appropriate) would have to be represented in a formal way. Second, it may also be the case that alteration of role behaviors in separate sectors will covary, for example, that changes in religious role behaviors will be accompanied by changes in recreational role behaviors. These are issues likely to become evident if such a framework were to be operationalized and implemented. Third, it should be apparent that alternative dimensions could have been selected in order to evaluate changes in role enactment. For example, instead of directly evaluating the performance of role, we could evaluate role enactment in terms of changes in the intensity of involvement with the duties subsumed by the role or changes in the amount of time devoted to such duties. The critical point to note is that in this particular behavioral framework, disease is articulated on the basis of deviations in the enactment of social roles.

On first impression, it might appear that the disease types outlined represent quasi-psychiatric types. This impression results from the current bias created by a dualistic conception of the nature of disease, a bias giving rise to the belief that since behaviors are used as units, then the entities defined on the basis of these units are psychiatric or "nonorganic." Furthermore, this "impression" overlooks the principal thrust of the analysis herein attempted. To repeat, in this framework we view verbalizations about the behavioral correlates of *all* types of health problems equivalently. In other words, the *variety* of ways in which actors rationalize and explain their health problems or their changes in behavior is not important, for the associated deviations in role enactment are seen as the critical units of the disease. Similarly, whether changes in sugar metabolism, toxic effects of an infectious or neoplastic disease, or anxiety and depression are judged by outsiders as the basis or cause of the associated changes in role behaviors is also irrelevant, for role behaviors *qua* behaviors are the critical units of "disease" in this frame-work. Disease types are thus *socially situated entities* comprised of changed interpersonal relations. Disease, in this framework, then, quite literally both expresses itself through and inheres in alterations in a person's enactment of his various positions in the social system.

On the Possible Logic of Behavioral Diseases

The preceding behavioral frameworks have been presented in order to demonstrate my rationale regarding alternative approaches to disease. Because these three frameworks together afford a different way of conceptualizing disease, and because they articulate social and phenomeno-logic matters (see Chapter 7), I shall refer to them as providing a *language of illness forms*. Clearly, other coordinates or variables may be employed in the effort to articulate such a language. We should entertain the possibility that a relatively culture-free language of illness can be devised (or discovered), and furthermore that its *grammar* may reveal to us something fundamental about the way man the biocultural animal functions and shows his dysfunctions (see the recent chapter by Leach [1972] in the book edited by Hinde for related matters). With regard to the notion of grammar, what needs to be uncovered is the sequence of changes that occur in illness, with illness formulated as a behavioral category. Illnesses, in other words, vary as to manifestations, and a useful way to quantify these has been by means of such concepts as severity, intensity, or degree. Behaviorally, we may judge severity as degree of spread or coverage of behavioral interferences. It is precisely in the way that an illness spreads out and ramifies into various behavioral spheres that we may find a grammar of the language of illness. The rules that underlie or explain regularities in the way illness unfolds may be termed the grammar of illness. A long-range aim of sociomedical inquiries (see Chapter 9) might then be to discover such a grammar of illness.

The notion of a grammar of illness leads us to modify statements made earlier in this chapter. A typology of illness is a hallmark of a synchronic description and/or characterization of illness. Types of behavioral interferences or illness forms are specified. However, were it to be shown that such types of illness forms are actually linked systematically, that is, that specific rules or laws explain the relationships between these types, then one would move beyond a synchronic typological analysis to develop a diachronic characterization. In this sense, then, the discovery of (or a search for) a grammar of the language of illness entails a shift from a synchronic to a diachronic mode of analysis and framework.

Some Implications of Viewing Disease in Behavioral Terms

We assume a priori that alternative ways of organizing phenomena within a domain offer the promise of revealing biases, contradictions, or the inutilities of premises implicit in a traditional orientation. Conversely, a new formulation of phenomena carries the potential for clarifying and possibly resolving problems that may be outcomes of traditional ways of conceptualizing a domain. In earlier chapters it was mentioned that contemporary physicians and social scientists generally tend to emphasize the relevance of behavioral factors in the study of disease, but that except for the writings of social epidemiologists (whose concern is primarily with questions of cause and distribution), few attempts have been made to explicate this relation further. The frameworks outlined and discussed in this chapter can be seen as a preliminary attempt to formulate and systematize how behavioral factors stand in relation to disease.

An obvious practical and pedagogical reason for developing a language of illness forms (that is, a behavioral framework of disease) is that it draws attention, in a very direct fashion and with rich detail, to the varied coordinates that can be used to evaluate an interruption in health status. Succinctly stated, *disease* is a term having varied meanings and referents, and in most instances we must assume that frameworks other than the biologistic are relevant. Just as a definition and indications of what a disease state represents in a specific instance can be seen as varied and complex, so must the plans for rectifying or modifying that state be multifaceted. Quite obviously, the full management or treatment of the disease in question requires close attention to the various components that indicate the disease. The *cost* of the disease and its *implications* can similarly be evaluated using the various frameworks outlined.

An additional reason for developing behavioral frameworks of disease is to arrive at a view of medical activity as constituted of social facts. In Chapter 3 I mentioned briefly that the traditional biological definition of disease poses problems for social analyses of medical matters since the category *disease* is imperfectly correlated with behavior. However, if the term *disease* were used to designate a behavioral or a social category, then studies demonstrating that certain disease types were distributed differently across social groups, or that the frequency of certain diseases was greater in particular subgroups, would be demonstrating *directly* social facts about those groups (or subgroups). For example, let us assume that a behavioral framework allowed defining and measuring occurrences of a behavioral disease B_1, which was indicated by minimal physical impairment or disability of work routines, minimal pain and bodily discomfort, high visibility of symptoms and signs, but no stigmatization or social discreditation. Similarly, let us assume that our framework specified a behavioral disease B_2, distinguished from the first only by its relatively high stigmatization. If a focused study demonstrated that subgroup X was associated with a higher frequency of disease B_1 as compared to subgroup Y, and, in addition, that disease B_2 was distributed in the subgroups in a converse manner, then we might conclude that the social burden of disease in subgroup Y was considerably higher. Knowledge of social characteristics of the two groups might allow us to entertain hypotheses about the "causes" of this state of affairs as well as the consequences of these very different disease pictures. In other words, a framework for defining behavioral diseases, together with a procedure for measuring or quantifying occurrences of these diseases, would allow determining in a direct fashion *sociomedical* facts about groups or populations we might want to study. This is the case because assessments regarding rates of behavioral disease would convey directly information about social phenomena (for example, work constraints, social discreditation) as well as medical phenomena (such as discomfort, disability, bodily complaints). Analyses and interpretations of the distribution and frequency of these types of disease using sociocultural variables, either as independent or dependent variables, would then constitute a truly social enterprise (see Chapter 9). Finally, specifying the relationship that exists between behavioral disease rates and rates derived from a biologistic framework would allow estimating in a general way the behavioral accompaniments of these diseases (for example, hypertension, coronary artery disease, diabetes, etc.). There is no reason not to believe that some degree of relatedness could be developed between disease profiles computed by means of contrasting medical frameworks.

It is important, however, to keep in mind the fact that the distribution of such "disease entities" would bear a systematic relationship to social categories and contexts. To clarify this point, let us review briefly considerations bearing on the biologistic framework. It should be evident that from the standpoint of studying the distribution of disease in human groups a strictly biologistic framework enjoys an unusual advantage. This is that the framework for defining disease does not in principle articulate logically with social categories. In other words, the study and evaluation of how disease relates to social categories (for example, social class, ethnic identity, occupational groupings, etc.) can in theory take place by means of concepts, variables, and relations that are logically independent of the unit that assigns medical meaning (or identity or status) to the individual. Given this logical separation between societal and medical dimensions, it is then possible to analyze empirically the relationship that exists between them, knowing that no systematic biases or errors will contaminate one's methods. (Psychiatric diagnosing, of course, is notoriously blameworthy in this regard, and there is much evidence that social factors directly influence and may in fact contaminate what presumably are medical affairs [Szasz 1961].) Clearly, were we to use a behavioral disease framework and then attempt to analyze how disease conditions are distributed in a social group we would be likely to observe that systematic relations obtain. Thus, keeping in mind the illustrative "behavioral indicators" introduced earlier, we can say that only persons who are family members can be evaluated in terms of performance of family role duties, only persons whose work requires heavy physical exertion can be evaluated on this task-action indicator, and only persons who are identified with a religious group can be evaluated with respect to role behaviors that attach to religious affiliation. Stated more directly, behavioral categories (from which behavioral indicators devolve) are distributed in patterned ways in a social system, and moreover, this patterning between social and behavioral dimensions results from what we might term logical considerations. Thus, a factor explaining a particular distribution of a behavioral disease in a social group would be the analytic link that obtains between that group and certain types of behaviors. A different way of making clear the logical independence that exists between social categories and a biologistic framework is to point out that biologistic indicators can all be used systematically and equivalently to evaluate persons (that is, blood sugars, lung parenchyma, and blood pressure levels are parameters that apply equally to all individuals), while behavioral categories of the type herein considered are not equally relevant to all persons.

We see, then, that analytic relations or biases can be expected to obtain between, on the one hand, the various social positions associated with a group and, on the other, types or categories of behaviors. Such biases significantly diminish the empirical value of studies designed to measure (behavioral) disease rates in any one social group. Since the behavioral indicators suggested previously are highly ethnocentric, similar biases make impossible and meaningless the attempt to evaluate disease in different sociocultural groups. In order to conduct cross-culturally meaningful studies of disease and behavior, what is needed is a logical analysis that would produce a listing of types of behaviors that are likely to be found in various social and cultural groups. In other words, behavioral categories or types (that is, disease indicators) need to be initially articulated in a highly abstract way such that the analogues or forms of these types can be identified cross-culturally.

Concluding Comment

The realization that physicians are urged to treat health crises and illnesses having no identifiable organic or biological substrate and that biological disease states often go unrecognized is compelling evidence that disease and human behavior as traditionally defined today are neither logically nor causally linked in any determinant manner. This indeterminacy between disease and behavior in fact must be regarded as a factor that limits the utility and relevance of behavioral science principles in the eyes of many medical students and educators. As long as biological changes are seen as necessary indices of disease, the form and content of behavior under these altered conditions must assume a secondary or auxiliary status. Medical planners and students of medical practice, however, see the indeterminacy differently. They acknowledge that in the day-to-day administration of care, physicians are dealing to a large extent with behavioral homologues of biological disease. In other words, a large proportion of patients merely *behave as if* they had a "disease." However, they remind us that the functions of the physician as they have evolved in Western society include helping and treating all of those who are ill regardless of the basis of the illness. In short, physicians must be concerned with treating "disease" regardless of how we choose to define this term. This latter position is used to support the appeal for behavioral science instruction. Conflict and confusion over the importance and relevance of behavioral science principles for the study of those problems physicians are repeatedly urged to deal with suggest that serious efforts be devoted to formulating how behavior and disease may be construed.

In this chapter I have attempted to organize and systematize the domain of human behavior and to link it with phenomena ordinarily classed as "disease." In these efforts, three independent analytic behavioral frameworks of disease were articulated. At this point in our analysis of sociomedical studies, the substance and form of these frameworks and the ease with which they can be operationalized are less important than the heuristic purpose for which they are intended. Undesirable person-centered deviations of the type we have come to judge as disease are associated with alterations in behavior, and when behavior is altered and persons are functioning suboptimally, analyses of alterations can proceed along phenomenologic, task-action, and role-enactment lines. At this stage of the development of knowledge about human biological functioning, behavioral organization, and dynamics of medical care, we can hope only to develop preliminary analytic efforts at formulating problems and charting the general direction of future efforts. Thus, I am not now interested in the judiciousness of such a "behavioral" approach to disease nor in exploring its many implications.

Rather, I wish to make explicit the logically alternative ways in which we could organize phenomena we see in our work as physicians and medical researchers. Current practices and research orientations in medicine are predicated on assumptions that ordinarily disregard such ontological matters; I believe that they need to be made clear and explicit before we can propose or judge specific medical policies.

Chapter 6 Toward a Model of Illness Behavior

In the last three decades behavioral scientists have developed a large body of concepts for the study of human behavior (Hall 1968, Ruesch and Bateson 1951, Scheflen 1967, 1968). Behavioral exchanges have been shown to have an inherent organization of their own, to be composed of units or segments that link with others to form hierarchically organized wholes (Harris 1964, Miller, Galanter, and Pribram 1960, Pike 1956). Most workers agree that, although the units and segments that comprise patterned forms of behavior are clearly relative to the groups studied, the likelihood of uncovering such things as behavioral plans, programs, or networks is very high; some go as far as to say that such social forms are probably universal attributes of human social groupings (Diebold 1968, Mitchell 1969). In short, given underlying similarities across human groups, behavioral scientists have been led to search for and expect some regularity in the way behavior is organized or programmed. In this light an aim of behavioral science research should be the persistent search for behavioral structures that occur transculturally, perhaps universally. Alternatively, scientists should strive to make clear the level of abstraction required in order to arrive at behavioral models or structures that are wide in their application.

Behavioral processes that are associated with occurrences of disease offer a relevant area of research to the behavioral scientist interested in investigating recurring features of human behavior. It has been pointed out that definitions of disease vary and ultimately rest on a set of historically selected symbols that are accepted as real. These symbols, in turn, form the basis for the actions that are taken vis-à-vis disease, actions often implemented by persons sanctioned with social power. Nevertheless, regardless of the framework that one might use as a basis for definition, members of all carefully studied contemporary human groups are prone to develop biological changes analogous to those that we term disease, and this has been the case for groups at all points in the evolutionary history of man (Brothwell and Sandison 1967, Cockburn 1967, Dunn 1968). Since occurrences of this type of disease are universal, this means that human groups are more or less regularly confronted with decremental changes in human functioning, which we assume are to some extent socially patterned. This in turn suggests that it should be possible to depict in an abstract way fundamental behavioral changes associated with an occurrence of disease. A first step in this direction would be the construction of an analytical model to account for the decisions that are made by a person during the time he is ill (Banton 1965, Cherry 1961, MacKay 1969, Raser 1969, Stogdill 1970, Willer 1967). We could term this a *model of illness behavior*. The purpose of this chapter is to put forth, in a preliminary fashion, an admittedly theoretical model of this decision-making process. The model to be discussed presumes, not to describe the actual way in which persons make decisions during illness, but rather to offer an abstract account of how such decisions may be interpreted or explained. Before presenting this model, however, it will be necessary to review briefly earlier thinking and work in the general area of medicine and social science and to use this material as a basis for discussing what requirements such a model must meet. In this review the term *disease* will refer strictly to biologically altered changes, and the broader term *illness* will refer to the social and behavioral correlates of these changes.

A theme implicit in previous chapters has been that if occurrences of disease can be linked more directly with actual behavior, then it should be possible to evaluate more directly the influence of social and cultural factors on medical issues and to develop a truly social formulation of these matters. We have seen that, heretofore, disciplinary emphases have held sway in the study of disease. Thus, although the prevailing conceptions generating research have been unileveled or analytically rigid regarding the entity disease, the combined findings have pointed to the complexity of factors that are implicated in occurrences of disease. A problem is thus created for those interested in explaining or developing theories about how disease and social happenings are interrelated. A model of illness, such as the one outlined in this chapter, because it is composed of elements that bear directly on human behavior, offers the possibility of studying more directly how socioenvironmental issues influence medical problems. Briefly, the model itself serves as a device for ordering and organizing social and cultural data tied to occurrences of illness that influence the behavior of the sick person. When it is used in conjuction with a method for similarly organizing data on the manifestations of disease (and here the frameworks described in earlier chapters are relevant), the stage may be set for meaningful analyses of medicine-society interactions. There is an additional and obvious benefit of having a model of illness behavior. If such a model *accurately* reflects behaviorally relevant factors that have their locus in persons who are ill, then the model may potentially aid those medical planners who are interested in developing health services that articulate meaningfully with the expectations and needs of the consumer of medical services (see Chapter 7). Finally, a practical implication of prior sociomedical studies is realized when the knowledge gained from these studies is used as background for the construction of a model of illness behavior.

The Problem of Modeling Aspects of Illness: Multiplicity of Factors
The large number of happenings and processes that can produce an instance of illness must be seen as the key factor that has heretofore impeded the development of an abstract statement or model of the behaviors associated with an occurrence of illness. An illness, of course, need not be associated with altered biological states. If it is, a number of different biological changes are possible, each associated with different types of causes (for example, chemical, structural). These biological changes vary by location, intensity, and effect. Persons obviously differ in the way they perceive and evaluate biological states. In other words, the information derived from the body which is evaluated during an instance of illness is subject to personal interpretations that are products of distinctive sociocultural traditions and ecological contingencies (Fabrega 1971b, Frake 1961, Franklin 1963, Gajdusek 1970b, Schacter 1971, Valins 1970, Vayda and Rappaport 1968). In addition, these interpretations form the bases of varied actions that have consequences that directly affect the person's many systems. We can summarize the preceding by saying that the recognition, definition, and responses associated with illness are variable, highly complex, and interconnected. Futhermore, time periods that underlie and demarcate an occurrence of illness differ in length, and the associated changes that take place vary as to rate. Changes that in the Western medical system we might label as meningitis can come on suddenly, whereas others we would term diabetes, cancer, or neurosis come on gradually and insidiously. The behavioral

consequences for the individual of these changes also differ markedly, suggesting that different types of evaluations and decisions can take place, each having consequences that in turn affect the illness. Recognition of changes we might term diabetes, for example, may allow work routines to be modified only slightly and infrequently; complex changes termed cancer may require constant and increasingly encompassing modifications in living routines; last, changes associated with meningitis, since they are usually sudden, all-encompassing, and rather drastic, may allow only limited behavioral alternatives. We must conclude, then, that the variable and fluid nature of illness and the many diverse ways in which persons are able to define and cope with it represent a formidable obstacle to those interested in modeling its salient characteristics.

The actual efforts of behavioral scientists to formulate and model the varied aspects of illness give evidence that the underlying problem is multifaceted and complex. Much social science theory and a number of concepts have been used in order to explicate social and behavioral dimensions. The concepts of role, deviance, career, labeling, and stigma are examples. Similarly, a host of new terms has been introduced, among them patient role, sick role, symptom experience, illness behavior, and patient career (Kasl and Cobb 1966a, 1966b, McKinlay 1971, Mechanic 1962, Parsons 1951a). By means of descriptive and analytic tools such as these, some efforts have been made to develop clear formulations of the social processes and behaviors underlying illness occurrences. However, investigators of this persuasion have usually not attempted to formulate or empirically study the progression and unfolding of events associated with illness but rather have been content to explicate in depth particular concepts or characteristics of discrete behavioral and social changes.

A notable exception is Suchman, who proposed a model drawn from empirical research of the social processes associated with illness (Suchman 1965a, 1965b, 1965c, 1967). In his model, Suchman attempted to capture structural factors, sociocognitive factors (such as attitudes, values, knowledge), group interaction factors, as well as actual behaviors associated with illness. In striving for comprehensiveness with regard to *levels* and *types* of happenings, however, Suchman sacrificed precision. He made no attempt to show how events in the illness-medical treatment cycle might be structured internally and across time and allowed for many different types of changes and endpoints. His "model," in other words, mainly describes and temporarily orders the possible events and processes associated with illness but makes no attempt to represent these in a theoretically abstract, systematic, and logically consistent manner.

Others, while contributing significantly to an understanding of illness behavior, have addressed themselves to only a segment of the relevant issues and have, consequently, tended to sacrifice scope. Rosenstock, for example, was principally interested in preventive behavior, wishing to account for or explain factors bearing on key decisions (Rosenstock 1966). Freidson's efforts have been directed mainly toward the examination of social and interpersonal issues that link lay persons with medical care systems; the illness state per se, or its behaviorally relevant dimensions, have not been given primary and systematic attention (Freidson 1960). Zola's work (1966) dealt only with specific types of problems and examined interpretations and responses associated with ethnic affiliation; how conceptions of illness affected key treatment decisions was not considered, nor was an effort made to see an illness as an occurrence that was temporally bounded and ordered. Andersen's work was aimed principally at explaining, in an empirical way, factors associated with treatment expenditures; illness behavior was simply not formulated as a process or sequence of actions that had an organization and logic of its own (Andersen 1968). A limitation of most analyses of illness behavior is that exclusive attention is given to events taking place in Western settings. The concepts and formulations used have not allowed including in any systematic fashion illnesses as they are defined and acted upon by persons living in preliterate settings.

A model of illness occurrences that is general in its application must somehow manage to represent the variable number and kinds of changes associated with illness in a precise and systematic fashion. First, these events and changes must be reduced or expanded so as to form a limited number of types. In the model to be described, I concentrate on the *information* that is evaluated and acted upon by the organism during an instance of illness. The problem of heterogeneity with regard to number and type of changes is thus resolved by focusing on only a finite number of events of one logical type. Second, the resulting types of changes and events must be temporally ordered in some consistent manner. Since almost all changes associated with illness are variable in terms of duration and rate of change, it is clearly not possible to order events using chronological time. Instead, we should strive to model "logical" time or "decision-making" time. In other words, stages of the model should be bounded by key events (that is, information-processing events) that are ordered in a logical plan or program, and not by amount of chronological time elapsed. Last, a model of illness occurrences should constrain the number of alternative resolutions that can associate with an occurrence of illness. Thus, instead of allowing processes and events to pursue alternative pathways, each yielding a potentially different endpoint in the health-illness-medical treatment cycle, a model should strive to achieve clarity, organization, and regularity in its ordering of stages and to culminate in one of a finite number of states that bears a relation to earlier stages. In the model to be described I attempt to achieve this type of ordering by employing an invariant and iterative procedure for processing medically relevant information.

A Model of the Information Processed during Illness

One potential way of ordering and simplifying the many factors associated with illness is to focus in an abstract way on the information that a person might be expected to process during an occurrence of illness. Concentrating in a theoretical way on informational correlates of illness can be seen as articulating a set of *rules* that *organize* the data of illness (that is, sensations, perceptions, beliefs, circumstances, etc.) and explain the culturally appropriate acts or behaviors associated with illness occurrences. As we shall see, this technique in effect leads to the formulation of a *decision theoretic model* of illness. In this section, the salient characteristics of this model are presented. We begin with a general description of the person.

An abstract outline of the person would include four analytically distinguished systems, which, however, are open or connected with each other. These systems are the biological, social, phenomenologic, and memory. The biological system includes chemical and physiologic processes; the social includes the relations between the person and other persons, groups, and institutions; and the phenomenologic involves states of awareness and self-definition. The unique history of the person, the product of a finite number of experiences in a specific spatial, temporal, and sociocultural setting, is represented in the memory system and includes earlier illness occurrences and associated medical attitudes, beliefs, associations, etc. Earlier impressions in the form of memories are seen as readily available to the person and are also believed to continually influence his evaluation of other systems. If systems were positioned along the vertical axis, then time could be represented along a horizontal axis. Although the temporal continuum would be partitioned into units or segments, it would be understood that each segment is continuous with and leads to the formation of each successive segment. At any one point in time (a vertical cross-section of this outline) the person is seen as a product or composite of the happenings in the various systems.

The phenomenologic system is seen as composed of informational categories or *coding units* that allow the person to encode happenings efficiently, thus reducing heterogeneity and variability and creating redundancy and continuity. In other words, the person's profile of information at a point in time is not simply the totality of previous informational inputs but rather is seen as composed of a much smaller set of categories by means of which it can efficiently encode inputs, assess and monitor happenings, and establish continuity and predictability. Information-coding categories can also be seen as serving as a series of norms or experienced levels of variation within which the person continually functions (Beck 1971).

Included among the categories of the memory system of the person are ones that represent *experienced* deviations in the configurations of the other three systems. We can term these *illness categories*. In addition, the person has available through participation in various learning situations a set of illness categories (not yet experienced) that represent additional potential states of illness. This open, interlinked, multisystemic representation of the person means that he is judged capable of continually monitoring happenings and processes in the functioning of the various systems. Judgment regarding a *new deviation* (that is, an illness occurrence I_i) is allowed precisely because of the availability of internalized norms, expectations, and categories that are derived from either experienced or learned configurations of information that represent deviations in functioning. The information available to the individual during an illness occurrence is processed in nine stages.

STAGE 1: ILLNESS RECOGNITION AND LABELING

The current states of the biological, social, and phenomenologic systems are evaluated in association with the memory system, in particular the various illness categories. Every person is believed to have a finite set of illness categories, which he is able to use for these purposes. The set can be termed his *taxonomy of illness*. The person is believed to judge himself as vulnerable to each and every illness of this taxonomy. When comparative analyses yield recognition that a current system's value has deviated and approximates that of an illness category, the person judges himself to be in a particular illness state I_i. In a parsimonious sense, then, the person is believed to be in an illness state when a reading of the phenomenologic system gives him a conviction that an undesirable deviation exists in the current values of the biological, social, or phenomenologic systems. Data internal to the person (biologic system conjoined with phenomenologic systems) or external to him (derived from appraisals of others, that is, social system conjoined with phenomenologic system) serve as the basis for illness definition. Illness as represented in the model, thus, is *subjective* and not objective in the sense of requiring biomedical verification. Since this is a model of *illness behavior,* it requires a conviction on the part of the person that an undesirable state of affairs exists, which in turn propels him to seek relief. It should be emphasized that recognition of an illness state I_i can result from a relabeling of some other pre-existing illness state I_h.

STAGE 2: ILLNESS DISVALUES

Every illness state that is experienced by a person leads to an evaluation by him of the illness's meaning and/or significance. In this evaluation, the person is believed to use information derived from current and past system values. At any point in time, the person can have more than one illness, each of which initiates an inquiry. Every illness is associated with a set of undesirable features or components. A person is believed to have available a set of dimensions A_i, each consisting of a negative component of illness, that he uses to evaluate illness states. These dimensions apply to all illnesses and can be termed *illness disvalues*. As he identifies and labels an illness state I_i, he also generates a vector of values for each A_i using disvalue units peculiar to him. Disvalues associated with an I_i are arrived at by evaluating the illness in the light of *current* system readings and *recollections* of related happenings that have occurred in the past or that the person has learned about from associations with other persons in his group. The following are illustrative dimensions: A_1 = presumed danger to life inherent in I_i, A_2 = degree of disability associated with I_i, A_3 = degree of discomfort associated with I_i, A_4 = degree of moral discreditation associated with I_i, A_5 = degree of sociopsychological passivity engendered by I_i, etc. To the illness state of Stage 1 is affixed a set of quantities that reflect the *disvalues* associated with the state arranged in vector form (units of disvalue reflect the relevance or seriousness of each disvalue dimension).

STAGE 3: TREATMENT PLANS

Each person is believed to have available a set of unit treatment actions U_i that can be implemented for purposes of combating illness. These treatment actions are products of learning and earlier experiences with illness. The following are illustrative ones: U_1 = home remedy (a), U_2 = home remedy (b), U_3 = modification in dietary intake, U_4 = patented medicine, U_5 = advice of family member, U_6 = advice of friend, U_7 = advice of folk practitioner, U_8 = advice of pharmacist, U_9 = advice of physician, etc. Every illness evaluation leads to the formation of a vector of mutually exclusive *treatment plans*. Each treatment plan T_i is composed of selected unit treatment actions U_i that have been combined in an optimal manner. These plans, in essence, represent the potential treatment responses of the organism and are composed of a compatible and nonredundant series of unit treatment actions, which (on the basis of experience) are judged as potentially efficacious for the I_i. (A treatment plan itself can be visualized as a vector whose entries are specifications of which or how much of the various treatment actions can enter into the treatment of a given illness.) In light of preceding considerations, then, the output or termination of Stage 3 is a set of treatment plans T_i that can be used for treating the illness I_i.

STAGE 4: ASSESSMENT OF TREATMENT PLANS

Each person is capable of estimating the probability that a treatment plan will alleviate a negative component or disvalue of illness. Again, the memory system of the person is believed to furnish the data for these estimates. To the set of illness disvalue dimensions is affixed a vector of probabilities that reflect the likelihood of effectively neutralizing the various disvalues by each treatment plan T_i. The result is a matrix of m (disvalue) rows and n (treatment plan) columns, each entry p_{ij} representing the probability that a disvalue dimension can be relieved by a treatment plan.

STAGE 5: TREATMENT BENEFITS

During this stage the person is believed to compute the potential benefits that can accrue from the various treatment plans. In essence, this entails that the probability matrix of Stage 4 be multiplied by the vector of illness disvalue quantities. The result is a vector yielding the amount of benefits potentially derivable from each treatment plan. In other words, the amount of disvalue that is eliminated by a treatment plan is taken as a measure of the benefit associated with that treatment plan. Each treatment plan is associated with a benefit quantity:

$B_j = \sum_i p_{ij} A_i$ (A_i = disvalue of illness; B_j = potential benefit of treatment plan j.)

STAGE 6: TREATMENT COSTS

During this stage the person is believed to compute the costs associated with treatment. Each person has available a set of cost factors c_i that he uses to evaluate treatment plans. Cost factors apply to all illnesses. Each treatment plan is evaluated with respect to factors such as time lost in implementing the corresponding actions, monetary cost, potential loss of personal control, etc. The costs attributed to each plan are believed to vary and be a function of time of year, resources available, situational factors, social contingencies, etc. Initially, a vector of costs c_i is associated with each treatment plan. These costs are summed, yielding a single quantity C_i for each treatment plan T_i.

STAGE 7: NET BENEFITS OR UTILITY

During this stage, the cost of each treatment plan (Stage 6) is subtracted from the potential benefits that can be derived from each plan (Stage 5). This stage thus yields a vector of residual benefits (or costs). Each T_i is associated with a quantity that represents the amount of overall benefit that can be derived from that treatment plan.

STAGE 8: SELECTION OF TREATMENT PLAN

The person is believed to possess various principles of choice that he can bring to bear in his efforts to combat illness. On the basis of the outputs of Stages 5, 6, and 7 he makes a decision to implement a given treatment plan T_i following a particular principle of choice. The following are illustrative principles of choice: (1) implement T_i having highest quantity in vector of Stage 5 (that is, highest benefits), (2) implement T_i having lowest quantity in vector of Stage 6 (lowest cost), (3) implement T_i having highest quantity in vector of Stage 7 (highest utility). The person also makes a decision to re-evaluate the effects or consequences of this treatment plan at t_{i+1}.[1] Time units here are not necessarily chronologic or metric but are, rather, behavioral. Thus, the expectation about the course of I_i in the light of the T_i that is implemented is what establishes the time unit, that is, when to re-evaluate I_i.

STAGE 9: SETUP FOR RECYCLING

The output of Stage 8 constitutes new information that yields an updated history for the person. Stage 1 is entered after a suitable time lapse (readings from current system values and from the memory system serve as data for the recycling and subsequent re-evaluation).

---

[1] It should be clear that both the computation of illness disvalues and the derivation and choice of treatment plans constitute processes that underlie phenomena ordinarily classified by other means. For example, concepts such as *sick role* and *patient role* refer to behavioral regularities that are contained within the more abstract notion of illness behavior as this is defined and modeled in this chapter. Such typological concepts are useful for the planning and execution of empirical studies dealing with the factors influencing the use of care facilities and for social analyses in general. Our interest here is different and involves formulating the dynamic, processual, and changing aspects of illness behavior.

Evaluation of the Model

A model of illness behavior has been presented. The kinds of information that are relevant to the person and considerations that need to be dealt with during the illness-medical treatment cycle have been given principal emphasis. In an abstract way, such a model portrays the way persons might be expected to behave during an occurrence of illness. In this section, we will examine how such a model might be used; the value that it would have in comparative studies, the accuracy of the model, the information needed for its implementation, and the likelihood of obtaining this type of information directly will be reviewed. In the next section I will summarize briefly a study currently underway, which was designed to evaluate empirically factors that correlate with critical treatment actions that are taken during illness occurrenes. That study, in short, aims to test in an empirical way some of the features of the model that was just presented.

LOGICAL AND STRUCTURAL LIMITATIONS

The model, as we have seen, borrows heavily from economics and elementary decision theory (Miller and Starr 1967). In this regard, the basic assumptions are that illness is undesirable, that illnesses are apprehended as discrete occurrences by means of a special language or taxonomy of illness, that persons are rational, that they will evaluate an instance of illness using economistic or utility considerations and reach a decision regarding the best or optimal action that might eliminate the illness (given the constraints or contingencies). Key reliance will be seen to be placed on the concept "illness," since its definition stipulates the property of undesirability or negativity. Persons, in other words, are assumed to prefer illness-free states. The model simply does not apply to those persons (or groups or cultures) who actually favor or deny the existence of illness altogether and who may disregard all such altered biologic states that we might term disease using external Western criteria. Second, the model is not particularly useful for explaining the behaviors of persons or groups for whom illness is a global, undifferentiated state that invariably produces similar and repetitive actions. For these, no complex and differentiated decision-making procedure accompanies illness, and hence Stage 1 (Illness Recognition) would simply be followed by habitual and mechanical behaviors. Similarly, if decisions associated with illness depend on purely random, idiosyncratic, and externally determined happenings (for example, dream content, atmospheric changes, cloud formations, judgments of outsiders, and purely chance happenings), the model's logical structure is not entirely applicable. In this instance, we would have to assume (or postulate) that a range of culturally specific situations gives rise to certain illness types, each of which has associated priorities or alternatives, which, however, depend on purely external contingencies for their resolution. To evaluate the predictability of these, empirical studies would be needed. In other words, the stages following illness definition and preceding that involving the actual selection of a treatment action would need to be formulated less precisely and systematically. Finally, the model is not useful in those instances when illness recognition or evaluation has no logical relation to illness treatment. (Further problems of a logical nature are discussed in a later section on measurement limitations.)

Illness behavior as here modeled bears a resemblance to what is discussed in the psychological literature as risk-taking behavior (for a review, see Slovic 1964). An illness can certainly be described as a situation of uncertainty that is associated with risk or the chance of loss. It differs from situations ordinarily studied by psychologists (like gambling) in that it is a common and repeatable exigency that persons and groups are forced to cope with and for which they have developed more or less explicit plans. It is these socially and culturally organized ways of dealing with illness that the model attempts to represent and offer a way of studying. One cannot, of course, exclude the fact that individual differences in risk-taking propensity (seen as features of personality) are additional factors that operate during illness. The application of this model in field studies would allow estimating the extent to which this is the case.

INFORMATIONAL OR CONTENT LIMITATIONS

Illness Recognition and Labeling The model is broad in its interpretation of illness states, allowing a variety of changes to be affixed with the label "illness." In our own culture, for example, headache, "hangover," overweight, or heart attack would qualify as instances of illness, thereby generating an evaluation cycle. The model also allows for constant monitoring and relabeling of illness states. What begins as a simple headache, for example, may in a short span of time be termed a different illness with the addition of fatigue or nausea. A relabeling of an illness state, in essence, becomes a new illness (with special memory correlates in the recent past) that generates a new evaluation.

A model such as the one outlined would have greater analytic and empirical value if it could be used in conjunction with or made dependent on a finite set of diseases or illnesses that are likely to be identified and measured reliably in all cultural contexts. In light of considerations discussed in the previous two chapters, this means that the value of the model would be enhanced if it could be used in conjunction with frameworks of disease that are systematic, exhaustive, universal, and easily implemented. To elaborate on this point let me first emphasize here once again that the model that was reviewed deals with *illness behavior*— what persons do about illness in the way of treatment or the seeking of relief. The model posits the existence of a native *taxonomy* that members of a group use to label or name particular occurrences of illness or disease. These occurrences when labeled become specific taxonomic types or what we have earlier referred to as folk illnesses. Such a taxonomy is based on native, culturally specific criteria of illness. A reason for developing a model of illness behavior is to have a device that can be used productively in comparative studies, that is, that will enable investigators to compare how different groups deal generically with disease or illness. The model that was articulated, were it to be used comparatively, could lead to a statement such as the following one: In Group 1 an illness occurrence is labeled by members of the group as I_{17}^1 and is associated with disvalues, behaviors, and treatment plans analogous to those associated with occurrences that are labeled I_9^2 by members of Group 2. In some sense, then, folk illnesses I_{17}^1 and I_9^2 can be described as similar—they are apprehended in such a way that they yield similar valuations and occasion similar treatments. However, the indicators of I_{17}^1 and I_9^2 may be entirely different. By indicators, I mean operational units that are associated with a particular framework of disease that the investigator brings with him to study illness occurrences cross-culturally. It must be recalled that I_{17}^1 and I_9^2 are folk illnesses or, as was implied earlier, taxonomic types. Occurrences of illnesses labeled as taxonomic types are presumed to possess various manifestations, components, and/ or characteristics, and it is these that the investigator focuses on in his effort to classify the occurrence as a *disease type*. Indicators of disease, then, should refer to observables and allow the researcher to equate a particular occurrence of illness with diseases that are articulated on the basis of his particular framework (see Figure 6.1). If these indicators of the

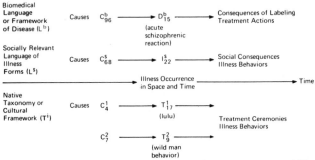

Figure 6.1 Logically separate ways of analyzing an occurrence of illness

folk illnesses I_{17}^1 and I_9^2 were known, then a statement such as the following could be made: In Group 1, a folk illness called I_{17}^1, which is indicated by or composed of Q_1-Q_6 (specific indicators associated with a particular disease framework), is evaluated and treated in the same way as is folk illness I_9^2 of Group 2, which is indicated by a different set of indicators, for example, $Q_{14}-Q_{22}$ (indicators associated with the *same* framework). In brief, illness occurrences marked by the indicators Q_1-Q_6 in Group 1 and illness occurrences marked by the indicators $Q_{14}-Q_{22}$ in Group 2 are associated with analogous valuations and treatment behaviors. Insofar as a framework of disease relies on indicators that reveal essential components of an illness occurrence, an explanation and interpretation as to why folk illness I_{17}^1 and I_9^2 occasion similar valuations and treatments are greatly facilitated by using such a framework in conjunction with the model, since this allows the researcher to pose questions that more directly examine the interplay between biology and culture. In other words, the values, meanings, and implications of particular organismic dysfunctions (that is, disease indicators) can be compared cross-culturally, and hypotheses as to why different organismic changes occasion similar or alternative valuations can be developed, when specifically identified disease entities (as articulated by a particular framework) can be related empirically to folk illness entities and to illness behaviors.

The availability of a framework of disease that is systematic, exhaustive, universal, and easily implemented when used in conjunction with a model of illness behavior also allows a researcher to compare and analyze the way in which a *specific disease* that the investigator marks or identifies by means of his framework is treated cross-culturally. For example, let us assume or hypothesize that a disease, which we will define primarily in terms of physiological behaviors and which consists of headaches, weakness, runny nose, sore throat, and coughing, is *universal* in its distribution.[2] (It should be clear that any of several frameworks for the definition of a disease could be used here. In other words, I could have used behavioral indicators as the basis for articulating a particular disease.) Furthermore, let us assume that occurrences of this disease are always labeled and apprehended more or less as a discrete entity by an individual or by members of a particular sociocultural group j (in this instance it is labeled I_{14}^{j}). Given these two assumptions, then, empirical studies using the model of illness behavior might allow one to compare the way this disease (indicated by the previously specified physiological behaviors) is evaluated cross-culturally and the factors that precede and follow the disease (such as modes of treatment). A review of extant research findings in medical anthropology, however, reveals that this degree of specificity in the way that diseases are evaluated often does not obtain. In a specific sociocultural grouping, the physiological symptom

---

[2] I should make explicit here a matter that bears on considerations alluded to in the preceding two chapters. That is, that *certain* organismic changes may approach what we would wish to describe as *universal indicators of illness*. I also referred to this directly in Chapter 3 when I mentioned the need for "visible" biobehavioral anchoring points that the investigator can focus on in order to uncover the native bases for marking and classifying folk illnesses. For example, seizures, vomiting, certain types of pain, and bleeding from various bodily orifices may be regarded as abnormal (that is, as indicators of illness) by most peoples. The interpretations given these indicators will of course differ, as will the illnesses that may be elaborated around them. The human body, in short, is to varying degrees a fixed entity with regard to its structure and physiological functioning, and we are led to believe that when it "breaks down" we have available only a limited number of ways in which we can recognize this, and some of these ways or manifestations may be to some extent universally seen as undesirable.

complex described might be termed on one occasion I^j_{14}, on another I^j_{95}, on another I^j_{25}, etc. In other words, any one symptom complex (which we have here specified as a disease by means of a suitable framework) may generate different taxonomic labels on different occasions, since for nonliterate peoples and many lay persons criterial features of an illness appear not to be clearcut symptoms. Furthermore, this symptom complex if encountered in a different cultural setting (k) is likely also to occasion varied responses (that is, it might be labeled I^k_7, or I^k_{16}, or I^k_{96}, where k now refers to an entirely different native taxonomic system). It is thus most difficult to compare cross-culturally how specified diseases are treated or evaluated since the bases for native forms of treatment are folk illnesses (derived from folk taxonomies), and these may bear little correspondence to disease types that the investigator articulates or categorizes on the basis of a particular framework of disease. Folk illness labels often seem to be applied in a random, haphazard manner, and public, observable features of an illness occurrence seem unrelated to this labeling process, although our lack of suitable means of coding illness occurrences in field situations using public and cross-culturally relevant indicators may account for this impression. If we could independently classify in a refined and precise manner each instanciation of a folk illness, we could begin to study how a particular disease is treated cross-culturally. Consequently, the employment of a universal or culturally pure framework of disease in conjunction with a model of illness behavior would allow the investigator to evaluate in a more refined way just how much variability persons of different cultural groups show when they diagnose and treat specific diseases. In particular, which types of disease occasion variability (at either the labeling stage, disvalue stage, or treatment stage) should be determinable.

To recapitulate, then, comparative use of a model of illness behavior, such as the one outlined in this chapter, requires two things. The first is an externally derived listing of diseases that are mutually exclusive and that are likely to be wide in their distribution (that is, a suitable disease framework). The second requirement is a procedure for equating diseases derived from such universalistic frameworks with folk illnesses as they are specified and defined in the native taxonomies of peoples. (It is these latter illnesses that are basic components of the model herein discussed.) In a tentative manner, one might put forth three independent lists of diseases (or disease frameworks): the classic medical epidemiologic, a biobehavioral, and a purely behavioral, such as the ones outlined in earlier chapters. The first listing of diseases requires specialized personnel as well as specialized diagnostic equipment and, as we saw in earlier chapters, is composed of units or entities that are neither mutually exclusive nor invariant with respect to behavioral consequences. For these reasons, such a listing and its corresponding framework is impractical and least valuable in comparative field studies. The second listing requires the development of an analytic framework and the generation of a typology of diseases composed of units dealing with specific bodily complaints and abnormalities. Insofar as physiological signs and symptoms vary as to intensity, a typology of diseases based on these types of signs and symptoms may need to take severity into account.[3] The last listing of diseases is derived from a behavioral framework of disease and is composed of categories of behavioral alterations. Provided behavior units are made general and abstract, the behavioral frameworks presented in the preceding chapter might be adapted for cross-cultural comparison. Careful recording of components of illness in field settings using external listings or frameworks such as these would yield a precise specification of how diseases are associated with particular native taxonomic labels, and such methods or procedures could then be used comparatively. This would, in essence, allow one to equate an *illness cross-culturally,* that is, specify which disease conforms to a given folk illness in a native nosological system, how it is evaluated and treated by representatives of the cultural group, and which folk illnesses (and treatment

---

[3] The fact that severity as well as other features of physiologic changes and/or bodily disturbances (for example, symbolic significance of body part) need to be taken into account in constructing such a framework of disease means that the standard items that make up the "review of systems" format of a medical history cannot be easily used to develop such a framework. In other words, the common symptoms and signs of disease imperfectly correlate with how people behave during illness and how they treat illness. A goal of cross-cultural sociomedical inquiries is to *compare* aspects of disease at the level of *social behavior.* Thus, a framework of disease should lend itself to field implementation and be focused on phenomena that are close to and bear on social behavior. It is these considerations that underlie the search for and development of a behavioral framework of disease.

plans, etc.) found in other cultural groups are analogous to it. Behavioral disease frameworks, in short, allow applying and testing the model that was proposed by means of comparative studies in order that broader explanations or theories might be developed. In the long run, such comparative studies of medical problems when supplemented by material involving social organization and cultural ecology would enable understanding the reciprocal influences between sociocultural happenings and the functioning of a group's medical care system (see Chapter 9).

Illness Disvalues Our assumption here is that each illness state is associated with undesirable characteristics (termed *disvalues*) that are threatening, objectionable, and otherwise unappealing to the person. The possibility that illness may be defined and hence labeled on the basis of these disvalues is not excluded, although for analytic purposes a logical distinction is made between illness labeling (that is, taxonomy) and illness disvalue determination. One requirement for cross-cultural application of the model is a comprehensive listing of illness dimensions that represent the "costs" or liabilities of illness. Several such listings can be suggested: we have already mentioned discomfort, disability, danger to life, and moral discreditation associated with illness. To this list, we could add implied loss of one's place in the scheme of things ("social disarticulation"), implied threat to one's living (or dead) relatives ("social communicability"), and implied long-range vulnerability to misfortunes. It should be clear that in using cross-culturally a model of illness having many illness disvalues, only a subset of these disvalues is likely to be applicable in any one social or cultural group. A comparative study might in fact reveal simply the different types of disvalue dimensions that are judged to be relevant with regard to illness occurrences. Alternatively, in using the notion of illness disvalues, we could use simply the amount of lost income entailed by the illness or the amount of general worry and concern occasioned by the illness. It will be seen, then, that what we have termed "illness disvalues" can be described as composed of several distinct units, or, conversely, it can be described as undifferentiated and constituted of only one dimension.

Action Alternatives In order to employ the model in comparative studies, a listing of the alternatives available for treating illness is needed. As in previous requirements, the listing should ideally be comprehensive and contain precisely defined units. In other words, the set of possible actions that can be taken to counteract an illness should be partitioned to yield treatment plans that are disjoint and exhaustive. Thus, an inventory of unit treatment actions would constitute the first requirement. Weightings and/or combinations of these in turn yield treatment plans, and paradigmatic forms of these need to be developed in order to conduct cross-cultural sociomedical inquiries. It is unlikely that these alternative treatment plans will be relevant in all settings, although it might be possible to develop a framework that would broaden coverage by organizing actions in some logical fashion. For example, a category "practitioner consultation" may be made to refer to a visit in one setting to a physician, in another to a shaman, in another to a pharmacist, etc., if there is data indicating that in the various settings these personnel function socially and symbolically in an equivalent manner. Another category, "special medicine," which might refer to preparations recommended by persons outside the family unit but not by a practitioner, may include in one setting a broth of tea and honey, in another an herbal preparation, and in still another a patented medicine. Regardless of whether conceptual equivalence was achieved by means of an analytical framework such as this, application of the model in diverse settings would still allow comparing the way different illness types were treated (for example, whether the rarity of an illness or its degree of disvalue bore a meaningful association with use of specialized personnel). An important feature of the model is its iterative character, since this feature allows one to formulate a research strategy aimed at systematizing the sequence of treatment actions that correlate with various illness disvalues and, as we saw in the discussion of illness labeling, with actual components of illness. A current need in sociomedical studies is such a procedure for retrieving and specifying the sequence of treatment actions and the patterning of medical care alternatives as these are actualized during illness occurrences.

A suitable listing of action alternatives would be needed in order to establish by means of field studies the cost and presumed efficacy of each action alternative. Problems associated with measuring such items as disvalues, costs, and utilities will be dealt with in the next section. With regard to the presumed efficacy of an action alternative, we are referring to subjective probability, that is, how likely it is that a specific treatment plan will produce a significant relief in a specific disvalue. This requires careful delineation of illness episodes and treatment alternatives and an inquiry process yielding culturally specific probability estimates for each illness-action pair. Issues discussed in the section on logical and structural limitations of the model are obviously relevant here, since it may well be the case that treatment alternatives are not selected and used on the basis of strict notions that involve probability of relief, although we assume a priori that actions are aimed at counteracting effects of illness or factors that contribute to the worsening of illness (Fabrega and Manning 1972b).

MEASUREMENT LIMITATIONS

If we assume that illness occurrences are associated with economistic evaluations, we are left with the problem of establishing units of measurement with which to test the model in field situations. Measurement, it will be recalled, is involved with regard to illness *disvalues, costs* of treatment actions, and *probability* estimates of how likely these actions are to relieve the various disvalues. Some illness disvalues can be conceptualized as constants, others as variables, which can change with respect to intensity (for example, pain) and can depend on social factors (for example, incapacitating illnesses can be more costly during harvest time). Thus, it is necessary to develop units of disvalue that are meaningful to the organism and that can be easily related to the changeable nature of illness and social contingencies. The problems of measuring utilities in situations of risk taking and in other contexts of decision making are quite complex, and no completely satisfactory way of resolving them has been developed (Cohen 1964, Edwards, Lindman, and Phillips 1966, Kogan and Wallach 1964). We can expect no less of a problem in the case of measuring the negative components of illness and measuring the costs associated with various action alternatives. Clearly, in certain settings some of these costs can be handled using monetary units of exchange, although the values of monetary units are known not to be linearly related to overall value nor comparable when individuals having different resources (let alone life-styles) are considered. At any rate, since these costs are likely to depend on the amount of resources available as well as on social factors, the cost units must be made readily interpretable in terms of situational contingencies. Implementation of the model in its present form also requires some procedure for converting units of illness disvalue into the units of costs for the various treatment actions, since these are summed during an illness occurrence. The simplest way of achieving this would be to employ the same units of measurement in both instances. Last, a measurement problem is posed by the use of the notion of probability that a treatment action will produce relief. Over and above the question of whether probability considerations are relevant from a logical standpoint or how one arrives at these estimates is the question of the *amount of relief* that can be expected from a treatment plan or that will be counted as "significant," as well as the amount of *time required for such relief.* Even if the question of amount of relief were to be related logically to the issue of probability (for example, *total relief* of disvalues A_i by action T_j means $p_{ij} = 1$, no relief means $p_{ij} = 0$), the problem posed by the time factor remains and would need to be dealt with in some systematic fashion. One way (the one followed here) is to allow the subsequent evaluation of the illness to take place when the memory system of the organism dictates that relief from the plan implemented should be forthcoming. In this way, the question of *when* relief can be expected is condensed logically with that of *amount* of relief and incorporated iteratively within the model.

It should be evident that in using the model in various settings the size of the various quantities—for example, disvalue units—in any one group or the relative differences in these quantities cross-culturally will furnish information of only modest theoretical usefulness, since it is unlikely that scales will have cross-cultural applicability. It is when one compares *across* cultural groups the relative importance of each scale's dimensions that more powerful analytic insights are likely to be gained. In other words, differences in the way groups construe the burden or cost of illness may be more directly reflected when disvalues or cost *rankings* are compared.

Empirical Application of the Model
The model as stated is designed to offer an abstract explanation of ill-

ness behavior. We have seen that direct use of the model in its present form is problematic, since the associated variables are difficult to specify and operationalize in a precise way. At this stage, the model can be used as an analytic device to plan empirical studies of illness behavior and to organize the data obtained from such studies. Suitable analyses of the resulting data should yield empirical estimates of key variables of the model, in particular, the frequency with which various treatment actions are taken during the illness-medical care cycle and the factors that correlate with such actions.

Figure 6.2 is an "illness graph" that I am using to collect information about illness occurrences among a panel of families residing in the city of San Cristobal de las Casas in Chiapas, Mexico (see also Chapter 8). Various competing medical traditions and associated care systems prevail in this setting—modern, spiritistic, herbalistic—thus providing a rich opportunity for investigating the dynamics of illness behavior. Each column of the figure designates a day within the two weeks preceding the interview, with the last column on the right representing the interview date. The purpose of the illness graph is to provide a means of recording the components of and treatment responses to all family-centered illnesses that have occurred during the two weeks preceding the interview date. The task of the interviewer is first to establish which family members have been ill. If there have been illness occurrences during the time interval, the interviewer then focuses on each occurrence and records the location and extension of the illness. This is done by inquiring about the components and treatment actions associated with the illness and "entering these" in the appropriate location on the illness graph. These "illness dimensions" are listed in Table 6.1 The capital letters in the figure designate the different types of dimensions. The items of information in this figure represent the answers given to questions actually asked of the female head of household about each illness occurrence. Most of the dimensions evaluated can be viewed as undesirable behaviors or symptoms that become manifest or "added" during the occurrence of illness. The interviewer records the positive answers to probes about these symptoms in the respective columns, each of which represents a day. Numbers 10 and 11 in Dimension D represent role behaviors of children and adults, respectively.

Table 6.1 Illness Dimensions

A. Severity
1. slightly sick
2. sick
3. very sick
4. gravely sick

B. Family Response to Illness
1. worried
2. angrily disturbed
3. ashamed
4. deeply concerned

C. Medical-Physiological Symptoms
1. cough
2. sore throat
3. weakness
4. abdominal cramps
5. fever and chills
6. dizziness and lightheadedness
7. headache
8. diarrhea
9. vomiting
10. chest pain
11. earache
12. shortness of breath
13. loss of appetite
14. rhinorrhea
15. nausea
16. low back pain
17. generalized aches and pains

D. Behavioral Changes
1. complained of discomfort
2. acted disoriented
3. stayed in bed
4. was restless
5. ate less
6. was irritable
7. avoided talking, wished silence

8. slept a great deal
9. stayed home all day
10. (children only)
  a. didn't go to school
  b. didn't feel like playing
  c. cried a lot
11. (adults only)
  a. did not meet religious obligations
  b. did not meet parental obligations
  c. did not (or could not) give advice to friends and relatives
  d. was unable to work outside of home
  e. did not do usual household chores
  f. was unable to meet responsibilities as a spouse
  g. was unable to pursue leisure activities

E. Treatment Actions
1. used medications available in the home
2. used standard herbs
3. sought family advice
4. sought advice of friends
5. sought curandero
  a. office call
  b. household call
6. sought additional curandero
  a. office call
  b. household call
7. went to pharmacy
8. went to federal health clinic
9. went to social security clinic
10. went to state health clinic
11. consulted private physician
  a. office call
  b. household call
12. consulted additional private physician
  a. office call
  b. household call

The illness occurrence depicted in Figure 6.2 began approximately eleven days prior to the interview date, lasted five days, was associated with the indicated reactions, symptoms, and role constraints, and

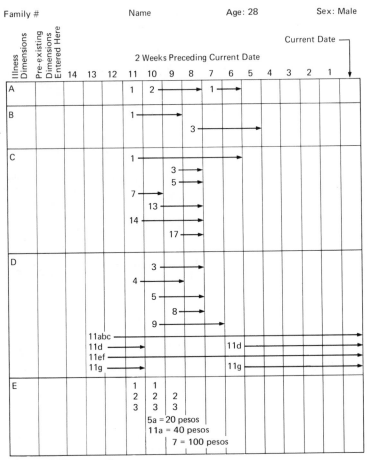

Figure 6.2 Illness graph

prompted the family on the second day to visit a curandero and then a physician (which cost them twenty and forty pesos, respectively) and finally, on day three, the drugstore (which was associated with an expenditure of one hundred pesos). Various household remedies were also used initially.

Repeated interviews with members of the panel over a sufficiently long time will yield a corpus of illness occurrences in adults and children of various ages. An initial baseline survey questionnaire administered to each family prior to illness occurrence evaluations provides relevant demographic and sociocultural information (social class, economic status, degree of acculturation, size of family), which will be used inductively to predict illness occurrences as well as associated illness behaviors.

The study thus furnishes several types of information that will allow specifying the following: (1) baseline demographic, sociocultural, and sociopsychological variables, which the literature suggests are related to illness occurrences and illness behaviors; (2) the family's general valuation of specific illness occurrences; (3) physiologic and behavioral correlates of these occurrences; and (4) actual treatment actions taken during the illness. I feel that analyses of this information will allow clarifying traditional problems tied to health services research. It will also yield a preliminary empirical articulation of issues dealt with analytically by our model, namely, (1) illness disvalues, (2) frequency of treatment actions (a form of probability estimates for these actions), (3) treatment plans (profiles of types of actions that are taken across time for various illnesses), and even (4) a sociomedical enumeration of illness types. Subsequent, more refined studies can be undertaken, which will include probing in greater depth aspects of decision making during illness. In this manner it should be possible to specify more precisely features of the analytic model described in this chapter.

Some Implications of Developing a Model of Illness

In earlier sections of this chapter the need for developing an abstract formulation of illness was discussed in relation to current activities in the subdisciplines of medical anthropology and medical sociology. Briefly, representatives of these disciplines who study medical problems rely, on the one hand, on a relativistic view of illness in which native perceptions, values, and medical categories hold sway. This particular view of illness is necessary and highly important in order to link medical happenings with exclusively sociocultural processes and events. However, a relativistic position has proven not to culminate in a systematic formulation, let alone theory, of how illness and medical care are structured cross-culturally and how these essentially medical concerns influence and express general sociocultural processes and happenings. The result has been a host of descriptive and highly specific analyses of medical problems in relation to the functioning of particular sociocultural units, but no theoretically incisive general picture of how illness and medical care are related to cultural dynamics or evolution has emerged.

A contrasting view of medical problems that is adopted by social scientists is the one underlying studies in social epidemiology and human biology. These sociomedical studies, which rely on a biomedical view of disease, have led to important findings in medicine, findings culminating in a more refined understanding of disease causation, prevention, and control. However, for those interested in studying the behavioral correlates of disease, an exclusively biomedical view of disease has disadvantages. These disadvantages are that biological disease categories are neither homogeneous nor stable with regard to their behavioral correlates, and furthermore, the categories on the whole are not mutually exclusive. This means that since biologically defined diseases vary in their implications, and since persons can be classified simultaneously in several ways, much redundancy and lack of precision will characterize statements about behavior that are made on the basis of this biomedical framework. In short, although social scientists employing a biomedical framework of disease have contributed importantly to an understanding of factors related to disease causation and distribution and to general social issues related to medical care, they have not sufficiently individuated the nature of their work and helped develop a view of illness and medical care that is anchored in social categories. A consequence of this is that a social formulation or theory of illness and medical care contingencies has not been realized. A model of illness behavior such as the one proposed in this chapter may help in efforts aimed at linking the study of medical problems with sociological concerns.

An obvious practical and pedagogical use of such a model of illness is to make explicit social correlates of disease that need to be evaluated for the effective treatment of disease. Succinctly stated, disease and illness are terms having varied meanings and referents. In most instances we must assume that the social and behavioral correlates of disease are critical since they promote the linkage that the sick person or potential consumer of health services has with the medical care system. Just as a definition and indication of what a disease or illness state represents in a specific instance can be seen as varied and complex, so must the plans for rectifying or modifying that state be judged as multifaceted. Quite obviously, the full management or treatment of a person who is diseased requires evaluating and modifying his behaviors, and this is facilitated by paying attention to the various informational components that underlie and guide this behavior. Thus, both the *effects* of the disease and its *implications* can be evaluated using the various parameters outlined in the model.

Part **III** Potential Contributions of
Sociomedical Study

Chapter 7 — Disease Concepts and the Organization of Medical Care

In Chapters 1 and 2 we reviewed some of the substantive findings and underlying assumptions of studies that examined the relations between, on the one hand, states variously classified as disease or illness and, on the other, processes or happenings that can be termed social and cultural. A critical posture was taken toward these studies, and some of their deficiencies were noted. Implicit in this review was the belief that a multidisciplinary, multileveled approach was needed if we hoped to gain a refined understanding of the nature of disease and its relations to environmental factors. Further deficiencies and limitations of studies that involve the relations between disease and sociocultural factors were discussed in Chapter 3. Perhaps as a result of this broad and interconnected view of medical matters the ontological status of "disease" was made to appear problematic, and a general frame of reference designed to orient the reader to alternative conceptualizations of disease and its relation to sociocultural happenings was presented.

In Chapters 4 and 5 we retraced our steps somewhat first by attempting to isolate fundamental generic properties of disease and then by arranging the multiplicity of substantive factors associated with disease in logically independent and self-contained frameworks. One way of separating out matters impinging on and interconnected with disease was to make explicit the various sorts of things that to varying degrees are implicated when physicians, psychiatrists, social scientists, and lay persons speak of "disease." During our efforts to fill in the analytic gap regarding behavioral correlates and modes of viewing disease, we touched on some of the advantages and disadvantages of employing behavioral frameworks of disease in an independent manner.

In Chapter 6 I presented a tentative descriptive model of illness behavior and indicated that application of such a model represented one way in which to investigate relations between disease and social factors. When used comparatively in various cultural settings, the model might facilitate the development of hypotheses about society-medicine interrelations, particularly if used in conjunction with a device for recording the manifestations of actual illness occurrences (for example, the various frameworks of Chapters 4 and 5). However, an analysis of the requirements of the model of illness behavior, together with an appreciation (alluded to in Chapter 5) of the difficulty of implementing disease frameworks, led me to emphasize the preliminary nature of these formulations.

In this chapter I will attempt to discuss some of the implications that conceptualizations of disease have for the way in which medicine is practiced. It is a truism, of course, that conceptualizations about disease have important social implications. Medicine, an institution of society, is defined in terms of its concern with disease. The very definition of disease, as I have implied, is a product of historically determined *social* happenings. Medical activities, thus, are rooted in socially structured categories. In addition, since definitions of disease seem to entail the phenomena of human suffering, consequences of medical activities bear directly or indirectly on the lives of members of society. So central and basic is a concern with disease in the minds of persons tied to medicine that, quite often, the meanings and logical properties of the term *disease* are taken for granted or left unexamined. Developments in contemporary society have brought into focus the organization and delivery of health services and challenged traditional medical orientations and goals. Problems involving the distribution and quality of medical care have been emphasized. Many of the problems that have been raised can be seen as reflections and even outcomes of the meanings of key medical terms, especially *disease*. It will prove instructive to examine these problems in medical care by relating them analytically to the concepts of disease reviewed earlier.

The Organismic View of Disease
To begin with, let me say that it is tempting to hypothesize that an absence of generally shared necessary *and* sufficient conditions for the proper designation of someone as having a disease or being diseased constitutes a key and determining reason for the problems associated with medical care delivery and practice. In other words, efficient and smooth functioning in a society's medical care system might be said to require that there be consensus about what disease "is." Clearly, other factors are involved in such smooth and orderly functioning. The demand for medical care should be matched by the supply available, and resources

should also be properly allocated. Yet in the absence of a clear consensus about what disease "is" there may be problems and disarticulations despite the fact that resources and expertise may be plentiful. Thus, I submit on a priori grounds that much of the confusion and social disarticulation involving the delivery of medical care is a consequence of ambiguities centering around what disease is and how it should be treated. One observes this conflict in primitive societies that are undergoing social change and in more complex and modern ones such as our own where, as I have implied, discrepant and contradictory definitions of disease obtain. These considerations argue for the need to work for a clear formulation or definition of disease. Sociomedical analyses (see Chapter 9) should thus be aimed at isolating the necessary and sufficient conditions that enable specifying what disease "is." The generic definition offered in Chapter 4 (that is, a temporarily extended undesirable deviation from both personal and group norms in the value of a characterization of a person) may serve as a useful starting point. Examinations of contrasting definitions (across time and cultures) are likely to be useful. It should be emphasized here that there is nothing unusual or unprecedented about conducting such a search for a refined definition of disease. Disease is and always has been a socially created entity, as our preoccupations with various cutoff points, norms, and research problems in general should make very clear.

In earlier chapters several independent frameworks for describing disease were reviewed. It was suggested that each framework could be used exclusively, thus enabling the grouping and description of phenomena having medical import. The first framework (see Chapter 4) represents the current biological approach to disease. The remaining frameworks, based on disease considered as a behavioral category, draw upon the findings of social scientists and also take into consideration the way actors in contrasting sociocultural units define and classify disease. At any point in time, a person or organism may be said to be normal or diseased in terms of any one or all four of the frameworks. *Although independent and logically self-contained, the frameworks are alike in three principal respects.* First, the unit of categorization is a discrete point in space, namely, a person or organism. Second, the frameworks suggest that disease is a qualitative state; that is, a particular instance of disease is described as if it were discontinuous or temporarily bounded. And third, implied is the view that disease is an undesirable state insofar as it constitutes a deviation and can be a source of human misery and suffering. These three properties, then, tie the previously described independent frameworks together. The fact that the frameworks share the three properties leads to their being easily confounded. At the same time, however, social processes and activities having medical import can be set in motion precisely because a measure of consensus across disease frameworks is allowed by the properties described. In large part because of its antiquity and conformance to common sense notions about illness, behavior, and how the body functions, the view of disease reflected by these shared properties and implied by the frameworks—namely, that disease is an undesirable person-centered deviation or discontinuity of some sort—appears implicitly to be used by many patients and medical personnel. This view of disease will be termed *organismic*.

Certainly it appears to be the case that the organization and functioning of the medical care system have heretofore been predicated on this traditional organismic view of disease. All persons appear to seek care when they or their immediate fellows reach a judgment that an undesired state or deviation exists. In some instances this discontinuity is judged impersonally and strictly physically, while at other times it is seen as highly personal and private, as well as interwoven with social matters. However, facilities and personnel are invariably spatially separated from the social group and located in settings designed to emphasize their distinctness and separation from regular social happenings; treatment is episodic and focused on discrete problems; payment is tied to a specific service aimed to resolve a certain problem; and more generally the implicit and often explicit premise guiding the medical transaction is that there is an endpoint to the concern, to the "disease." Writings of social scientists dealing with the role of the person who is sick have emphasized the activities and responsibilities of the patient to work to get well, to cooperate with the physician's efforts to terminate the "state of illness" (Parsons 1951a). Woven into the fabric of medical care and practice, then, appears to be the view that disease is person centered, temporally bounded, and discontinuous. On the other hand, medical care *could* be conceptualized analogically as if it represented health surveillance with physicians seen as supervisors, transactions as elements of a continuous monitoring process, and payment as rent or investment. If this model were followed, many of the features of present medical care delivery would be structured differently. An organismic view of disease with its emphasis on boundedness and separation, then, promotes a discrete and segmental approach to medical care that requires an episodic focus and encourages the practice of fees for service and a concentration on salient and describable deviations.

Problems of Present Health Care Systems

Many of the present problems in health care and its delivery may be traced, at least in part, to problems stemming from the dominating influence of an organismic conception of disease.[1] As implied previously, an episodic view of disease indicates episodic treatment and militates against the comprehensive and continuous evaluation that some patients require. When the disease "appears" as defined by a set of symptoms, the person may then seek help, have his discomfort validated, and pay for it on the basis of a completed service. The patient, of course, seeks help for what he judges or suspects is a discontinuity (that is, a "disease") of some unspecified sort. However, the way in which medicine is practiced and medical care structured is premised not only on the proposition that diseases are biological entities but also on the assumption that differences between diseases exist. Segmenting the body and its problems in terms of a biologistic framework has the effect of fragmenting services and can also relegate more general concerns to an ancillary status, blurring the boundaries of the physician's responsibilities. The patient's felt discontinuity, which is often unitary and lodged in an alternative framework, may be left out of focus.

These issues when magnified and concentrated account in part for the dilemmas surrounding the management of the "problem" patient. Patients may unwillingly attract this label by conflicts with the physi-

---

[1] The assumption that a formulation about disease contributes in part to problems of medical care and practice in no way minimizes the contributions of other factors to these problems. Economic, transportation, and structural factors, for example, can obviously contribute to problems in medical care delivery independent of any conceptual issues.

cian in the course of negotiating an illness diagnosis or by the sheer persistence of their needs (Balint 1957, Fabrega, Moore, and Strawn 1969, Von Mering and Early 1966). Factors that seem to lead to many of these specific difficulties in patient management are similar to those already alluded to involving differences in medical orientations. The "problem" patients tenaciously hold on to their conviction that they have a disease despite a medical workup that fails to demonstrate a bodily abnormality. The problems *posed* by these patients can be seen as consequences of the combination of essentially conflicting frameworks within an organismic view of disease. The individual, feeling disarticulated in a social or psychological sense, concludes that he is diseased. The physician, relying on a different framework but on the same organismic conception of disease, cannot validate this label. A referral to a psychiatric clinic can often accomplish professional validation. Motivationally oriented psychiatrists, on the other hand, may view this type of patient as "displacing" or "converting" his psychological problems onto the body ("somatizing"), perhaps as the result of "cancer phobia." The emphasis here is often on the "anxiety" that is expressed in or as bodily preoccupations. Sometimes the term *somatic delusions* may be employed. The possibility that the "symptoms" of the patient may represent his naïve attempts to fuse contrasting orientations is not entertained.[2] In these instances, then, it is not the "existence" of a person-centered discontinuity that is at issue but instead the framework that should be adopted to label it.

A great deal has been written about the impersonality of the physician, his alleged disinterest and detachment, his tendency not to "care" about his patient. Criticisms state that a physician, instead of seeing a person in distress, tends to see a mechanical and isolated body or ma-

---

[2] The validity of psychoanalytic theory is not being questioned. Quite obviously, the application of psychoanalysis to medical problems has led to significant insights regarding the mechanisms of disease. However, the use of psychoanalytic formulations in dealing with patients unaccustomed to this manner of conceptualizing phenomena that are believed to be implicated in the disease process requires great skill and tact. Working-class patients, for example, typically persist in formulating their medical problems using the language about the body, and it is frequently necessary to learn their perspective about the "disease" needing resolution before therapeutic gains can be made.

chine that is abnormal. Since alleviating human suffering is currently viewed as a principal goal of medical activity, then it inescapably follows that physicians need to concern themselves instrumentally with this objective. It should be noted in passing that the conception that disease is or involves suffering often leads to the converse assertion—namely, that suffering is or involves disease. Matters usually labeled psychological, social, or economic have in recent years often entered the sphere of medicine as though they were (or should be seen as) disease. These matters of labeling and definition cannot be merely tossed off as semantic, trivial, or irrelevant, for they are at the root of the dilemmas now confronting the "medical" institutions of society. In one sense, such matters are consistent with what social groups have always done—namely, set standards about what sorts of things are to be *treated* as problematic. From another standpoint, these efforts at labeling touch on fundamental matters involving the hazy boundaries between the biological and the social and bear on the essence of social control. The implications of these particular issues, thus, are currently very far-reaching and cannot be discussed fully at this juncture. We will return later to related themes. However, given that the alleviation of human suffering in a broad sense is seen as a principal feature or object of medical transactions—the so-called "ministerial function" of the physician—then the criticisms about the physician's alleged preoccupation with bodily centered happenings and his tendency to discount humanistic and social concerns quite obviously reflect conflicts in the prevailing view of disease. If we view the language of scientific medicine (particularly the terms, propositions, and directives that follow from a biologistic conception) as a set of symbols to which attach dispositions, attitudes, and other behaviorally relevant prescriptions, then the formalistic and stereotypical aspects of the physician's demeanor that underlie such criticisms seem understandable. An organismic view of disease, when biological issues are given salience, contains a picture or a "construction of reality" (Berger and Luckmann 1967). In this picture the individual who is ill and seeking help often appears as a changed organism. He may be treated as a potential "case," his body searched for abnormalities, and the totality of his humanness subordinated. What assumes importance are his complaints, his pains, his physical limitations, and his habits as they may pertain to his medical (that is, bodily) condition. His relatedness to the world is probed and dissected, not for its humanity, but as part of a "medical history." The stripping down, the systematic reduction of the person and his transformation into a set of diagnostic possibilities, can be viewed as a necessary and perhaps desirable process that enables the precise thinking and rigorous inquiry that constitutes a medical evaluation. My intent here is not to judge the merits of this process but to point out that this particular process conflicts with the processes expected by persons holding other frameworks (behavioral or phenomenological) that are formally comparable to the biologistic view. Stated more succinctly, the reciprocal expectations of physician and patient are mediated by an organismic view of disease, but the underlying frameworks that each participant follows differ, thus creating friction in the transaction. Criticisms about the physician's demeanor and mode of relating, then, can be traced to basic disagreements in the underlying and guiding frameworks that happen to be fused in and concealed by an organismic view. The fact that the various disease frameworks share formal properties allows for the illusion that expectations about conduct and behavior are also shared, when in fact they are not.

Inconsistent interpretations of disease that are obscured by an organismic view, as well as features of this view itself, also account for problems of articulating other types of health services with consumers. The implementation of "preventive" programs is hindered by a consequence of the dominating organismic view, namely, the insistence that diseases are discrete and recognizable discontinuities or deviations. A logical consequence, of course, is the lack of a concept of health that is different from that of "absence of disease." (The paper by Audy [1971] on the concept of health is highly recommended to the reader.) Here, in other words, the view that treatment is directed at disease, an undesirable state that somehow needs to be recognized in order to "exist," proves problematic. The definition of the patient as a person who seeks help for what he judges is a discontinuity clouds the issue of whether, for example, an undetected instance of diabetes is actually a disease or not and whether treatment is required. These issues in turn underlie the confusion that medical students demonstrate when asked if the person with an asymptomatic or "silent" chest lesion "has a disease." Indeed the tendency to see disease as a changed state of the organism accounts in part for the disbelief that persons sometimes experience when, following a routine evaluation, they are told that they "need" an operation or treatment. The implicit premise behind the person's reaction seems to be that, if his body is diseased, he should "know" about it. The organismic view of disease appears to assume that social processes simply funnel or propel patients directly to physicians once they are aware that they "have" a disease; the social rootedness of disease, or, more precisely, the fact that there are different frameworks contained within the prevailing organismic view, is forgotten.

These issues are equally relevant to delays in seeking care and problems in adhering to medical advice. As already mentioned, the organismic view suggests that only identified personal discontinuities require evaluation and attention. The organismic conception also implies that since disease represents an abnormality that is atypical, it may be distinct from the person. This, in turn, tends to militate against openness about and acknowledgment of the body's function, as well as its dynamic relation to everyday situations. In other words, acceptance of the body as a component of the self, a domain that is subject to modification, change, and levels of functioning (which in turn are affected by social and psychological matters) might facilitate attending to its care. One could say that much of the mystery that persons attribute to the body, their tendency to compartmentalize and isolate it and to avoid responding to its needs, may be attributed to consequences of the traditional organismic view, which ascribes to disease features of a discontinuity that is somehow apart from the person. Conversely, it should not be forgotten that the view that disease is somehow separate and atypical may also be an outgrowth of the mystery and fear with which individuals reflect upon the functioning of the body, a heritage stemming from times when the capacity to control its function was minimal. Social meanings about disease and the body, in short, are intertwined, products of historically structured traditions, and frequently at variance with refined views of related phenomena made possible by subsequent intellectual developments. In a similar vein, problems associated with aging, the connotations of death, and the multifaceted problems of "managing" patients with terminal illnesses can be viewed as both determinants and results of these implications tied to and devolving from the traditional organismic view of disease.

It can also be argued that some of the undesirable social and psychological consequences that individuals experience as a result of receiving medical care (that is, having the label of disease applied to them) stem from the properties of the organismic view of disease. The implication of separation, discontinuity, and alteration that this view seems to attach to a disease concept can very often have the effect of promoting in the patient a feeling of being separate, different, and abnormal. The connotation that disease may represent a change in personal identity can promote social withdrawal and lead to new self-definitions that may prove deleterious to the individual regardless of whether the biological correlates of the disease actually interfere with function. Much has been written about the sick role, the set of behaviors and dispositions that are adopted by persons who are ill and that are sanctioned for them by others as a result of illness. In many instances, of course, such roles can be adaptive and actually necessary or inevitable. Diseases that are acute in onset, short-lasting, and accompanied by much distress and disability no doubt require social redefinitions and informal contractual realignments in order to dampen their effects on established social equilibrium and patterns. I suspect, however, that in a number of instances, sick-role behaviors and dispositions can be activated even though they are inapplicable, and, furthermore, that their sociopsychological correlates can prove to be harmful to individuals classified as diseased (and to their families). This may be the case, for example, with the so-called "chronic diseases," which in many ways could be seen merely as involving modifications of habits and psychologic processes, rather than as "disease" as traditionally viewed. Diseases classified as "psychiatric" are known to have pernicious effects that stem from matters associated with social meanings and symbols. To this must be added diseases such as tuberculosis, syphilis, and cancer. Indeed, such attributive forms as "diabetic," "asthmatic," and "epileptic" remind us that relatively common diseases can be associated with, if not the cause of, altered personal identities. The literature dealing with the discrediting and stigmatic effects of disease should be consulted for further details (Goffman 1963).

The point I wish to emphasize is that some of the sociopsychologically undesirable consequences of receiving care stem from features implied by symbolic correlates of the traditional organismic view of disease.

The Linguistic Dilemma in Medicine

We have reviewed briefly some of the problems attending the practice and delivery of medical care, concentrating on the role played by contrasting frameworks of disease or what I now wish to describe as contrasting *languages* of disease or medicine (see Chapter 5). Because there exist different languages that allow us to describe, talk about, and explain disease, and because we often are confused between types of languages, I shall refer to this state of affairs as a *linguistic dilemma in medicine.* In this section I will attempt to outline in a more direct manner some of the sources and consequences of the linguistic dilemma that underlies and reflects problems surrounding the delivery and organization of medical care. For heuristic purposes, it will be useful to formulate more precisely and also more strongly the nature of this dilemma, and to this end I offer the following propositions. (For purposes of brevity, I will fuse all behavioral disease frameworks and will henceforth signify them as sociophenomenologic.)

DEFINITIONS

1. A language (L) is defined as a system of lexical terms and rules that enable man to describe and communicate about phenomena.

2. All phenomena, including persons, can be described by means of specific and different logical calculi, termed *languages,* each of which refers to entities, particulars, processes, situations, changes, etc., that are of the same logical type.

3. The languages of (2) are logically discontinuous and self-contained (that is, the terms of L_j may be equated with those of L_i only coarsely, with difficulty, and in some instances not at all).

4. Entities, processes, and changes that are signified by terms of the biomedical language (L_b) are impersonal and mechanical and are equivalent to those involving complex, nonliving machines (such as clocks, tractors, automobiles, airplanes, thermostats, computers, etc.).

5. Entities, processes, and changes that are signified by terms of the sociophenomenologic medical language (L_{sp}) derive from or are tied (directly or indirectly) to living persons and include an actor's own person and

body, other persons, and social symbols of various sorts (religious, familial, racial, etc.).

ASSUMPTIONS

1. All of the impersonal "things" referred to by terms of L_b (that is, bodily systems) encroach upon and can potentially affect (and/or be affected by) all of the "things" referred to by terms of L_{sp}.

2. Persons communicate (with themselves and with others) by means of a language that includes terms drawn from both L_b and L_{sp}.

3. When communications between or within persons take place by means of terms drawn from L_b, the *process of communication* itself is, to some extent, invested with the significance attached to communications undertaken by means of L_{sp}.

4. Although persons using L_b are allegedly referring to mechanical and impersonal "things," they respond as though the "things" referred to were those of L_{sp}.

With the linguistic dilemma outlined by means of these propositions, it becomes a relatively easy matter to describe and analyze the various problems reviewed earlier involving medical care and practice. People, it would appear, have always conceptualized, experienced, and "related" to disease as though it were a personal, social, and moral matter—that is, by means of L_{sp} and as though the "things" denoted had the significance that are implied by this language and which are inevitably implicated when this language is used. This language (and its various forms) is our fundamental heritage as human beings, and it continues to function in a "primary" way. By this it is meant that man as a social animal *evolved with* a means of communicating about and controlling rather fundamental, existential, and for this reason essentially sacred matters. Languages continue to have this function and effects: that is, to enable us to control a nature that we respond to as mysterious and threatening, to implicate these sorts of things, and to arouse in us reactions and experiences that are personally inciting and vital precisely because of their fundamentally self-preservative character. Impediments, dangers, and threats to life itself (for example, floods, droughts, accidents, antagonists, predators, "disease," etc.) have always contained, by definition as well as empirically, a profound significance for us. Our means of coding and referring to these "things" by the use of L_{sp} have aroused or been associated with direct and almost tangible significance (that is, anxiety, fear, sadness, pain, disappointment) because they threatened vital matters. Natural languages, in other words, arose in the context of and are inextricably linked with matters invested with significance to the person and to the group, and our means of referring to threats to our existence partake of this significance on the basis of two *interrelated* considerations: (1) The language itself initially served to describe personal and group-centered things of importance, and (2) some of the environmental matters to which the terms of the language came to be applied were themselves threatening to the individual and group and consequently also invested with personal and group significance.

The language of biomedicine, however, like all technological languages (for example, those of physics, chemistry, and mechanics), is an "impersonal" language in that the things it refers to and the processes it describes and explains are artifically constructed. In a very real sense, the entities and processes signified by this language are technologically created. Their existence may have been made possible by and contingent upon the personal efforts (and frustrations, pains, etc.) of others, but the ontology or nature of these entities and processes has a secondary, abstracted character; strictly speaking, they exist as logical things, almost as though they were divorced and uncoupled from human (personally inciting) matters. The language of biomedicine is for this reason *in principle* and *fundamentally* an impersonal and abstracted language. Yet since this language (or its terms) can and does serve as a *human language,* as a device by means of which people can communicate with others and with themselves about life-related matters, it partakes of, refers to, and arouses in us very human and personal sorts of experiences. Physicians in their work use L_b to a large extent in a technological sense, but when communicating with patients, they tend to overlook the fact that L_b (or its terms) is being perceived and responded to as L_{sp}. Conversely, patients may use L_b but often seem to mean L_{sp}. Any communication device— more precisely, any communication *between* and *within people*—partakes of these fundamental linguistic correlates, and the use of the biomedical language for these communication purposes continues to have this personalistic and humanistic dimension. Furthermore, the things the language of biomedicine refers to (those abstracted and impersonal entities and processes) are vital to and interwoven with the highly personalized sorts of things ordinarily implicated by the natural languages or what we have termed the sociophenomenologic medical language.

To summarize, then, I assert that human and social problems surrounding medical care and practice are reflected in and perpetuated by (1) the use of the language of biomedicine for communication purposes *and* (2) the use of the categories and entities coded by the language of biomedicine as a basis for the organization and structure of medical practice and care, especially *when* (3) there is a concomitant devaluing of or inattention to the more basic and fundamental sociophenomenologic language of medicine. This is a source of difficulties *because* (4) persons respond to phenomena (including bodily changes, communications about "disease," etc.) on the basis of the personalized categories that are coded by this sociophenomenologic language, *and* (5) we assume that processes and changes that take place in persons, regardless of their level or in which language they are conceptualized, are integrally related. In short, we communicate about disease and organize ourselves to treat it in terms of an abstracted and technologically "artificial" language and lose sight of the fact that social and personal problems are what disease means and always has meant to persons. (See Douglas 1970 for a discussion relating language, symbols, and social relations.) It is thus possible to say that communications about disease and its control take place by means of alternative languages that articulate differing ontologies and which also possess distinctive phylogenies. The problems created by this "linguistic dilemma" underlie and sustain problems in medical care.

Practical Functions Served by a Language of Illness Forms
One way of conceptualizing medical care as it is conducted today is to see in its actualization two fundamental processes: on the one hand, the attempt to alter human conduct—to change another's way of behaving —and, on the other, to comfort (that is, minister to) the person suffering from personal difficulties that are occasioned by or fused with "disease"— that is, to help another person live with, cope with, or adjust to human problems posed by disease. In a rather basic sense, practicing physicians have to get persons to take medicines, agree to operations, acknowledge negatively toned feelings, re-orient themselves to given constraints, re-

turn for a follow-up visit, eat less, check their urine, limit (or increase) physical exertion, etc. Each of these instances, I submit, involves convincing another that a particular new form of behavior is desirable and useful, and at the same time (according to tradition) it often requires that the physician comfort or help another with the personal difficulties occasioned by the realization that the "old" image, identity, habits, or ways are wanting and require modification in the best interests of maintaining one's existence and socially valued entities (for example, resources, leisure, work, etc.). Furthermore, we note that these essentially *sociophenomenologic tasks* are interwoven with persons and in social relations (such as patient-doctor, patient-significant other, patient-boss, patient-self, etc.), and, important to our theme, a particular and natural language (L_{sp}) mediates, captures, and in a sense embodies these entities and processes. Persons interpret and respond to disease in terms of this "language," and in this sense it is correct to say that this language and its domain register what disease "is."

A way to counter the problems stemming from and reflected by what I have termed the *linguistic dilemma* of medicine is to attempt to develop and formalize a language of disease that will in fact mark in a systematic and inclusive manner the altered social and phenomenologic processes involved in disease. To emphasize that such a language will refer to altered behaviors (which include verbalizations and actions) and register what are essentially social matters, I term it, as I did in Chapter 5, a *language of illness forms*. This language is defined as articulating illnesses on the basis of classes of (altered) behaviors that persons show, point to, seek help for, and/or wish to amend. Disease in this language or paradigm then quite literally is constituted by forms of behaviors that persons find undesirable and wish to modify or eliminate or, conversely, judge as desirable and would like to be able to engage in but are excluded from because of various (potentially remediable) conditions. Since the term *language* is used here also in an informal way to signify a communication system, it should be clear that what is required is a set of behavioral dimensions or coordinates on the basis of which one could partition in a formal way and then classify the myriad of specific socially problematic behaviors that persons demonstrate when they judge themselves (or are judged by others) as sick. Such behavioral dimensions or coordinates await development, and the reader should refer to Chapter 5 for preliminary efforts along these lines.

Here I would like to suggest some of the practical consequences that could accrue to the field of medicine were a suitable language of illness forms developed. To the extent that such a language adequately captured the kinds of problems that are posed by disease and that require behavioral changes of a particular class, the language could serve as the basis for the organization and structure of medical care and practice. For example, obese persons wishing to lose weight, persons classified as diabetic who wish to alter their diet, and others termed hypertensives struggling to limit their salt intake, etc., could be treated in one setting or by one type of practitioner, since they may be seen as requiring changes in eating behavior. Persons classified as peptic ulcer patients, others having coronary artery insufficiency, and still others showing what is now termed an irritable colon or early ulcerative colitis may also be "treated" together or using analogous methods and procedures to teach them about their emotional vulnerabilities and help them develop ways of modulating their "affective involvements." These examples are trivial, and the reader should not be deterred from seeing the more important general point: Once a medical diagnosis is accurately made, medical care as now practiced involves the physician in the attempt to change another's way of behaving, commits him to these behavioral tasks, and requires him to support the patient and alleviate the difficulties entailed by the behavioral processes set in motion. The latter set of tasks and processes can be encompassed logically as involving a bounded socio-phenomenologic domain, which can in turn be systematically partitioned and made a basis for types of medical treatment regimens. The reader will discern in this brief exposition that the form of medical care being suggested here entails classifying types of problems in terms of *task requirements* rather than in terms of (biological) disease entities. In other words, the generic changes being sought or implemented, rather than the diagnosis or anatomical entity involved, would constitute the care organizing units. Thus, not only may it be desirable for different biomedical diseases to be associated together vis-à-vis treatment requirements and tasks at a given point in time, but the logic of the rationale also means that the same disease at different points in time or in its several manifestational forms might be placed in altogether different "treatment categories."

To summarize, the preceding illustrates one potential application of a language of illness forms. It should be clear that an incisive logical analysis of behaviors that can potentially *prefigure* disease and/or that *reflect the early phases of disease* could yield a typology or a classification of illness behaviors that could in turn serve as the basis of organizing medical *diagnostic practices*—that is, the settings to which ill persons first turn for help could be organized in terms of relevant sociophenomenologic categories. By drawing attention to these sociophenomenologic matters, rather than abstracted categories such as cancer, tuberculosis, or diabetes, such a classification scheme and its correlated organizational structure would be addressing the principal social and phenomenologic ingredients that persons find problematic about disease, and which often underlie what prompts the initial evaluation. I submit that the availability of such a basis for disease conceptualization, or language, could serve additional practical medical aims, such as providing a means of evaluating the quality of medical care and estimating the social costs and burdens of disease. In short, a language of illness forms represents a formal way in which behavioral facets of disease can be conceptualized for purposes of grounding medical care practices in social and phenomenologic categories. The development and use of such a "language" is thus one way in which the various frameworks of disease could be used practically. Presently, we shall consider another such possibility.

Effects of Narrowing the Meaning of Disease

A theme implicit throughout this book has been that conceptualizations about disease are responsive to, mirrored by, and reflected in social attitudes, values, and perspectives. Similarly, what is done about disease and how it is done bear a systematic relationship to the way in which disease is defined. Specifically, insofar as conceptions of disease underlie and pattern medical practice and care, alternative conceptions present challenges to the underlying basis of the profession and institution of medicine. This underlying basis has been considered a mandate and includes: (1) a fundamental definition of the role of the professional; (2) his ethics, or the norms of practice usually developed into a professional code; (3) the etiquette, or rules about the nature of the client relationship; and (4) a perspective regarding the aim of medical treatment. The mandate of medicine is typically defined as curing disease and maintaining health or, more dramatically, dealing with life and death. In practice, through the mediation of the view of disease we have termed *organismic*, attention seems to be narrowed down to the treatment dimension of the mandate. This narrowed conception is reflected by the location of the physician in individual, entrepreneurial roles, which tie him to the daily demands of his patient population and which require, ironically, that he respond to *their definitions* of disease. As was discussed earlier, some of the problematic aspects of medical care and health services delivery can be seen as stemming from ambiguities, inconsistencies, and current implications of an organismic view of disease. It must not be concluded, however, that the problems that have been linked to an organismic view of disease cannot be resolved in such a way that the advantages of continuing to work with this view of disease are retained. The delineation of these problems is an obvious first step toward their resolution. An important reason for striving to maintain an organismic view, it can be emphasized, is that it does articulate with the rather basic expectations and conceptions of medical consumers. In Western settings and in preliterate settings, common sense notions about the body's function, disease, health, and treatment partake of the view that disease is person centered, temporally bounded, and undesirable.

It is, of course, not the case that all physicians and students of disease generally hold to the conception that disease represents a time-bound, person-centered discontinuity. In the first place, it is simplistic to assume that any one view of disease is shared by all physicians or students of disease. What obtains, instead, are views and perspectives composed of elements that shift and fluctuate according to clinically relevant situations. Nevertheless, to the extent that orientations share general features, it is permissible to use the notion of a general view of disease. The second reason for expecting that medical perspectives are not rigidly dominated by an organismic conception of disease involves the influences that are no doubt being felt as a result of research in the psychosomatic field. In Chapter 4 I indicated that a prevailing paradigm toward disease is the one entertained by systems theorists, namely, the unified view of disease, which admits of many factors. I would like to return briefly to this particular conception.

We have seen that an apparent logical consequence of the unified or systems view of disease is the disappearance of the traditional concept of organism and discontinuity, as well as the notion of separation between systems (see Chapter 4). Stated succinctly, what we respond to or label as "medically" relevant and salient is described as systems that are disequilibrated. However, they are subsystems of larger systems that also are involved in any disease process. An implication of this view of disease might be that practitioners of medicine at the very least must become biological systems experts; yet given the hierarchic, multileveled, and mutually influencing nature of medical phenomena, it would appear that practitioners might need also to become experts in various other areas of knowledge. Clearly, a view of disease that emphasizes holism, interconnectedness, and continuity among "systems" does away with the traditional organismic features that seem to be implicit in the organization of medical practice, and it also broadens significantly the expertise required of the physician. Thus the rigorous application of a unified conception of disease might lessen problems discussed earlier involving the delivery of care, problems stemming from symbolic correlates of an organismic conception. Furthermore, the findings of recent social and cultural studies of disease reviewed in Chapters 1 and 2 would seem to justify the adoption of the unified view of disease.

However, the consequence of institutionalizing a general systems conception of disease would have far-reaching implications for medical practice and education, precisely because its emphasis on hierarchy, holism, and interconnectedness seems to blur the boundaries between types of problems or sufferings. The use of such a unified view in order to organize medical care and practice would appear to raise questions regarding (1) the composition, location, organization, and structure of treatment and/or prevention units; (2) the significance and role of persons administering medical care; (3) the nature of the information base required of such persons; (4) the actual processes of diagnosis and administration of care; and (5) the linkage of the preceding with the remainder of society's institutions. To reiterate, since reversibility, modifiability, and compensability are hallmarks of the systems paradigm, we are forced to adopt a rather broad or inclusive view of what medicine and disease encompass. The systems view thus appears to require that equal emphasis be given to all the components or levels that appear to be implicated in an instance of what it terms *disease* as well as to matters currently viewed as external to and separate from disease.

Preceding considerations, when viewed from the pedagogical standpoint, are seen to constitute the core of the argument that prevails today to the effect that physicians, the medical care agents, need to be knowledgeable in and responsive to all facets (social, behavioral, biologic, phenomenologic, etc.) of disease. In other words, if disease is seen as having its "causes" and manifestations embedded in various systems, attempts to prevent, control, or treat disease would seem to entail understanding of how systems function and interrelate so that judicious interventions can be effected. An inescapable conclusion is that physicians need to be trained in the social as well as in the biological sciences. On the other hand, were one to conclude that the outcomes of such a broad "medical" education rested on fallacious logic, that on empirical grounds it failed to provide the desired products, or that the costs involved (in time, money, etc.) rendered its pursuits invaluable from an economistic standpoint, then alternative emphases in medical education and patterns of service organization might be entertained. We might, for example, consider training different types of experts, each knowledgeable in the functioning of narrowly defined systems, and labeling the concerns that are tied to each "separate" system differently. Let me elaborate on this point.

The way in which a particular conceptualization about disease can relate generally to social phenomena, and specifically to the manner in which medical care and practice are organized and conducted, can be further illustrated by considering in greater detail the strictly biologistic framework that was discussed in Chapter 4. It appears reasonable to believe that, with sufficient time, it might be possible to begin to apply this biological framework in quantitative terms. The application of this particular framework of disease in such a fashion could yield a number or measure, which could be assigned to individuals on the basis of a medical evaluation; such a measure would represent the amount of a "disease" (that is, a disease score) that X has. Indeed, since what is being measured is a continuum underlying any disease process, it becomes more accurate to speak of diabetic scores, hypertensive scores, etc. (For a very lucid analysis of issues related to the point being illustrated here, the reader is urged to consult Israel and Teeling-Smith 1967.) For example, the various "biological" indicators that signal different diseases could each be quantified whenever possible, and on the basis of a suitable formula wherein indicators appear as variables, a number could be computed for each person (not patient). The following form is suggested:

D = "amount" of diabetes = $a_1 Q_1 + a_2 Q_2 + \ldots + a_n Q_n.$

a_i = weighing constants ("how much" each indicator or variable contributes to D).

Q_i = an indicator of D specified in appropriate units.

The use of a biological framework in this fashion would avoid the suggestion that disease is a (qualitative) changed state. Thus, logical problems such as that of "determining" whether X has or does not have D are avoided; since everyone has D, the question becomes how much of D and how the D score can be lowered so as to promote certain desired ends (such as less malaise, less pain, longer life expectancy). If sufficient knowledge were available about the causes of D, its manifestations, its mechanism, and how to modify bodily processes and indicators reflecting or showing D, then treatment plans could also be specified in terms of formulas containing quantitative variables, that is, how much of and how long X needs to take A, how much he needs to do of B, etc. In the long run, the use of this framework in this fashion could lead to the conception that all individuals can be characterized by numbers, each of which reflects the status and level of a biological functioning (embodied conceptually as "disease scores"), which in turn contribute to decrements of desired ends; correspondingly, to each individual would attach formulas or treatment plans. The orientations and values required to support such a view of disease and the social implications and consequences of adopting this conception and manner of evaluating disease would obviously be profound.

A state of human affairs wherein the preceding notions are actualized would probably require a different type of medical consumer, as well as sharp differences in the way that medical care and practice are organized. First of all, it would be important for persons to demonstrate some knowledge about the implications of these disease scores. The body's function would have to be made a relevant area of concern for people, and accurate information about biological matters would have to be made available and, more importantly, desirable. Motivation to maintain scores within acceptable ranges could become a domain of greater personal responsibility if individuals were systematically educated about individual differences in how their bodies function, about determinants of bodily changes, and about the short- and long-range implications of alterations in scores. Provided this attitude was encouraged early in life, systematically, by means of educationally sound procedures and with optimal social values placed on this type of human activity, there is reason to expect that the enterprise could be successful.[3] The result might then be a population of persons, each of whom is interested in and informed about his body's function and the wear and tear that it is subject to and committed to the notion of his responsibility for its care. The management of disease could then become a highly technical, impersonal, and computerized affair. Regular evaluations would provide a profile of score values together with a printout containing a list of modifications in living habits that are required in order to reach particular desired ends. Short-term flare-ups of different "disease scores" might require some form of external supervision and surveillance by technicians or biological engineers skilled and trained in the methods of reducing "elevated" scores. A variety of different types of technicians and engineers can be imagined, all regularly situated in specialized facilities that service bounded population segments. The man-

[3] The use of the word *optimal* in this sentence condenses what needs to be seen as a relatively complex set of notions. To conceptions about the body, its function, its fluids, and its emanations, are attached a variety of values and prudential interests that are incorporated in and form an integral part of routine social prescriptions. Attitudes and orientation toward *disease* are reflected in these valuations and conceptions about the body. A social system that institutionalizes a biologistic conception of disease in the manner outlined would likely require orientations and dispositions toward bodily affairs that are different from those currently reflected in what is termed acceptable discourse and behavior. These new orientations and dispositions would need to be reflected in any educational efforts aimed at changing the prevailing view of disease.

agement of chronic elevations, of course, would be systematically woven into routine daily habits and practices that all persons continually engage in.

Dealing with the emotional and psychological correlates of disease could be retained as a feature of the obligations of the "physician"; this view of the physician's role is highly consistent with the current position of many medical educators and theoreticians. However, this facet of what is currently viewed as a requirement of good *medical* care could be regarded as logically independent of concerns just discussed. For example, social and psychological difficulties that stem from or involve work situations, economic constraints, interpersonal relationships, life cycle adjustments, and the physical constraints and bodily abnormalities associated with disease score changes could be defined a priori as distinctly separate realms of human activity and concern. "Human relationship experts" might be the title of personnel skilled and trained in helping others with these types of problems. The notion that these everyday living concerns (although problematic, painful, and disorganizing to human productivity and social equilibrium) constitute diseases would, of course, have to be eschewed. Disease, to repeat again, would be defined in terms of biological system malfunction and indicated by the type of information reviewed earlier. Insofar as brain changes are capable of effectuating social and psychological changes that mimic typical problems that might confront the human relationship experts, the latter personnel (or subtypes of these) would need to scan computer printouts of their clients in order to define those in need of more specialized forms of help. On the other hand, the visit to these human relationship experts could be made contingent on regular evaluations by the biological engineers.

One consequence of implementing such a system is that it would separate notions that today are viewed as indivisible, namely, that disease involves suffering and suffering involves disease. A premise of the program would be that elevated scores can be associated with human suffering and in fact for this reason need to be closely regulated and monitored. The prevailing view of and orientation toward suffering, however, would be that it represented an affair different from that of disease, and consequently that it needed to be dealt with differently.

Specifically, "diseases" would be treated as strictly biologistic affairs, whereas the sufferings traceable to "disease," together with other types of sufferings, would be seen as altogether different concerns. It needs to be emphasized that the values and traditions that link with and stem from "disease" as it is currently conceptualized and handled could hardly accommodate the separation of services as outlined. The form and expression of disease and its attendant problems, as well as approaches to their treatment, are outgrowths of historical and social contingencies. In brief, the type of problems tied to disease, the anticipations of consumers, and their satisfactions or dissatisfactions with medical care are embedded in formulations of disease that are anchored in social categories. New ways of handling disease and its problems such as those touched on here would for this reason require quite different social contexts (see Parsons 1951b for a background discussion).

The preceding discussion has considered one possible way of implementing disease frameworks. Some of the requirements for and the consequences and implications of this approach have been mentioned, and others can be inferred. The main point of this discussion is that how we choose to define disease can have profound implications for how we go about actually dealing with disease. Our current taxonomy and nosology are outgrowths of our attempts to identify disease and treat it biologically. However, there is no one "natural" meaning of disease. Biomedical diseases are not species in the systematics sense, which ascribes to taxa or categories the status of a group of "real" entities in nature differentiated along phylogenetic lines. Neither is there a powerful theory, such as evolutionary theory, that underlies the current taxonomy of disease (Simpson 1961, Mayr 1970). In the absence of this type of basis for classification, *we are free to adopt conceptions and classifications of disease that prove useful or desirable for different reasons and purposes.* We have seen that a strict or narrow biologistic definition in many ways commits us to viewing physicians as biological engineers and technicians. If this paradigm is followed, then, many of the social and political aspects of the physician's role in contemporary society are eliminated and made the province of others, among these possibly the human relationship experts. Conversely, we could choose to adopt the holistic or unified view of disease expounded by systems theorists. Although this view commits us to an educational and social policy vis-à-vis medical affairs that might be costly, cumbersome, impractical, and difficult to implement, it has the profound advantage that it stems from or is isomorphic with our current refined understanding of the causes of disease and also that it maintains continuity with the traditional functions and responsibilities of the physician.

Contemporary American medicine is currently experiencing a crisis of sorts manifested in two different but related spheres. First, it is becoming increasingly clear that although the technology and expertise for controlling disease is at hand, the means by which these are applied leave much to be desired, particularly among certain sectors of the population (see Herman 1972 for a review). Second, and in large measure as a result of this first point, medical institutions and personnel are broadening their emphases and reaching into the community to deal with medical problems as they are socially situated. A number of instances have been recorded where these well-intentioned though impulsive efforts have been repelled after occasioning much conflict (Cumming and Cumming 1957). In short, we have the technology and knowledge that enable us to control different facets of disease but lack the necessary frame of reference for applying these in a manner that is socially useful. I submit that these considerations, which in part point to deficiencies in the way disease is conceptualized vis-à-vis medical care practices, argue that critical attention must be given to alternative disease definitions and to ways of implementing these as a basis for organizing medical care.

General Considerations

In a society or culture, activities and considerations subsumed under the rubric "medical" have as their principal and fundamental object dealing with disease in a socially productive way. Yet "disease," we have seen, is an elusive, ambiguous, and complex term, which moreover rests on social and historical developments. How the term is defined and consequently what sorts of phenomena are considered to be worthy of predication and hence attention as "disease" are products of sociohistorical arrangements, which include scientific developments. Furthermore, the personnel that societies set apart and empower with the task and mandate of controlling and/or eliminating "disease" have their duties and functions delineated and in turn sanctioned by a socially arrived at consensus, which, importantly, entails a particular definition of what disease is.

The morphology of a modern society's medical institutions and practices and the emphases that guide them are outcomes of fundamental sociobiological changes associated with the processes of urbanization and industrialization. These changes can be summarized as follows: (1) Man as a biological specimen was formed under social conditions radically different from those of modern Western nations; (2) processes described as cultural evolution have culminated in the development of complex social systems and, together with the concomitant growth of scientific knowledge, have allowed man to control the bulk of factors that previously claimed more lives at earlier ages; (3) as a result of (2), more people are able to complete an expanding life trajectory, leading to (4) the prevalence of "diseases" whose control, elimination, and indeed meaning is highly problematic and to (5) an aged and almost by definition diseased population whose function, contribution, or purposes in society are equally problematic; and last, (6) more and more, man is freed from direct and arduous livelihood activities, which, in turn, challenges him to develop ways of finding meaning in nonlivelihood or "recreational" and "leisure" activities. Activities in this domain also, interestingly, become problematic in their own right, and our socially derived medical logic seems to force us in the direction of searching for and finding there as well *new* disease entities. Thus although we may be said to have eliminated many of the diseases common to nonliterate man, we manage to find new ones in our very different and largely self-created world. The question of disease prevalence and incidence in different social systems is therefore highly problematic. This tendency to find and create new diseases, as well as the nature of some of these new diseases, must suggest something about the nature of *social systems* just as much as it sheds light on the nature of the biological genome.

When one examines disease, in many ways one is focusing on a phenomenon that society and its members view as costly and problematic, a phenomenon, moreover, that is, literally, defined for the purpose of its own elimination. In other words, in "disease" we have a *socially con-*

structed entity that we as members of society are in many ways *committed to eliminate and control* by means of our self-created medical institutions. The underlying premises that give form and content to "disease" thus reflect fundamental norms about what is desirable and undesirable, and these norms in a sense articulate and delimit that which we wish to eliminate.

We have seen that contemporary definitions of "disease" inhere in various frameworks and domains, which, although logically independent, are often viewed as empirically interrelated if not indivisible. In some instances we are unquestionably correct in assuming isomorphism across domains or frameworks (or, as system theorists would say, across system levels); some "diseases," in other words, are in fact indicated or marked by discontinuities or undesirable deviations in several if not all of the logically separable frameworks. Often, in basing medical activities and preoccupations on empirical findings lodged in only one "disease" framework, we physicians seem to overlook the fact that these activities can have repercussions elsewhere and hence literally cause human dilemmas or "disease" in altogether separate spheres of social life—dilemmas that, ironically, on the grounds of our medical logic we claim were inevitable or necessary and for which we are consequently not responsible. This occurs, for example, when we misjudge the havoc brought about by a mastectomy, reconstructive procedure, or by the communication of a certain type of diagnosis. At other times, although we address ourselves to phenomena that on empirical grounds are organized by matters of literally only one framework or type, we assume implicitly an isomorphism across frameworks and treat as "disease" a problem of social adjustment or a matter that is merely a personal and private dilemma. The rationale for viewing these activities as medical or disease-centered is often questioned, and it is certainly the case that many of the tasks of society's other institutions are made more difficult and cumbersome by the socially sanctioned processes set in motion by the application of self-created definitions of disease. Recently, under the protection and rationalization of the label "medical" or "disease-centered," society has concerned itself with modifying intrafamily and community issues as well as with the life-styles, attitudes, and value positions of its members. The consequences of these activities, particularly because they are sanctioned as *medical,* form an interesting chapter in the exploration of society's self-constructed medical history and preoccupations.

By concentrating on the logical skeletons of disease, then, one draws attention to fundamental bases for a society's medical activities. In isolating the principal logical "location" of a disease definition that is entailed by a particular medical course of action, one often uncovers explanations and justifications for that action; and by systematically examining the relationship between frameworks or logical skeletons, one is afforded a graphic demonstration of the sometimes unexpected and perhaps unwanted social consequences that devolve from those medical actions. One observes that social consequences of medical actions can be justified by an appeal to considerations allegedly isomorphic to those actions but frequently logically independent from them, sometimes simply because the person undertaking that action has competence and knowledge in the separate sector. By thus emphasizing the historical and social bases of disease definitions, the logical independence of these definitions from one another, and the implications that can follow from or that are implied by the mixing of logical types in this fashion, we may provide for ourselves the conditions for more rationally resolving dilemmas and problems associated with being alive and having to create conditions for survival.

Chapter 8 Ladino Theories of Disease: A Case Study in Psychosomatic Medicine

The previous chapter discussed the implications of definitions of disease for the organization of medical care. Analysis was by and large restricted to matters that are germane to Western, complex, and urbanized societies. This chapter will consider related issues involving disease definitions and theories but as these are exemplified in non-Western groups. A host of different questions and implications about disease definitions are made apparent by such material.

The chapter reviews selected but critical aspects of beliefs about disease and medical care that prevail among Spanish-speaking peoples of the highland region of the state of Chiapas in southeastern Mexico. The material reviewed represents, on the one hand, a theoretical orientation toward disease that is part of the culture and, on the other, an abstract statement of the way feelings and conceptions of individual persons of the area are organized and patterned during actual occurrences of illness. The term *disease,* which, as we have seen, has frequently been used dualistically to indicate alterations of body or mind, in this region is actually used holistically and includes happenings and processes that observers would view as both sociopsychological and physiological. Briefly stated, a nondualistic and integrated theory of disease obtains in this region, a theory that includes reference to emotions, interpersonal relations, naturalistic processes, and bodily changes. The native theory of disease contrasts sharply with that associated with the modern system of medical care. These differences in orientation toward medical problems are a source of difficulty for persons who seek medical relief in the clinics of the city. We shall see that the conflicts between these two logically independent theories of disease raise questions about the study of disease (viewed generically) in more complex and urban societies, questions that are also germane to the theory and practice of psychosomatic medicine. Discussion of these issues will lead to a further illustration of the social and medical influences and implications of prevailing theories of disease. In general, analyses conducted in the chapter should make clearer how medical institutions function and also how changes in social organization and medical practices (and policies) interact as societies evolve.

Psychosomatic Questions and Ethnomedical Data

It needs to be stressed once again that theoretical developments associated with the psychosomatic approaches to disease are typical products of Western biomedicine and as such must be seen as recent outgrowths of a distinct sociohistorical tradition (Ackerknecht 1955, Lipowski 1967a). More specifically, one can say that the study of the mentalistic correlates of biomedical happenings as though these constituted a separate domain is a recent development in the field of medicine, a field that following the social and theoretical revolutions of the 17th and 18th centuries has been closely tied to the growth of Western biological science (for a review of the philosophical presuppositions of biology and its unique concepts and modes of explanation, see Simon 1971). One can trace the unfolding of this attention aimed at linking mind and body functioning in early psychoanalytic writings, and to many, the problems and formulations of "psychosomatic medicine" represent natural and highly creative extensions of psychoanalytic thought (however, see Veith 1965 and Klibansky, Panofsky, and Saxl 1964).

We have reviewed in earlier chapters some of the negative consequences of holding a rigid dualistic position toward disease. Our orientation has been that altered processes we may term disease all have both emotional and bodily correlates. A definition of disease that emphasizes a discontinuity between these types of changes militates against effective treatment. In pointing to the simplicity of the earlier closed and dualistic orientation, investigators have emphasized the theoretical influence of historically bound scientific paradigms such as that associated with developments in microbiology. In the last analysis, however, a society's theory of disease is more than an explanation of how a person changes during a phase of life we may term illness. An orienting perspective adopted here, and one that I hope to elaborate upon later, is that a theory of disease is also like a map or blueprint that provides the outline of what members of a culture accept as real. Theories of disease, then, not only explain but also structure the expectations and behaviors of persons during illness itself, thereby directly affecting the nature of the experiences and manifestations of disease. The contemporary unified or systems view of disease expounded by medical theoreticians is in this sense an outgrowth of observations and inferences made by physicians during the course of treating patients who themselves interpreted and reported their problems within the dualistic mold. It is thus possible to see earlier dualistic notions as providing the necessary background against which the unified perspective emerged.

Examining human dispositions and experiences with regard to disease in a group that is guided by alternative medical orientations, such as that studied and reported upon here, offers the student of disease and human behavior an opportunity to study basic characteristics of how man responds to and copes with stress, just as it affords the possibility of uncovering problematic correlates of our own contemporary framework of disease. Like all historically bound paradigms, this framework constitutes our guiding approach to disease and serves to organize if not constrain our questions and observations (Kuhn 1970). What physicians ask of and look for in patients is determined by our preconceptions of what disease "is." Potentially enriching insights about the nature of disease and human functioning may be anticipated when problems associated with crises, stress, and disordered bodily functioning are probed in a setting such as the one to be described shortly. For here we can observe the operation of an indigenous Mayan approach to disease (which is sociobiologic and nonmental) and its interpenetration with a colonial Spanish culture that largely antedates developments of Western biological science (Foster 1960, Beltran 1963). The material to be described in this chapter, in other words, will examine altogether different approaches to illness and disease, approaches that should prove insightful, since comparative analyses of this material may point to characteristics of human functioning that are tied to and concealed within the prevailing Western biomedical and dualistic mold. In this context, it is notable that workers of the psychosomatic persuasion do not often examine biosocial and psychosocial aspects of disease in non-Western cultural settings.

Although the study of medical problems in nonliterate settings can be seen as a potentially fruitful endeavor from the standpoint of the problems associated with the psychosomatic mode of approach toward disease, our review of the literature of the field of medical ecology and medical anthropology disclosed that investigators all too often ignore this aspect of medical issues. Much of this work, as I have indicated, is of an epidemiological sort, in which the investigators are attempting to delineate the distribution of disease in various social groups. Insofar as the investigator begins his study with a fixed preconception of the disease or diseases he intends to uncover in the field, his framework may be considered closed. He is not likely to look for or notice, much less record, the way in which actual persons experience and orient to the various, complex changes and processes that are associated with an actual occurrence of disease. It is often the case that the investigator does not actually see or talk with the person that may later (after suitable samples of his blood or stool specimens are examined) be classified as a "case." Even the work of recent epidemiologists who are very sensitive to the pernicious effects that a closed-systems approach to disease can have for understanding the nature of disease in human groups manifests little concern for carefully searching for hidden, possibly unique correlates of a disease process. The result is, then, that fixed categories vis-à-vis disease are perpetuated, and the way the persons of the group experience, explain, and orient to the disease process is left out of focus. It is precisely in this latter arena—namely, the domain of bodily sensations, emotions, and cognitions—that the student of disease is likely to find material to enrich the field of psychosomatic medicine. For it is here that the investigator is likely to learn about the reciprocal influences that sociocultural factors have on bodily happenings.

Culturally oriented anthropologists who study medical issues from the perspective of their traditional discipline represent another group of investigators who are potentially able to contribute to an enrichment of the field of psychosomatic medicine. Our review of the literature in the field of ethnomedicine, however, indicated that these anthropologists have been content simply to examine medical issues at the sociocultural level. The deleterious effects that this has had for social science and for medicine generally have already been outlined. Suffice it to say that the bodily correlates of other types of "disease," and by this I mean the physiological symptoms and the way in which these are experienced and evolve through time, have not been described. The guiding assumption appears to have been that at most, social, cultural, and psychological categories merely elaborate upon that which is biologically "given." Physicians and biologists conversant with the literature of psychosomatic medicine can anticipate that the effect that culture has on human disease is more pervasive insofar as the relation between psychological factors and biological happenings is direct and continuous.

Research Setting and Methods

The research was conducted in and around San Cristobal de las Casas, a city of some 33,000 people in the highlands of Chiapas in southeastern Mexico. The city is the commercial, social, and religious center for a hinterland that contains about 175,000 Indians of Mayan descent. Within this geographic setting there are three principal ethnic groups: *ladinos,* who are said to be of direct Spanish descent; *mestizos,* or people of mixed Indian and Spanish descent (these two groups speak fluent Spanish, wear Western clothing, and identify with the values and institutions of the Mexican government); and the numerically dominant (outnumbering the other two by 6 or 7 to 1) but socially subordinate group, the heterogeneous *indigena* (Indian). The characteristics that distinguish the groups are not exclusively genetic or biological but rather social and cultural (wealth, power, education, style of dress, etc.).

The data upon which part of the report rests were gathered by means of a technique of ethnographic investigation and description that is current in anthropology (Tyler 1969). The procedures employed were largely those of systematic elicitation from informants and can be briefly characterized as directed toward discovering native-language questions that regularly and successfully constrain informant responses to a limited set (Fabrega, Metzger, and Williams 1970). Questions that are adequate in this sense are termed frames, and the regularly associated answers are called responses. The frame and responses constitute a unit in the description, and such units may be seen as related to each other in a variety of ways within the description as a whole. Within a shared framework of communication (Spanish was always used), the initial goal is to search for the specific and relevant frames in the domain of interest, namely, illness. These frames are used in the subsequent elicitation process when choices, contrasts, and cognitive boundaries are sought. Such a form of description is a step toward the final goal, the production of an intraculturally valid ethnography, that is, an ethnography in which significant categories and relations are derived from intracultural analysis rather than from externally imposed rubrics. That is, one begins with the assumption that prior knowledge and experience, derived from one's own cultural background or other cultures previously studied, is potentially different from the knowledge and experience of these informants, and the task becomes the discovery of the knowledge that people of the culture under study use to identify, evaluate, and respond to circumstances in which they find themselves. A description that accurately displays what is believed to be the "knowledge" of these informants should allow the anticipation (if not prediction) of events and behavior in circumstances specific to the culture under study in ways that match the expectations of the informants. Appropriateness or inappropriateness of anticipations based on the description is the means of actually testing the description.

In the following research, lay individuals of the region as well as sick persons, physicians, and folk practitioners were interviewed regarding relevant experiences with medical problems. Persons of both ladino and mestizo background served as subjects. In the substance of the chapter, no attempt is made to differentiate between these two social groups, and in line with the conventions adopted by social scientists who study in the Chiapas area, the term *ladino* is used.

The Humoral Background and the Mayan Inheritance

From a historical perspective, the ladino-mestizo medical care system and the beliefs on which it is based represent a culmination of a developmental process issuing originally from Iberian culture, which was transformed and synthesized by contact with indigenous Mayan cultures (G. A. Foster 1960, Beltran 1963, G. M. Foster 1953, Harwood 1971). The most notable aspect of the highlands is its conservative atmosphere, a tribute to the power and durability of native values and traditions. The ideas current in the highlands can be traced to Spanish conceptions of health and illness. One of the principal paradigms organizing these conceptions is the Greek humoral theory, associated with Hippocrates. Related views are prevalent throughout Hispanic cultures. Originally introduced to Latin America in the 16th and 17th centuries and taught in medical schools established by the Spanish in Mexico and Peru, the ideas were spread by missionaries and subsequently diffused throughout

Mexico and Central and South America. The four humors (blood, phlegm, yellow bile, and black bile) are normally in a state of equilibrium in the person's body. Natural adjustments are made to everyday events and changes in physical demands, but health is signified by a warm, moist body maintaining a balance among the four basic elements. In contrast, illness is believed to result from humoral imbalance said to be caused by an excess of one of the four and reflected metaphorically in an excessively hot, cold, moist, or dry body. There is a strong culturally sanctioned emphasis upon the restoration of balance. Foods, drinks, herbs, and medicinal substances, themselves also classified into hot or cold categories, may be used to maintain health or to return the body to a previous healthful state. An extension of the notion of balance is the concern with the emotions, which are seen as a reflection of the degree of balance obtained in social relations and "inside" a given person. Previous investigators have not adequately explicated the extensiveness and universality of the conception of balance and holism in Latin cultures. Often they have taken a basically cartesian dualism abroad. In these types of analyses, it is assumed that body and mind, because they have an independent logical status, are also viewed as empirically separated, with changes confined to one or the other domain.

The various Mayan groups that reside in townships surrounding the city of San Cristobal are agriculturalists who cling tenaciously to traditional ways despite government efforts to assimilate them to Mexican national values. Like other nonliterate groups, the Mayas do not manifest a medical care system that is delimitable as an independently functioning unit within their society. Thus, despite a rather broad definition of what constitutes illness, native Mayan practitioners are the objects of requests for consultations and advice about a variety of problems that outside observers and the Mayas themselves would not ascribe to illness or disease. Conversely, problems that we as physicians would ascribe quite unambiguously to disease are not the exclusive concern of medical practitioners but, as we shall see, are given political and social importance by civil authorities and village elders.

What can be described as a *sociological* theory of disease prevails among the Mayan Indians of the Chiapas highlands. This does not mean that illness is not a personalized event of significance to the individual, nor that phenomenologic experiences do not punctuate and in fact guide and mediate the behaviors of persons who are ill. For, as has been pointed out in earlier research publications, this experiential dimension of illness is quite striking and salient among the various Mayan groups that have been studied carefully (Fabrega 1970a, 1971a). What should be emphasized about an occurrence of illness, however, is the extent to which it provides the context for the acting out of a drama having important social implications and functions for the group. For illness is usually taken to represent (1) a sign that an individual has sinned and has been dutifully punished by the gods or (2) an indication that a known or suspected antagonist or enemy has in fact plotted with the devil and witches to inflict harm on the person or family member who is ill. In the first instance, the event of illness leads village elders to bring pressure on the sick person who has misbehaved. As a result, either because of external prodding or because of a purely inward motivation, the sick individual and his family will make the necessary social, moral, and/or religious amends. In the second instance, the occurrence of illness may serve one or both of the following functions: It may allow an individual to justifiably direct his aggression and hostility at the identified human agent believed to be responsible for the illness, either through witchcraft, violence, or personal insults. On the other hand, an occurrence of illness may actually constitute the necessary *evidence* that an act of malevolence has been perpetuated, in which case the afflicted person merely has to report the illness to the civil authorities for appropriate decision and action. If the social friction involving the "assailants" is clear and easily documented, or if an independent "medical evaluation" by a shaman confirms the nature of the underlying illness, the suspected person will be reprimanded, physically punished, or placed in jail (see Fabrega and Silver 1973 for details).

We see, then, that an instance of illness constitutes a socially constructed episode that involves individuals and various workings of the social system. We could depict illnesses and responses to them graphically as patterns that extend across space and time; an element of the pattern may constitute an individual's impaired functioning, but the significance of this element cannot be appreciated if it is not examined in the *context* of other elements and social processes that give the pattern its design and meaning. In support of this view of disease among the Maya are observations and interview data about the causes and consequences of disease, participation with families in activities aimed at resolving the illness, and material describing how individual Mayas view their bodies and their own personal identity. The latter issues require some elaboration, since their implications involve ladino beliefs and orientations and bear on aspects of disease and medical care that will be discussed subsequently.

The Mayas do not view their bodies as units that are constituted of complex elements that in turn can be differentiated as to mechanism and function and which together harmoniously interact in an integrated fashion. The body, for the Maya, may be depicted as a "black box"— undifferentiated, unarticulated, and unrefined. It represents a very general repository for evil, and it crudely signals when this evil or abnormality is assuming concrete form. People may swell, have pain, and experience changes in bodily function even of a very radical nature. These "evils," however, do not represent the disordered workings of a machine that is capable of variable levels of functioning and interdependence. Instead, visible changes in bodily appearance and function assume relevance when they are associated with the "experience of illness." With regard to what an outside observer may term bodily functioning, then, illness in the last analysis is diagnosed when disordered function produces or is associated with an altered experiential state: a state evolving changes in the level of awareness, consciousness, self-definition, and strength, which in turn signify social happenings. This diagnostic judgment then initiates the systematic unfolding of a socially significant episode. Precisely because Mayas see an illness as a direct or indirect extension of the workings of the social system and in time act upon the illness itself as if it represented a specimen of social fact, one can term their view "sociological." In this type of "theory" of illness, the body is not seen as a functional entity having an *exclusive* importance to the self, to one's personal identity, nor is it judged to be subject to appreciable influence, modification, and control by the person. To state the matter succinctly, Mayas do not regard their bodies as merely physical or spiritual extensions of themselves; the body reflects social goings-on and mirrors states having a locus outside the individual.

Mayas also seem to lack a conception of the self that is internally housed, autonomous, and separate from that of other "objects" (persons, things, deities, animals). The person is seen as tied to his family, his land, and his activities; he is closely and invariably a member of a group, rather than a unique person. Furthermore, he "is" pretty much as he behaves and acts. Concepts of a self, a personality, and/or a mind standing somehow separate from the concrete person, which can have the function of monitoring and controlling human actions, are not in evidence. Each person's essence, his "animal spirit," is capable of wandering, but this essence is seen as a passive agent (Fabrega, Metzger, and Williams 1970). It can be the object of injury and harm (which in turn is reflected personally), but it is not described either as a controlling agent or as being under the direct influence of the person. Mayas do not believe that feelings are independent entities housed within the person, entities that in turn are capable of affecting choice, exerting influence on bodily concerns or human motivations, and existing as circumscribed reactions to interpersonal or impersonal occurrences. Instead, the prevailing view appears to be that pain, sadness, anger, happiness, envy, etc., are concomitants of life that are rooted in social or interpersonal occurrences that are inevitable; persons experience these reactions in certain types of situations, and these in turn channel the person in particular directions promoting similarly valued actions. One might describe the Maya's view of self and person as equally "spread out" over the family and group. Just as with the body, the self (or "mind") appears reflected in and responsive to the social system.

The preceding considerations may perhaps make clearer the assertions of social scientists that illness and medical care are bound up in the processes of social control. For what we observe in these Mayan communities are beliefs and consequent actions about illness that indicate that persons and bodies are working participants of the social system. An occurrence of illness is an affliction experienced by the person and his body and is in turn the reflection of how the social system functions. Furthermore, insofar as the illness serves as evidence that leads the person, elders, or the actual civil authorities to engender punishment and retribution, it allows for the implementation of social sanctions and rules. Illness, in short, is the context for the expression of personal wishes and actions and serves to control the behaviors and actions of others within the bounds deemed appropriate by the culture. In a metaphorical sense, then, illness and bodily states may be seen as parts of the processes that lead to the implementation of norms, just as the fear of punishment and other legal sanctions (as symbolized in part by illness outbreaks) serves to promote harmony and the resolution of conflicts, should these occur. In this light, one could view the treatment of an illness as the occasion not only for removing pain and discomfort and restoring function to a person but also for the execution of social, legal, and moral precepts.

These general comments on Mayan medicine are presented for two reasons. The first is simply their heuristic interest and value. Illness and disease, which in our society may be viewed (depending on our medical ethic) as either relatively impersonal occurrences or as the manifestations of personal crises laden with dysphoric and physically consequential feelings, are in this region the very substance of sociological affairs. Any comprehensive theory of illness, disease, and mind-body functioning would consequently need to encompass and explain this aspect of what we might conservatively term medical affairs. A second reason for discussing Mayan medicine is that the set of beliefs and presuppositions about disease dictated by this medical "system" exert, as we shall soon see, an important influence on ladino and mestizo medicine. The ladino culture of this region must be seen as profoundly influenced by traditional indigenous values and orientations. Mayas participate daily in the commercial and social activities of the ladino (Mexican or Spanish-speaking) world. Ladino culture is continually being infused with new indigenous sources in the form of Mayas who migrate to the city and begin to identify with urban and nationalistic ways. Even should one insist that these acculturating Mayas are marginal, nontraditional, and somewhat "modern" in orientation when compared to those who remain in their villages and hamlets, it is a fact that their manner of orienting to the demands of the ladino world is profoundly affected by their background. Furthermore, though these Mayas occupy low-rung positions in the social system of the ladino, their beliefs and orientations are influential at all levels.

The Etiology of Illness

According to ladinos, an outbreak of illness constitutes evidence that a person's strength, termed by them *consistencia*, has been overrun or depleted. *Consistencia* refers to various aspects of a person that, importantly, are thought of as conjoined, including his inherited constitution. Here, ladinos have in mind not only attributes that are passed on through generations but also factors stemming from the physical, psychological, and moral status of the parents during the time of conception and throughout the pregnancy. Both body and mind fall within the intention of the term. Bodies that are strong, resilient, constituted of "good food," rest, exercise, and, in the case of men, proper amounts of sexual energy show high *consistencia*. A person's *caracter*, which designates a mentalistic entity—roughly, personality—contributes to a person's strength or *consistencia*. Together with one's intelligence, education, and previous experiences, personality is believed to contribute to level-headedness. These enable a person to anticipate and deal effectively with life demands. During times of crisis these traits become more relevant, since they allow the person to discharge emotion and tension in a constructive way so that the mind and body are not harmed by excesses of emotion (see the next section). One last feature of mind is relevant here. A person with a strong *consistencia* is one who does not allow himself to become *sugestionado*. Here, ladinos refer to the ability to withstand suggestions from others as well as preoccupations and worries of any sort. In a setting where persons are always potential targets of envy, anger, spiritistic influences, superstitions, and the general interpersonal machinations of others, a strong person is one who is not overcome by these influences. Thoughts, worries, and preoccupations are seen as potentially harmful to both mind and body.

Centrality of Emotions and Interpersonal Relations

In the causation of illness and disease, ladinos ascribe principal importance to the emotions. Indeed, in ladino theories of disease one can equate the emphasis on emotions with that on "germs" in the Western biomedical germ theory of disease. The amount ("dosage") and noxiousness ("virulence") of the various *sentidos* (roughly, emotions, feelings) are differentiated and are believed to affect proneness to disease, as well as the seriousness and actual type of disease that develops. Emotions can actually be ranked as to their pathogenicity, and it is also possible to associate causally illness types with each of the various emotions. Inspection of the list of emotions that are described as pathogenic indicates that the pleasantness and unpleasantness are not critical factors. Rather, the amount of a certain emotion and its persistence in the individual across time appear to be critical. Emotions and feelings are viewed as inevitable, but when present they should be discharged (in action, talk, or thought) or neutralized (as with alcohol) so that the body at no one time carries an excessive load. For emotions, when present in this way, are seen to have deleterious bodily extensions. Related to the pathogenicity of the emotions is the importance that ladinos ascribe to interpersonal relations. Arguments, separations, envy, love triangles, intensely satisfying exchanges, etc., all have medical relevance precisely because they give rise to excessive feeling. The personality types, or *caracteres*, assume relevance here, since they reflect an individual's habitual mode of conducting and responding to interpersonal situations.

In contrast to Mayan conceptions, then, in the ladino theory of disease one finds a concept of "person," which refers to a distinct psychological, social, and physical being. Furthermore, all of these related aspects of being are seen as connected and affected in important ways by the emotions. A person's inner "self," for example, is believed not only to respond passively to external situations and occurrences but also to mediate and monitor actions so as to maintain both consistency with and proper amounts of the emotions. This "self," however, is not limited to social and psychological factors but has bodily attributes. In the following section, ladino views about the body will be discussed. Suffice it to say here that the body is described as differentiated, the organs are named, their functions described, and their influence on disease recognized and explicitly stated. It is not the scientific correctness of these views that is important here, but rather the fact that they are taken into account and figure importantly in formulations and prescriptions for social action. Diseases and emotions, in short, are believed to have specific loci in the organs of the body, which are consequently altered and damaged, causing the signs and symptoms of disease. The body, instead of being conceived simplistically as a passive repository for evil, as in the indigenous Mayan medical system, is seen instead as a complex entity composed of separate parts that function together in an integrated manner. Body and mind, then, are conjoined and represent the essence of a person, responding to and regulating his various activities.

We may illustrate the relations between these notions by examining outbreaks of illness. The *consistencia* of the person and his personality form a baseline that determines vulnerability. A critical factor is the influence of certain types of interpersonal situations. A frightening occurrence or an embarrassing or shameful incident, for example, are common causes of illness among women but will rarely affect men who are judged as more resistant along these emotional axes. Arguments and altercations, on the other hand, can affect both sexes. Unless resentments are discharged (by fighting, insulting, or acting out a plan of revenge), they will subsequently produce physical harm. Hostility is associated with the shortest "incubation period," and furthermore, its effect is judged as rapid and direct. The same is true of excitements and intensely satisfying or happy situations. Illnesses can result in days or hours, and although these can be lethal, they often are short-lasting episodes. Sadness and envy, on the other hand, produce illness gradually and insidiously; the components or manifestations of the illness, in addition, are general, diffuse, and less dramatic, but longer-lasting and less easily removed. The type of illness that develops as well as its gravity are a function of the constitution and character of the person and the evolving interpersonal situation. Cleverness and intelligence are traits that modify the severity and duration of emotional states insofar as they enable one to discharge the emotion in a reasonably productive or adaptive way.

Illness conditions can affect groups (families or friends) that are exposed to or participants of inciting interpersonal situations. In this sense, the illness may be described as "contagious." Likewise, it follows that friends and relatives occupy important roles in the genesis and development of illness. For they, by intensifying or modifying the reactions of others, are believed to affect the level of emotion and hence its virulence and pathogenicity. By giving advice, offering to perform chores, or by otherwise simply supporting those bound up in emotionally trying circumstances, they are said to have strategic influences on illness. It remains to be emphasized that communities or periods of time characterized by social unrest are especially deleterious from a medical standpoint. By contributing to low morale, unhappiness, and worry, they can so debilitate the person that they render him vulnerable to frequent and/or more serious illness. Illnesses that cluster as a result of these factors can be seen as reflecting an "epidemic" of sorts.

Additional Factors in Illness Occurrence

Besides reflecting emotional and interpersonal considerations, illness is judged by the ladino also to result from naturalistic factors. Excessive heat, cold drafts of air (especially when an individual is angry or otherwise emotionally excited), insufficient, improperly prepared, or spoiled food, unduly prolonged fastings, excessive sexual or other form of physical activity, and insufficient or inadequate rest and exercise (or sexual activity) may all be invoked as relevant factors in the explanation of an occurrence of illness, although they are usually given secondary importance. The ladino theory of disease accommodates most of the usual causes of disease that are expounded in the competing modern system. Thus, genetic factors, pathogenic microorganisms, or physiological dysfunctions may be (and often are) included as contributory explanations. However, careful interviewing discloses that emotional-interpersonal issues underlie these factors and are considered basic.

Acts of malevolence attributed to witches are frequently said to be sources of illness, though persons differ as to how frequently they resort to this type of explanation. The degree of acculturation seems to be a factor, since more Westernized and urbanized ladinos invoke this cause less frequently. Acculturation is neither a necessary nor a sufficient condition for belief in witchcraft, however. A person's level of morality, distrust, and suspiciousness are related, though this is partly a tautology, since in this cultural setting the form assumed by distrust is precisely that of accusations and suspicions of witchcraft. Sources of alleged witchcraft are fellow ladinos and especially the *indigena*. Most ladinos view him as the ultimate irrational and malevolent agent who holds a potential influence on their well-being. Meaningless or otherwise unexplainable outbreaks of serious disease are eventually attributed to his "senseless" actions.

Attitudes toward the Body

Ladino views on illness and disease must be seen as extensions of their beliefs and attitudes about their bodies. A person's body, in many ways viewed as a machine, symbolizes that which is complex, delicate, and above all sacred in the human being. As one of my informants stated, "Our bodies indicate that we carry a portion of God with us. They are the source and focus of our feelings, our energies, and our personalities." Regardless of how much antagonism and resentment may be felt toward someone, a ladino maintains awe and respect for his corporeal self. Mystery also attaches to the body, for with the body one is said to be able to apprehend the pain of a loved one, his physical constraints, his disease. "His pain I can feel as my pain" is an assertion that ladinos invoke as proof of the capacity of the body to apprehend and "receive" communications from the bodies of others. In other words, what we may view as sensitivity, empathy, or simply suggestibility, the ladino views as the body's way of actually apprehending and communicating changes in the physical states of others. The fact that sadness, happiness, and other emotions can replace the pain of a disease or the awareness of sensations associated with physiological processes (for example, weakness, hunger) is considered proof of the continuity or unity of body and mind, for the body's physically compromised state is believed to be actually altered by these experiences. The body can dominate the self in other ways. Attractive and strong bodies are sources of pride and admiration, whereas heavy, unkempt ones bring shame and discredit. Gaining weight is something ladinos claim can be felt and, since it is associated with changes in the blood, can be harmful to one's health. Furthermore, extra weight is associated with a changed personality—one becomes less energetic, slower, lazier, more cautious and restrained as a result of gaining weight. To the ladino, another person is not merely a psychological or social type. There is a particular individuality and uniqueness in others, which involves their bodily constitution.

Social exchanges between close persons are thus also occasions for inquiries about the condition of one's body and health in general. The fatigue of a long journey or the stiffness produced by the strain of a trip allow relatives an opportunity to directly (through massage and heat) or indirectly (by preparation of herbs, the giving of folk preparations, etc.) relate to and enter into the physical essence of others. In these and other ways, then, ladinos manifest a continual awareness and acceptance of their bodies as extensions of their minds and selves.

A dramatic illustration of the various influences that are associated with bodily constitution and state is afforded by the condition of pregnancy. First of all, women are accorded a number of social and psychological entitlements and prerogatives as a result of becoming pregnant. Family members significantly modify their expectations of and demeanor toward pregnant women, just as they are likely to show a great deal of tolerance for peculiarities of their temperament. Pregnant women are also the locus of unusual powers. Since their bodies contain more heat and are altered in complex ways, they are able to effectuate medical cures denied nonpregnant women. Sprains, joint tenderness, bone pains, or any other reasonably well-localized pains believed to be the result of drafts of cold air are particularly susceptible to the ministrations of pregnant women; it is believed that the heat of the woman and fetus can capture and extract the air, thereby relieving if not curing the ailment. This power, however, is not without its liabilities. Women who are pregnant are also dangerous sources of illness. The heat of their bodies can "infect" others, causing either an outbreak of illness or worsening of one due to other causes. Insofar as women involuntarily acquire this strength or power during pregnancy, they are not held responsible for its untoward effects on others. It behooves the individual, however, to exercise care and constraint when dealing with women who are pregnant. Ways of dissipating the effects of this heat, such as by selecting proper foods and clothing and maintaining physical distance, are consequently enjoined.

The Experience of Pain

The unity between mind and body, feeling and biological state, and the linkage of these with social processes can be illustrated in the way ladinos speak about and describe pain. The *sensation* of pain does not appear to be differentiated. One does not obtain descriptions of pain experiences such that the quality of this experience as a mentalistic entity is differentiated and seen as separate from the locus, extensions, and presumed source of the pain. "I have a crampy pain in my stomach" or "The pain I am having is continuous" are not assertions likely to be proffered by ladinos. Rather, we hear remarks such as "I am having the pain of X." Probing the meaning of this statement, we obtain "It is the pain of my liver, located here, which was brought on by doing Y after having experienced Z, and the pain is like someone is squeezing me inside, and the vomiting and headache that I am also having are part of the same malady." Physical and social metaphors abound in attempts to elaborate about the pain associated with various conditions, which may be seen as focused in discrete anatomical parts. In short, pain as a distinct sensation or feeling is not given independent status. What exist, instead, are pains of X, Y, Z, etc., where these are diseases, emotions, anatomical entities, or even situations. Even the word "pain" itself (*dolor*) has limited extension. What we observe frequently are "heaviness," "burningness," "squeezingness," etc., which (although viewed as instances of pain by the observer) are often seen as phenomena different from "pain" by the ladino. The uniqueness of these units is not limited to their sources or locations but includes the mode of physiological, social, and interpersonal handling. In this broad sense, we may say that what we as physicians think of as pain, ladinos conceptualize, talk about, and experience as complex wholes, that is, as chains of behavior, or situations, or critical episodes. Thus, description of the pain of X will likely include an emotional and/or interpersonally inciting cause, the mechanism and components of the processes that result, a description of the characteristics of the pain viewed as a bodily, psychic, and social entity, the duration of these, and the various ways of controlling the pain and bringing the pain episode to a close.

The Mechanism of Disease

The manner in which the ladino explains the relations among the multiple factors that are implicated in an occurrence of illness can be described as homeostatic. An optimal range of function and structural integrity underlies health. Each of the classes of factors discussed earlier represents sources of disturbances that can upset this range. The various factors can combine with or oppose the others, so that notions of balance and equilibrium are also implicated in health and illness.

The linkages among the various classes of factors that underlie and affect health are mediated by the person's blood and by his nervous energy or activity. The latter two elements are viewed almost as isomorphic. Emotional excitement, physical essences reflecting the state and strength of the body, and deleterious exogenous influences that affect health all directly affect the blood and in fact are judged as part of the blood. Native practitioners, consequently, by pulsing the sick person learn from the blood the nature of the disease and its cause. The blood, then, is seen as literally carrying the emotions throughout the body and in this way affecting the structure and function of the organs. At times the blood is described as a form of nervous activity that can be communicated to various parts of the body and bring about movement and sensation.

An Integrated Theory of Disease

The preceding considerations should indicate that in contrast to the views held by the Mayas of this region, for ladinos disease (or illness) is a relatively complex entity. Among Mayas, disease is conceptualized abstractly, and the influences of body, social relations, and supernatural factors are condensed and fused. The social and legal consequences of illness are salient. Among the ladinos, on the other hand, a number of factors (seen as related) are identified and almost invariably held to be implicated in an occurrence of disease. These rest on rather elaborate, if not complex, notions about human functioning. The causes of disease, in short, touch on aspects of personality and social relations, as well as strictly biological functioning, all of which are seen as linked in an almost homeostatic and feedback manner. The self or personality and the body emerge as complicated entities. Furthermore, we observe that disease—as a time-bound state denoting compromised human functioning—is likewise highly differentiated. Ladinos distinguish between disease types on the basis of rate of onset, duration, and severity as well as symptom components. While it may be the case that these aspects of disease are associated causally with personality, interpersonal relations, biophysical constitution, and prevailing situation, nevertheless, a more refined entity is envisioned by ladinos when they speak about disease. This is also reflected in their description of the manifestations of disease, for they elaborate not only on the kinds of physiological behaviors (symptoms) that can take place but also on the many different types and levels of constraints imposed by disease. What persons do and do not do during an illness state is as much a function of the causal factors that are invoked as of the type of disease that has developed.

The ladino theory of disease can be labeled "integrated" because a number of alternative domains frequently viewed in an analytic sense by others as separate and exclusive are treated by them as conjoined and continuous. Among these domains we may include mind versus body, naturalistic versus supernaturalistic, genetic versus environmental, and social versus psychological. Attention was drawn to the unified way in which ladinos view their bodies and their *caracteres*. Just as these two domains overlap and fuse, so also do the naturalistic and supernaturalistic. It will be recalled that physical factors as well as spiritistic or diabolical influences are given importance in disease causation. These two classes of happenings likewise appear to be fused. Various "natural" occurrences, for example, are viewed by the ladino as evidence of the mysterious and occult. A broken glass, window, or plate indicates that something evil and tragic will occur soon. The broken fragments are consequently placed in water in order to neutralize their effects. Portions of garlic are kept attached to doors, undergarments may be worn inside out, and holy water sprinkled across windows and doors to keep spiritistic emanations from intruding. A barking dog at night, a flying vulture, or a screeching owl are not only animals but also the transformed essences (*naguales*) of the devil himself or of persons who have a compact with the devil. Dreams are critical openings into the supernatural and the mysterious; their content portends, causes, or reflects bodily changes of a harmful and threatening sort. In these and innumerable other ways, then, the natural and supernatural "orders" are connected by the ladino and are treated by him as phenomena that are conjoined. In an analogous fashion, ladinos combine the points of view that are entailed in the "nature versus nuture" conflict. Environmental and genetic factors are given equal and related roles in disease causation, with these two classes of occurrences affecting and modifying the other in a Lamarckian manner. In the area of health and disease, children profit in a genetic and physicalistic sense from the habits and experiences of their parents.

The integrated view of disease that prevails among ladinos is manifest in still another manner. In an earlier study the striking characteristics that ladinos from the town of Tenejapa ascribed to what we would term psychotic disturbances were outlined (Fabrega and Metzger 1968). The causes of this type of illness are not judged as different from those of other types of illness. Furthermore, although ladinos may view the psychotically disturbed person as altered and changed in important ways during the time that he is ill (and this would include bodily changes), no stigma or other form of social discreditation (or differentiation) attaches to the person following recovery. Mental illness, in short, is not the occasion for morally censuring an individual—it is judged as an illness similar to others. Related to this, we observe that many behavioral alterations that an outside observer might describe as psychiatric—depressive or paranoid reactions, antisocial outbursts, character disorders, etc.—are frequently also judged by ladinos as indications of illness, though the nature of this illness is not differentiated in any special way. The illnesses, in other words, would not be described by them as purely emotional, although these psychological (as well as social) aspects would be acknowledged. Illnesses of this type may even be called excessive envy or greed or sadness due to painful separations, etc., with the situational and interpersonal roots included as indications of the illness state. Importantly, however, discussions with ladinos disclose that they consider the afflicted person or persons as also *physically* changed and ill; specific organs as well as the blood are described as altered and diseased. We observe, then, that among ladinos of the Chiapas region psychiatric illness in the way that we think of this entity has no unique and separate status. Attitudes and dispositions about its causes and attributes are continuous with those of other illnesses, and, in addition, the belief that it reflects dysfunction of only one type of system (mind as opposed to body) is eschewed.

Medical Treatment

The fact that illness in the Chiapas highlands is seen as a state having many diverse but interconnected facets has logical implications for medical treatment. For one thing, requesting treatment from a practitioner is the occasion for the sharing of a host of personal concerns, which, as I have tried to indicate, are viewed as components of the illness. Data about how the body is functioning represent simply one type of information that is exchanged. Furthermore, personal relations with the practitioner become critical; his humanity, trustworthiness, and alleged powers in various domains that outsiders may view as separate from if not irrelevant to disease are critical. In other words, what one might term as technical competence is but one of many attributes that a practitioner must possess. Ladinos believe that one who knows about the mysteries of the body must know about the mysteries of the soul, of the spirits, of the proper forms of conducting social relations, and of the future itself. This follows from the "sacredness" that surrounds the body, from the fundamental role that it has in reflecting and mediating self-consciousness and a social reality that includes the supernatural, and from the identity that these sociobiologic issues have with what we would term "medical issues." Thus, the transaction between the practitioner and his patient is the focus of social, psychological, and moral as well as bodily matters. Insofar as illness refers to and reflects both personal and interpersonal issues, the self-presentation of each participant is critical: morality, illness, and self, in other words, are fused, and all three are continuous with how one behaves. During medical treatment, practitioner and patient both become parties to a crucial situation that has roots in and effects on highly private and socially meaningful issues. The transaction, thus, must establish consensus vis-à-vis blame, shame, malevolence, and propriety. In this context, trust and distrust become critical. This is the case because a medical evaluation entails the examination of motives, the evaluation of character, and the opportunity to judge the espousal of norms; diagnosis is in part equivalent to socially and morally judging another; and treatment brings the opportunity to share in and help resolve another's crisis of living by modifying his conduct.

A person's view or theory of disease naturally determines what he will do in order to get well. If the theory is broadly shared by members of the culture, as it is in the highlands, it will also determine the kind of treatment that he receives from a folk practitioner. In the case of ladinos, we note that the native theory directly implicates domains that medical theorists currently believe importantly affect the cause, components, persistence, and resolution of disease. Stated succinctly, if it is desirable to handle and treat disease in terms of the various separate but linked systems that are believed to be implicated in any one instance or occurrence, then ladinos (because of their native theory of disease) to some extent accomplish this among themselves. Thus, not only do they view disease as having a holistic basis, they also treat it in this fashion. Assuming the validity of the view of disease expounded by medical theorists, and presuming that ladinos can point to sources of psychosocial tension and interference in a reasonably accurate manner, we can infer that ladinos to some extent deal effectively with disease (see next chapter also). What they lack, of course, are effective ways of directly modifying physiologic and chemical changes that are also associated with disease. It is the ability of modern medicine to affect this domain that draws many ladinos to seek care from physicians. This visit to a physician, however, often has interesting and sometimes ironic consequences.

When a ladino visits a physician he encounters a "modern" view that fractionates his own holistic and integrated view of disease. There he is probed in a very precise and intensive way about his body (its appearance, function, and sensations) but not about his feelings, moods, dispositions, and social relations. Little confidence and trust can be placed in procedures and strategies that stem from a framework and orientation that is judged as highly formal and mechanistic, especially when these procedures are coordinated by an impersonal individual who appears uninterested in the varied personal and social goings-on that the ladino believes cause alterations in bodily states and give these their significance. For the ladino patient, the result of having his medical problems reduced in this fashion and of receiving interpretations about bodily matters that are not only discordant but frequently viewed as insufficient and simplistic is skepticism, alienation, and a lack of compliance with medical regimens. A search for a more "understanding" practitioner follows; and the result is often a deterioration of a problem for which there is an "available" cure. Countless instances can be recorded of persons who have withdrawn from "modern" treatment when no immediate cure was forthcoming, with consequent deterioration in health status, because of the physician's neglect of the relevant areas of concern.

Research indicates that ladinos themselves and their native practitioners have available various modes for effectively dealing with alterations in most of the system components that we (abstractly) may judge as implicated in an occurrence of disease. Their mode of care lacks refinement in one of these components, namely, the strictly biological. It is in this narrow segment of the spectrum of disease that physicians can be most effective. However, physicians lack "competence" or credibility in the other system components or portions of the spectrum of disease that ladinos judge as logically contained in and indicated by an occurrence of disease. Thus they are often not visited, or their advice is ignored precisely because of their narrow approach to disease.

Many factors can be invoked to explain why folk systems of medical care are supplanted by Western biomedical conceptions and practices. We can classify these roughly into two types: (1) patent limitations of the folk system (objectified as high infant mortalities, high disease prevalence, etc.) and (2) evidence (visible and inferential) that Western "modern science" can profoundly change, alter, and control nature (not just illness matters). However, the spread of modern medicine should be seen, not as a process that simply erodes and takes the place of native views and practices, but rather as a pervasive undermining (with consequent disarticulation) of established modes of thinking, feeling, and behaving. In the highlands, conceptions about disease, indeed experiences of and with disease, are isomorphic with those that articulate one's personal identity and also give meaning to social relations. What is more, all of these form the fabric of what we may term "medical care." It is not surprising, then, that the intrusion of Western medicine into such a setting brings with it more than decreased infant mortality and rates of infectious diseases; it brings with it the destruction of the previously mentioned unity in social relations, body, and self. Insofar as it operates through specialized occupational and sub-occupational groups (nurses, internists, psychiatrists, surgeons, etc.), medicine tends to segmentalize the person in various ways. Each of these groups has a perspective that is organized by separate premises, obligations, and explanations, all of which are in conflict with native understandings. Problems are somewhat arbitrarily divided into "mental" versus "physical," "social" versus "medical," "natural" versus "superstitious," thereby producing disarticulations. In other words, what to ladinos is a single crisis having broad ramifications is in this new system or view a heterogeneous collection of "problems," each of which has a separate cause and locus. In this process of differentiation and specialization, Western medicine not only fragments and undermines the native cultural system, thereby creating conflict, but it also brings with it the rigid dualistic notions that many physicians see as being central to the disaffection patients often feel with medical care in urbanized societies. Table 8.1 lists the contrasting ways in which medical matters are viewed in these two social systems.

Relevance of Ladino Theories of Disease for Contemporary Sociomedical Study

In assuming the strict biomedical framework of disease, which rests on quite rigid dualistic assumptions, researchers often see "cultures" or "values" as contributing to the cause of disease or to its expression. In the study of the cultural patterning of presenting symptoms, to cite one example, specific diseases are used as a control, or independent fact, with "expression" of symptoms (for example, pain) a dependent variable associated with membership in Irish, Anglo-Saxon, or Italian ethnic groups. Anglo-Saxons and Irish report more fever, more sharply focused and located symptoms, and less intense pain (Zola 1966). We can interpret this set of findings in a fashion consistent with inferences drawn from the findings of the study reported here. Anglo-Saxons, coming from a tradition that both spawned and supported the leading medical advances in past centuries, may have learned to see their bodies within a more impersonal, dualistic framework, identifying illness as a bodily or physical experience. The "discrepant" behaviors of Latins and Ital-

Table 8.1 Contrasting Views on Health and Illness in Two Social Systems

Impersonal System	Personal System

A. Self and Body

Impersonal System	Personal System
1. The body and the self are seen as distinct entities, logically and socially.	1. The body and self form a continuum. Changes in one produce and cannot be separated from changes in the other.
2. Health and illness, or "normal and sick," may be applied to either the body or the self in a logically consistent fashion.	2. Health and illness cannot be considered logically to be located exclusively in the body *or* the self.
3. Social relationships tend to be partitioned, segmented, and situational, that is, there are many selves and roles, which are seen as discontinuous.	3. Social relationships tend to be nonpartitioned, diffuse, encompassing; there are fewer roles and selves, and those that do exist are intimately linked.
4. Social relationships are relatively formal, impersonal, and are evaluated without a consistent moral-judgmental framework.	4. Social relationships are less formal, more personal, and are contained within a consistent moral framework, which is legitimated by a higher, that is, sacred, authority.
5. The body is described within a biological framework; everyday discourse about health concerns is heavily punctuated by the use of biological categories and explanations derived from scientific sources.	5. The body is not seen as an independent entity separated from interpersonal relations; everyday discourse contains few biological terms derived from scientific sources.
6. The body is understood as a complex biological machine.	6. The body is seen as a holistic, integrated aspect of self and social relations that is vulnerable and may easily be affected by feelings, other people, natural forces, or spirits.
7. The body's structure and function are partitioned logically into specific parts and systems. The level of functions and interdependence is differentiated in a relatively precise manner.	7. Categories referring to the body are unrefined. The body as an anatomic and physiologic entity is only generally partitioned. A simple view of function, extension, and meaning of parts is held.
8. *Health* and restoration to health are perceived as dependent on and logically referring to the body as a physical entity, or alternatively, to the self as a mentalistic entity.	8. *Health* is equivalent to social equilibrium. In addition to having bodily correlates, restoration to "health" is seen as a product of re-equilibrated or more harmonious social relationships, purging of emotional and spiritualistic forces, and/or restoring equilibrium in socioritualistic bonds.

9. *Personality* is seen as a salient factor in interpersonal relationships; it is the means by which one shows a "consistent self," and it is conceptualized almost as a distinct entity that explains behavior.

9. *Personality* does not exist as a separate entity; all relationships are transactional and multibounded, and the guiding emotional tone and interpersonal style as revealed in these relationships is what is considered characteristic of the individual.

10. *Character types* and personality styles are only minimally significant in the diagnosis and treatment of disease. Such labels as "moody," "insensitive," "silly" exist and are socially relevant, not biologically so.

10. *Character types* and self-presentation are intrinsic or isomorphic to the cause, type, diagnosis, and cure of disease.

11. Disease exists apart from these modes of self-presentation.

11. Disease cannot exist apart from these modes of self-presentation.

B. Conceptions of Health and Illness

1. Although sometimes viewed as continuous, health and illness or disease are regarded as mutually exclusive.

1. Illness is a nonsegmentalized process punctuated by "key events," the consequences of which are seen morally and interpersonally.

2. *Disease* is universal in form, progress, and content. It can be logically partitioned into stages, with beginning and end points.

2. *Illness* to a significant extent is idiosyncratic in form, progress, and content. It can be understood only in the context of the social relations of the sick person.

3. The consequences of disease are seen intersystemically and organically.

3. The consequences of illness may be seen in virtually every facet of the person's transactions, activities, and concerns.

4. Disease and behavior are logically discrete.

4. Illness and behavior are linked, logically and empirically.

5. The clock and mechanical forces govern the progress of disease; the unfolding of disease is inexorable unless medical intervention is mobilized.

5. Spirits, evil forces, and people govern the progress of illness. The unfolding of illness depends on the cause; these beliefs in turn determine the options of intervention.

6. Specific, identifiable causal processes are known, based upon accumulated chemical and biological evidence.

6. Generalized categories of cause exist, but they lack technical bases and precise delimitation.

7. Almost all diseases are caused naturalistically (biologically). Diseases are classified scientifically by type of system or tissue involved, type of cause, and form.

7. Illness is caused by spirits, emotionally laden transactions, malevolent people, natural forces, and/or "genetic" or constitutional weakness. Types of illness are determined by the source or cause.

Impersonal System	Personal System
8. "Mental illness" exists as a category of illness that affects the self.	8. "Mental illness" is one possible manifestation of processes causing other disturbances in the person's universe of bodily and sociomoral relationships. All illnesses affect the self and the body.
9. Illnesses or diseases, since they are seen as abstract entities with specifiable properties and a recurring identity, can be treated at any time and in any place, provided the necessary technical perquisites are present.	9. Since illnesses are personalized, idiosyncratic, and mysterious and involve complex forms and processes, they require treatment in special and varying locations, during highly "critical" portions of the time cycle, and with many symbolic and multivalued elements.

C. The Character of the Health Care System

Impersonal System	Personal System
1. Help-seeking is rationalized by scientific labels and explanations involving biological categories and terms.	1. Help-seeking is cloaked in moral symbols; patterns of help-seeking and sources of help are largely determined by perception of the locus of causation: evil forces, persons, naturalistic events, spirits, etc.
2. The aim of help-seeking is to restore bodily function.	2. Help-seeking actualizes the need to re-establish or re-equilibrate physical, emotional, and social structures, which are seen to some extent as fused.
3. Medical specialization is based on precisely defined knowledge, technique, and procedures, all of which are discontinuous from ordinary social processes.	3. Specialization of health care providers is based on types of *cause;* for example, illness resulting from witchcraft can be effectively treated only by a witch; bodily malfunction can be treated by an herbalist, etc. Rationale of treatment types is continuous with ordinary social processes.
4. The risk a practitioner may incur as a result of accepting responsibility for treatment of a disease is *collectively* distributed by: (a) legal systems (b) professional associations (c) insurance (d) referral systems (horizontal) (e) specialization (vertical) (f) collective "business" organizations, for example, group practice, partnership, hospital, etc.	4. The risk a practitioner may incur as a result of accepting responsibility for treatment of an illness is individualized and *personal:* (a) A person's "self" is his most significant possession and cannot be protected by formal means. (b) Legal controls on provisions of health care are minimal or nonexistent. (c) No professional associations or collective means of distributing risk exist. (d) Little referral by curers exists, and there are no interdigitated practice systems.

5. Referral is highly patterned and rationalized, differentiated (horizontally and vertically), and rule oriented.

5. Referral is "unpatterned," that is, personalized, idiosyncratic, localistic, and lay dominated. It is nonhierarchical and undifferentiated.

6. Time is purchased in discrete units, it is contractually shared, and the clock governs the availability of physician; time is highly segmented: 15-minute time units, 8- to 10-hour day, 6-day week, 11-months practice per year.

6. Time is judged analogically, jointly owned and shared, and partitioned complexly, for example, in terms of "moral" or "intersubjective" time, time since the event "causing" the illness, and general time of day for appointments. The day is segmented into 3 to 4 units.

7. Treatment procedures are universal, formal, learned, and impersonal and are not altered significantly by time and place of the treatment nor by personality of physician.

7. Treatment procedures are personalized, idiosyncratic, and based on the particulars of the transaction and have an interpersonal basis.

D. The Curer-Client Relationship

1. Relationship is highly patterned and based on formal, almost contractual role prescriptions. It is:
  (a) instrumentally oriented
  (b) universalistic
  (c) neutralistic
  (d) focused.

1. Relationship is informal, diffuse, noncontractual, semicontinuous with everyday life. It is:
  (a) expressively oriented
  (b) particularistic
  (c) affectively charged
  (d) diffuse.

2. Confidence or trust is to a considerable extent pre-established by formal means: titles, credentials, certification of legal right (license), membership in professional organizations.

2. Confidence or trust is transactional; it must be situationally legitimated by the self-presentations of both curer and patient. Trust varies as to time, place, person, day, and symbols used.

3. Self-presentation and body presentation are separated for all practical purposes, and the relationship is directed to either.

3. Body and self are seen as presented together, and relationship is directed to these but in the context of varied factors.

4. In most instances transactions tend to be limited to those intended to produce a change in the body, while the self is often secondary. Alternatively, if self is treated, body is considered unaffected and often left unattended.

4. Medically situated transactions always involve body and self in relation to others. Therefore, treatment and diagnosis tend to be holistic and integrated. They affect human relationships and spiritual forces simultaneously.

5. The role of the curer is highly differentiated, segmented, professionalized:
  (a) It is a full-time occupation.
  (b) Extensive formal training is required.

5. The role of the curer is not differentiated:
  (a) It is a part-time occupation.
  (b) Little or no formal training is required.

Impersonal System	Personal System
(c) Specialization is high. (d) Technical skill is high. (e) Knowledge base is complex and extensive. (f) Political control over access to the profession is high.	(c) There is little specialization in curing occupations. (d) Technical skill is low. (e) Knowledge base is limited. (f) Access to curing role is almost "open."
6. Basis of power and authority over clientele is *science*.	6. Basis of power and authority over clientele is personal *charisma* as conveyed by repute, appearance, and curing performance.
7. Relationship is symbolized by distance, coolness, formal relations, use of abstract concepts (jargon).	7. Relationship is symbolized by closeness, shared meaning, warmth, informality, concreteness of reference (use of "everyday language").
8. Recruitment to curing role is based on choice, skill, performance, knowledge, and endowment.	8. Recruitment to curing role tends to be based on ascribed criteria (family associations), "personality," or natural qualities. Skill and knowledge are relatively unimportant.
9. Only for "mental illness" does curing process involve self-expressive, self-modifying components.	9. For all illnesses curing process involves symbolization of self and expression of a placement in sociomoral order.
10. Responsibility of curer appears to be principally to the patient, and scientific and legal-judicial communities verify this obligation.	10. Responsibility of curer is to patient, his family, to the community, and often to the gods.
11. Responsibility and aim of curer is principally to remove disease (biomedically defined) but also to alleviate discomfort.	11. Responsibility and aim of curer is principally to undo harm, punishment, or evil that is basis for "disease" but also to alleviate discomfort.
12. Only in rare instances (for example, mental illness) do curer's decisions, actions, and judgments directly affect workings of social system.	12. Curer's decisions, actions, and judgments can intimately act, reflect, and feed back on workings of social system.
13. Curer is geared to probe impersonal entity (that is, disease) using abstracted and technological "language."	13. Curer constantly assesses morality, guilt, and "character" as a basis for deciding to treat and choosing mode of treatment and uses language of social relations.
14. Curer may acknowledge inability to cure by specifying nature and extent of "pathology" of disease.	14. Curer may acknowledge inability to cure by specifying nature and strength of evil in the "disease" or illness.

15. Curer in principle is obligated to help when consulted.

15. Curer is afforded option of noninterference when consulted.

16. Curer influences patient actions (compliance) by invoking (biomedical) knowledge of disease unfolding as validity of his advice.

16. Curer influences patient actions (compliance) by invoking (spiritual) knowledge of illness and capacity to directly aggravate illness.

17. Patient does not (in principle) fear curer retaliation.

17. Patient always fears curer retaliation.

E. Tools, Symbols, and Settings of Curing

1. Tools and procedures are specialized, discontinuous from and unavailable to the person in everyday life (otoscopes, X rays, lab analysis techniques).

1. Tools and procedures are not specialized but are continuous with and available to the person in everyday life (candles, flowers, drink).

2. Tools and procedures are aimed at revealing, probing, cutting a mechanical entity, that is, the body.

2. Tools and procedures are intrinsic to social relations and are consistent with other symbolizations of social relations.

3. Settings are segregated; home is separate from office.

3. Settings are multipurpose; curing setting is home and also a religious place.

4. Treatment settings are rationally rule governed. Specific staff with special roles is used. Paperwork dominates procedures. Setting is hierarchical and authoritative.

4. Treatment settings are loci for diffuse, overlapping, multipurpose transactions. There is no special staff, no paperwork, little or no formal authority over staff: family structure is replicated in organization of treatment.

5. Curing resources are technological and scientific, purchased, manufactured and complex, and available in complex systems, such as hospitals.

5. Curing resources are proximal—many are available naturally. Some are purchased, others (drink, herbs) are handmade or grown. Simple and few specialized systems are needed for obtaining curing resources.

ians when they are sick may in part reflect current and past differences in the way concepts about disease are understood and acted upon in Hispanic and Mediterranean cultures. The latter groups may not share the Anglo-Saxon attachment to a sharp body/mind distinction, and in this sense, the expression of pain or discomfort may be not simply a result of emotional or temperamental factors as these are affected by a universal biological entity (that is, "disease") but rather the expression of fundamentally different conceptions of what disease represents. Interpretations of illness "behavior" in modern settings, by both social scientists and physicians, may thus be traced to implicit biomedical assumptions (the universality and precise identity of disease) combined with simplistic, if not naïve, identification of a cultural tradition.

Modern psychosomatic medicine and the unified view of disease, seen in light of these historic and logical considerations, may represent an attempt to reconstruct in a highly refined manner a view of illness that (1) was previously dominant at a particular point in time and perhaps only in selected cultures (principally those that are glossed by the terms "Latin," "Mediterranean," or "expressive") and (2) is presently held in variable degrees by subcultural groups, for example, Italian-Americans, Mexican-Americans, and Puerto Ricans. Furthermore, as mentioned earlier, this modern systems view of disease must be seen as a response to the earlier dualistic one, which itself was a product of historical circumstances. In other words, observations of persons showing disease who themselves believed that a physicalistic alteration was responsible may have furnished the "data" necessary for investigators to develop the modern unified perspective. Taken together, the dualistic and unified views of disease dramatize the point that facts taken logically as evidence of disease in one framework are nondisease or epistemologically nonexistent in the other. In other words, attention is drawn to the social and historical bases of what disease "is." This point has interesting implications. If one assumes that the natural biological tendency of man is to view and respond to crises and stress in some integrated or at least undifferentiated way, then one can posit that rigid conceptions about what these crises are may affect how one in fact behaves and responds during them. Theories about or views of these "crises" (that is, disease), then, literally contribute to the very essence of what is indicated by them. One is thus drawn to the position that the "natural history of disease" is not invariant and fixed but rather a consequence of changes in the functioning of connected systems, *each of which is affected by symbolizations about the meaning of and bases for these changes* (see Chapter 9).

There are additional implications that can be drawn from the material presented in this chapter. As I have indicated, there is much confusion and ambiguity in contemporary American society about where medical matters begin and end and also about the nature of the boundary between the medical and the social. This is partly symbolized by beliefs regarding whether mental illness is real like other (bodily) diseases or simply a "myth." No clear solutions to these dilemmas are forthcoming, though factors underlying the dilemmas may perhaps be better understood in the light of the material reviewed.

In many ways, features of the contemporary problems of health and illness, of deviance and welfare, of social control and crime, may be seen as residues of the fractionation of the more holistic and integrated system associated with simple folk societies such as those of the Chiapas highlands. Here I refer to confusion about whether an individual is healthy or diseased, whether he is responsible for his behavior, whether he is to be discredited for his actions, and whether he is to be seen as a pawn of bodily or mental forces over which he has no control or as a volitional being. Since these concerns are often framed in terms of possible disease, and since persons (we are told) cannot be held responsible for disease, physicians and the medical profession are brought in to "clarify" the situation, though we observe that this is not always accomplished. To the extent that portions of one's behavior can be ascribed to "disease" and/or to autonomous units that are fostered by rigid dualistic notions (such as hormone levels, unconscious conflicts, etc.), individuals are able to claim lack of responsibility for something that in a compelling way is a feature of the self. However, in a setting where notions that self and body cannot be dissolved, that both are in fact intimately and inextricably linked in social relations, behaviors we may gloss or label as mental or physical illness, crime, deviance, and alcoholism (to name a few) are not separated and distinctly marked. In these settings, such behaviors are not isolated and viewed as unwilled and determined in some impersonal way, nor are they a source of ambiguity and confusion to the individual or to the social system. Instead, the behaviors are interpreted and given significance within the integrated and comprehensive view of self-body and social relations that prevails, that is, within the integrated theory of "disease" that I have described. In other words, the consequences and causes of "mental illness" or "deviance" or whatever else we may wish to label these behaviors can seemingly never be separated from an equation involving both *external* relations (friendships, kinship ties, social associations) and the *condition of the body and the self* as perceived and defined. These behaviors are thus viewed as an inseparable part of the individual, his family, and his group and are matters of their doing and for which they are responsible. They may be viewed as complex, lethal, and unfortunate but rarely as ambiguous, unwilled, or confusing. It may be then that contemporary dilemmas about medicine and society and ambiguities about ways of dealing with them result in part from the fractionation that is a feature of the modern view, a fractionation that is associated with the creation of separate domains, each of which has causes that are somehow beyond the individual's control.

Chapter 9   On the Form and Course of Sociomedical Inquiries

Social scientists, as the preceding chapters have indicated, have a long-standing interest in the study of medical problems. However, previous investigators have devoted comparatively little attention to the description and analysis of actual disease occurrences and, importantly, have seldom viewed these occurrences as social facts and processes that express matters germane to social theory. It is my conviction that the study of this social dimension of disease can bear on theoretical questions pertinent to social science and medicine as well as on practical exigencies that currently face both of these disciplines. Disease, in other words, can be conceptualized as a social occurrence, and such a form of conceptualization allows studying cultural systems as well as traditional medical questions.

The general theme of the chapter is that social scientists, especially anthropologists, have not sufficiently asserted themselves in the study of medical problems, particularly with respect to the entity disease in its special social sense. As regards the comparative study of medical problems, I would assert that social scientists have either (1) wholly accepted or borrowed the biomedical and epidemiological framework of disease (which has in many instances proved very useful to medicine, though not necessarily to social science) or (2) pursued legitimate and socioculturally relevant questions that touch on medical problems but in a manner that has precluded comparisons and the cumulation of knowledge. The relativistic view that each culture is unique and separate, in other words, has obscured the search for basic forms that can be used to compare illness and medical practice cross-culturally. In large part because traditional paradigms within medicine and social science have dictated these particular orientations (each with its own questions, needs, purposes, etc.), social scientists have been kept from exploring what I would describe as theoretical aspects of society-medicine interrelations. This limitation of traditional sociomedical studies is demonstrated, first, by the emphases in ethnomedical inquiries on traditional sociocultural questions that are of relevance to anthropology and which basically disregard the centrality of disease and, second, by the highly pragmatic and ultimately correctionistic aims of social epidemiological approaches, which seek to understand causes of disease (viewed within the biomedical paradigm) and do not investigate social system functioning as it is reflected in and feeds back on medical matters. The potential that inheres even within this particular paradigm for the development of social theory has been neglected.

Emics and Etics as Applied to Medical Activities

A central preoccupation of social scientists and especially anthropologists is with developing concepts that will allow an accurate description and comparison of various cultural activities or practices (Goodenough 1970). In this effort the characterization of concepts and descriptions as belonging to the classes termed *emic* and *etic* has proven valuable. Suitable (etic) concepts that will allow one to decompose and/or organize the basic native (emic) concepts in an accurate manner are a primary requirement. With regard to medical issues, what is needed is (1) an initial enumeration of basic forms that are assumed to have cross-cultural extensions (for example, disease, medical practitioner, medical procedures, medicines, etc.) and (2) a framework (or a set of related ones) that will allow for the accurate definition of those fundamental features of these forms that are necessary and sufficient for meaningful cross-cultural analysis. Stated differently, this requirement entails a suitable *language* that can be used to accurately describe and compare basic medical forms that are importantly implicated in the medically related experiences of peoples. These forms, I maintain, should be specified in such a fashion that their analysis will lead to the examination of questions about the functioning of social and cultural systems. The empirical use of a language (or disease framework—see Chapters 4 and 5) of this type in various cultural settings should yield a pool of information about medical matters that will accomplish several basic aims; among these aims are (1) accurate description of medically related expectations, practices, procedures, behaviors, etc., and (2) accurate placement of features of (1) in specific sociocultural units whose demography, patterns, values, change potential, history, ecological setting, etc., are already known or can be adequately described. Once these two aims are accomplished, it should be possible to develop a body of propositions about culture-society-medicine interrelations that can be incorporated within a theory and science of man.

My conviction, as this book has indicated, is that the fundamental form that is in need of accurate definition in order to conduct cross-cultural medical studies is that which in our own culture we label *disease*. I opt for this form for two related reasons. First of all, members of all carefully studied contemporary human groups develop biological changes analogous to those we term disease. As I emphasized in Chapter 6, I assume that the manifestations of these changes in space and time possess behavioral organization and social meaning that can be described, formalized, and compared. In a sense, I believe that disease when viewed as a sociobehavioral occurrence (and from this standpoint the term "illness" is more appropriate) offers a key to medical and social scientists that allows access to important theoretical and practical discoveries. Cultural anthropologists, like other social scientists, see the potential of focusing directly on human behavior, for it is in this domain that the set of rules or expectations that are subsumed under the term *culture* are richly and vividly exemplified. Consequently, concepts that will enable one to describe and analyze in a formal way an *occurrence of illness* (that is, the social aspects of a disease occurrence) afford a handle on a significant aspect of medical matters that, importantly, is rooted in behavior. An accurate depiction of illness using a behavioral (and hence, indirectly, cultural) framework thus accomplishes two things at once. It focuses on processes that reflect cultural rules as well as changes, and it also allows more static or structural analyses insofar as the components or elements of these behaviors can be mapped or coded in some abstract way. Another reason for the emphasis on "illness" as the fundamental form needing accurate description is that I see an illness occurrence as the central fact around which other medical forms and activities cluster. Medical practices and the activities of medical practitioners are brought to bear on an illness occurrence. Illness occurrences interrupt social processes, cause alarm, require attention, can initiate changes in the organization of a group, and can alter relations between groups. The focus, it seems to me, of all that is medically relevant in a social group is an occurrence of illness.

Certain issues need to be made explicit about my conviction regarding the centrality of "illness" as the medical form needing accurate definition. One could say that much of what is medically relevant in a sociocultural unit involves protecting against or warding off the *potential* occurrence of an illness. In other words, a great many organized human activities that reflect the application of cultural rules and that are important from a medical standpoint are demonstrated or are in actual operation in the absence of an actual occurrence of illness. In this light, it might be argued that the medical form most in need of definition is "medical practitioner," or beliefs about "illness causes," or beliefs about "illness consequences," or characteristics of the "medical procedures" brought to bear on the control of disease, or the way medical care and practice is organized, or a host of other medical forms designed to respond to actual *and* potential occurrences of illness and hence equally if not more crucial for cross-cultural description and comparison. I will attempt, briefly, to indicate why I feel this is not the case.

First, a number of considerations of fundamental concern to all social scientists are very salient precisely during actual occurrences of illness and less so or not at all at other times. In addition to the ones mentioned earlier, I would simply add questions of cost viewed economically and questions bearing on issues such as function, purpose, and efficacy. Illnesses cost people and groups important resources and hence have important social consequences, and their control or treatment allows social scientists to evaluate the effectiveness of a sociocultural unit's institutions or practices or whatever else we may wish to call a group's organized attempts to meet universal crisis situations. Furthermore, during illness occurrences these matters are expressed in a dynamic way, thereby allowing processual analyses. It seems to me, then, that this costly item, which has functional implications, should be made retrievable in some refined and systematic way that facilitates cross-cultural comparisons, since this will allow social scientists to relate the occurrence to other important cultural events and processes and hence to evaluate important questions about the functioning of social and cultural systems. In order to retrieve these occurrences we need to be able to define them, specify and measure their types and/or components, and eventually analyze factors associated with their cost, prevalence, consequences, etc., as a prelude to cross-cultural comparisons. Focusing our analytic effort on concepts and methods for describing illness occurrences thus seems fundamental. With regard to matters of priority, the other medical forms mentioned previously seem to be less efficient or central. Furthermore, I believe that a meaningful set of concepts that can be used for the description and analysis of illness occurrences still allows one to make sense of those culturally related activities directed at potential occurrences. It is actual occurrences, or actual experiences vis-à-vis discrete illness occurrences, that persons and groups draw on to model their medically relevant activities and practices as well as the duties of medical personnel, all of which are designed to protect against potential occurrences. If we understood in some meaningful and comprehensive sense what particular illnesses or what aspects about illnesses concern members of groups, we would be far in the direction of explaining what, how, and why they organize themselves the way they do to protect against possible illness occurrences. Furthermore, a suitable language or model for describing illness that allows the investigator to bridge the gap between social and biological systems may offer a convenient node around which other medical forms might be suitably organized such that questions germane to social science can be fruitfully entertained.

Because our language for describing disease (the previously described biologistic framework) is at present so coarse and socially inappropriate, it is often difficult to tie in the connections that may exist between disease and social context. A suitable language of illness, in other words, by also incorporating social correlates of illness, can take into account important contextual factors surrounding illness occurrences that influence the consequences and implications of the occurrence. In brief, a set of refined concepts about illness would *indirectly* enable one to analyze many of the issues that can be approached by means of other important medical forms; furthermore, these concepts would *directly* allow evaluating processes and consequences associated with actual occurrences that do occupy an analytically strategic locus for problems central to social science.

To recapitulate, then, it seems that in activities that fall under the rubric "medical" anthropologists have material that lends itself in some important sense to the development of theories about human behavior, its underlying cultural rules and guidelines, and about social systems proper. Several forms that are basic to medical activities stand in need of precise description in order to facilitate meaningful comparative studies. The long-standing concern within social science, especially anthropology, for developing suitable concepts and frameworks for the comparative analysis of social and cultural forms should be applied to these medical activities and forms. Because problems posed by illness are in many ways the foci of all medical activities, I have emphasized the importance of establishing a set of cross-culturally relevant concepts about illness. Since actual illness occurrences also facilitate and enable investigating structural, processual, and functional aspects of cultural systems, concepts about illness that facilitate the description, analysis, and comparison of these occurrences will in turn provide an opportunity for the analysis of theoretical questions about culture.

Possible Areas of Cross-Cultural Medical Study

I have argued that requirements for the cross-cultural study of medical problems include a suitable language of illness that would allow investigators to label precisely and describe illness occurrences in various social settings. In Chapter 5 I suggested that since the manifestations of an occurrence of illness involve behavior, and, furthermore, since these behaviors may reflect how the individual and the group "read" the illness, such a language of illness should rely on behavioral indicators. Furthermore, it was pointed out in Chapter 6 that in order to describe and analyze responses to an occurrence of illness, investigators should strive to develop a model of illness behaviors. The model outlined, despite the limitations of its present form, offers an example of the kind of logic that can be followed. Some of the concepts of the model (illness disvalues, treatment actions, treatment plans) may be useful in these efforts.

Additional requirements for the comparative study of medical problems can be surmised. I will limit this and the ensuing discussion to questions that are germane to nonliterate social groupings. The next section will touch briefly on the task of formulating related questions that apply to complex, industrialized nation-states. With these boundaries clearly in mind, then, I suggest the following items as requirements for cross-cultural medical studies. It would appear useful to develop a classification of medical taxonomies. The complexity of these taxonomies, the number and diversity of taxonomic types, and the richness as well as number of treatment plans that are prescribed for each type need to be suitably specified, so that cultural groups can be compared in terms of their manner of structuring medical experiences. At the very least, some procedure for evaluating the kinds of dimensions that people use to describe illness, in particular, the causes of illness, needs to be developed. I mention causes because these often specify the value or significance attached to the illness. The model described in Chapter 6, of course, offers an example of how dimensions of illness can be evaluated. Thus, the disvalues and treatment plans associated with a taxonomic type represent a more or less culturally specific value and significance given to that type. Additional ways of ordering taxonomic types and treatment plans of people obviously enrich the comparative analysis of medical taxonomies. From the standpoint of enhancing our understanding about illness in general, it would be interesting to know which bodily symptoms (or signs) of disease are singled out for ritualistic attention and also the way in which these are handled symbolically by native peoples. Turner has provided rich detail about how the Ndembu people, by means of sympathetic and contagion magical notions, link various aspects of illness with therapeutic actions (Turner 1967). To the extent that we know more generally which components of illness are singled out and how these are worked on by peoples in conformance with cultural rules, we approach a more comprehensive understanding of illness.

Insofar as medical studies, as herein described, would make important use of the social happenings that prefigure and succeed illness occurrences, some procedure for ordering and classifying these happenings would appear desirable. Illness occurrences that follow negatively valued happenings in a group may be labeled and treated in highly selective ways when compared to illness that follows neutral or positive happenings. Similarly, since illness labeling may bear a relationship to who gets sick and when in the life trajectory one gets sick, it would appear desirable to develop ways of classifying the status of persons as well as their prior medical histories. Clearly, no elaborate way of accomplishing these goals is possible, but then again a highly elaborate scheme may not be needed. The social analysis and interpretation of illness may be significantly enhanced simply by being able to make distinctions globally based on the sex, age, or social status of people.

Cross-cultural studies, or, more precisely, social analyses of illness and medical care conducted across cultural groups, are seen as anchored in social categories. In contrast to social epidemiological studies, which examine the (independent) social bases of illness specified in terms of *biological* categories, cross-cultural medical studies as herein described seek to arrive at a *social* formulation of medical problems—that is, to explain the causes, the manifestations, the interpretations, and the consequences of illness using data about social life and about social system functioning and change. Anthropology, in its quest to develop a science of man, has had a traditional interest in explaining how man, his behavior, and his actions are affected by social and cultural systems and how these latter entities evolve and function. Cross-cultural studies of medical problems seek to facilitate and enrich traditional aims of anthropological inquiry by opening the domain of illness and medical care to social analysis. In order to illustrate the substance of what can characterize such studies, I offer a set of research questions that can be entertained.

At the level of the individual, the following problems would seem to require clarification: What are the changes produced by or associated with an occurrence of illness that lead subjects to label the illness the way they do? Given an occurrence of illness of a particular type, how much variability is shown by members of a culture when they label this occurrence? What are the kinds of factors (for example, personal status or history, situation or context, social organization, etc.) that best predict how members of a culture will label and interpret an occurrence of illness? Is the course of illness in a particular individual significantly affected by the way the members of the group label (and hence respond to) the particular occurrence? How do interpretations about an occurrence of illness change during the course of an illness, and what types of factors best explain these changes? What is the relationship between the kind of interpretation given a particular occurrence of illness (as revealed by the taxonomic label applied to it) and the form of treatment? Do certain illness labels invariably occasion distinctive treatments as opposed to others, which may be associated with particular treatment *profiles,* or is the relationship between all taxonomic illness types and treatments variable and problematic in a particular cultural group? What are the factors, biological or social, that explain which medical practitioner will be selected during an illness occurrence? In a particular cultural group, do individuals die from only certain types of illnesses? If so, at what point during the course of an illness occurrence (and as a consequence of what type of factors) is this particular type of illness label applied to the individual? What effects does a death in a particular family have on the subsequent medical history of the family?

Questions involving disease and other medical problems can be framed at the level of the group: Do social groups that are undergoing rapid social change show a greater frequency of illnesses characterized by distinctive labels, disvalues, or treatments? If we assume (as others have done) that a group's medical care system is significantly implicated in the process of social control, how is this form of control actualized at the levels of illness labeling, diagnosis, and treatment? Are illnesses (of a particular type?) more frequent during certain phases or stages of a group's development? How are illness types and treatment plans distributed across prestige or power status positions in a cultural group? How are illness occurrences, and, more importantly, the diagnosis and interpretation of these occurrences, related to existing relations among group members as opposed to nearby (perhaps competing) groups? In situations of contact between cultures, what is the relationship between cultural change (as measured in terms of level of literacy, use of money economy, type of clothing, value identification, etc.) and frequency with which particular taxonomic illness labels are used and treatment plans implemented that involve practitioners and medicines of competing medical care systems? Are groups that function at marginal levels of subsistence characterized by particular kinds of illness labels and/or treatment plans as opposed to other groups with similar forms of social organization but having more plentiful resources? In reference to this particular question it should be understood that in a broad sense treatment plans include not only who formally administers to the ill and what is done but also *how* sick persons are treated by family and group members. Can groups with a predominantly patrilineal form of organization be differentiated at the level of illness frequency, illness typing, treatment plan formulation and implementation, etc., from groups more accurately labeled matrilineal? How are these essentially medical considerations distributed across gender lines in these two types of social groupings? How do groups economize on the energies of their members? How do they capitalize on the remaining strengths of their sick members? This question considers the possibility that illness diagnosing and treatment plan formulation and implementation bear a relation to biosocial components of illness occurrences as well as to sociostructural and functional needs of the group, that is to say, that the functioning of the group is reflected in its medical activities.

The comparative study of medical problems in various cultural settings would seem to allow the anthropologist an opportunity to examine a variety of theoretical questions about the nature of cultural systems. Some examples will be provided, but first it must be appreciated that many of the questions discussed in the previous paragraph can be tested and refined by carrying out studies in several cultural settings. The insights that are gained by being able to generalize across groups in this fashion, insofar as they inform us about medical aspects of cultural organization, maintenance, and change, would make a substantial contribution to cultural theory. In this regard, we may also ask the following: Do groups characterized by distinctive forms or levels of organization show similarities in their beliefs about illness or in the kinds of illnesses that they define? As groups change in their level of organization and complexity, how do their ways of defining and treating illness change? Do groups sharing a form of social organization but differing as to geographic locale have similar ways of explaining and dealing with illness? Is the amount of illness prevalent in a group related to the degree of the variety of illness terms and treatment plans that their members bring to bear on illness, or are these latter factors traceable to the complexity of the group's form of organization? Is there a relationship between the amount or type of illness that is found in a group (measurable by means of a universalistic language as well as in terms of the group's own categories of meaning) and the way in which they provide for the care of the young or, more broadly, structure marital and familial obligations? Do groups in competition with other groups for limited resources explain illness as a consequence of this competition? How does a group's system of medical care change during a period of time when it may be said to be borrowing from a larger, more complex group as opposed to when it may be described as isolated and rejecting (or devaluing) of contacts with the other? The types of treatment and care that are given to persons plagued by illnesses of long duration probably vary; in this light, what features of a group best explain continuity of intense medical care as opposed to brief and token kinds of care? What characterizes cultures that draw significant distinctions (which need to be specified) between illnesses having physiological symptoms and those of a purely psychologic nature (that allow for the type "mental illness")?

The Construction of Sociomedical Theory Using Epidemiologic and Ecologic Data

In this section I will try to summarize how matters involving societal functioning have heretofore been related to those having to do with disease pictures and, importantly, with disease now viewed along traditional nosological lines. As I have emphasized, the information produced by epidemiological and ecological studies has ordinarily been addressed principally to overriding biological and practical concerns, such as the nature of man and the control of disease. The pressing nature of these kinds of questions has had the effect of obscuring how epidemiological data could be brought to bear on questions relevant to social theory. Because the concept of disease in biomedicine is essentially independent in a logical sense from those concepts describing social behavior (see Chapters 3 and 5), considerations to be discussed here involve larger-scale and more abstract aspects of society-medicine relations. It appears that in efforts to use epidemiological data productively for the development or refinement of social theory, larger groups, such as nation-states or civilizations, have served as analytic units, and time segments have correspondingly been expanded. Disease, in short, has been seen in terms of population dynamics; and demography has served as the analytic paradigm. Thus, behavioral elements of disease in space and time and the immediate social responses that these occasion—problems requiring alternative approaches to disease measurement and evaluation —are not in focus. Explanations here are addressed not to the behavioral changes of individuals but rather to the functioning of social systems.

Efforts at sociomedical theory building using this type of analytic paradigm have been anchored in the awareness of the strikingly different population characteristics of groups showing different levels of social organization. Some data reviewed in Chapter 2, for example, suggest that hunter-gatherer groups have a small number of elderly persons and may have evolved a form of population control. Groups at this level typically demonstrate only certain kinds of infectious diseases, namely, those characterized by chronicity, those propagated vertically across generation lines as well as horizontally across space, and those having vectors and/or reservoirs in the animal and insect groups with whom man has intimate contact. In a similar fashion, more settled agricultural groups, and especially those types made possible by the growth of urban centers, tend to show an altogether different population structure and correspondingly provide opportunities for the spread and persistence of different kinds of microorganisms. Epidemics as we have come to know them are a feature of these larger and more permanent urban-centered groups (see Fenner 1970).

The interactions between environmental characteristics, themselves affected by cultural practices, and the biological traits of the population that importantly affect the group's persistence and freedom from disease have figured importantly in these formulations. The hemoglobin S-malaria cycle touched on in Chapter 2 is a paradigmatic instance of these sociobiologic interactions. Although disease outbreaks, some of which have lethal implications, are in a sense promoted and made possible by social advances (and the fact that social considerations *determine* biologic disease will have to be incorporated in this type of sociomedical theory), one observes that the social system characteristically regains ascendancy. This is demonstrated, first, by the sewage disposal, hygienic, and sanitary practices and, later, the chemotherapeutic and immunologic advances that have been developed in the last century, which have had the effect of controlling and largely eliminating the earlier health hazards associated with industrialization. As implied in earlier chapters, we could be said to be now in the midst of a new cycle, namely, that involving the outbreak of chronic and degenerative diseases (a consequence of changing life habits and extended life span) as well as those that we have come to call "emotional" or "mental" diseases. Indeed, the recent controversies over environmental pollutants, the drug abuse "problem," and the apparent broadening definition of disease itself demonstrate rather graphically how societal advances are followed by and/or cause various "disease pictures."

The preceding considerations are, of course, well known and have already been the subject of speculation and much careful discussion (see Dubos 1965, Dunn 1968, Cockburn 1971, Alland 1970, Boyden 1970a, and Burnet and White 1972). What has not heretofore been demonstrated in these efforts, however, is an awareness of the necessity of adopting a sociohistorical framework, of constructing types of societies and patterns of environmental adaptation, of developing indices or measures of how disease pictures can be marked and their consequences graded, of specifying how population-disease interaction "time paths" can be formalized, and of articulating these general social organization-disease outbreak-disease control relations with more specific ones having to do with sociostructural arrangements, including the various modalities of medical care and practice of the different nation-states. Thus, characteristics of how societies organize themselves vis-à-vis medical care and practice, themselves no doubt related to a number of additional sociostructural and historical facts that can be made clearer by developments in comparative sociology, need to be seen as another form of response that social systems make to biomedical contingencies. In this light, it is interesting that contemporary theoretical developments in sociology show that relatively little attention is being given to these sociomedical matters.

By way of summary, I will list what appear to be the general assumptions and orientations that characterize contemporary efforts to develop sociomedical theory using the frame of reference of biology and medical ecology. For heuristic purposes, these assumptions are arranged by subject matter and also by degree of generality. The first set of assumptions, for example, presents fundamental sociobiologic principles, whereas the fourth set of assumptions is more specific and precise and captures what appear to be the projected boundaries of sociomedical theory.

ASSUMPTIONS INVOLVING HUMAN FORMS

1. All forms of life strive toward a state of equilibrium with their "natural" environments.

2. At a certain stage in the development and evolution of life forms, a variety of biological adaptations interrelated with cultural ones (such as bipedalism, expansion of neocortex, ability to use language, capacity to recall and apply past experiences to present ones, emphasis on social rules, elaborate hunting practices) came to characterize Homo sapiens, or man as we know him.

3. At any given point in time, the environment of a group differs with regard to characteristics that require adjustment on the part of the group and its individual members; these characteristics E_i include degree of rainfall, temperature, food resources, predators, parasites, microorganisms, atmospheric pollutants, etc.

4. The biological characteristics of man, like those of other animals, are a response and adaptation to the characteristics of the environment (the E_i); a subset of these biological characteristics B_i may be termed defenses (for example, immunological reactivity, hormonal responsivity, cardiovascular reflexes, capacity for symbolic and emotional transformations), since they protect man from or enable him to adjust to environmental changes or hazards that are capable of causing undesirable organismic changes, or *disease*.

5. All groups are characterized by population parameters P_i (such as age structure, fertility, and sex ratio), which are themselves a result of the group's existing balance with the environment, and actual or potential untoward biological changes (disease) figure importantly in forging these parameters; the P_i are significantly affected by each new balance that the group reaches with its environment (or vis-à-vis disease control) and are reflected in given distributions of B_i.

ASSUMPTIONS INVOLVING DISEASE

1. Members of all human groups G_i are capable of developing a finite number of diseases D_i, which are a result of temporary setbacks in the group's efforts biologically and culturally to establish mastery over the environment; the group's geographic location and climate importantly affect the subset of possible diseases.

2. Diseases prevalent in a group are named, described, and interpreted by the group, often by selected members of the group, for example, elders, experienced members, practitioners, etc.; the identities of diseases, thus, are not given as such but in the broadest sense are created by the group.

3. Diseases vary with regard to their effects on members of the social group and also with regard to their effects at different points in the life cycle of the person; the effects that diseases have depend on the environment and its degree of order and on the corresponding net protection afforded by the B_i. The prevalence of disease and the distribution of B_i in the group, given a set of E_i, importantly affect the P_i. Population biologists attempt to formulate the structure of the population at a given point on the sociocultural evolutionary continuum in terms of P_i and B_i and, in particular, in terms of how these population and biological characteristics relate to the existing environmental conditions (the E_i).

4. A subset of diseases (D_j) produces mainly short-lasting interferences, whereas others (D_k) can lead to the death of a person. Social scientists and biologists strive to make explicit how many and what type of forms diseases can take. In other words, although diseases may be defined in biological terms, their morbidity or social effects on the group need to be specified and quantified in precise terms and in a manner that reflects on the society's capacity to persist, for example, as they affect fertility, capacity to mate, longevity, etc.

5. The number of diseases prevalent in a group as well as their effects are directly and indirectly affected by changes in the way the group is organized both internally and externally (that is, vis-à-vis environmental contingencies).

ASSUMPTIONS INVOLVING DISEASE–SOCIAL GROUP RELATIONS

1. For heuristic purposes, a group's social rules or practices S_i can be divided into three types: (1) socioattitudinal—those that establish social values and affect how members relate to each other (for example, vis-à-vis family, religion, economic pursuits, etc.); (2) sociolegislative—those policy decisions of the group that directly affect the welfare of the community (for example, development of public facilities, medical care practices, sanitation, education, etc.); and (3) socioecologic—those practices that affect how energy from the environment will be extracted, processed, and used (for example, hunting and food distribution practices, food storage practices, access to and manner of using fossilized energy resources, etc.). Changes in any of these social practices are seen as potentially able to bring about effects that can cause new diseases and exacerbate old ones, since they can by definition disrupt the group's equilibrium.

2. A group's practices are constantly being refined, modified, and created; some of these changes can bring about immediate negative organismic consequences, while others can contribute to long-range ones.

3. A group, by modifying its old practices or by developing new ones, is able to undo changes that have resulted in or caused disease outbreaks.

4. A group constantly strives to develop new practices to enable it to control and eliminate disease.

5. The new balances that groups develop, the corresponding disease pictures that these balances entail, and related (or unrelated) changes or developments in social practices "feed back" on the group and can affect the P_i and the B_i and other S_i (for example, attitudes toward aging and disease can affect what is done with the aged and how terminally ill persons are treated, and these in turn affect the P_i, B_i, etc.).

ASSUMPTIONS INVOLVING THE PUTATIVE
DOMAIN OF SOCIOMEDICAL THEORY

1. Social theorists should strive to make explicit the social practices that at different points in time characterize groups and the way in which these change in response to sociohistorical developments; the historical paths that groups traverse vis-à-vis changing social practices are assumed to be finite in number and capable of being formulated; they may be termed H_i.

2. All G_i are associated with a subset of S_i and E_i as well as a population structure P_i characterized by a specific subset of B_i; its members are vulnerable to a subset of D_i. Social theorists should strive to describe accurately each G_i in terms of these parameters.

3. Social theorists should strive to make explicit how each G_i is linked with an H_i, how the unique features of G_i–H_i coupling (that is, vis-à-vis B_i, D_i, and S_i) affect disease outbreaks, and, in turn, how these outbreaks affect the group.

4. There exists a set of general propositions or laws that explain the various sociomedical pathways that groups traverse, and this set of laws remains to be discovered.

To summarize, sociomedical theory as described in this section has involved delineating group characteristics—in terms of social practices (S_i), biological parameters (B_i), population parameters (P_i), and historical time paths (H_i)—that have a bearing on a group's successes and failures in its attempt to achieve mastery of or new equilibrium with the environment. These positions vis-à-vis the environment (specific E_i) are reflected as disease prevalence and incidence. However, it must be re-emphasized that diseases have not yet been described in a socially meaningful way. Some way of equating disease entities (as biomedically articulated) with social costs or burdens needs to be developed in order to use epidemiological data productively for purposes of developing social theory. Similarly, some way must be found of articulating and comparing specific practices aimed at undoing or controlling disease; and these practices will need to be construed broadly and generically. In other words, a way of grouping diverse things, such as sanitation efforts, immunologic practices, medical practices, and types of medical insurance programs, will have to be developed. These matters, of course, need to be related systematically to relevant social practices and histories of various groups (that is, in terms of the forms that social and economic institutions take). It should be emphasized that in a positivistic sense sociomedical theorizing of this type cannot help but be rather general and abstract. In a later section I will touch on a related problem, namely, that of evaluating the efficacy of a group's theory of disease, and will indicate the severe limitations imposed on anyone interested in specifying disease pictures of societies. In a strict sense, levels of disease at a point in time reflect the changing and imperfect understandings that people have about medical matters as revealed by their current definitions of disease. Procedures for measuring disease obviously are tied to these definitions. Consequently, theorizing as described in this section requires that the analyst avail himself of historical documents and infer about past disease pictures using contemporary knowledge and definitions. This particular manner of going about explaining (or theorizing about) how groups relate to their environment and the role of disease in this adaptation is thus essentially sociohistorical. In other words, rather broad macro-level trends are sought, formulated, and then hopefully explained in a formal manner. The concepts referred to earlier (that is, P_i, B_i, S_i, etc.) obviously need to be specified more precisely and refined. As already mentioned, the explanations of society-medicine relations touched on in this section are to be contrasted with the more fine-grained requirements of sociomedical explanations and theorizing described earlier in this chapter and in various portions of the book, which deal with actual occurrences of illness, illness behaviors, and the immediate socio-organizational as well as sociointerpersonal consequences that devolve from these occurrences. In the last section of this chapter I will articulate in a more direct way how this particular behavioral discussion of human disease can also be related to socioecologic matters.

The Use of Sociomedical Data in Operations Research

I would like to turn now to a more practical domain, namely, the field of sociomedical planning. This field is one toward which more and more operations research persons are being drawn. A desire and need of such researchers, it seems to me, is the development of a formal description or model of a society's medical care system. By such a model I shall mean an abstract representation of (1) the components of a society's medical care system, including various institutions and their practices, and (2) a representation (descriptive or mathematical) of how such components are interrelated. Such a model should, for example, include *types of medical personnel,* how personnel are *"produced,"* how they *practice,* and how they are *recompensed.* It should also represent the nature of the *educational institutions* that do the "producing" and the costs associated with this process. Similarly, the *structures* wherein medical care takes place will need to be represented formally such that the outcomes of the several forms of medical care and practice therein contained can be related systematically to the outcomes of other components of the medical care system. Once such a model is designed and operationalized, it should be possible by simulation experiments to estimate effects of alternative sociomedical policies as well as optimal ways of allocating resources for given ends.

It should be clear that a fundamental desideratum of a realistic model of a society's medical care system is the equating of the previously mentioned components and processes of the system with (1) the population served and (2) the various consequences or endpoints of medical care and practice. I would like now to demonstrate that in order to accomplish this requirement, the planner or operations researcher will be forced to develop a procedure for equating biomedical disease categories with social ones, and that, in essence, he will be faced with problems analogous to those described earlier in this chapter. In order to demonstrate this, it will prove instructive to extend fully in one direction the paradigm of social epidemiology. In the following discussion, the reader is referred to Figure 9.1, where much of the material is represented diagrammatically.

We start with a bounded population unit and assume that this pop-

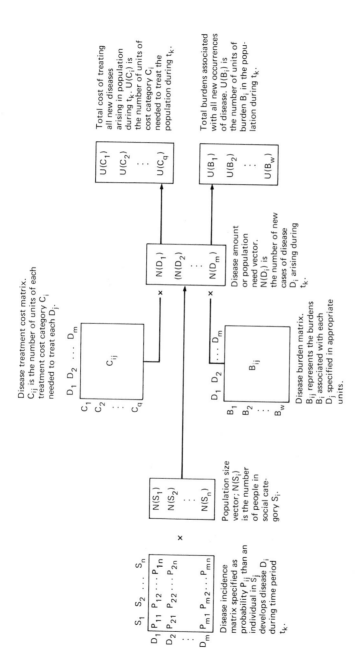

Figure 9.1 Disease-society relations and operations research

ulation can be partitioned exhaustively into mutually exclusive social categories or cells that are relevant from the standpoint of disease incidence (such as age, sex, ethnicity, social class, etc.). Various diseases are believed to develop among members of this population. Thus, by drawing on the established knowledge of social epidemiology it might become possible to develop a disease incidence matrix composed of m disease rows and n socially relevant categories or columns, each entry P_{ij} in this matrix representing the probability that an individual in social category j develops disease D_i during a suitable time interval t_k. By multiplying such a matrix by a vector descriptive of the size of the population (that is, the number of persons in each social category), we arrive at the amount of disease expected in the population during time interval t_k specified in terms of numbers of each D_i anticipated. Let us call this a *disease amount vector*. Two projections of this scheme will be illustrated: one descriptive of the costs associated with the treatment of disease, the other descriptive of the burdens occasioned by disease.

In order to compute the costs to the population of treating diseases, we will assume that studies of the process of medical care have furnished us with the capability of developing a *disease treatment cost matrix* composed of q rows involving relevant treatment cost categories (for example, physician man-hours, drug costs, nursing time hours, equipment time) and the m disease columns previously articulated. An entry C_{ij} in the matrix constitutes the cost of treating an average occurrence of disease j using units of treatment cost category i. It should be emphasized that it might become possible to articulate several matrices, each describing different ways in which treatment resources can be distributed in the various categories. Alternatively, relying on just one way of distributing treatment resources in the treatment of a given disease, different matrices might describe different endpoints one might wish to use in the treatment process. In short, the idea of such a matrix should bring to mind any number of types of matrices that can be developed as well as the various uses these may be expected to serve. Obviously, by multiplying such a matrix by the disease amount vector just mentioned, one obtains the costs to the population of implementing these various treatment strategies during the time interval.

For purposes of estimating the burdens to the population occasioned by disease, let us assume we have available a *disease burden matrix* composed of w rows, each describing a disease burden category (for example, number of workdays actually lost, number of days of impairment in fulfilling work duties), and the previously articulated m disease columns, an entry B_{ij} in this matrix describing the social burdens i to the population (specified in appropriate units) that are occasioned by an average occurrence of disease j. By multiplying such a matrix by the previously developed disease amount vector, one could in theory estimate the total burdens to the population occasioned by new disease occurrences during the specified interval of time. Again, one can imagine any number of forms that such a matrix can take as well as different ways in which it could be used.

The preceding discussion has a number of weaknesses and limitations, and I emphasize that its purpose is purely heuristic, that is, to illustrate some of the potential uses of social epidemiologistic data and how operations research persons and other social planners might be expected to use such data in order to study disease in relation to the functioning of social systems.[1] The important point is that the schemes discussed will be seen to require bridging across what we can now label precisely as the biological and the social frames of reference. Thus, in the present context, let us assume that alternative costs of treating a particular disease

[1] The limitations of modeling a society's medical care system along the rather abstract lines outlined above are legion. Here I will mention only a few of these: (1) there are problems associated with defining relevant disease treatment and burden categories as well as providing units of measurement; (2) problems associated with how the relevant categories are numerically interrelated remain to be solved; (3) costs of treating disease to different endpoints and burdens occasioned by disease are not unitary sorts of quantities but can be expected to vary across social groupings; (4) disease categories are empirically interrelated, and it can be anticipated that the attempt to compute the burdens or costs of treating clusters of related diseases will encounter grave difficulties; (5) for modeling medical care, the scheme assumes (falsely) that each person seeking care has or shows a disease; (6) the processes involved in the pursuit of care are collapsed within the notion of "probability" that an individual develops a disease; (7) furthermore, each and every new occurrence of a disease is simply assumed to receive treatment; (8) every person with a disease when brought to a care facility and linked to a treatment cost scheme is assumed to stay in treatment until optimal (or arbitrarily specified) benefits have been derived (this is clearly a false assumption, as the literature on compliance with medical regimens shows); and (9) the scheme simply overlooks the many factors that compete in the individual's mind with the desire to pursue and stay in medical treatment.

specified biologically can be developed (for example, cost of treating $D_i = aC_1 + bC_2 + \ldots + nC_n$, where $a, b, \ldots, n$ are constants specifying amounts of each treatment cost category $C_1, C_2, \ldots, C_n$ needed to treat D_i). Now, if the uses or endpoints of treatment involve social considerations (for example, removal of a certain amount of disability, alleviation of weakness, reinstating the physical capacity for limited work), then it becomes clear that the computation of such costs requires equating biological factors with social ones. The need for developing a procedure that allows one to meaningfully equate biological categories with social ones becomes even clearer when we consider what was referred to previously as a disease burden matrix, for in order to articulate the burdens of a disease to a population, one is confronted with the need of translating an occurrence of a particular disease into relevant social and behavioral constraints and incapacities. This problem can be symbolized by examining the kind of mathematical expression that in a futuristic spirit one might expect will be developed in the effort to express the burden(s) of an average occurrence of a given disease: Burden $B_i = f(I_1, I_2, \ldots, I_n)$, where B_i is a relevant social burden, and $I_1, I_2, \ldots, I_n$ represent biological parameters or indicators of a given disease. Here, in short, the problem of crossing the biological (that is, I_1, I_2, etc.) and the social (B_i) frames of reference is symbolized by the f of the equation, which signifies that the particular social burden of the disease is a function of the parameters indicating that disease. Clearly, present knowledge about disease manifestations and consequences does not allow one to construct such a mathematical expression, and I argue that the imprecision, if not illogicality, of crossing the social and biological domains is a contributing factor.

I close this section by pointing out once again that if the intent of an operations researcher is to conduct social analyses of disease and medical care, then he is limited if he relies exclusively on the traditional biomedical definition of disease and on contemporary social epidemiological data. Indeed, in the various reviews conducted in Chapters 1 and 2 and in the additional critique of discipline-centered sociomedical studies, we have been led to appreciate the many sorts of processes and changes that are associated with disease occurrences and that are simply left out of focus because disciplinary questions do not require their articulation. We see now that many practical exigencies and needs confronting medicine are difficult to realize precisely because of such disciplinary biases.

On the Evaluation of the Efficacy of a Group's Theory of Disease

Diseases, we have seen, are ubiquitous in nature and have always been found regularly associated with human groups. Furthermore, since diseases by definition are problematic and costly to members of groups, they inevitably are made the focus of corrective actions. By *a group's theory of disease* I am referring to those concepts and laws that members of a group avail themselves of in explaining the prevalence and mechanisms involved in the development of disease. In addition, in explaining the fundamental reasons for the existence of disease, such theories also implicitly or explicitly set forth the means by which members go about controlling and/or eliminating disease, and in this sense the theory's efficacy could in principle be evaluated. In view of the important and central role played by theories of disease in a society's efforts to maintain itself, it is striking that few investigators have addressed themselves directly to the range of issues associated with how theories of disease grow and function. It is evident that when analyzing the factors that determine how theories of disease develop and function, one probes the very essence of how societies exert control over nature. Even given this straightforward statement regarding the central and fundamental role of a group's theory of disease and the strategic value of studying related matters, we should expect that the study of disease in this light poses special problems. First of all, a group's theory of disease changes through time and bears an obvious relation to a range of social and historically bound processes. Furthermore, in the absence of empirical data regarding the prevalence and distribution of disease (*that is, disease as defined by the particular group*) we can anticipate that only the efficacy of a limited segment of a group's theory of disease is amenable to analysis. Add to this the fact that a theory of disease is like a sign or emblem that marks what the group values, disvalues, and, more generally, preoccupies itself with; and it is apparent that a rather formidable obstacle is presented to one interested in analyzing and comparing the efficacy of various disease theories. Consequently, we shall have to set some realistic boundaries to the problem at hand.

We will limit this discussion to contemporary nonliterate groups and omit the difficult problem of evaluating the success of earlier historical groups' efforts at controlling disease. In this light, a theory of disease can be described as a social group's explanation of the causes of disease and of the kinds of changes associated with states so labeled. To the extent that the theory guides activities that diminish the burdens of disease, it is effective. There are at least two points of reference that can be adopted in this evaluation: that of individual persons and that of the group as a whole. A theory of disease may contribute to low morbidity and/or mortality at the level of individuals but prove deleterious to the group as a whole; on the other hand, in promoting the persistence and continued functioning of the group it may prove disadvantageous to certain individuals. In each of these cases, the evaluation of efficacy requires one to judge whether the theory leads to behaviors that prevent the onset, limit the spread, diminish the intensity, promote the eradication, and/or control the manifestations of disease. Here, attention is given only to whether the individual is affected positively, and benefits at the group level are not discussed. It is of course obvious that nonliterate and peasant groups typically do not have the technical knowledge and resources of industrialized nations, and this lack is reflected in the limited understanding that they have about the physiological bases of disease. Nevertheless, one cannot exclude the possibility that folk remedies might have physiological consequences that are desirable. This dimension of a theory's "usefulness," however, is also not discussed here.[2]

2 It should be evident that a multidisciplinary investigation of the way members of a cultural group conceptualize and use herbs and folk preparations of various sorts will afford a clarification of a number of problems central to a "psychosomatic" understanding of disease. Briefly, by delineating (1) the chemical constituents of herbs, (2) their physiological actions under controlled and experimental conditions, (3) their psychological effects under socially and culturally appropriate circumstances, and (4) the social consequences of their use in the group of the person who is sick, it should be possible to clarify the reciprocal influences between cultural and biological systems. An examination of this sort, then, not only clarifies the question of the efficacy of a group's theory of disease (which prescribes the various herbs) but

Even within the constraints just outlined it is still possible to evaluate the effectiveness of a particular theory of disease, by determining whether the theory promotes treatment actions that are effective. An evaluation of this type presupposes that there is some standard against which the group's theory can be compared, since we lack empirical data about the "real" or cultural disease pictures of the corresponding groups. In this regard, the unified or systems view of disease will be used as a standard, and attention will be given to the role of psychological factors. The unified view of disease can be summarized by the following fundamental proposition:

Disturbances in any system can cause disturbances in other systems, and all systems are manifestationally implicated in any occurrence of disease (where systems are represented by the biochemical, the social, the psychological, the interpersonal, etc.).

Since the organism is depicted as a set of hierarchically linked open systems, it follows that a disturbance or stress in any one system can bring about deleterious changes in others; the totality of these changes we may term *disease*. For example, the anxiety or guilt associated with a discordant personal relationship (psychological system) has associated hormonal and/or psychophysiological changes that can eventuate in structural bodily damage. A theory that identifies *correctly* the psychological conflicts that contribute to the development of a disease will be judged effective, since treatment actions entailed by that theory are likely to resolve the conflicts. This evaluation follows from the more general assumption that a particular form of medical practice can be termed effective to the extent that it first identifies those changes in a system's functioning that actually cause or initiate disease processes and then restores these during treatment.

In order to use the fundamental systems proposition to examine a group's theory of disease, one must first specify the kinds of interpretation that can be given to this proposition. Two interpretations will be distinguished:

---

also makes explicit the many ways in which cultural factors influence body functioning and bodily sensations.

1. *A behavior-specific interpretation:* Discrete and highly specific behavioral events can be held to be causally significant. For example, if an individual's father dies or if his or her spouse deserts, then this can bring about changes in various bodily systems.

2. *An event-class interpretation:* Only events of a certain type (that is, emotionally significant ones) can cause disease. In this form, the kinds of values and meanings that are attached to specific events will determine whether these events will in turn cause or contribute to disease. This is to say that the culture of a people must be taken into account in evaluating which situations or behaviors have medical significance.

With the preceding considerations serving as background and, importantly, using the systems or unified view of disease as a standard, one may then go on to evaluate the effectiveness of a group's theory of disease.

BEHAVIOR-SPECIFIC INTERPRETATION

The systems or unified view of disease is true in terms of specific behaviors. A consequence of this particular interpretation of the unified view of disease is that in *any* society or group, regardless of its culture, certain behavioral occurrences may lead to changes in a person's physiological systems; these changes can be termed *disease*. One may anticipate some difficulty in initially defining who the equivalent of "spouse" or father is in a particular culture, but having done this one should be able to predict potential medical consequences in line with our proposition. It follows then that *if* a sociocultural unit's theory of disease proposes that such specific behavioral occurrences can cause disease and, furthermore, if treatment practices entail resolving the associated crises, *then* one can regard the theory in that sense as adaptive or positive vis-à-vis medical issues. In other words, to the extent that people (1) acknowledge this "fact" in their beliefs about interpersonal relations and medical matters (that is, that highly specific interpersonal or social occurrences can cause disease) and, furthermore, (2) reflect these beliefs in their actual behaviors and dispositions toward medical treatment, then (3) to that extent they can be viewed as espousing a view of disease that is adaptive and positive. In short, an interpretation of the unified view of disease that stresses its truth in this behavior-specific form allows one to evaluate very directly the adaptiveness of a people's theory of disease, and this is the case because in assuming the validity of this form of the systems view, one can make *universal statements* regarding the medical consequences of highly specific social and behavioral events (such as deaths, unresolved separations).

EVENT-CLASS INTERPRETATION

The unified or systems view of disease is true but in a more general form, namely, that only "emotionally significant events" can cause disease. In this instance, to evaluate properly how closely a group's theory of disease conforms to the standard, it would appear that the general cultural and value orientation of a group as well as its specific theory of disease should be taken into account. For purposes of analysis, then, one needs to distinguish analytically three items of information: (1) the systems or unified theory of disease as articulated in this more general form, (2) the general value or cultural orientation of a group (that is, the set of symbols and patterns of expectations that guide the actions of members of a group and, in particular, the emotional valuations that are placed on events, occurrences, and behaviors of various types, and, related to (2) insofar as it represents a unit within the culture, (3) the theory of disease that is articulated by the culture of the group, in particular, the sets of symbols, expectations, assumptions, and emotional valuations that are associated with occurrences of disease and with the treatment of disease.

It should be emphasized at the outset that the systems proposition in this general form can be interpreted tautologously to mean that treatment practices of all groups or cultures must be to some extent effective. Thus, by definition, medical treatment involves ritualistic actions and practices of various sorts that are designed to eliminate or control those factors that are thought to cause disease. Since these practices are invested with emotional significance and in a cognitive sense are believed to be curative, they can be seen as resolving or discharging in a culturally appropriate way the anxiety and emotional stress triggered by or associated with the causal factors regardless of what content these factors may have in the culture. This is the case because *by definition* illness is assumed to be problematic, that is, emotionally upsetting. In other words, the definition of what brings on the illness or what is awry is a culturally specified "fact," and experts of the culture articulate such facts. Furthermore, treatment entails dealing with this problematic and stressful "reality" in a rational and emotionally involving way. The psychiatrist who in treating an ulcer patient tries to help by getting him to acknowledge and/or resolve feelings associated with an interpersonal crisis (that he believes is causing the illness) is acting in ways analogous to a folk practitioner or shaman who is guiding and instructing a sick person in the proper execution of a treatment ritual in order to overcome or neutralize the factors that (he judges) are causing the disease. Both practices are aimed at removing or resolving the underlying disturbance that is judged as causing the disease, and both practices accomplish this aim by the use of methods and symbols that are invested with emotional significance for the sick person. One may of course say that the etiological factors identified by the psychiatrist are valid or "correct" (since he relies on the scientific method), whereas the factors identified by the shaman are not necessarily the correct ones (since he does not rely on the scientific method). A reply might be *either* that the psychiatrist often heals despite the fact that he has identified the wrong cause precisely because of his influence *or* that shamans usually heal because, on intuitive grounds, they have managed to identify correctly a psychological, or interpersonal, conflict that underlies a particular disorder. Issues bearing on this point have led a number of psychiatrists and psychologically oriented anthropologists to propose that primitive medical treatment constitutes a form of ("folk") psychotherapy.[3] These issues will not be pursued further here. Suffice it to say that if one holds that the systems or unified view of disease is true in the general form enunciated earlier in this section, then since all treatment practices are to some extent *rational* and *affectively* involving, in certain ways they can be judged analytically as effective.

[3] It should be mentioned that determining in a compelling way whether this is in fact the case poses a formidable empirical problem—it requires one to find out precisely: (1) what emotional factors "truly" underlie and contribute to a disease; (2) what emotional factors are judged by the practitioner to underlie the disease; (3) the degree of correspondence between (1) and (2); and (4) the degree of effectiveness of resolution of (1), whether this is accomplished directly or indirectly by (2). Each of these four component tasks entails a delineation of affectively charged interpersonal issues in a culture *different from* the one in which the investigator has been socialized. Consequently, an assertion that simply glosses over these tasks and states that primitive medicine is "folk psychotherapy" must be regarded only as a working hypothesis.

It is when one distinguishes between, on the one hand, the valuation of those symbols that are fundamental and basic in a culture and, on the other, the valuation of those other, more specific symbols that are involved in the explanations and cures of disease that one is afforded the opportunity of evaluating in a more precise way the effectiveness of a particular group's theory of disease. In this light, one can hypothesize that emotional significance or valuation can be equated with economic significance or value. Thus, the monetary value associated with the function, purpose, or significance of something (that is, how much an event, occurrence, person, transaction, etc., ends up costing an individual) is equivalent to its emotional significance. With this thesis in mind, one can delineate two hypothetical groups or cultures:

Culture X: Supernatural events or occurrences as these are revealed in natural occurrences (such as cloud formations) determine economic prosperity. Human relations are comparatively less valuable. Human relationships, in fact, are highly formalized and ritualistic, and the network of these is so extensive and diversified that any one relationship or type of relationship has relatively low economic value (that is, emotional significance).

Culture Y: The satisfactions derived from interpersonal relationships are in an economistic and emotional sense the most valuable and significant. Environmental resources are relatively constant and plentiful, so that the efficiency and harmony implicit in social relationships determines subsistence level and success. Furthermore, these social relationships are invested with great significance. Supernatural events and occurrences are of comparatively smaller value and significance, and reflections of these in nature (for example, atmospheric conditions) are likewise of comparatively little value.

At the same time, let us for purposes of simplicity posit two basic theories of disease that we wish to evaluate:

Theory A: The gods and ancestors cause disease and reveal themselves exclusively through weather changes.

Theory B: Problems of an interpersonal nature cause disease, and these are reflected in the stream of social life.

With these considerations in mind, one may proceed with the analysis. Figure 9.2 relies on the two variables (cultural orientation and theory of disease) and illustrates the logical possibilities. If one assumes as

	Theory of Disease	
	A	B
Culture — X	1	2
Y	3	4

Figure 9.2 Relationship between cultural orientation and theory of disease

true the fundamental systems proposition in the form that states that emotionally significant occurrences can cause disease, then cells 1 and 4 show a complementarity or isomorphism between a group's general cultural orientation and its theory of disease. That is, in cells 1 and 4 that which at a fundamental level is economically and emotionally significant in the culture is also held to be causative of or directly implicated in disease. To the extent that members of the group have ways of dealing with disease that are cognitively and emotionally significant, ways that are articulated by and *congruent with* their theory about the causes of disease, then they may be said to deal with disease adaptively and positively. In other words, in investing personal concern in treat-. ment practices and symbols that are isomorphic to those general symbols most highly valued in the culture, members of the group are acting *congruently:* medical treatment practices and activities draw on the most important cultural symbols. On the other hand, cells 2 and 3 show a disjunction between what is economically (or emotionally) significant and what is causative of disease. Medical treatment, in these instances, does not draw on the fundamental and basic symbols of the group. Since (1) it is assumed that the psychosomatic proposition is true (that is, emotionally significant events cause disease), and (2) since the group's theory of disease articulates causes that (in terms of its own ideology) are less economically (that is, emotionally) significant in a fundamental way, then (3) there is an *incongruity* or relative lack of isomorphism between its theory of disease and its underlying value orientation. In this sense, the theory can be described as less adaptive or positive.

The previous discussion must be viewed only as a heuristic exercise. The discussion has obvious limitations, if not inconsistencies, some of which have already been noted. For example, disease is a central pre-occupation of all people, and important, that is, emotionally significant, symbols are usually brought to bear on its control. Similarly, in all cultures social relations are invested with emotional significance. Nevertheless, the discussion has merit insofar as it points up several issues that stand in need of clarification in the theory and practice of psychosomatic medicine. First, in articulating the systems or unified view of disease, in particular, the fundamental psychosomatic proposition regarding the causal influence of psychological factors, one needs to make specific the form in which the proposition is believed to hold—that is, either with regard to specific behavioral events or in a more abstract form, which specifies the type of event. Second, in thinking about how cultural patterns influence disease, one needs to distinguish analytically among (1) culturally specific theories of disease; (2) within (1), the emotional valuations that are attached to different types of events that are believed to cause disease (and which may be the focus of medical treatment); and (3) within the general cultural orientation, the different kinds of emotional valuations and behavioral prescriptions that are associated with universal interpersonal occurrences (death of spouse or parents, altercations in nuclear families, etc.). Third, one must analyze in an uncompromising way the basis and source of the systems or unified view of disease, a task that may require a form of historical analysis. The relevant question here is, Does the fundamental psychosomatic proposition articulate what one may term *a law of nature,* or does it simply enunciate an empirical generalization born of clinical observations and careful studies of disease that have been conducted recently in a particular (Western, humanistic, Judeo-Christian) culture—itself heavily influenced by earlier dualistic notions vis-à-vis disease—or in cultures of a particular type variously termed "Mediterranean" or expressive"? Tied to this latter issue, of course, is the assumption that a group's cultural orientation may affect its view of disease, and that furthermore, both of these affect what its members do about disease. Taken together, these points can lead to a rational and more refined evaluation of the effectiveness of a group's theory of disease. One may, of course, be led to wonder through what mechanism a group's culture and value orientation actually influence the kind of view and theory of disease that is developed by its members. Last, the previous discussion should make evident the pressing need that exists in psychosomatic medicine for cross-cultural research, both in the general realm of how culturally specific views and theories of disease, viewed as formulas of *psychosomatic mediation,* affect treatment practices and actual occurrences and, more specifically, with regard to the cross-cultural validity of the systems or unified view of disease itself. By identifying the type or theory of disease *and* the types of emotionally relevant events articulated in the cultures of different peoples, cross-cultural medical studies may eventually enable one to assess the validity of the fundamental psychosomatic proposition.

On the Psychological Manifestations of Neuropsychiatric Entities

In this section I will continue to discuss theoretical matters in social medicine. I will deal with a question that has intrigued psychiatrists and behavioral scientists for some time, namely, that of how the so-called "psychiatric diseases" are expressed cross-culturally. I have already emphasized the problems implicit in the way this question is ordinarily posed and studied (see Chapters 1–3). There it was mentioned that people who study this question often adopt a narrow frame of reference that inappropriately constrains field observations and analysis, and also that conditions for proper assessment of behavior cross-culturally are frequently not met. Assuming that these difficulties are overcome or properly controlled, the question of the purely psychological manifestations of psychiatric diseases in other cultures remains, and it is an interesting one, which unfortunately has not been studied in any great detail.

It should be emphasized that evaluating how Western disease types, such as schizophrenia or depression (or any other so-called psychiatric disease for that matter), are manifested at the psychological level in contrasting cultural settings offers the researcher a rich opportunity to clarify fundamental aspects about human behavior. Traditional approaches to this problem have involved studying socialization patterns in relation to processes of personality functioning, the latter construed in motivational and dynamic terms. Perceptual-cognitive aspects of this same issue, namely, that of the form and expression of psychiatric disease in contrasting cultures, have been relatively underemphasized. Yet it is precisely the careful evaluation of such processes that is currently receiving a great deal of attention in anthropology, as I have emphasized repeatedly in this book. If properly applied to the study of psychiatric disorders, such evaluations would offer an opportunity for the testing of prevailing assumptions about both psychiatric disease and the influence of culture on psychological functioning. Culture, in this light, may be defined as the shared cognitive processes of a people; these, to be sure, encompass ordinary rules of conduct; however, such rules need to be seen as grafted onto basic perceptual-cognitive constancies that grow out of how people represent the physical and nonphysical world. Let us posit that persons, in relating to their physical and social environment, employ a finite number of perceptual categories by means of which they order sensory input. Perceptual categories are an outgrowth of both biological attributes and culturally programmed learning experiences and can be seen as furnishing the raw units of experience. These categories may be described as ordered into various classes, and the ordering or patterning of these, in turn, may be said to form a "cognitive map" of the world. The learned meanings of a group or culture can be seen as represented in and by such a map. Through the execution of various rules that are culturally specific, individuals are believed to process in a meaningful and consistent way the data of experience, that is, the meanings furnished by the cognitive map of the world (Wallace 1961b, 1962). Now, a group's language must be judged as intimately connected with the paradigm of culture just presented. The exact nature of this connection is problematic, and we cannot go into this aspect of the problem here. Suffice it to say that perceptual categories can be analogized to the encoding and transferability of basic information by means of *lexical* items, and the cognitive map as well as the rules of operation performed on the information contained in the map can be compared with the syntactic and semantic structures of language. Linguistic relativism and the Sapir-Whorf hypothesis are the names given to the ways in which relations among language, thought, and culture have heretofore been formulated. Although there is controversy as to whether thought actually derives from language, there is little doubt that language influences cognition through memory and may actually guide perception under conditions of ambiguity (Cole et al. 1971, Lloyd 1972).

Let us now see how this formulation may be used to understand the way in which culture and psychiatric disease might be related. It is the positing of such relations, their articulation in the form of hypotheses, and the subsequent testing of these in the field that may help clarify basic aspects of behavior and disease. I will concentrate on so-called psychoses, adopt for heuristic purposes a purely psychological approach, and compare depression with schizophrenia. I will posit that depression is a bona fide disease entity that primarily affects the individual's coloring of experience and level of activity; and, in particular, that a feeling tone we term "sadness" is a component of this entity depression. According to many, sadness constitutes one of the primary emotions of man—a biological verity, if you will. Cultures may differ with regard to what produces sadness, but that such emotional tones are realized is generally accepted. Following the registration of the emotions in the central nervous system, there is an activation of distinctive facial muscular groups by what is termed a "facial affect program"; however, situational factors and cultural conventions are believed to influence the possible activation of such muscles (Ekman 1972). In brief, the consequences of emotions, their meanings, their elaborations into behavior, and the way in which they are expressed are affected by culturally specific display rules, although all people everywhere are believed to share and recognize to some extent the workings of the "facial affect program."

Given the essentially complex way in which the primary emotions get reworked and channeled by culture, an altered psychobiologic organismic state that is long-lasting and that includes sadness and diminished activity can be expected to assume various "appearances" cross-culturally. I will assume, nevertheless, that changes brought about during an instance of depression do not alter the basic ordering or form of the individual's cognitive apparatus. The model of culture reviewed earlier is not seen as structurally altered during an instance of depression. Perceptual categories, the orderings of these into a cognitive map, and the rules of operation are judged as structurally intact in depression at least in its early stages. The manifestations of the disease are believed instead to reflect quantitative alterations in the functioning of the cognitive apparatus. Thus, a slowing of bodily processes and information processing together with changes in the coloring of an individual's experiencing of his world will, I anticipate, be expressed in habitually ordered ways. In other words, when viewed against the prevailing cultural norms, the form of behavior during depression is preserved, though exaggerations or deviations in content are to be expected. The investigator wishing to find and understand depression is thus required first to construct a model of the culture by means of an analysis of the prevailing language and then to use both the model and the language to infer how behavior is ordered in the culture, since it is in terms of such habitual behavioral patterns that the changes of the disease processes are likely to be channeled and expressed. Alternatively, by analyzing the behavior of disturbed or deviant individuals, he is expected to infer the meanings of various segments (such as actions, verbalizations, etc.) using the understanding of the culture generated by his model and command of the language. Once this is accomplished, he is then in the position to see which of these behaviors might correspond to behaviors ordinarily felt to indicate depression. The investigator, for example, is required to study the culture and learn the various emotional terms, the meanings and interpretations given to these, how emotions are likely to be expressed behaviorally in the light of such meanings, the ways in which sensory information about the body and physical world is ordered and represented cognitively, the interpretations placed on fundamental physical and biological processes, etc., for it is in terms of these culturally shared perceptions, cognitions, and culturally based theories of the world (that is, existential premises) that the individual will experience and express the effects produced by the profound psychological changes seen in depression. Using this paradigm, then, we would say that cross-cultural differences in the manifestations of depression are a direct expression of, and consequently deducible from, differences in the prevailing cultures (as represented in our models or maps of these cultures). For this reason, the manifestations of depression could be hypothesized to be derivable, in a systematic and direct way, from fundamental perceptual-cognitive categories and rules of operation that differ cross-culturally but that retain their form and order during the disease process.

For purposes of contrast, let me posit that schizophrenia is also a bona fide disease entity, that it affects the way in which the individual regulates attention (specifically, that the disorder involves the stimulus-response process), and that failure to regulate and selectively inhibit attention brings about a breakdown in perceptual constancies, or, stated differently, a change in the individual's perceptual categories (McGhie and Chapman 1961, Shakow 1971). In schizophrenia, thus, I anticipate a loosening or outright alteration in the ordering and form in which experience is cast. Thought, mood, and behavioral changes in schizophrenia are seen as consequences of, or responses to, these fundamental perceptual-cognitive alterations. Now the pattern of a culture or a "cognitive map" can also be expected to influence how schizophrenia is expressed but in a way that differs from depression. Since such a map is judged as formally unaltered during depression, its structure and central organizing themes will bear a direct, almost isomorphic, relation to the structure and organization of behavior during an instance of disease. In schizophrenia, on the other hand, key "nodes" or concepts in the map that determine how the individual defines his position vis-à-vis the world become differentially important, since it is these that regulate attention and in turn determine the overall meaning given to the information furnished by the perceptual categories as a result of the channeling of attention. In other words, I assume that man, like other animals, attends to the world and processes sensory data by means of perceptual categories that are biologically constrained. However, the information furnished by these categories is interpreted on the basis of fundamental conceptions of who he is, where he is, and what he is. These fundamental explanations implicitly guide and give significance to any experience that is sustained by the activation of the perceptual categories, and these explanations, furthermore, are part of what culture is all about. In our culture, for example, a central concept or node is that of the person who is articulated as though somehow separated from the world and also as composed of differing sorts of elements and processes, for example, mind as opposed to body. Attention is regulated and perceptual categories formed on the basis of a "cognitive map" that isolates the individual from his world and even body, and which gives him a separated, controlling, almost superordinate position in the web of experience. Failures in the regulation of attention and the consequent breakdown in perceptual constancies, which are assumed here to be hallmarks of the schizophrenic process, are interpreted in the light of what they mean about or portend for the person who in our culture is defined as someone who is supposed to be centrally and autonomously "placed" in a world of space and time and who judges himself as a master or controller of sorts. We must assume that other cognitive maps and linguistic systems do not articulate such a view of self or person, and that consequently attentional regulation and perceptual constancies are not predicated and dependent on this view of self and personhood. Consequently, processes that disrupt how attention is regulated and how perceptual categories function (in this case, an instance of schizophrenia) will be expressed differently—partially in terms of the substance or content of the categories, partially in terms of the organization and form that they take on in the cognitive map, and partially in terms of the central assumptions and premises that give the information that they furnish symbolic and structural significance. We anticipate, then, that manifestations of schizophrenia in a particular culture will represent a complex function of the group's cognitive map, and that such manifestations will not preserve in a systematic way the form and orderings of the perceptual categories observed. Behavior changes traced to schizophrenia, when compared cross-culturally, then, would not necessarily be duducible from propositions that directly express the form and content of a culture's perceptual categories and cognitive map (as in the case of depression) but instead would indirectly and complexly reflect fundamental changes in the orderings and form of these and, in particular, in terms of those basic notions of self that articulate experience. The task of the investigator studying schizophrenic disease cross-culturally can for this reason be expected to be very complex, since it requires him not only to obtain an accurate cognitive map of the culture but also to uncover and specify those underlying and fundamental premises about self in terms of which he channels attention and which give meaning to any information that is furnished by the perceptual categories.

The psychological study of neuropsychiatric entities such as depression and schizophrenia in various cultures thus presents the researcher with an opportunity of probing the very essence of how culture articulates and "rationalizes" for man his unique position in the world. The one "disease" disturbs his basic level of activity and, most importantly, his degree of satisfaction with himself and his position; whatever emotional quality attaches to the experience of being a participating member of culture (and we must assume that this quality is a product of the unique cultural map that the individual draws on to explain his position in the world) is hedonically despoiled and undermined in depression. The other "disease" shatters or at least alters drastically the fundamental perceptual constancies that the individual draws on to sustain the unique position and role in the world that his culture endows him with; whatever structure, organization, and meaning the individual is provided by or draws from culture, they all require perceptual regularities for their articulation, and it is precisely these regularities that schizophrenia disturbs. It should be clear, then, that when studying these neuropsychiatric entities the researcher is placed in a strategic position to uncover elemental aspects about man's conception of his place in the world. Indeed, it is because these matters are so elementally tied to notions of self, identity, and meaning vis-à-vis the world that they require very rigorous methods of inquiry for their elucidation.

The preceding discussion has many limitations that need to be made explicit. In the first place, I am assuming for heuristic purposes that the fundamental processes signified by the term *depression* involve psychological changes, and furthermore, that these include a distinctive alteration in mood as described. Clearly, any disease process (especially the one selected here) is associated with a whole range of types of changes, and these develop and express themselves in complex ways (always influenced to some extent by culture). We could instead, for example, hold that the fundamental changes of this disease, although spanning the various systems of the person, do not mark any distinctive mood. The sadness and despair that are hallmarks of "depression" could be judged as simply a "Western version" of this disease. This would then leave for further cross-cultural study clarification of what the basic mood changes marking this disease are. A second limitation is that the view of the respective "psychoses" contained in the discussion is an overly simplified one. Thus, in psychotic depressions one obviously can find associated perceptual and cognitive difficulties, and, on the other hand, persons classified as schizophrenic manifest perceptual cognitive changes in an emotionally charged context, which can include sadness and despair. I do not mean to imply either that thought and emotion can be easily separated or that each is reflected in the absence of the other. In this discussion, then, I could be said to be dealing with the early changes in the psychoses (as we have come to understand them), analytically treating thought and cognition as though these were separate and adopting an essentially descriptive (as opposed to dynamic and etiologic) approach. I also do not mean to suggest that only in schizophrenia are notions of self and identity relevant. Clearly, fundamental existential premises about self and identity must be assumed to play an influential role in *both* depression and schizophrenia. I assume, however, that the changes brought about in these diseases are substantially different, and that they affect the individual's sense of identity differently, as I have indicated. Last, the preceding discussion has proceeded on the a priori assumption that entities we term depression and schizophrenia are universal, and moreover, that the fundamental processes that they disturb are those that *we* in Western culture have identified as significant. As I have tried to emphasize throughout this book, assumptions of this type are either erroneous or fraught with difficulties and also essentially beg the very questions that can be seen as requiring clarification cross-culturally, that is, those concerning the influences of culture and social systems on human disease. Assumptions such as these that involve the nature of what depresssion and schizophrenia "are," thus, cannot be other than mere *working assumptions*. Indeed, the task of the researcher is that of *refining* his understanding of depression or schizophrenia by cross-cultural analyses. Only by continued work along this line will a broadly grounded theory of human disease emerge.

Toward a Theory of Human Disease

Disease has been with man throughout his evolutionary history. It is by definition the successful coping with the burdens of disease that has contributed to man's phylogenetic identity. This biological significance of disease, however, should not be seen only as limiting the capacity of groups to reproduce, a type of mechanical view of the relations among disease, man, and social systems. In a broader view, it is because of associated changes in the way people behave in relation to the physical environment and their comembers that disease initially shows itself, and it is by altering the organization of groups and limiting their capacity to establish an equilibrium with their ecosystem (which involves a social dimension) that disease continues to have relevance. This includes, but is not limited by, the concept of "reproductive potential." It is in terms of this social modality that disease is rooted phylogenetically in the human genome and biological matrix. This is the basis for the claim enunciated in this and earlier chapters that disease–man–behavior comprise a "natural" whole, and that this whole must be assumed to have a biocultural significance.

Assuming that disease does have a "natural" and essentially direct connection with human behavior, and that it reflects broadly environmental adaptation, we are led to inquire as to how this holistic trait or complex is organized and expressed. What are the components, attributes, or patterns of this whole? Are there prototypical ways in which the relations among disease, man, and behavior are constrained or compromised (that is, as reflected in a given occurrence of disease in space and time)? Social medicine is concerned with seeking regularities in the way people behave in the context of disease. Earlier efforts, however, have mainly sought to understand, in a narrowly defined context, the *causes* of disease in order to allow treating specific occurrences of disease. The typical time interval that occupies investigators can be termed ontogenetic. In order to understand and explain a particular occurrence of disease, investigators have looked back into the individual's own (often very immediate) past. Clues derived from the present evaluation of disease and behavior in an individual are used to infer about antecedent life circumstances, and vice versa. Phenomena contained in such a time scheme have, moreover, been organized purely on the basis of cause, in conformance with certain accepted biomedical paradigms.

As I have emphasized in this book, however, one is not required to look at phenomena only from the exclusive standpoint of the perspectives that happen to govern now in modern biomedicine. One can choose instead to look at disease and human adaptation more broadly, and in doing so certain things become immediately evident. For one, I hold as axiomatic that the human genome was constructed or developed in a continuous evolutionary manner, and that its current form was to a large extent "set" under more elementary forms of social organization. In such groups, environmental pressures were jointly experienced by members, and furthermore, the social effects of disease were visibly manifest. Under these circumstances, then, an occurrence of disease did not simply incapacitate or eliminate an individual in some mechanical sense. Rather, we must assume that besides reflecting the group's overall adaptation, disease was (and obviously still is) reflected in the individual's behavior, and that it possessed a social form such that its short- and long-term effects may have been "communicated" in the group. Countless numbers of disease-producing circumstances, some potentially lethal to man, must be presumed to have transpired, each of these contributing to and leaving its traces on a "sociophenomenologic language" of disease. In other words, the matrix of disease–behavior that is the locus of selective forces was shaped by a myriad of circumstances, and since such forces bear on man as a social animal, I assume that they are reflected in what I would term *behavioral programs*. The totality of such programs can be viewed as a language that possesses a distinctive biocultural form and meaning.

I am led to assume, then, that programmed in man is such a "language" that communicates the social basis and effects of disease, a kind of symbolic code and regularity inherent in the way in which disease unfolds and ramifies across various social and behavioral spheres. Such a language and its "grammar" must be judged a biocultural trait, since its roots are in phylogeny and its bases dependent on and demonstrated in a sociocultural context (see Chapter 5). In this light we should begin to see culture as only partially constraining this more generic biosocial dimension of disease and, on the other hand, as altering in only limited ways the outward appearance or morphology of the form in which disease is expressed in social groups. Our "scientific" culture has approached the study of disease using a rather rigid dualistic mold, and such a paradigm affects not only what we choose to observe but also how organismic alterations are communicated and to some extent expressed. Furthermore, in the prevailing view the biological effects of disease are judged in a mechanical way—that is, in terms of effects on a fertility measure of the population. This Western scientific cultural paradigm has unquestionably allowed posing and answering important questions about man; but its limitation is that it fixes and limits how we view disease in relation to social systems. The point I wish to emphasize is that we need to begin to look at disease not only as reflecting person-centered and narrowly defined biological effects in an ontogenetic time frame (and with the exclusive aim of uncovering immediate causes in order to determine treatment) but also as reflecting other, more basic and essentially phylogenetic factors about man in relation to social systems.

Briefly stated, in given occurrences of disease we must be prepared to find a type of biocultural communication about the person, his group, and the status and adjustment of both in relation to the environment. Across the spectrum of human disease, we should work to uncover, understand, and systematize how disease and behavior are interwoven in an ecologic sense. Clearly, for this task new ways of looking at disease are needed, as well as new heuristic devices for examining and codifying phenomena. The material presented in earlier chapters can be taken as initial efforts in this direction. The following outline is intended to summarize these and related matters.

A. Persons can be represented as though they were constituted of a hierarchic array of open and interconnected systems (molecular, chemical, physiological, psychological, social, etc.).

B. A disease is a person-centered, time-bound, undesirable deviation in the way a person functions (or is characterized by himself and/or others) in any of these systems.

C. At a fundamental level, diseases stem from disarticulations in the way the person (and group) relate to the environment and for this reason can be seen as involving adaptational setbacks.
   1. Adaptational setbacks are caused by environmental irritants that overwhelm the individual's capacity to function and sustain himself.
      a. Environmental irritants are potentially inherent in virtually every facet of the person's modes of establishing contact with his physical and social world.
      b. Environmental irritants stem from (or are framed in the context of) distinctive social, cultural, and ecologic forms of adjustment.
      c. Environmental irritants differ in terms of which system they affect most strongly.
D. Disease affects all systems concomitantly, though certain systems are more saliently affected than others.
E. Diseases assume a *behavioral form,* which depends on the nature of the environmental irritant, the kinds of systems disturbed, and various *behavioral programs* that structure behavior during the period of disturbance.
   1. Behavioral programs are cast in a "culture-free" biosocial (that is, phylogenetic) matrix.
      a. Such a matrix sets the general outlines of the behavioral form of the disease.
      b. Such a matrix is designed to program the disease so that to varying degrees the irritants and systems involved are made clearer and the import of the disease to the person and group is also made clearer.
      c. The behavioral form of the disease is dependent on and conditioned by the apparatus of the body and its modes of functioning.
      d. The form of the disease is affected by symbolizations prevalent in a given sociocultural unit about the following:
         (1) Categories relevant to how the person, as an organism, is structured and constituted internally
         (2) Categories relevant to how the social and nonhuman en-

vironments, both natural and supernatural, are structured
  (3) Explanations or theories about how persons function vis-à-vis other persons and the environment
  (4) Explanations or theories about how the environment functions in relation to persons
  (5) Rules (such as norms, standards) relevant to how persons should relate to other persons and to the social institutions of the group
  (6) Rules relevant to how persons should relate to the environment
2. Behavioral programs are finalized in terms of shared meanings and symbols of the group, so that disease is articulated in a culturally contextualized manner.
  a. The culture's way of specifying items in (E, l, d) contributes to the form and determines the symbolic content of a given disease.
  b. The culturally specific versions of (E, l, d) are incorporated in the organism's language system, which in turn serves to order, structure, and mold the individual's experiences and expectations.
  c. To a variable extent, then, the group's language, considered as its cognitive map and calculus of the world, articulates what environmental irritants exist, how and why these irritants lead to disease, what behavioral forms such diseases take, and what the diseases portend for the person and group.
F. The culturally specific behavioral forms of human disease allow members of the group to express their problematic adjustment in ways that are understandable in the culture.
  1. Such forms of disease are also indications of and give clues about the personal difficulties that members of the group face in the context of their social and physical environment.
    a. By identifying areas of difficulty for the individual (and by extension, for the social group), culturally specific behavioral forms of disease serve to direct attention and concern to specific problem areas inherent in the group's social rules and ways of relating to the environment.

b. Eventually such forms of disease bring about group attempts to control or eliminate the problem areas. These efforts often produce unanticipated consequences, which are then defined and viewed as problematic, and the cycle is repeated.

G. The behavioral forms of a disease can be analyzed by means of *behavioral frameworks* (for example, task-action, role enactment, phenomenologic), which address various behavioral dimensions, and such analyses should help uncover generic features of diseases and their role and influence in the social and cultural unit.

H. The use of the behavioral frameworks of (G) in the study of disease occurrences in various cultural contexts should allow developing a broad sociomedical theory that explains why diseases are produced, what the generic types of disease are and how these are related to each other (this is equivalent to the language and grammar of illness forms discussed in Chapter 5), how diseases happen to develop the culturally distinctive behavioral forms that they do, what they portend for the group, and how groups in coping with disease have developed and functioned in relation to their environments.

Bibliography

Ackerknecht, E. H. 1942a. Problems of primitive medicine. *Bulletin of the History of Medicine* 11:503–521.

———. 1942b. Primitive medicine and culture pattern. *Bulletin of the History of Medicine* 12:545–574.

———. 1943. Psychopathology, primitive medicine and primitive culture. *Bulletin of the History of Medicine* 14:30–67.

———. 1945a. On the collecting of data concerning primitive medicine. *American Anthropologist* 47:432–437.

———. 1945b. Primitive medicine. *New York Academy of Sciences, Transactions II* 8:26–37.

———. 1946a. Natural diseases and rational treatment in primitive medicine. *Bulletin of the History of Medicine* 19:467–497.

———. 1946b. Contradictions in primitive surgery. *Bulletin of the History of Medicine* 20:184–187.

———. 1947. Primitive surgery. *American Anthropologist* 49:25–45.

———. 1955. *A short history of medicine.* New York: Ronald Press.

———. 1965. *History and geography of the most important diseases.* New York: Hafner.

Adelstein, A. M. 1963. Some aspects of cardiovascular mortality in South Africa. *British Journal of Preventive and Social Medicine* 17:29–40.

Ahluwalia, H. S., and J. T. Ponnampalam. 1968. The socio-economic aspects of betel-nut chewing. *Journal of Tropical Medicine and Hygiene* 71:48–50.

Alland, A. 1966. Medical anthropology and the study of biological and cultural adaptation. *American Anthropologist* 68:40–51.

———. 1967. *Evolution and human behavior.* Garden City, New York: Natural History Press.

———. 1970. *Adaptation in cultural evolution: An approach to medical anthropology.* New York: Columbia University Press.

Allison, A. C. 1968. Genetics and infectious disease. In *Haldane and modern biology,* ed. K. R. Dronamraju, Chapter 4. Baltimore: Johns Hopkins.

Alpers, M. 1970. III. Kuru in New Guinea: Its changing pattern and etiologic elucidation. *American Journal of Tropical Medicine and Hygiene* 19:133–137.

Alpers, M., and D. C. Gajdusek. 1965. Changing patterns of Kuru: Epidemiological changes in the period of increasing contact of the Fore people with Western civilization. *American Journal of Tropical Medicine and Hygiene* 14:852–879.

Andersen, R. 1968. A behavioral model of families' use of health services. University of Chicago Graduate School of Business, Center for Health Administration Studies, Research Series 25.

Anderson, Odin W. 1963. The utilization of health services. In *Handbook of medical sociology*, eds. Howard E. Freeman, Sol Levine, and Leo G. Reeder, pp. 349–367. Englewood Cliffs, New Jersey: Prentice-Hall.

Antonovsky, A. 1968. Social class and the major cardiovascular diseases. *Journal of Chronic Diseases* 21:65–106.

Ashley, D. J. B. 1968. "Welshness" and disease. *Human Biology* 40:517–533.

Audy, J. R. 1971. Measurement and diagnosis of health. In *Environmental essays on the planet as a home,* eds. P. Shepard and D. McKinley. Boston: Houghton-Mifflin.

Baker, P. T. 1966. Human biological variation as an adaptive response to the environment. *Eugenics Quarterly* 13:81–91.

Baker, P. T. and J. S. Weiner, eds. 1966. *The biology of human adaptability.* Oxford: Oxford University Press.

Balikci, A. 1963. Shamanistic behavior among the Netsilik Eskimos. *Southwestern Journal of Anthropology* 19:380–396.

Balint, M. 1957. *The doctor, his patient, and the illness.* New York: International Universities Press.

Banton, M. 1965. *The relevance of models for social anthropology.* London: Tavistock Publications.

Beck, H. 1971. Minimal requirements for a biobehavioral paradigm. *Behavioral Science* 16:442.

Beltran, G. A. 1963. *Medicina y magia.* Mexico: Instituto Nacional Indigenista.

Berger, P. L., and T. Luckmann. 1967. *The social construction of reality: A treatise in the sociology of knowledge.* New York: Doubleday (Anchor Books) .

Bergner, J. F., Jr. 1964. Intestinal parasites in an Aborigine village in southeast Taiwan. *American Journal of Tropical Medicine and Hygiene* 13:78–81.

Berlin, B., D. E. Breedlove, and P. H. Raven. 1968. Covert categories and folk taxonomies. *American Anthropologist* 70:290–299.

———. 1973. General principles of classification and nomenclature in folk biology. *American Anthropologist* 75 (No. 1):214–242.

Berlin, B., and P. Kay. 1969. *Basic color terms.* Berkeley and Los Angeles: University of California Press.

Bertalanffy, Ludwig von. 1968. *General system theory*. New York: George Braziller.

Beveridge, W. I. B. 1972. *Frontiers in comparative medicine*. Minneapolis: University of Minnesota Press.

Blackard, W. G., Y. Omori, and L. R. Freedman. 1965. Epidemiology of diabetes mellitus in Japan. *Journal of Chronic Diseases* 18:415–427.

Bloom, S. W. 1965. *The doctor and his patient: A sociological interpretation*. New York: Macmillan (Free Press).

Boyden, S. V. 1970a. Cultural adaptation to biological maladjustment. In *The impact of civilisation on the biology of man*, ed. S. V. Boyden, pp. 190–218. Toronto, Canada: University of Toronto Press.

————. 1970b. The human organism in a changing environment. In *Man and his environment*, ed. R. T. Appleyard, pp. 1–20. Nedlands, Western Australia: University of Western Australia Press.

————. 1972. The environment and human health. *Medical Journal of Australia* 1:1229–1234.

Boyer, L. B. 1962. Remarks on the personality of shamans with special reference to the Apache of the Mescalero Indian reservation. In *The psychoanalytic study of society*, eds. W. Muensterberger and S. Axelrod, vol. 2, pp. 233–254. New York: International Universities Press.

————. 1964. Further remarks concerning shamans and shamanism. *Israel Annals of Psychiatry and Related Disciplines* 2:235–257.

Boyer, L. B., B. Klopfer, F. B. Brawer, and H. Kawai. 1964. Comparisons of the shamans and pseudoshamans of the Apaches of the Mescalero Indian reservation: A Rorschach study. *Journal of Projective Techniques and Personality Assessment* 28:173–180.

Boyer, L. B., R. M. Boyer, H. Kawai, and B. Klopfer. 1967. Apache "learners" and "nonlearners." *Journal of Projective Techniques and Personality Assessment* 31:22–29.

Brazelton, T. B., J. S. Robey, and G. A. Collier. 1969. Infant development in the Zinacanteco Indians of southern Mexico. *Pediatrics* 44:274–290.

Bronks, I. G., and E. K. Blackburn. 1968. A socio-medical study of haemophilia and related states. *British Journal of Preventive and Social Medicine* 22:68–72.

Brothwell, D. R. 1963. *Digging up bones*. London: British Museum of Natural History.

Brothwell, D. R., and A. T. Sandison, eds. 1967. *Diseases in antiquity: A survey of the diseases, injuries, and surgery of early populations*. Springfield, Illinois: Charles C. Thomas.

Bruch, H. A., W. Ascoli, N. S. Scrimshaw, and J. E. Gordon. 1963. Studies of diarrheal disease in Central America: V. Environmental factors in the origin and transmission of acute diarrheal disease in four Guatemalan villages. *American Journal of Tropical Medicine and Hygiene* 12:567–579.

Bruhn, J. G., B. Chandler, M. C. Miller, S. Wolf, and T. N. Lynn. 1966. Social aspects of coronary heart disease in two adjacent, ethnically different communities. *American Journal of Public Health* 56:1493–1506.

Buchler, I. R. 1964. Caymanian folk medicine: A problem in applied anthropology. *Human Organization* 23:48–49.

Buck, A. A., T. T. Sasaki, and R. I. Anderson. 1968. *Health and disease in four Peruvian villages: Contrast in epidemiology.* Baltimore: Johns Hopkins.

Buck, A. A., T. T. Sasaki, J. J. Hewitt, and A. A. Macrae. 1968. Coca chewing and health: An epidemiologic study among residents of a Peruvian village. *American Journal of Epidemiology* 88:159–177.

Buck, A. A., R. I. Anderson, K. Kawata, T. T. Sasaki, F. M. Amin, and I. W. Abrahams. 1970a. *Health and disease in rural Afghanistan: An epidemiological study of four villages.* Baltimore: Johns Hopkins.

Buck, A. A., R. I. Anderson, T. T. Sasaki, and K. Kawata. 1970b. *Health and disease in Chad: Epidemiology, culture, and environment in five villages.* Baltimore: Johns Hopkins.

Buckley, W. F., ed. 1968. *Modern systems research for the behavioral scientist: A source-book.* Chicago: Aldine.

Burnet, M., and D. O. White. 1972. *Natural history of infectious disease,* 4th edition. New York: Cambridge University Press.

Cartwright, F. F., and M. D. Biddiss. 1972. *Disease and history.* New York: Thomas Y. Crowell.

Cassel, J. 1964. Social science theory as a source of hypotheses in epidemiological research. *American Journal of Public Health* 54:1482–1488.

Cassel, J., R. Patrick, and D. Jenkins. 1960. Epidemiological analysis of the health implications of culture change: A conceptual model. *Ann. N.Y. Acad. Sci.* 84:938.

Castaneda, C. 1968. *The teachings of Don Juan: A Yaqui way of knowledge.* Berkeley and Los Angeles: University of California Press.

Cawte, J. E. 1964. Tjimi and Tjagolo: Ethnopsychiatry in the Kalumburu people of north-western Australia. *Oceania* 34:170–190.

Cherry, C. 1961. *On human communication.* New York: John Wiley and Sons, Science Editions.

Ch'i, I., and R. Q. Blackwell. 1968. A controlled retrospective study of Blackfoot disease, an endemic peripheral gangrene disease in Taiwan. *American Journal of Epidemiology* 88:7–24.

Chomsky, N. 1965. *Aspects of the theory of syntax*. Cambridge, Massachusetts: MIT Press.

Chowdhury, A. B., G. A. Schad, and E. L. Schiller. 1968. The prevalence of intestinal Helminths in religious groups of a rural community near Calcutta. *American Journal of Epidemiology* 87:313–317.

Chowdhury, A. B., and E. L. Schiller. 1968. A survey of parasitic infections in a rural community near Calcutta. *American Journal of Epidemiology* 87:299–312.

Clements, F. E. 1932. Primitive concepts of disease. *University of California Publications in American Archeology and Ethnology* 32:185–252.

Cockburn, T. A. 1971. Infectious diseases in ancient populations. *Current Anthropology* 12:45–62.

———, ed. 1963. *The evolution and eradication of infectious diseases*. Baltimore: Johns Hopkins.

———, ed. 1967. *Infectious diseases: Their evolution and eradication*. Springfield, Illinois: Charles C. Thomas.

Coe, R. M. 1970. *Sociology of medicine*. New York: McGraw-Hill.

Cohen, J. 1964. *Behaviour in uncertainty*. New York: Basic Books.

Cole, Michael, John Gay, Joseph A. Glick, and Donald W. Sharp. 1971. *The cultural context of learning and thinking: An exploration in experimental anthropology*. New York: Basic Books.

Colson, Anthony C. 1971. The differential use of medical resources in developing countries. *Journal of Health and Social Behavior* 12:226–237.

Conklin, H. C. 1955. Haunuoo color categories. *Southwestern Journal of Anthropology* 11:339–344.

Cornell, J. B. 1971. Review of A. Alland, *Adaptation in cultural evolution: An approach to medical anthropology*. *Human Biology* 43:173–177.

Cravioto, J. 1968. Nutritional deficiencies and mental performance in childhood. In *Biology and behavior: Environmental influences*, ed. D. C. Glass, pp. 3–51. New York: Rockefeller University Press and Russell Sage Foundation.

Cruz-Coke, R., R. Etcheverry, and R. Nagel. 1964. Influence of migration on blood-pressure of Easter Islanders. *Lancet* 1:697–699.

Cumming, E., and J. Cumming. 1957. *Closed ranks: An experiment in mental health education*. Cambridge, Massachusetts: Harvard University Press.

Currier, R. L. 1966. The hot-cold syndrome and symbolic balance in Mexican and Spanish-American folk medicine. *Ethnology* 5:251–263.

Devereux, G. 1956. Normal and abnormal: The key problem of psychiatric anthropology. In *Some uses of anthropology: Theoretical and applied*, eds. J. B. Casagrande and T. Gladwin. Washington, D.C.: Anthropological Society of Washington.

————. 1963. Primitive psychiatric diagnosis: A general theory of the diagnostic process. In *Man's image in medicine and anthropology*, ed. I. Galdston, pp. 337–373. New York: International Universities Press.

Diebold, A. R., Jr. 1968. Anthropological perspectives: Anthropology and the comparative psychology of communicative behavior. In *Animal communication*, ed. T. A. Sebeok. Bloomington: Indiana University Press.

Dobzhansky, T. 1962. *Mankind evolving: The evolution of the human species*. New Haven: Yale University Press.

Dohrenwend, B. P. 1966. Social status and psychological disorder: An issue of substance and an issue of method. *American Sociological Review* 31:14–34.

Dohrenwend, B. P., and B. S. Dohrenwend. 1969. *Social status and psychological disorder: A causal inquiry*. New York: Wiley-Interscience.

Donabedian, A. 1966. Evaluating the quality of medical care. *Milbank Memorial Fund Quarterly* 44:166–206.

Douglas, M. 1970. *Natural symbols: Explorations in cosmology*. New York: Pantheon Books (Random House).

Draguns, J. G., and L. Phillips. 1971. *Psychiatric classification and diagnosis: An overview and critique*. New York: General Learning Press.

Dubos, R. 1965. *Man adapting*. New Haven: Yale University Press.

————. 1968. *Man, medicine, and environment*. New York: New American Library.

Dunn, F. L. 1965. On the antiquity of malaria in the Western hemisphere. *Human Biology* 37:385–393.

————. 1966. Patterns of parasitism in primates: Phylogenetic and ecological interpretations, with particular reference to the Hominoidea. *Folia Primatologica* 4:329–345.

————. 1968. Epidemiological factors: Health and disease in hunter-gatherers. In *Man the hunter*, eds. R. B. Lee and I. Devore, pp. 221–228. Chicago: Aldine.

————. 1970. Natural infection in primates: Helminths and problems in primate phylogeny, ecology, and behavior. *Laboratory Animal Care* 20:383–388.

————. 1972. Intestinal parasitism in Malayan aborigines (Orang Asli). *Bull. Wld. Hlth. Org.* 46:99–113.

Dunn, F. L., B. L. Lim, and L. F. Yap. 1968. Endoparasite patterns in mammals of the Malayan rain forest. *Ecology* 49 (No. 6):1179–1184.

Durell, Jack. 1973. Introduction. In *Biological psychiatry*, ed. Joseph Mendels, pp. 1–14. New York: John Wiley & Sons.

Edgerton, R. B. 1966. Conceptions of psychosis in four East African societies. *American Anthropologist* 68:408–425.

Edwards, W., H. Lindman, and L. D. Phillips. 1966. Emerging technologies for making decisions. In *New directions in psychology II*, ed. T. M. Newcomb. New York: Holt, Rinehart and Winston.

Ekman, Paul. 1972. Universals and cultural differences in facial expressions of emotions. In *Nebraska Symposium on Motivation*, ed. James Cole. Lincoln: University of Nebraska Press.

Elder, R., and R. M. Acheson. 1970. New Haven survey of joint diseases. XIV. Social class and behavior in response to symptoms of osteoarthrosis. *Milbank Memorial Fund Quarterly* 48:449–502.

Engel, G. L. 1960. A unified concept of health and disease. *Perspectives in Biology and Medicine* 3:459–485.

———. 1970a. Pain. In *Signs and symptoms*, 5th ed., eds. C. M. MacBryde and R. S. Blacklow. Philadelphia: Lippincott.

———. 1970b. Sudden death and the "medical model" in psychiatry. *Canada Psychiatric Association Journal* 15:527–538.

Engle, R. L. 1963a. Medical diagnosis: Present, past, and future. II. Philosophical foundations and historical development of our concepts of health, disease, and diagnosis. *Archives of Internal Medicine* 112:520–529.

———. 1963b. Medical diagnosis: Present, past, and future. III. Diagnosis in the future, including a critique on the use of electronic computers as diagnostic aids to the physician. *Archives of Internal Medicine* 112:126–139.

Engle, R. L., and B. J. Davis. 1963. Medical diagnosis: Present, past, and future. I. Present concepts of the meaning and limitations of medical diagnosis. *Archives of Internal Medicine* 112:512–519.

Erasmus, C. J. 1952. Changing folk beliefs and the relativity of empirical knowledge. *Southwestern Journal of Anthropology* 8:411–428.

Evans-Pritchard, E. E. 1937. *Witchcraft, oracles and magic among the Azandes.* Oxford: Clarendon Press.

Fabrega, H., Jr. 1970a. On the specificity of folk illnesses. *Southwestern Journal of Anthropology* 26:305–314.

———. 1970b. Dynamics of medical practice in a folk community. *Milbank Memorial Fund Quarterly* 48:391–412.

———. 1971a. Some features of Zinacantecan medical knowledge. *Ethnology* 9:25–43.

————. 1971*b*. The study of medical problems in preliterate settings. *Yale Journal of Biology and Medicine* 43:385–407.

Fabrega, H., Jr., and P. K. Manning. 1972*a*. Disease, illness, and deviant careers. In *Theoretical perspectives on deviance*, eds. R. A. Scott and J. D. Douglass, pp. 93–116. New York: Basic Books.

————. 1972*b*. Health maintenance among Peruvian peasants. *Human Organization* 31:243–256.

Fabrega, H., Jr., and D. Metzger. 1968. Psychiatric illness in a small ladino community. *Psychiatry* 31:339–351.

Fabrega, H., Jr., D. Metzger, and G. Williams. 1970. Psychiatric implications of health and illness in a Maya Indian group: A preliminary statement. *Social Science and Medicine* 3:609–626.

Fabrega, H., Jr., R. J. Moore, and J. R. Strawn. 1969. Low income medical problem patients: Some medical and behavioral features. *Journal of Health and Social Behavior* 10:334–343.

Fabrega, H., Jr., and R. E. Roberts. 1972. Social-psychological correlates of physician use by economically disadvantaged Negro urban residents. *Medical Care* 10:215–223.

Fabrega, H., Jr., A. J. Rubel, and C. A. Wallace. 1967. Working class Mexican psychiatric outpatients: Some social and cultural features. *Archives of General Psychiatry* 16:704–712.

Fabrega, H., Jr., and D. Silver. 1970. Some social and psychological properties of Zinacanteco shamans. *Behavioral Science* 15:471–486.

Fabrega, H., Jr., and D. Silver. 1973. *Illness and shamanistic curing in Zinacantan: An ethnomedical analysis.* Stanford, California: Stanford University Press.

Fabrega, H., Jr., and C. A. Wallace. 1967. How physicians judge symptom statements: A cross-cultural study. *Journal of Nervous and Mental Disease* 145:486–491.

Feinstein, A. R. 1967. *Clinical judgment.* Baltimore: Williams and Wilkins.

————. 1968*a*. Clinical epidemiology: I. The populational experiments of nature and of man in human illness. *Annals of Internal Medicine* 69:807–820.

————. 1968*b*. Clinical epidemiology: II. The identification rates of disease. *Annals of Internal Medicine* 69:1037–1061.

Feldman, J. F. 1960. The household interview survey as a technique for the collection of morbidity data. *Social Psychiatry* 5 (No. 2) : 84–91.

Feldman, R. A., K. R. Kamath, P. S. Sundar Rao, and J. K. Webb. 1969. Infection and disease in a group of South Indian families. I. Introduction, methods, definitions and general observations in a continuing study. *American Journal of Epidemiology* 89:364–374.

Fenner, F. 1970. The effects of changing social organisation on the infectious diseases of man. In *The impact of civilisation on the biology of man,* ed. S. V. Boyden. Toronto, Canada: University of Toronto Press.

Ferster, C. B. 1963. Essentials of a science of behavior. In *An introduction to the science of human behavior,* eds. J. I. Nurnberger, C. B. Ferster, and J. P. Brady, pp. 199–345. New York: Appleton-Century-Crofts.

Fishman, J. 1960. Systematization of the Whorfian hypothesis. *Behavioral Science* 5:323–339.

Florey, C. and R. R. Cuadrado. 1968. Blood pressure in native Cape Verdeans and in Cape Verdean immigrants and their descendants living in New England. *Human Biology* 40:189–211.

Foster, G. A. 1960. *Culture and conquest: America's Spanish heritage.* Viking Fund Publications in Anthropology, 27. New York: Wenner-Gren Foundation.

Foster, G. M. 1953. Relationships between Spanish and Spanish-American folk medicine. *Journal of American Folklore* 66:201–217.

Foucault, M. 1965. *Madness and civilization.* New York: Random House.

Fox, John P., Carrie E. Hall, and Lila R. Elveback. 1970. *Epidemiology: Man and disease.* London: Macmillan Company, Collier-Macmillan Ltd.

Frake, C. O. 1961. The diagnosis of disease among the Subanun of Mindanao. *American Anthropologist* 63:113–132.

———. 1962. The ethnographic study of cognitive system. In *Anthropology and human behavior,* eds. T. Gladwin and W. C. Sturtevant, pp. 72–93. Washington, D. C.: Anthropological Society of Washington.

Frank, J. D. 1961. *Persuasion and healing.* Baltimore: Johns Hopkins.

Franklin, K. J. 1963. Kewa ethnolinguistic concepts of body parts. *Southwestern Journal of Anthropology* 19:54–63.

Freed, S. A., and R. S. Freed. 1964. Spirit possession as illness in a North Indian village. *Ethnology* 3:152–171.

Friedrich, Paul. 1969. On the meaning of the Tarascan suffixes of space. *International Journal of American Linguistics* (Part II) 35 (No. 4):1–48.

Freidson, E. 1960. Client control and medical practice. *American Journal of Sociology* 65:374–382.

———. 1971. *Profession of medicine: A study of the sociology of applied knowledge.* New York: Dodd, Mead.

Fulmer, H. S., and R. W. Roberts. 1963. Coronary heart disease among the Navajo Indians. *Annals of Internal Medicine* 59:740–764.

Gajdusek, D. C. 1963. Kuru. *Transactions of the Royal Society of Tropical Medicine and Hygiene* 57:151–166.

———. 1964. Factors governing the genetics of primitive human populations. *Cold Spring Harbor Symposia on Quantitative Biology* 29:121–135.

———. 1970a. Introduction to papers presented at the Intercongressional Plenary Session No. 5 of the Eight International Congresses on Tropical Medicine and Malaria. *American Journal of Tropical Medicine and Hygiene* 19:127–129.

———. 1970b. Physiological and psychological characteristics of Stone Age man. *Engineering and Science* 33:26–33, 56–62.

Geiger, H. J., and N. A. Scotch. 1963. The epidemiology of essential hypertension: A review with special attention to psychological and sociocultural factors. I. Biologic mechanisms and descriptive epidemiology. *Journal of Chronic Diseases* 16:1151–1182.

Gelfand, M. 1966. The general or constitutional symptoms in S. Mansonia infestation: A clinical comparison in two racial groups. *Journal of Tropical Medicine and Hygiene* 69:230–231.

Gibbs, C. J., and D. C. Gajdusek. 1970. IV. Kuru: Pathogenesis and characterization of virus. *American Journal of Tropical Medicine and Hygiene* 19:138–145.

Glick, L. 1967. Medicine as an ethnographic category: The Gimi of the New Guinea Highlands. *Ethnology* 6:31–56.

Goddard, D., S. N. De Goddard, and P. C. Whitehead. 1969. Social factors associated with coca use in the Andean region. *International Journal of Addictions* 4:577–590.

Goffman, E. 1959. The moral career of the mental patient. *Psychiatry* 22:123–142.

———. 1963. *Stigma: Notes on the management of spoiled identity.* Englewood Cliffs, New Jersey: Prentice-Hall.

———. 1969. The insanity of place. *Psychiatry* 32:357–388.

Goldstein, M. S. 1969. Human paleopathology and some diseases in living primitive societies: A review of the recent literature. *American Journal of Physical Anthropology* 31:285–294.

Goodenough, W. H. 1957. Cultural anthropology and linguistics. In *Report of the seventh annual round table meeting on linguistics and language study,* ed. P. L. Garvin. Monograph Series on Language and Linguistics, No. 9. Washington, D. C.: Georgetown University Press.

———. 1970. *Description and comparison in cultural anthropology.* Chicago: Aldine.

Gordon, G. 1966. *Role theory and illness.* New Haven: College and University Press.

Gordon, J. E., and T. H. Ingalls. 1958. Medical ecology and the public health. *American Journal of Medical Science* 235:337–359.

Graham, D. 1967. Health, disease and the mind-body problem: Linguistic parallelism. *Psychosomatic Medicine* 29:52–71.

Graham, S., R. Gibson, A. Lilienfeld, L. Schuman, and M. Levin. 1970. Religion and ethnicity in leukemia. *American Journal of Public Health* 60:266–274.

Graves, T. D. 1966. Alternative models for the study of urban migration. *Human Organization* 25:295–299.

———. 1967. Acculturation, access and alcohol in a tri-ethnic community. *American Anthropologist* 69:306–321.

———. 1970. The personal adjustment of Navajo Indian migrants to Denver, Colorado. *American Anthropologist* 72:35–54.

Grover, N. 1965. Man and plants against pain. *Economic Botany* 19:99–112.

Gussow, Z. 1964. Behavioral research in chronic disease: A study of leprosy. *Journal of Chronic Diseases* 17:179–189.

Gussow, Z., and G. S. Tracy. 1968. Status, ideology, and adaptation to stigmatized illness: A study of leprosy. *Human Organization* 27:316–325.

Haddad, N. A. 1965. Trachoma in Lebanon: Observations on epidemiology in rural areas. *American Journal of Tropical Medicine and Hygiene* 14:652–655.

Hall, E. T. 1968. Proxemics. *Current Anthropology* 9:83.

Hallowell, A. I. 1963. Ojibwa world view and disease. In *Man's image in medicine and anthropology,* ed. I. Galdston. New York: International Universities Press.

Hamer, J., and I. Hamer. 1966. Spirit possession and its sociopsychological implications among the Sidamo of Southwest Ethiopia. *Ethnology* 5:392–408.

Handelman, D. 1967. The development of a Washo shaman. *Ethnology* 6:444–464.

———. 1968. Shamanizing on an empty stomach. *American Anthropologist* 70:353–356.

Hanson, F. A. 1970. The Rapan theory of conception. *American Anthropologist* 72:1444–1447.

Harper, E. B. 1964. Ritual pollution as an integrator of caste and religion. *Journal of Asian Studies,* Volume XXIII.

Harris, M. 1964. *The nature of cultural things.* New York: Random House.

Harwood, A. 1971. The hot-cold theory of disease. *Journal of the American Medical Association* 216:1153–1158.

Hempel, C. G. 1965. *Aspects of scientific explanation.* New York: Free Press.

———. 1966. *Philosophy of natural science.* Englewood Cliffs, New Jersey: Prentice-Hall.

Henderson, L. J. 1935. Physician and patient as a social system. *New England Journal of Medicine* 212:819–823.

Henry, J. P., and J. C. Cassel. 1969. Psychosocial factors in essential hypertension: Recent epidemiologic and animal experimental evidence. *American Journal of Epidemiology* 90:171–200.

Herman, M. W. 1972. The poor: Their medical needs and the health services available to them. *Annals of the American Academy of Political and Social Science* 399:12–21.

Hinde, R. A., ed. 1972. *Non-verbal communication.* New York: Cambridge Univ. Press.

Hinkle, L. E. 1961. Ecological observations of the relation of physical illness, mental illness, and the social environment. *Psychosomatic Medicine* 23:289–297.

Hobson, W. 1969. *The theory and practice of public health,* 3rd edition. London: Oxford University Press.

Hoeppli, R., and C. Lucasse. 1964. Old ideas regarding cause and treatment of sleeping sickness held in West Africa. *Journal of Tropical Medicine and Hygiene* 67:60–68.

Hogarty, Gerard E., and Marvin M. Katz. 1971. Norms of adjustment and social behavior. *Archives of General Psychiatry* 25:470–480.

Holland, W. R., and R. G. Tharp. 1964. Highland Maya psychotherapy. *American Anthropologist* 66:41–52.

Holland, W. W., ed. 1970. *Data handling in epidemiology.* London: Oxford University Press.

Honey, R. M., and M. Gelfand. 1962. *Urological aspects of bilherziasis in Rhodesia.* Edinburgh, Scotland: E. & S. Livingstone.

Horowitz, I., and P. E. Enterline. 1970. Lung cancer among the Jews. *American Journal of Public Health* 60:275–282.

Hoskin, J. O., L. G. Kiloh, and J. E. Cawte. 1969. Epilepsy and guria: The shaking syndromes of New Guinea. *Social Science and Medicine* 3:39–48.

Howard, A., and R. A. Scott. 1965. Proposed framework for the analysis of stress in the human organism. *Behavioral Science* 10:141–160.

Hudson, E. H. 1965. Treponematosis and man's social evolution. *American Anthropologist* 67:885–901.

Hughes, C. C. 1963. Public health in non-literate societies. In *Man's image in medicine and anthropology,* ed. I. Galdston, pp. 157–233. New York: International Universities Press.

Ibrahim, M. A., C. D. Jenkins, J. C. Cassel, J. R. McDonough, and C. G. Hames. 1966. Personality traits and coronary heart disease: Utilization of a cross-sectional study design to test whether a selected psychological profile precedes or follows manifest coronary heart disease. *Journal of Chronic Diseases* 19:255–271.

Imperato, P. J. 1969. Traditional attitudes towards measles in the Republic of Mali. *Transactions of the Royal Society of Tropical Medicine and Hygiene* 63:768–780.

Imperato, P. J., and D. Traore. 1968. Traditional beliefs about smallpox and its treatment in the Republic of Mali. *Journal of Tropical Medicine and Hygiene* 71:224–228.

Ingham, J. M. 1970. On Mexican folk medicine. *American Anthropologist* 72:76–87.

Israel, S., and G. Teeling-Smith. 1967. The submerged iceberg of sickness in society. *Social and Economic Administration* (London) 1:43–55.

Jain, S. K. 1965. Medicinal plant lore of the tribals of Bastar. *Economic Botany* 19:236–250.

Jarcho, S. 1966. *Human palaeopathology*. New Haven: Yale University Press.

Jelliffe, E. F. P., and D. B. Jelliffe. 1963. Plasmodium Malariae in Ugandan children. I. Prevalence in young children in rural communities. *American Journal of Tropical Medicine and Hygiene* 12:296–297.

Kamath, K. R., R. A. Feldman, P. S. Sundar Rao, and J. K. G. Webb. 1969. Infection and disease in a group of South Indian families. II. General morbidity patterns in families and family members. *American Journal of Epidemiology* 89:375–383.

Kartman, L. 1967. Human ecology and public health. *American Journal of Public Health* 57:737–750.

Kasl, S. V., and S. Cobb. 1964. Some psychological factors associated with illness behavior and selected illnesses. *Journal of Chronic Diseases* 17:325–345.

————. 1966a. Health behavior, illness behavior, and sick-role behavior. I. Health and illness behavior. *Archives of Environmental Health* 12:246–266.

————. 1966b. Health behavior, illness behavior, and sick-role behavior. II. Sick-role behavior. *Archives of Environmental Health* 12:531–541.

Katz, J. J., and P. M. Postal. 1964. *An integrated theory of linguistic descriptions*. Cambridge, Massachusetts: MIT Press.

Katz, Martin M., Jonathan O. Cole, and Walter E. Barton. 1968. The role and methodology of classification in psychiatry and psychopathology. DHEW Publ. No. (HSM) 72–9015.

Katz, Martin M., J. O. Cole, and H. A. Lowery. 1969. Studies of the diagnostic process: The influence of symptom perception, past experience, and ethnic background on diagnostic decisions. *American Journal of Psychiatry* 125 (No. 7) : 109–119.

Katz, Martin M., H. Gudeman, and K. Sanborn. 1969. Characterizing difference in psychopathology among ethnic groups: A preliminary report on Hawaii-Japanese and Mainland-American schizophrenics. In *Mental health research in Asia and the Pacific*, eds. W. Caudill and T. Lin. Honolulu: East-West Center Press.

Katz, Martin M., and S. B. Lyerly. 1963. Methods for measuring adjustment and social behavior in the community: I. Rationale, description, discriminative validity and scale development. *Psychological Reports* 13:503–535.

Katz, S. H., and E. F. Foulks. 1970. Mineral metabolism and behavior: Abnormalities of calcium homeostasis. *American Journal of Physical Anthropology* 32:299–304.

Kennedy, J. G. 1967. Nubian Zar ceremonies as psychotherapy. *Human Organization* 26:185–194.

————. in press. Cultural psychiatry. In *Handbook of social and cultural anthropology,* ed. J. Honigmann.

Kerley, E. R., and W. M. Bass. 1967. Paleopathology: Meeting ground for many disciplines. *Science* 157:638–644.

Kerr, M., and D. G. Trantow. 1968. Perspectives—and a suggested framework—for defining, measuring, and assessing the quality of health services. In *Health services and mental health administration,* pp. 38–76. Washington, D. C.: U.S. Public Health Service.

Kessler, Irving I., and Morton L. Levin. 1970. *The community as an epidemiological laboratory: A casebook of community studies.* Baltimore: Johns Hopkins.

Kiev, A. 1966. Obstacles to medical progress in Haiti. *Human Organization* 25:10–15.

————. 1969. Transcultural psychiatry: Research problems and perspectives. In *Changing perspectives in mental illness,* eds. S. C. Plog and R. B. Edgerton, pp. 106–127. New York: Holt, Rinehart and Winston.

————, ed. 1964. *Magic, faith, and healing.* New York: Free Press of Glencoe.

King, Lester S. 1963. *The growth of medical thought.* Chicago: University of Chicago Press.

————. 1971. *The medical world of the eighteenth century.* Huntington, New York: Robert E. Krieger.

King, S. H. 1962. *Perceptions of illness and medical practice.* New York: Russell Sage Foundation.

Klibansky, R., E. Panofsky, and F. Saxl. 1964. *Saturn and melancholy: Studies in the history of natural philosophy, religion and art.* London: Thomas Nelson and Sons, Ltd.

Koch, K. 1968. On "possession" behavior in New Guinea. *Journal of the Polynesian Society* 77:135–146.

Kogan, N., and M. A. Wallach. 1964. *Risk taking: A study in cognition and personality.* New York: Holt, Rinehart and Winston.

Kourany, M., and M. A. Vasquez. 1969. Housing and certain socioenvironmental factors and prevalence of enteropathogenic bacteria among infants with diarrheal disease in Panama. *American Journal of Tropical Medicine and Hygiene* 18:936–941.

Kuhn, T. S. 1970. *The structure of scientific revolutions.* Chicago: University of Chicago Press.

Kupferer, H. J. K. 1965. Couvade: Ritual or real illness. *American Anthropologist* 67:99–102.

Kutner, B., H. B. Makover, and A. Oppenheim. 1958. Delay in the diagnosis and treatment of cancer: A critical analysis of the literature. *Journal of Chronic Diseases* 7:95–120.

Langness, L. L. 1965. Hysterical psychosis in the New Guinea Highlands. A Bena Bena example. *Psychiatry* 28:258–277.

———. 1967a. Rejoinder to R. Salisbury's "Possession on the New Guinea Highlands: Review of literature" and "Possession among the Siane (New Guinea)." *Transcultural Psychiatric Research* 4:125–130.

———. 1967b. Hysterical psychosis: The cross-cultural evidence. *American Journal of Psychiatry* 124:143–152.

Lasker, G. W. 1969. Human biological adaptability: The ecological approach in physical anthropology. *Science* 166:1480–1486.

Last, J. 1965. Evaluation of medical care. *Medical Journal of Australia* 2:781–785.

Laughlin, W. S. 1963. Primitive theory of medicine: Empirical knowledge. In *Man's image in medicine and anthropology,* ed. I. Galdston, pp. 116–140. New York: International Universities Press.

Leach, E. 1972. The influence of cultural context on non-verbal communication in man. In *Non-verbal communication,* ed. R. A. Hinde, pp. 315–347. New York: Cambridge University Press.

Lehman, E. W. 1967. Social class and coronary heart disease: A sociological assessment of the medical literature. *Journal of Chronic Diseases* 20:381–391.

Leighton, A. H. 1955. Psychiatric disorder and social environment: An outline for a frame of reference. *Psychiatry* 18:367–383.

———. 1959a. *My name is legion: Foundations for a theory of man in relation to culture.* New York: Basic Books.

———. 1959b. Mental illness and acculturation. In *Medicine and anthropology,* ed. I. Galdston, pp. 108–128. New York: International Universities Press.

———. 1969. Cultural relativity and the identification of psychiatric disorders. In *Mental health research in Asia and the Pacific,* eds. W. Caudill and T. Lin, pp. 448–462. Honolulu: East-West Center Press.

Leighton, A. H., and J. H. Hughes. 1961. Cultures as causative of mental disorder.

In *Causes of mental disorders: A review of epidemiological knowledge*, pp. 341–383. New York: Milbank Memorial Fund.

Leighton, A. H., and J. M. Murphy. 1965. Cross-cultural psychiatry. In *Approaches to cross-cultural psychiatry*, eds. J. M. Murphy and A. H. Leighton, pp. 3–20. Ithaca, New York: Cornell University Press.

Leighton, A. H., T. A. Lambo, C. C. Hughes, D. C. Leighton, J. M. Murphy, and D. B. Macklin. 1963. *Psychiatric disorder among the Yoruba*. Ithaca, New York: Cornell University Press.

Leighton, D., J. S. Harding, D. B. Macklin, A. M. MacMillan, and A. H. Leighton. 1963. *The character of danger*. New York: Basic Books.

Lemert, Edwin. 1951. *Social pathology*. New York: McGraw-Hill.

———. 1967. *Human deviance, social problems, and social control*. Englewood Cliffs, New Jersey: Prentice-Hall.

Leonard, H. S. 1967. *Principles of reasoning: An introduction to logic, methodology and the theory of signs*. New York: Dover.

LeVine, R. A. 1973. *Culture, behavior and personality: An introduction to the comparative study of psychosocial adaptation*. Chicago: Aldine.

Levine, S. B., R. E. Sampliner, P. H. Bennett, N. B. Rushforth, T. A. Burch, and M. Miller. 1970. Asymptomatic parotid enlargement in Pima Indians: Relationship to age, obesity, and diabetes mellitus. *Annals of Internal Medicine* 73:571–573.

Lewis, I. M. 1966. Spirit possession and deprivation cults. *Man* 1:307–329.

Lieban, R. W. 1965. Shamanism and social control in a Philippine city. *Journal of the Folklore Institute* 2:43–54.

———. 1966. Fatalism and medicine in Cebuano areas of the Philippines. *Anthropological Quarterly* 39:171–179.

———. 1967. *Cebuano sorcery: Malign magic in the Philippines*. Berkeley: University of California Press.

Lilienfeld, Abraham M., Einar Pedersen, and J. E. Dowd. 1967. *Cancer epidemiology: Methods of study*. Baltimore: Johns Hopkins.

Lipowski, Z. J. 1967a. Review of consultation psychiatry and psychosomatic medicine. I. General principles. *Psychosomatic Medicine* 29:153–171.

———. 1967b. Review of consultation psychiatry and psychosomatic medicine. II. Clinical aspects. *Psychosomatic Medicine* 29:201–224.

———. 1968. Review of consultation psychiatry and psychosomatic medicine. III. Theoretical issues. *Psychosomatic Medicine* 30:395–422.

———. 1969. Psychosocial aspects of disease. *Annals of Internal Medicine* 71:1197–1206.

Livingstone, F. B. 1958. Anthropological implications of sickle-cell genes distribution in West Africa. *American Anthropologist* 60:533–562.

————. 1967. *Abnormal hemoglobins in human populations: A summary and interpretation.* Chicago: Aldine.

Lloyd, B. 1972. *Perception and cognition: A cross-cultural perspective.* Middlesex, England: Penguin Books, Ltd.

Lounsbury, F. G. 1969. Language and culture. In *Language and philosophy,* ed. S. Hook. New York: New York University Press.

Lyons, F. 1972. Human language. In *Non-verbal communication,* ed. R. A. Hinde. New York: Cambridge University Press.

McGhie, A., and J. Chapman. 1961. Disorders of attention and perception in early schizophrenia. *British Journal of Medical Psychology* 34:103–115.

McGregor, I. A., A. K. Rahman, B. Thompson, W. Z. Billewicz, and A. M. Thomson. 1968. The growth of young children in a Gambian village. *Transactions of the Royal Society of Tropical Medicine and Hygiene* 62:341–352.

McGregor, I. A., A. K. Rahman, A. M. Thomson, W. Z. Billewicz, and B. Thompson. 1970. The health of young children in a West African (Gambian) village. *Transactions of the Royal Society of Tropical Medicine and Hygiene* 64:48–77.

MacKay, D. M. 1969. *Information mechanism and meaning.* Cambridge, Massachusetts: MIT Press.

————. 1972. Formal analysis of communicative processes. In *Non-verbal communication,* ed. R. A. Hinde. New York: Cambridge University Press.

Mackenzie, R. B. 1965. Epidemiology of Machupo virus infection. I. Pattern of human infection, San Joaquin, Bolivia, 1962–1964. *American Journal of Tropical Medicine and Hygiene* 14:808–813.

McKinlay, J. B. 1971. The concept "patient career" as a heuristic device for making medical sociology relevant to medical students. *Social Science and Medicine* 5:441.

Maclean, C. M. U. 1965a. Tradition in transition: A health opinion survey in Ibadan, Nigeria. *British Journal of Preventive and Social Medicine* 19:192–197.

————. 1965b. Traditional medicine and its practitioners in Ibadan, Nigeria. *Journal of Tropical Medicine and Hygiene* 68:237–244.

————. 1966. Hospitals or healers? An attitude survey in Ibadan. *Human Organization* 25:131–139.

————. 1969. Traditional healers and their female clients: An aspect of Nigerian sickness behavior. *Journal of Health and Social Behavior* 10:172–186.

MacMahon, B., and T. F. Pugh. 1970. *Epidemiology: Principles and methods.* Boston: Little, Brown.

Mann, G. V., R. D. Shaffer, R. S. Anderson, and H. H. Sanstead. 1964. Cardiovascular disease in the Masai. *Journal of Atherosclerosis Research* 4:289–312.

Margetts, E. L. 1965. Traditional Yoruba healers in Nigeria. *Man* 65:102.

Marsden, P. D. 1964. The Sukuta project: A longitudinal study of health in Gambian children from birth to 18 months of age. *Transactions of the Royal Society of Tropical Medicine and Hygiene* 58:455–482.

Marsh, G. H., and W. S. Laughlin. 1956. Human anatomical knowledge among the Aleutian Islanders. *Southwestern Journal of Anthropology* 12:38–78.

Marwell, G., and J. Hage. 1970. The organization of role relationships: Systematic description. *American Sociological Review* 35:884–900.

Mata, L. J., C. Albertazzi, A. Negreros, and R. Fernandez. 1965. Prevalence of shigella, salmonella, and enteropathogenic escherichia coli in six Mayan villages. *American Journal of Public Health* 55:1396–1402.

Mates, B. 1965. *Elementary logic*. New York: Oxford University Press.

Mathai, K. V. 1970. VI. Amyotropic lateral sclerosis and parkinsonism dementia in the Marianas. *American Journal of Tropical Medicine and Hygiene* 19:151–154.

May, J. M. 1960. The ecology of human disease. *Annals of the New York Academy of Sciences* 84:789–794.

Mayr, E. 1970. *Populations, species, and evolution*. Cambridge, Massachusetts: Belknap Press of Harvard University Press.

Mazzur, S. 1970. Behavior and disease: A possible approach. *American Journal of Physical Anthropology* 32:309–313.

Mead, M. 1947. The concept of culture and the psychosomatic approach. *Psychiatry* 10:57–76.

Mechanic, D. 1962. The concept of illness behavior. *Journal of Chronic Diseases* 15:189–194.

———. 1968. *Medical sociology: A selective view*. New York: Free Press.

Mendels, Joseph, ed. 1973. *Biological psychiatry*. New York: John Wiley and Sons.

Merskey, H., and F. G. Spear. 1967. *Pain: Psychological and psychiatric aspects*. London: Bailliere, Tindall and Cassell.

Metzger, D., and G. Williams. 1963. Tenejapa medicine: The curer. *Southwestern Journal of Anthropology* 19:216–234.

———. 1966. Some procedures and results in the study of native categories Tzeltal "firewood." *American Anthropologist* 68:389–407.

Miall, W. E., P. F. Milner, H. G. Lovell, and K. L. Standard. 1967. Haematological investigations of population samples in Jamaica. *British Journal of Preventive and Social Medicine* 21:45–55.

Miller, D., and D. Starr. 1967. *The structure of human decisions.* Englewood Cliffs, New Jersey: Prentice-Hall.

Miller, G. A., E. Galanter, and K. H. Pribram. 1960. *Plans and the structure of behavior.* New York: Henry Holt.

Miller, J. G. 1965. The organization of life. *Perspectives in Biology and Medicine* 9:107–125.

———. 1971. The nature of living systems. *Behavioral Science* 16:277–301.

Mishler, E. G., and N. A. Scotch. 1965. Sociocultural factors in the epidemiology of schizophrenia. *International Journal of Psychiatry* 1:258–295.

Mitchell, J. C., ed. 1969. *Social networks in urban situations.* Manchester, England: Manchester University Press.

Morgan, W. L., and G. L. Engel. 1969. *The clinical approach to the patient.* Philadelphia: W. B. Saunders.

Morton, J. F. 1968a. A survey of medicinal plants of Curacao. *Economic Botany* 22:87–102.

———. 1968b. The Calabash (Crescentia Cujete) in folk medicine. *Economic Botany* 22:273–280.

Nash, J. 1967a. The logic of behavior: Curing in a Mayan Indian town. *Human Organization* 26:132–140.

———. 1967b. Death as a way of life: The increasing resort to homicide in a Maya Indian community. *American Anthropologist* 69:455–470.

Neel, J. V. 1970. Lessons from a "primitive" people. *Science* 170:815–822.

Neel, J. V., and F. M. Salzano. 1964. A prospectus for genetic studies of the American Indian. *Cold Spring Harbor Symposia on Quantitative Biology* 29:85–98.

———. 1967. Further studies on the Xavante Indians. X. Some hypotheses–generalizations resulting from these studies. *American Journal of Human Genetics* 19:554–574.

Neel, J. V., W. M. Mikkelsen, D. L. Rucknagel, E. D. Weinstein, R. A. Goyer, and S. H. Abadie. 1968a. Further studies of the Xavante Indians. VIII. Some observations on blood, urine, and stool specimens. *American Journal of Tropical Medicine and Hygiene* 17:474–485.

Neel, J. V., A. H. Andrade, G. E. Grown, W. E. Eveland, J. Goobar, W. A. Sodeman, G. H. Stollerman, E. D. Weinstein, and A. H. Wheeler. 1968b. Further studies of the Xavante Indians. IX. Immunologic status with respect to various diseases and organisms. *American Journal of Tropical Medicine and Hygiene* 17:486–498.

Neel, J. V., W. R. Centerwall, N. A. Chagnon, and H. L. Casey. 1970. Notes on the effect of measles and measles vaccine in a virgin-soil population of South American Indians. *American Journal of Epidemiology* 91:418–429.

Negrete, J. C., and H. B. Murphy. 1967. Psychological deficit in chewers of coca leaf. *Bulletin on Narcotics* 19:4.

Newman, L. 1966. The Couvade: A reply to Kupferer. *American Anthropologist* 68:153–155.

Newman, P. L. 1964. "Wild man" behavior in a New Guinea Highlands community. *American Anthropologist* 66:1–19.

Niswander, J. D. 1967. Further studies on the Xavante Indians. VII. The oral status of the Xavantes of Simoes Lopes. *American Journal of Human Genetics* 19:543–553.

Norman-Taylor, W., and W. H. Rees. 1963. Blood pressures in three New Hebrides communities. *British Journal of Preventive and Social Medicine* 17:141–144.

Obeyesekere, G. 1963. Pregnancy cravings (dola-doka) in relation to social structure and personality in a Sinhalese village. *American Anthropologist* 65:323–342.

O'Nell, C. W., and H. A. Selby. 1968. Sex differences in the incidence of *susto* in two Zapotec pueblos: An analysis of the relationships between sex role expectations and a folk illness. *Ethnology* 7:95–105.

Osgood, K., D. L. Hochstrasser, and K. W. Deuschle. 1966. Lay midwifery in Southern Appalachia: The case of a mountain county in Eastern Kentucky. *Archives of Environmental Health* 12:759–770.

Otten, C. M. 1967. On pestilence, diet, natural selection, and the distribution of microbial and human blood group antigens and antibodies. *Current Anthropology* 8:209–226.

Pan American Health Organization. 1968. Biomedical challenges presented by the American Indian. Scientific Publication No. 165. Washington, D. C.: Pan American Health Organization, Pan American Sanitary Bureau, Regional Office of the World Health Organization.

Panoff, F. 1970. Maenge remedies and conception of disease. *Ethnology* 9:68–84.

Parker, S. 1962. Eskimo psychopathology in the context of Eskimo personality and culture. *American Anthropologist* 64:76–96.

Parsons, T. 1951a. Illness and the role of the physician. *American Journal of Orthopsychiatry* 21:452–460.

———. 1951b. *The social system.* New York: Free Press.

Paykel, Eugene S., and Myrna M. Weissman. 1973. Social adjustment and depression. *Archives of General Psychiatry* 28 (No. 5) :659–663.

Paykel, Eugene S., Myrna M. Weissman, Brigitte A. Prusoff, and Clive M. Tonks. 1971. Dimensions of social adjustment in depressed women. *Journal of Nervous and Mental Disease* 152 (No. 3) : 158–172.

Petroni, Frank A. 1969. Influence of age, sex and chronicity in perceived legitimacy to the sick role. *Sociology and Social Research*, Volume LIII: 180–193.

Petrov, P. A. 1970. V. Vilyuisk encephalitis in the Yakut Republic (USSR). *American Journal of Tropical Medicine and Hygiene* 19:146–150.

Phillips, Leslie. 1968. *Human adaptation and its failures.* New York: Academic Press.

Pike, K. 1954. *Language in relation to a unified theory of the structure of human behavior.* Glendale, Illinois: Summer Institute of Linguistics.

———. 1956. Towards a theory of the structure of human behavior. Mexico, D. F., Estudios Antropologicos Publicados en Homenaje al Doctor Manuel Gamio.

Pimentel, D. 1961. Animal population regulation by the genetic feedback mechanism. *American Naturalist* 95:65–79.

———. 1968. Population regulation and genetic feedback. *Science* 159:1432–1437.

Polgar, S. 1963. Medical problems from an evolutionary view. *Journal of Social Research* (Ranchi, India) 6:11–20.

———. 1964. Evolution and the ills of mankind. In *Horizons of anthropology*, ed. S. Tax, pp. 200–211. Chicago: Aldine.

Potter, R. G., J. B. Wyon, M. New, and J. E. Gordon. 1965. Fetal wastage in eleven Punjab villages. *Human Biology* 37:262–273.

Press, I. 1969. Urban illness: Physicians, curers and dual use in Bogota. *Journal of Health and Social Behavior* 10:209–218.

Price, D. L., and C. J. Lewthwaite. 1963. Plasmodium malariae in Ugandan children. II. Malaria parasites in children at Mulago Hospital in Kampala. *American Journal of Tropical Medicine and Hygiene* 12:298–299.

Price, D. L., G. V. Mann, O. A. Roels, and J. M. Merrill. 1963. Parasitism in Congo Pygmies. *American Journal of Tropical Medicine and Hygiene* 12:383–387.

Pridan, D., and H. Navid. 1967. Correlating diseases, causes and practitioners: A theoretical model. *Transactions of the Royal Society of Tropical Medicine and Hygiene* 61:553–558.

Prince, R., ed. 1968. *Trance and possession states.* Montreal, Canada: R. M. Bucke Memorial Society.

Quine, W. V. 1960. *Methods of logic.* New York: Holt, Rinehart and Winston.

———. 1965. *Elementary logic.* New York: Harper Torchbooks, The Science Library.

———. 1969. *From a logical point of view,* 2nd ed. New York: Harper and Row Torchbooks.

Rabin, D. L., C. R. Barnett, W. D. Arnold, R. H. Freiberger, and G. Brooks. 1965. Untreated congenital hip disease: A study of the epidemiology, natural history, and social aspects of the disease in a Navajo population. *American Journal of Public Health* 55:1–44.

Raser, J. R. 1969. *Simulation and society: An exploration of scientific gaming.* Boston: Allyn and Bacon.

Reed, D., D. Labarthe, and R. Stallones. 1970. Health effects of Westernization and migration among Chamorros. *American Journal of Epidemiology* 92:94–112.

Reed, D., S. Struve, and J. Maynard. 1967. Otitis Media and hearing deficiency among Eskimo children: A cohort study. *American Journal of Public Health* 57:1657–1662.

Riese, Walther. 1959. *A history of neurology.* New York: M. D. Publications, Inc.

Rivers, W. H. R. 1924. *Medicine, magic and religion.* London: Kegan Paul.

Robins, Eli, and Samuel B. Guze. 1972. Classification of affective disorders: The primary-secondary, the endogenous-reactive, and the neurotic-psychotic concepts. In *Recent advances in the psychobiology of the depressive illnesses,* pp. 283–293. DHEW Publ. No. (HSM) 70–9053.

Robson, J. R. K. 1964. Haemoglobin levels in apparently normal men, women, and children in Tanganyika. *Journal of Tropical Medicine and Hygiene* 67:282–283.

Rodrigue, R. B. 1963. A report on a widespread psychological disorder called lulu seen among the Huli linguistic group in Papua. *Oceania* 33:274–279.

Rogers, E. S. 1962. Man, ecology, and the control of disease. *Public Health Reports* (Washington, D. C.) 77:755–762.

Rohrl, V. J. 1970. A nutritional factor in Windigo psychosis. *American Anthropologist* 72:97–101.

Romano, I. O. V. 1965. Charismatic medicine, folk-healing, and folk-sainthood. *American Anthropologist* 67:1151–1173.

Rosen, G. 1968. *Madness in society.* Chicago: University of Chicago Press.

Rosenstock, I. M. 1966. Why people use health services. *Milbank Memorial Fund Quarterly* 44:94–127.

Rubel, A. J. 1960. Concepts of disease in Mexican-American culture. *American Anthropologist* 62:795–814.

————. 1964. The epidemiology of a folk illness: *Susto* in Hispanic America. *Ethnology* 3:268–283.

Ruesch, Jurgen. 1969. The assessment of social disability. *Archives of General Psychiatry* 21:655–664.

Ruesch, J., and G. Bateson. 1951. *Communication: The social matrix of psychiatry.* New York: W. W. Norton.

Ruesch, Jurgen, and Carroll M. Brodsky. 1968. The concept of social disability. *Archives of General Psychiatry* 19:394–403.

Rutstein, D. D. 1967. *The coming revolution in medicine.* Cambridge, Massachusetts: MIT Press.

Rutstein, D. D., and M. Eden. 1970. *Engineering and living systems: Interfaces and opportunities.* Cambridge, Massachusetts: MIT Press.

Salisbury, R. 1966a. Possession on the New Guinea Highlands: Review of literature. *Transcultural Psychiatric Research* 3:103–108.

————. 1966b. Possession among the Siane (New Guinea). *Transcultural Psychiatric Research.* 3:108–116.

————. 1967. Reply to rejoinder by L. L. Langness. *Transcultural Psychiatric Research* 4:130–134.

Salmon, W. C. 1970. Statistical explanation. In *The nature and function of scientific theories,* ed. R. D. Colodny, pp. 173–232. Pittsburgh: University of Pittsburgh Press.

Salomon, J. B., J. E. Gordon, and N. S. Scrimshaw. 1966. Studies of diarrheal disease in Central America. X. Associated chickenpox, diarrhea and kwashiorkor in a Highland Guatemalan village. *American Journal of Tropical Medicine and Hygiene* 15:997–1002.

Sarbin, T. R. 1968. Ontology recapitulates philology: The mythic nature of anxiety. *American Psychologist* 23 (No. 6) : 411–418.

Sarbin, T. R., and V. L. Allen. 1969. Role theory. In *The handbook of social psychology,* Volume III, eds. G. Lindzer and E. Arson, pp. 223–258. Reading, Massachusetts: Addison-Wesley.

Sargent, F. 1966. Ecological implications of individuality in the context of the concept of adaptive strategy. *International Journal of Biometeorology* 10:305–322.

Savage, C., A. H. Leighton, and D. C. Leighton. 1965. The problem of cross-cultural identification of psychiatric disorders. In *Approaches to cross-cultural psychiatry,* eds. J. M. Murphy and A. H. Leighton, pp. 21–63. Ithaca, New York: Cornell University Press.

Schacter, Stanley. 1971. *Emotion, obesity and crime.* New York: Academic Press.

Schappere, D. 1966. Memory and scientific change. In *Mind and cosmos: Essays in contemporary science and philosophy*, ed. R. G. Colodny. Pittsburgh: University of Pittsburgh Press.

Scheff, T. J. 1966. *Being mentally ill: A sociological theory*. Chicago: Aldine.

Scheffler, I. 1963. *The anatomy of inquiry*. New York: Alfred Knopf.

Scheflen, A. E. 1967. On the structuring of human communication. *American Behavioral Scientist* 10:8.

————. 1968. Human communication: Behavioral programs and their integration and interaction. *Behavioral Science* 13:44.

Schilder, P. 1950. *The image and appearance of the human body*. New York: John Wiley and Sons, Science Editions.

Schmale, A. H. 1972. Giving up as a common pathway to changes in health. In *Advances in psychosomatic medicine, Volume 8, Psychosocial aspects of physical illness*, ed. Z. J. Lipowski, pp. 20–41. New York: S. Karger.

Schofield, F. D. 1970. VIII. Some relations between social isolation and specific communicable diseases. *American Journal of Tropical Medicine and Hygiene* 19:167–169.

Schofield, F. D., and A. D. Parkinson. 1963*a*. Social medicine in New Guinea: Beliefs and practices affecting health among the Abelam and Wam peoples of the Sepik district, Part I. *Medical Journal of Australia* 1:1–10.

————. 1963*b*. Social medicine in New Guinea: Beliefs and practices affecting health among the Abelam and Wam peoples of the Sepik district, Part II. *Medical Journal of Australia* 1:29–33.

Schofield, F. D., A. D. Parkinson, and D. Jeffrey. 1963. Observations on the epidemiology, effects and treatment of *tinea imbricata*. *Transactions of the Royal Society of Tropical Medicine and Hygiene* 57:214–227.

Schwartz, L. R. 1969. The hierarchy of resort in curative practices: The Admiralty Islands, Melanesia. *Journal of Health and Social Behavior* 10:201–209.

Scotch, N. A. 1963*a*. Medical anthropology. In *Biennial review of anthropology*, ed. B. J. Siegel, pp. 30–68. Stanford, California: Stanford University Press.

————. 1963*b*. Sociocultural factors in the epidemiology of Zulu hypertension. *American Journal of Public Health* 53:1205–1213.

Scotch, N. A., and H. J. Geiger. 1962. The epidemiology of rheumatoid arthritis: A review with special attention to social factors. *Journal of Chronic Diseases* 15:1037–1067.

————. 1963. An index of symptom and disease in Zulu culture. *Human Organization* 22:304–311.

Scrimshaw, N. S., J. B. Salomon, H. A. Bruch, and J. E. Gordon. 1966. Studies of diarrheal disease in Central America. VIII. Measles, diarrhea, and nutritional deficiency in rural Guatemala. *American Journal of Tropical Medicine and Hygiene* 15:625–631.

Scrimshaw, N. S., M. Behar, M. A. Guzman, and J. E. Gordon. 1969. Nutrition and infection field study in Guatemalan villages, 1959–1964. IX. An evaluation of medical, social, and public health benefits, with suggestions for future field study. *Archives of Environmental Health* 18:51–62.

Scriven, M. 1959. Truisms as the grounds for historical explanations. In *Theories of history,* ed P. Gardiner, pp. 443–471. New York: Free Press.

Searle, J. R. 1970. *Speech acts—An essay in the philosophy of language.* New York: Cambridge University Press.

Shakow, David. 1971. Some observations on the psychology (and some fewer on the biology) of schizophrenia. *Journal of Nervous and Mental Disease* 153 (No. 5): 300–316.

Shekelle, R. B., A. M. Ostfeld, and O. Paul. 1969. Social status and incidence of coronary heart disease. *Journal of Chronic Diseases* 22:381–394.

Sheldon, A., F. Baker, and C. P. McLaughlin, eds. 1970. *Systems and medical care.* Cambridge, Massachusetts: MIT Press.

Shiloh, A. 1965. A case study of disease and culture in action: Leprosy among the Hausa of Northern Nigeria. *Human Organization* 24:140–147.

———. 1968. The interaction between the Middle Eastern and Western systems of medicine. *Social Science and Medicine* 2:235–248.

Shimkin, D. B. 1970. Man, ecology, and health. *Archives of Environmental Health* 20:111–127.

Sievers, M. L. 1967. Myocardial infarction among Southwestern American Indians. *Annals of Internal Medicine* 67:800–807.

Sigerist, H. E. 1951. *A history of medicine—Primitive and archaic medicine,* Volume I. Fair Lawn, New Jersey: Oxford University Press.

———. 1961. *A history of medicine—Early Greek, Hindu, and Persian medicine,* Volume 2. Fair Lawn, New Jersey: Oxford University Press.

Silverman, J. 1967. Shamans and acute schizophrenia. *American Anthropologist* 69:21–31.

Simmons, L. W., and H. G. Wolff. 1954. *Social science in medicine.* New York: Russell Sage Foundation.

Simmons, O. G. 1955. Popular and modern medicine in mestizo communities of coastal Peru and Chile. *Journal of American Folklore* 68:37–71.

Simon, M. A. 1971. *Matter of life: Philosophical problems of biology*. New Haven: Yale University Press.

Simpkiss, M. J. 1968. Birth weight, maternal age, and parity among the African population of Uganda. *British Journal of Preventive and Social Medicine* 22:234–237.

Simpson, G. G. 1961. *Principles of animal taxonomy*. New York: Columbia University Press.

Skinner, B. F. 1953. *Science and human behavior*. New York: Macmillan.

Skyrms, Brian. 1966. *Choice and chance: An introduction to inductive logic*. Belmont, California: Dickenson.

Slovic, P. 1964. Assessment of risk taking behavior. *Psychology Bulletin* 61:220–233.

Snell, Bruno. 1960. *The discovery of the mind: The Greek origins of European thought*. New York: Harper Torchbooks.

Solien de Gonzalez, N. L. 1963. Some aspects of child-bearing and child-rearing in a Guatemalan ladino community. *Southwestern Journal of Anthropology* 19:411–423.

———. 1964. Lactation and pregnancy: A hypothesis. *American Anthropologist* 66: 873–878.

———. 1966. Health behavior in cross-cultural perspective: A Guatemalan example. *Human Organization* 25:122–125.

Sprague, H. B. 1966. Environment in relation to coronary artery disease. *Archives of Environmental Health* 13:4–12.

Stark, L. R. 1969. The lexical structure of Quechua body parts. *Anthropological Linguistics* 11:1–15.

Stevenson, H. N. C. 1954. Status evaluation in the Hindu caste system. *Journal of the Royal Anthropological Society* 89: Parts I and II.

Stogdill, R. M., ed. 1970. *The process of model-building in the behavioral sciences*. Columbus: Ohio State University Press.

Stopp, K. 1963. Medicinal plants of the Mt. Hagen people (Mbowamb) in New Guinea. *Economic Botany* 17:16–22.

Suchman, E. A. 1965a. Social patterns of illness and medical care. *Journal of Health and Human Behavior* 6:2–16.

———. 1965b. Stages of illness and medical care. *Journal of Health and Human Behavior* 6:114–128.

———. 1965c. Social factors in medical deprivation. *American Journal of Public Health* 55:1725–1771.

————. 1967. Preventive health behavior: A model for research on community health campaigns. *Journal of Health and Social Behavior* 8:197–209.

Susser, Mervyn. 1973. *Causal thinking in the health sciences: Concepts and strategies of epidemiology.* Oxford: Oxford University Press.

Syme, S. L., M. M. Hyman, and P. E. Enterline. 1964. Some social and cultural factors associated with the occurrence of coronary heart disease. *Journal of Chronic Diseases* 17:277–289.

————. 1965. Cultural mobility and the occurrence of coronary heart disease. *Journal of Health and Human Behavior* 6:178–189.

Syme, S. L., and L. G. Reeder, eds. 1967. Social stress and cardiovascular disease. *Milbank Memorial Fund Quarterly* 45: Part 2.

Szasz, T. S. 1957. *Pain and pleasure: A study of bodily feelings.* New York: Basic Books.

————. 1961. *The myth of mental illness: Foundations of a theory of personal conduct.* New York: Hoeber-Harper.

————. 1964. *The myth of mental illness.* New York: Harper and Row.

Talbot, N. B., J. Kagan, and L. Eisenberg. 1971. *Pediatric medicine.* Philadelphia: W. B. Saunders.

Temkin, Owsei. 1971. *The falling sickness: A history of epilepsy from the Greeks to the beginnings of modern neurology,* 2nd edition. Baltimore: Johns Hopkins.

Tenzel, J. H. 1970. Shamanism and concepts of disease in a Mayan Indian community. *Psychiatry* 33:372–380.

Terespolsky, L. S., and J. Yofe. 1965. Epidemiological study of hospital admission in a community of new immigrants. *British Journal of Preventive and Social Medicine* 19:30–37.

Thompson, B. 1966. The first fourteen days of some West African babies. *Lancet* 2:40–45.

————. 1967a. Early childhood in a West African village. *Maternal and Child Care* 3:545.

————. 1967b. Childbirth and infant care in a West African village. *Nursing Mirror,* pp. 1–4.

Thompson, B., and D. Baird. 1967a. Some impressions of childbearing in tropical areas. Part I. *Journal of Obstetrics and Gynecology of the British Commonwealth* 74:329–338.

————. 1967b. Some impressions of childbearing in tropical areas. Part II. Pre-eclampsia and low birthweight. *Journal of Obstetrics and Gynecology of the British Commonwealth* 74:499–509.

————. 1967c. Some impressions of childbearing in tropical areas. Part III. Outcome of labor. *Journal of Obstetrics and Gynecology of the British Commonwealth* 74:510–522.

Thompson, B., and A. K. Rahman. 1967. Infant feeding and child care in a West African village. *Journal of Tropical Pediatrics* 13:124–138.

Thomson, A. M., W. Z. Billewicz, B. Thompson, R. Illsley, A. K. Rahman, and I. A. McGregor. 1968. A study of growth and health of young children in tropical Africa. *Transactions of the Royal Society of Tropical Medicine and Hygiene* 62:330–340.

Thomson, A. M., W. Z. Billewicz, B. Thompson, and I. A. McGregor. 1966a. Body weight changes during pregnancy and lactation in rural African (Gambian) women. *Journal of Obstetrics and Gynecology of the British Commonwealth* 73:724–733.

Thomson, A. M., W. Z. Billewicz, B. Thompson, I. A. McGregor, and A. K. Rahman. 1966b. Growth of children in West Africa: Effects of nutrition and disease. In *Somatic growth of the child: Proceedings of a Boerhaave course for postgraduate medical teaching*, pp. 165–173. Lieden, Holland: H. E. Stenfert, N. V. Kroese.

Topley, M. 1970. Chinese traditional ideas and the treatment of disease: Two examples from Hong Kong. *Man* 5:421–437.

Tromp, S. W. 1963. Human biometeorology. *International Journal of Biometeorology* 7:145–158.

Turner, V. W. 1963. Lunda medicine and the treatment of disease. Publication of the Rhodes-Livingstone Museum (Livingstone, Northern Rhodesia). Lusaka, Northern Rhodesia: Government Printer.

————. 1967. *The forest of symbols: Aspects of Ndembu ritual.* Ithaca, New York: Cornell University Press.

————. 1968. *The drums of affliction: A study of religious process among the Ndembu of Zambia.* Oxford: Clarendon Press.

Tyler, S. A. 1969. *Cognitive anthropology.* New York: Holt, Rinehart and Winston.

Tyroler, H. A., and J. Cassel. 1964. Health consequences of culture change. II. The effect of urbanization on coronary heart mortality in rural residents. *Journal of Chronic Diseases* 17:167–177.

Valins, S. 1970. The perception and labeling of bodily changes as determinants of emotional behavior. In *Physiological correlates of emotion*, ed. Perry Black, Chapter 11. New York: Academic Press.

Vayda, A. P., and R. A. Rappaport. 1968. Ecology, cultural and non-cultural. In *Introduction to cultural anthropology*, ed. J. A. Clifton, pp. 476–497. Boston: Houghton Mifflin.

Veith, Ilza. 1965. *Hysteria: The history of a disease.* Chicago: University of Chicago Press.

Von Mering, O., and L. W. Earley. 1966. The diagnosis of problem patients. *Human Organization* 25:20–23.

Walker, A. R. P. 1969. Coronary heart disease—Are there differences in racial susceptibility? *American Journal of Epidemiology* 90:359–364.

Wallace, A. F. C. 1961*a*. Mental illness, biology, and culture. In *Psychological anthropology: Approaches to culture,* ed. F. L. K. Hsu, pp. 255–295. Homewood, Illinois: Dorsey Press.

————. 1961*b. Culture and personality.* New York: Random House.

————. 1962. Culture and cognition. *Science* 135:351–357.

Wapner, S., and H. Werner, eds. 1965. *The body percept.* New York: Random House.

Ward, R. H., and J. V. Neel. 1970. Gene frequencies and microdifferentiation among the Makiritare Indians. IV. A comparison of a genetic network with ethnohistory and migration matrices; a new index of genetic isolation. *American Journal of Human Genetics* 22:538–561.

Weakland, J. H. 1968. Shamans, schizophrenia, and scientific unity. *American Anthropologist* 70:356.

Weaver, T. 1970. Use of hypothetical situations in a study of Spanish American illness referral systems. *Human Organization* 29:140–154.

Weinerman, E. R. 1966. Research into the organization of medical practice. *Milbank Memorial Fund Quarterly* 44:104–145.

Weinstein, E. D., J. V. Neel, and F. M. Salzano. 1967. Further studies on the Xavante Indians. VI. The physical status of the Xavantes of Simoes Lopes. *American Journal of Human Genetics* 19:532–542.

Weissman, Myrna, Eugene S. Paykel, Rise Siegel, and Gerald L. Klerman. 1971. The social role performance of depressed women: Comparisons with a normal group. *American Journal of Orthopsychiatry* 41 (No. 3) : 390–405.

Wells, C. 1964. *Bones, bodies, and disease: Evidence of disease and abnormality in early man.* New York: Frederick A. Praeger.

White, K. L. 1968. Organization and delivery of personal health services. *Milbank Memorial Fund Quarterly* 46:225–258.

Wiesenfeld, S. L. 1967. Sickle-cell trait in human biological and cultural evolution. *Science* 157:1134–1140.

Willer, D. 1967. *Scientific sociology: Theory and method.* Englewood Cliffs, New Jersey: Prentice-Hall.

Wilson, P. J. 1967. Status ambiguity and spirit possession. *Man* 2:366–378.

Winokur, G. 1973. The types of depressive disorders. *Journal of Nervous and Mental Disease* 156:82–95.

Wolff, B. B., and S. Langley. 1968. Cultural factors and the response to pain: A review. *American Anthropologist* 70:494–501.

Wolff, H. G. 1962. A concept of disease in man. *Psychosomatic Medicine* 24:25–30.

Wolff, R. J. 1965. Modern medicine and traditional culture: Confrontation on the Malay Peninsula. *Human Organization* 24:339–345.

Worth, R. M. 1963a. Health in rural China: From village to commune. *American Journal of Hygiene* 77:228–239.

———. 1963b. Health trends in China since the "great leap forward." *American Journal of Hygiene* 78:349–357.

Yap, P. M. 1967. Classification of the culture-bound reactive syndromes. *Australian and New Zealand Journal of Psychiatry* 1:172–179.

———. 1969. The culture-bound reactive syndromes. In *Mental health research in Asia and the Pacific,* eds. W. Caudill and T. Lin, pp. 33–53. Honolulu: East-West Center Press.

Yase, Y. 1970. VII. Neurologic disease in the Western Pacific Islands, with a report on the focus of amyotropic lateral sclerosis found in the Kii Peninsula, Japan. *American Journal of Tropical Medicine and Hygiene* 19:155–166.

Zborowski, M. 1958. Cultural components in responses to pain. In *Patients, physicians and illness,* ed. E. G. Jaco, pp. 256–268. New York: Free Press of Glencoe.

———. 1969. *People in pain.* San Francisco: Jossey-Bass.

Zigas, V. 1970. II. Kuru in New Guinea: Discovery and epidemiology. *American Journal of Tropical Medicine and Hygiene* 19:130–132.

Zola, I. K. 1966. Culture and symptoms: An analysis of patients' presenting complaints. *American Sociological Review* 31:615–630.

———. 1972. Studying the decision to see a doctor: Review, critique, corrective. In *Advances in psychosomatic medicine, Volume 8, Psychosocial aspects of physical illness,* ed. Z. J. Lipowski, pp. 216–236. New York: S. Karger.

Index

Oppenheim, A., xv
Organismic view of disease, 196–199, 200–205, 212
Osgood, K., 38
Osteoarthrosis, 84–85
Ostfeld, A. M., 49
Otten, C. M., 70

Pain, 86, 143–144, 239–240
Paleopathology, 71
Panama, study of enteropathogenic bacteria in, 57
Panoff, F., 6
Panofsky, E., 78–79, 224
Papua, study of *lulu* in, 19
Parker, S., 16, 96
Parkinson, A. D., 81–82
Parsons, T., 27, 102, 167, 198, 218
Patient role, 105, 121, 174n
Patrick, R., 47–48
Paul, O., 49
Paykel, Eugene S., 153
Pedersen, Einar, 92
Personal norms, *def.*, 128
Petroni, Frank A., 102n
Petrov, P. A., 74
Phenomenologic framework of disease, 142–148
Phillips, L. D., 184
Phillips, Leslie, 53, 153
Pike, K., 44, 164
Pimentel, D., 70
Polgar, S., 67
Ponnampalam, J. T., 53–54
Postal, P. M., 119n
Potter, R. G., 76
Pregnancy, 75–76, 87, 239
Press, I., 15, 23, 30, 91
Pribram, K. H., 74, 164
Price, D. L., 55, 57
Pridan, D., 8–9
Primitive medicine, ethnomedical studies of, 24–25
Prince, R., 20
Psychiatric approach to medicine
 in epidemiological studies, 51–53
 in ethnomedical studies, 39–42
 in folk illness diagnosis, 27, 33, 96–98, 99–101
Psychiatric illness, 51–52, 108, 134–135, 142, 243
 cross-cultural analysis of, 95, 288–296

Psychoanalysis, application to medical problems, 200n
Psychosis, beliefs about, 6
Psychosomatic approaches to disease, 224–227, 254
Psychosomatic medicine, 138, 287–289
Pugh, T. F., 45, 92, 121

Quechua, analysis of body-part concepts in, 10
Quine, W. L., 120n, 124

Rabin, D. L., 56
Rahman, A. K., 75–76
Rappaport, R. R., 67, 166
Raser, J. R., 165
Raven, P. H., 42
Reed, D., 55, 57
Reeder, L. G., 49
Rees, W. H., 56
Riese, Walther, 78
Risk-taking behavior, 176
Ritual pollution, 129–130
Rivers, W. H. R., 24
Roberts, R. E., xv
Roberts, R. W., 49
Robins, Eli, 108
Robson, J. R. K., 56
Rodrique, R. B., 19
Rogers, E. S., 46
Rohrl, V. J., 41
Role enactment framework of disease, 152–157
Role relationship, *def.*, 152
Romano, I. D. V., 27–28
Rorschach tests, 34–35
Rosen, G., 136n
Rosenstock, I. M., xv, 58, 168
Rubel, A. J., xv, 16, 17–18
Ruesch, Jurgen, 153, 164
Rupert, Henry, 37
Rutstein, D. D., 121, 139

Sadness, 290
Salisbury, R., 21
Salmon, W. C., 127
Salomon, J. B., 57
Salzano, F. M., 72
Sanborn, K., 52
San Cristobal de las Casas, Chiapas, Mexico
 study of illness behavior in, 186–189